MORALITY

AND

MORAL THEORY

MORALITY
AND
MORAL THEORY

A Reappraisal
and
Reaffirmation

ROBERT B. LOUDEN

New York   Oxford
OXFORD UNIVERSITY PRESS
1992

Oxford University Press

Oxford   New York   Toronto
Delhi   Bombay   Calcutta   Madras   Karachi
Petaling Jaya   Singapore   Hong Kong   Tokyo
Nairobi   Dar es Salaam   Cape Town
Melbourne   Auckland

and associated companies in
Berlin   Ibadan

Published by Oxford University Press, Inc.
200 Madison Avenue, New York, NY 10016

Oxford is a registered trademark of Oxford University Press

Library of Congress Cataloging-in-Publication Data
Louden, Robert B., 1953–
Morality and moral theory : a reappraisal and reaffirmation /
Robert B. Louden.
p.   cm.
Includes bibliographical references and index.
ISBN 0-19-507145-X
ISBN 0-19-507292-8 (pbk.)
1. Ethics.   I. Title.
BJ1012.L67   1992
170—dc20   91-21428

"Train in the Distance" © 1981 Paul Simon.
Used by permission of the Publisher.

2 4 6 8 9 7 5 3 1

Printed in the United States of America
on acid-free paper

In Memory of Two of My Teachers

WARNER A. WICK

(1911–1985)

ALAN DONAGAN

(1925–1991)

What is the point of this story
What information pertains
The thought that life could be better
Is woven indelibly
Into our hearts and brains

PAUL SIMON, "Train in the Distance"

Acknowledgments

I would like first to thank the following friendly critics who read earlier drafts of this book and who contributed greatly toward its improvement. Robert Roberts and Robert McCauley each worked his way through an early version of the entire manuscript and mailed me copious criticisms. Louis Pojman and Mark Johnson provided numerous comments on the first half. Norman Dahl, Eugene Garver, John Kekes, Larry May, Steven Tigner, Derek Phillips, Michael Howard, James Robinson, Tony Smith, Mark McPherran, Larry Simon, and Bart Gruzalski all criticized various versions of different chapters.

The reader for Oxford University Press, Joel Kupperman, also offered a number of extraordinarily helpful criticisms and suggestions. In this regard I would also like to thank my editor, Cynthia Read, particularly for her initial interest in the project; Peter Ohlin, assistant editor, for his prompt responses to a variety of queries; and Michael Lane, copy editor, for a job well done.

The writing of this book was made possible by a 1989–90 American Council of Learned Societies fellowship, a 1989 National Endowment for the Humanities (NEH) summer stipend, and a 1989–90 sabbatical leave from the University of Southern Maine. I am very grateful to all three institutions for their support. I would also like to thank the late Alan Donagan, Martha Nussbaum, Lawrence Blum, and my colleague Jeremiah Conway for their support in writing recommendation letters for my fellowship applications.

Some of the Kantian flavors in the first half of the manuscript were greatly enhanced by an invitation from Amelie Rorty to speak on Kant's views about virtue before the participants of her 1989 NEH summer seminar at Radcliffe College, Virtues and Their Vicissitudes.

In the years immediately preceding the writing of the manuscript, I was fortunate enough to be a participant in three different NEH–funded summer institutes and seminars: Kantian Ethics: Historical and Contemporary Perspectives (directed by J. B. Schneewind and David Hoy, Johns Hopkins University, 1983), The Practical Value of the Study of Ethics in Ancient Greek Thought (directed by Martha Nussbaum, Wellesley College, 1985) and Aristotle's Metaphysics, Biology, and Ethics (directed by Michael Frede, John Cooper, and Allan Gotthelf, University of New Hampshire, 1988). In hindsight these "summer camps for professors" have proved to be the most enjoyable as well as the most edifying part of my philosophy education, for it was here that I was able to study and converse with many of our most outstanding contemporary Kant and Aristotle scholars. Their writings have profoundly influenced my approach to many of the issues in this book.

This study develops a number of ideas (and borrows an occasional phrase or two) from several of my previously published articles. Part I grew out of "Can We Be Too Moral?" (*Ethics* 98 [1988]: 361–78) and, to a lesser extent, "Kant's Virtue Ethics" (*Philosophy* 61 [1986]: 473–89). Traces of part II can be detected in "Virtue Ethics and Anti-Theory" (*Philosophia* 20 [1990]: 93–114).

Finally, a few less scholarly debts should also be noted: to my father, for helping me upgrade my computer system and guiding me through its mysteries and for reminding me that he wrote a book when he was my age (while his son practiced electric guitar in the adjoining room); to Yves Dalvet, for his precise piano playing at our Wednesday morning sonata sessions, which (I like to think) not only improved my meager violin abilities but also gave me a better sense of how things (including philosophy books?) should fit together; and last and most, to my wife, Tama, not only for watching our daughters, Elizabeth and Sarah, while I hid out in the attic behind a computer monitor and several small mountains of books and journal articles, but also for her work on the book cover and for her insistence that the project was not too crazy.

Marburg, Germany   R.B.L.
July 1991

Contents

Abbreviations

References to Aristotle's and Kant's writings are given in the body of the text; all other references, in notes. For Aristotle, I use the standard Bekker numerals and generally rely on the revised Oxford translation of his works. The following abbreviations of Aristotle's works are used:

Cael	*De Caelo*
De An	*De Anima*
Gen An	*De Generatione Animalium*
EE	*Ethica Eudemia*
Hist An	*Historia Animalium*
Meta	*Metaphysica*
MM	*Magna Moralia*
NE	*Ethica Nicomachea*
Pol	*Politica*
Rhet	*Rhetoria*
Top	*Topica*

For Kant, I cite the volume and page number in the standard German Akademie edition of his works, followed by a page number in a corresponding English translation of his work. Details on English translations are in the bibliography. The following abbreviations of Kant's works are referred to:

A	*Anthropology from a Pragmatic Point of View*
C1	*Critique of Pure Reason* (references are to page numbers first of the 1781 A edition and then of the 1787 B edition)
C2	*Critique of Practical Reason*
C3	*Critique of Judgment*
DV	*The Doctrine of Virtue*
E	"An Answer to the Question: What Is Enlightenment?" (in *"Perpetual Peace" and Other Essays*)
End	"The End of All Things" (in *Perpetual Peace and Other Essays*)
Ed	*Education*
G	*Grounding of the Metaphysics of Morals*
L	*Logic*
LE	*Lectures on Ethics* (first page references here are to Paul Menzer's German edition, *Eine Vorlesung Kants über Ethik*)
R	*Religion Within the Limits of Reason Alone*
Science	*Metaphysical Foundations of Natural Science*
TP	"On the Common Saying: This May Be True in Theory, but It Does Not Apply in Practice" (in *Kant's Political Writings*)

MORALITY

AND

MORAL THEORY

Introduction

> Morality is a subject that interests us above all others: We fancy the
> peace of society to be at stake in every decision concerning it; and 'tis
> evident, that this concern must make our speculations appear more
> real and solid, than where the subject is, in a great measure, indifferent
> to us.
>
> H U M E, A Treatise of Human Nature

This is a book about morality and moral theory—about how, upon reflection, we
ought to understand the nature and aims of morality and moral theory and about
why the two are fundamentally important in human life. These are large topics;
but readers who are wary of books about large topics may be relieved to hear that
it is not my intent to offer an exhaustive, systematic analysis of either morality or
moral theory. Rather, I shall be exploring certain select areas within the broad terrains of morality and moral theory, areas where I believe contemporary assumptions are unsatisfactory and in need of replacement. The areas to be investigated
were chosen as part of a larger strategy for coming to grips with a variety of recent
philosophical criticisms of both morality and moral theory.

Contemporary philosophers have grown increasingly skeptical toward both
morality and moral theory. The skepticism concerning morality stems from arguments that moral considerations are not always the most important considerations and that it is not always better to be morally better. The skepticism
concerning moral theory stems from arguments that moral theory is a radically
misguided enterprise, one that does not illuminate moral practice and fulfills no
useful functions. *Morality and Moral Theory* is a response to the arguments of both
"antimorality" and "antitheory" skeptics. My aim is to defuse such skepticism by
putting forward alternative conceptions of morality and moral theory, conceptions that owe more to central texts within the canon of Western philosophical
ethics (particularly Kantian and Aristotelian) than to sheer conceptual virtuosity.

Reappraising Morality

Again, the skepticism concerning morality with which I shall be concerned stems
from recent arguments that moral considerations are not always the most im-

3

portant considerations—that we sometimes admire immorality more than mo- rality, prefer to be less moral rather than more moral, recognize that aesthetic or personal or prudential ends may take precedence over moral concerns, care more about nonmoral ideals than about moral ideals, or believe with justification that we ought to do what is morally wrong.[1]

At first glance, these antimorality arguments may not seem new: Thrasyma- chus, in book 1 of Plato's *Republic,* argues that injustice is better than justice; and history is riddled with intellectuals who advocate immoralist doctrines. However, the contemporary philosophical skeptics about morality whose ar- guments are the subject of the first half of this book are not immoralists who stand outside the pale of all moral considerations. They recognize that morality has a place within human life—indeed, a significant place. Their view is, rather, that moral considerations are not the only important considerations to which human beings are subject: morality is not the only game in town. This is a softer view than Thrasymachean immoralism; and many readers may find it sensible, noncontroversial, and perhaps even trivially true. Still, for those of us who were taught (and continue to believe) that morality is supremely important in human life, it is a deeply troubling view.

When we situate this scholarly debate concerning morality within contem- porary American culture, the irony of a society obsessed with the morality and immorality of its politicians and business people in which accusations on both sides are fueled by frequent editorial warnings that we have lost our collective moral compass is difficult to ignore. Current academic as well as popular discourse reveals a great deal of talk about morality but little reflection concerning what it is we are talking about when we profess to be talking about morality.[2]

When I speak of "putting forward alternative conceptions of morality," I do not mean to imply that it is my view that moral conceptions are normally the sorts of things that people simply *choose* to pick up or discard at a moment's notice. On this point I agree with Bernard Williams that

> we cannot take very seriously a profession of [moral principles] if we are given to understand that the speaker has just *decided* to adopt them. The idea that people decide to adopt their moral principles seems to me a myth. . . . We see a man's genuine convictions as coming from somewhere deeper in him than that; and . . . what we see as coming from deeper in him, he—that is, the deciding "he"—may see as coming from outside him.[3]

At the same time, I also believe that Alasdair MacIntyre is largely correct when he asserts that many contemporary U.S. citizens possess mere fragments of competing ethical conceptions, "simulacra of morality" for which we lack the historical understanding of their various origins[4]—*largely* because, unlike MacIntyre, I do not think this state of affairs necessarily implies that our culture is in a state of "grave disorder." Morality *is,* in a sense, up for grabs at present; and while this is "a disquieting suggestion" for some, it may also be the case that we at this particular time and place are confronted with unique opportunities for conceptual exploration of moral territories. There are, as it were, different moralities out there, and in such a situation a certain amount of choice concerning one's moral conception is certainly possible and perhaps even inevitable.

Reaffirming Morality

Briefly, the alternative moral conception to be developed and defended herein is a broader, richer one. In chapter 1, I argue, in opposition to most modern theorists, that morality ought to be understood primarily as a matter of what one does or does not do to oneself rather what one does or does not do to others. Adoption of this self-regarding conception of morality enables us to bridge the gulf that many antimorality critics claim exists between morality's demands and the personal point of view, thereby defusing one prominent source of recent philosophical opposition to morality.

In chapter 2, I argue that morality's primary[5] evaluative focus ought to be on agents and their lives rather than on right acts or optimific consequences of acts. Adoption of this agent or virtue conception gives morality a richness and pervasiveness that literally encompasses all voluntary and even indirectly voluntary aspects of people's lives, thus enabling us to draw upon a much wider body of moral resources. Here the gulf between the moral and the nonmoral is bridged by showing that all aspects of our lives over which we exercise at least some voluntary control have indirect (if not direct) moral relevance.

In chapter 3, I argue, contra contemporary antimorality critics, that it is "always better to be morally better" and that we should strive to make our society as morally good as possible.[6] Once morality is properly understood, we see that it does not make good sense to claim that individuals or societies can ever be "too moral." This commits me to what is often called a "maximizing" conception of morality, albeit one that is radically opposed to dominant consequentialist conceptions of moral maximization. Unlike most consequentialists,[7] I do not believe that morality should be construed as an attempt to maximize values in action at all. Rather, I argue that the most moral persons are those who are more strongly disposed than the rest of us to stand fast by their reflectively chosen principles and ideals when tempted by considerations that are morally irrelevant. Additionally, morally excellent individuals recognize that certain fundamental constraints stemming from duties concerning the development of human capacities, beneficence, and promotion of justice must be placed on the content of chosen ideals and principles if they are to count as distinctively moral in character. Adopting this particular conception of moral maximization serves both to undercut the standard objections to morality as an object of maximal devotion and to reclaim the importance of ideals and aspiration in the moral life.

Finally, in chapter 4, I contend that recent critics, as well as defenders, of the claim that morality is supremely important in human life have failed to appreciate

the relevant properties of morality that make it important. The central importance of morality in human life stems not from the "nonoverridingness" of moral
interests vis-à-vis other competing sets of narrowly defined interests but rather
from the fact that it is much more pervasive throughout human life than other
interests, that it has, as Aristotle argued, an "architectonic" authority that other
human interests lack, and from what Kant called the "primacy of the practical"
over all other human interests. Science—and, indeed, all forms of critical
thought—presuppose and depend on a commitment to basic moral norms.
Morality is supremely important not because it "stands above" everything else
but because it is literally underneath, as well as continually embedded in, all
human cognitive efforts. Recent attempts to show that we would be "better off
without morality" are thus revealed to be suicidal.[8]

Reappraising Moral Theory

The contemporary skepticism concerning moral theory with which I shall be
concerned might appear to be a relatively distinct phenomenon, one that is
perhaps of interest only to philosophers and other intellectuals who believe that
theory is important and that theories about morality can and do perform valuable
functions. For it is quite conceivable that someone could come to believe that
morality itself is vitally important without also believing that we need moral
theories. But on my view, part of the linkage between the morality and moral
theory halves of this project lies precisely in the concept of importance. It is
partly because morality is so important that we need to develop better moral
theories. Theorists ought to devote their energies to developing theories about
important, rather than trivial, matters.

In the second half of this book I respond to the basic argument that we ought
not to engage in moral theorizing or turn to existing moral theories for practical
guidance—that the aims of moral theory are radically misguided and impossible
to fulfill because moral thought and practice are not the sort of phenomena that
theory can illuminate. What is needed are people with *moral sensitivity* rather
than people with moral theories, and exposure to theory is by no means a
prerequisite to—indeed, is often an impediment to—the acquisition of moral
sensitivity.[9] Here, too, there is a sense in which such claims do not seem new.
Many of Socrates' contemporaries thought he was wasting his time in trying
to disclose the nature of virtue, and numerous critics have noted that the collective achievements of subsequent moral theories are slightly less than stag-
gering. What makes the current antitheory movement somewhat novel is that
it is an academic philosophers' movement: professors who teach and write about
ethics are themselves calling for the end of moral theory.

Just as current philosophical doubts about the place of morality in human
life reveal a great deal of disagreement and uncertainty as to what exactly is
meant by *morality,* so, too, do contemporary skeptical attacks on moral theory
serve to underscore the fact that *moral theory* itself is a contested concept. There
exists no detailed, univocal definition of the term that is employed faithfully by

all who have professed to be moral theorists. And just as my basic strategy in part I is to offer an alternative moral conception that will provide us with stronger reasons to affirm the supreme importance of morality in human life, so my strategy in part II is to offer an alternative conception of moral theory that will defuse the antitheorists' objections to moral theory and allow us to reaffirm the significance of moral theory.

A further parallel should also be noted. Just as the conception of morality I shall advocate is one that is closer to a classical and widely accepted understanding of morality than are contemporary philosophical constructs (or so I shall argue), so the particular conception of moral theory to be advocated in this book is one that captures more of the essential features of the best work done in the canon of Western moral theory than do current assumptions concerning the nature of moral theory. In both cases, certain peculiarly modern assumptions regarding both morality and moral theory are in need of replacement. The alternative conceptions of morality and of moral theory to be advocated in this book are therefore not entirely constructions of my own making: they are not made out of whole cloth. Rather, this undertaking is in part an exercise in recollection. I am asking the reader to recall certain occasionally forgotten chapters in our moral history, and I believe such an effort will demonstrate that to some extent we *already possess* the conceptual resources to defuse contemporary moral skepticism.

The occasional excursions into canonical texts in Western philosophical ethics are therefore not meant as scholarly meanderings but rather as amplifications of the central argument. At the same time, my references to older works in moral theory are quite selective and, some may feel, idiosyncratic. I am primarily concerned with Aristotelian and Kantian ethics—two philosophical traditions that for many of us represent the highest achievements within ancient and modern ethical theory, respectively. At present it is widely assumed that Aristotelian and Kantian ethics differ radically from one another. Indeed, an important subtheme in much of the recent antimorality literature is that contemporary "Kantian" moral conceptions (if that is what they really are) need to be replaced by a less problematic Aristotelian notion of the practical. My opposing view is that the moral conceptions of Kant and Aristotle share much more in common with one another than contemporary wisdom allows; and while I am strongly sympathetic to the recent reappreciation of ancient Greek moralists by contemporary ethical theorists, I do not believe that allegiance to this tendency, in most instances, necessitates rejection of Kantian-influenced moral conceptions. Much contemporary argument in ethics depends on oversimplified pictures of Aristotle and (particularly) Kant. Such argumentation posits exhaustive alternatives that fit neither Aristotle nor Kant but only lesser thinkers. An available richness is therefore missing from current moral argument, and part of my aim is to recover it.

But it should also be noted that my own views about morality and moral theory are in many ways quite different from those of either Aristotle or Kant. For instance, to a much stronger degree than either of them, I am a pluralist in ethics in the following two senses:

1. I believe that moral evaluation needs to incorporate fundamentally different kinds of values, values that cannot always be compared to one another on a common scale.
2. I believe the existence of conflicting types of ethical theories is both intellectually healthy and close-to-inevitable.

Similarly, in appealing to certain aspects of a classical moral conception and to canonical texts within this tradition, I do not wish to be interpreted as asserting that only "the good old Great Books approach" can save us, that students should read canonical books about morality and no others, or that people "cannot hear what the great tradition has to say" as long as they listen to rock and roll.[10] Rather, my view is simply that certain aspects of these older traditions are arguably superior to contemporary moral conceptions and that we have good reason to reappropriate them (in our own way, in our own time, to address our own needs) once we reexamine their merits in light of current concerns.

I remarked earlier on the irony of a culture that apparently enjoys the ubiquity of the word *morality* but in which the word itself has very little determinate meaning. A similar irony is evident with respect to moral theory. During the same time in which contemporary philosophers have been aiming some extremely heavy artillery at the very notion of moral theory, educational reformers have succeeded in instituting required ethics courses in many of our country's graduate professional schools. Many of these courses are taught by moral philosophers who loan themselves out to schools of law, medicine, business, and public policy; all are at least taught by academicians who have suffered severe exposure to moral theory. If moral theories are useless, impossible, and (as one antitheorist puts it) "threats to moral sanity and balance,"[11] it would seem that those who teach such courses are committing an enormous act of bad faith.

Reaffirming Moral Theory

The alternative conception of moral theory defended in part II is a less reductionistic and more empirically sensitive conception than that assumed by antitheorists—one that recognizes both the irreducible plurality of moral values and the reality of unresolvable moral conflict and one whose interest in moral deliberation is not distorted by an extremist faith in a universal decision procedure. At the same time, this alternative conception—or so I shall argue—is in fact much closer to Aristotelian and even Kantian understandings of moral theory than is that of contemporary antitheorists.

Part II begins by asking what exactly antitheorists have in mind when they talk about moral theory. In chapter 5, I analyze numerous antitheory writings with an eye toward this basic question, concluding that by *moral theory* their authors mean a project that adopts six assumptions and aims:

1. All correct moral judgments and practices are deducible from universal, timeless principles, to articulate which it is theory's job.
2. All moral values are commensurable; that is, they can be compared with one

another on a common scale of measurement. Theory's task is to construct the requisite scale and then to show which value wins in each particular value conflict and why it wins.

3. All moral disagreements and conflicts are rationally resolvable. There is one right answer to every moral problem, which it is theory's job to find.

4. The correct method for reaching the one right answer involves a computational decision procedure. It is the task of moral theory to provide such a mechanism.

5. Moral theory has no descriptive or explanatory role to play in human life but presumes instead to be able to tell people what to do and how to live. Moral theory is entirely normative.

6. Moral problems are solved best by moral experts, that is, by people who know what rules to apply to the case at hand and who have been trained successfully in formal academic settings in deducing right answers by means of rules.

The antitheorist movement is not a unified camp. Certainly, not every writer associated with this tendency holds that each of these six aims and assumptions constitutes a necessary part of moral theory. However, I do believe that we can take the target of their criticisms to be any intellectual project in ethics that satisfies a simple majority of these conditions, without treating any one of them as strictly necessary.

In chapter 6, I turn again to Aristotelian and Kantian texts, this time in an attempt to show that neither Aristotle nor Kant is guilty of moral "theorizing"; neither of them, that is, subscribes to a majority of the six basic assumptions summarized in the previous paragraph. We are thus able to cast serious doubt on the antitheoretical conception of moral theory, not by pointing to an alleged logical flaw on which it rests but by showing that it is historically inaccurate. Any conception of moral theory that does not reflect accurately what two of the most influential practitioners of moral theory were trying to do is an inadequate conception.[12]

Chapter 7 presents an alternative conception of moral theory, a conception that is constrained both by a desire to reflect accurately some of the basic assumptions and aims of Aristotelian and Kantian ethical theories and a qualified appreciation for several antitheory criticisms of formalist programs in moral theory. The aim of this chapter is not to offer a detailed defense of a specific, worked-out moral theory but rather to elucidate and to defend some basic assumptions and aims that *any* acceptable moral theory ought to possess. Here again, the six focal areas analyzed in chapter 5 are used to structure the discussion.

Finally, in chapter 8, I attempt to show that moral theories are humanly necessary insofar as they uniquely satisfy certain genuine and indispensable human needs that would remain unsatisfied in the absence of moral theories. Moral theories are necessary to explain and interpret many mundane aspects of human thought and action, to uncover the basic concepts and categories in terms of which the moral thought and experience of any given culture understands itself, to defend the moral practices that survive reflective scrutiny and criticize those that do not, to enlarge the moral imagination and present new possibilities for moral growth, and to serve as vehicles for giving expression to our abiding curiosity concerning our place in the universe.

Like much philosophy, this book is largely a collection of arguments, explanations, and attempts to view things differently, each of which is intended to help persuade the reader to take my side rather than my opponents'.[13] Without at all wishing to diminish the adversarial nature of the project, I should confess before proceeding that I have borrowed much from my opponents. In many cases I have found myself in agreement with their attacks on morality and moral theory, or, rather, their attacks on *a certain conception of* morality and moral theory. However, in such cases I have tried to apply their arguments toward positive ends by asking whether there exists a different kind of morality and moral theory that can survive skeptical assaults, a kind of morality and moral theory that we would want to defend and to consult as a means by which to guide our lives. In this task I like to believe I have been successful.

In the following chapters, the reader is offered a broader and richer moral conception, one that embraces important areas of life that other moral conceptions slight. By reappraising morality in this manner we are able to reaffirm its accustomed role as the sole and final arbiter of how to live and act. In the second half of the book, the central strategy behind the reappraisal of moral theory is not so much to broaden our conception of theory as to slim it down—to offer a more humble, more reasonable conception of moral theory that captures more of the essential aims of the best work in the tradition than do most contemporary portraits but is still unmistakably a plea for theory rather than antitheory.

Even in the numerous cases where I have not been convinced by my opponents' arguments and have thus not sought to appropriate them for my own ends, the force of their objections has forced me to think harder (and hopefully better) about morality and moral theory. Many other readers of these same skeptical writings have undergone similar philosophical journeys of their own. Here, too, there may be irony. The long-term result of the current proliferation of skeptical attacks on morality and moral theory may well be to spur others to construct stronger cases for more sensible and substantive conceptions of morality and moral theory. Rather than achieve their intended goal of ushering in a culture without moral theory where moral considerations have no dominant place in human life, contemporary skeptics may in fact be contributing to the arrival of something quite different. But that is for the future to decide. Let us turn now to the issues at hand.

I
MORALITY

I who called myself magus or angel, exempt from all morality, I am thrown back to the earth.

RIMBAUD, *A Season in Hell*

1
Morality and Oneself

Are you not ashamed of your eagerness to possess as much wealth, reputation and honors as possible, while you do not care for nor give thought to wisdom [*phronēsis*] or truth, or the best possible state of your soul?... Be sure that this is what the god orders me to do.... For I go around doing nothing but persuading both young and old among you not to care for your body or your wealth in preference to or as strongly as for the best possible state of your soul, as I say to you: "Wealth does not bring about virtue [*aretē*], but virtue brings about wealth and all other public and private blessings for human beings."

P L A T O, *Apology*

Self-command is not only itself a great virtue, but from it all other virtues seem to derive their principal lustre.

A D A M S M I T H, *The Theory of the Moral Sentiments*

Far from ranking lowest, in actuality our duties to ourselves rank highest and are the most important of all [*die wichtigsten unter allen*], for...what can be expected of a man who dishonors himself? He who violates a duty to himself loses his humanity and becomes incapable of performing his duties to others. A man who performed his duties to others badly, who lacked generosity, kindness and sympathy, but who nevertheless did his duty to himself by leading a proper life, might yet possess a certain inner worth; but he who has violated his duty to himself, can have no inner worth whatever.

K A N T, *Lectures on Ethics*

Our Bias Toward Others

One of the loudest complaints issued against morality by contemporary critics is that it downgrades personal concerns by requiring of moral agents that they adopt an impersonal, exclusively other-regarding point of view that alienates them from their own deepest projects and convictions.[1] The most moral agent, according to Susan Wolf's influential account, is the one whose life is "dominated by a commitment to improving the welfare of others or of society as a whole," the result being that said agent is "too good for his own well-being."[2] Such a person devotes all of his energies to cultivating exclusively other-regarding moral virtues and thus (if successful in achieving his or her aim) winds up with a lopsided personality in which there is little if any room left for the development of self-regarding and/or nonmoral traits. The person who adopts such a life plan successfully is not only quite unlikely to become a gourmet cook, concert violinist, or champion tennis player but, more importantly for antimorality critics, quite likely to become extremely boring and uninteresting in the process. Little wonder, then, that Wolf is led to complain that the way "in which morality, unlike other possible goals, is apt to dominate is particularly disturbing, for it seems to require either the lack or the denial of the existence of an identifiable, personal self."[3] Similarly, in Bernard Williams's much-discussed Paul Gauguin example, the painter's desertion of his family to pursue his own artistic career raises the specter of immorality for many readers but also leads Williams himself to salute Gauguin's decision even while conceding that he "perhaps" lacks a moral justification for his actions. Gauguin's artistic success shows us, Williams claims, that we have "in fact deep and persistent reasons to be grateful" that we do not live in a world in which morality is universally respected.[4]

But why should morality be construed as an exclusively other-regarding affair? Why must we, upon hearing the word *moral,* necessarily block out self-regarding concerns and devote ourselves 100 percent to the concerns of others? In this chapter I shall challenge the "bias toward others" assumption that underlies much contemporary antimorality skepticism, arguing that morality ought rather to be regarded as a fundamentally self-regarding project. If we can succeed in replacing the exclusively other-regarding conception of morality that currently enjoys hegemony among contemporary philosophers with one that is primarily self-regarding, an entire class of the stock-in-trade objections to morality will become irrelevant. No longer will critics be able to dismiss morality on the ground that it has no place for the personal; for morality, properly understood, *is* intensely personal.

Care of Soul

As the epigraphs indicate, morality has certainly not always been construed as an exclusively other-regarding affair. On the contrary, until quite recently, the exact opposite was the case.[5] According to most earlier conceptions of morality, self-perfection rather than the welfare of others is the most important moral commitment. The most famous example here is Socrates' parting plea to his Athenian jurors to recognize that care of one's soul (*psuchēs epimeleia*) is one's highest moral obligation. Classicist John Burnet, in his note on the passage, remarks: "Socrates appears to have been the first Greek to speak of the *psuchē* as the seat of knowledge and ignorance, goodness and badness. . . . It followed that the chief duty of man was to 'care for his soul.' . . . This rule of *epimeleia psuchēs* was the fundamental thing in the teaching of Socrates."[6]

The emphasis on self-perfection is also clearly central in Kantian ethics, as the epigraph from his *Lectures on Ethics* indicates. Philip Hallie writes, "Kant is very careful to point out—and this care makes him one of the greatest figures in the history of the classic conception of ethics—that what we do to or for others is not central to ethics; the orderly conception of our own souls, our character, is what ethics seeks to achieve, and praises when it succeeds."[7] In a parallel passage in the *Doctrine of Virtue*, Kant argues that if there were no duties to oneself, then

> there would be no duties whatsoever [viz., duties to others], and so no external duties either. For I can recognize that I am under obligation to others only in so far as I, at the same time, obligate myself, since the law by virtue of which I deem myself obligated always proceeds from my own practical reason; and in being necessitated by my own practical reason, I am also the necessitating subject in relation to myself. (*DV* VI 417–18/80)*

The Socratic conception of ethics as fundamentally self-regarding follows fairly directly from three assumptions:

1. The *psuchē* is the most important feature (morally as well as epistemologically) of a human being.
2. Each individual is ultimately responsible for the state of his or her soul.
3. Ethics is an extremely broad-ranging concern, encompassing the multiple terrains of practical, prudential, and what most moderns call *moral* choices under the general query of how one ought to live.

As Socrates remarks, "The argument concerns no casual topic, but how one must [*chrē*] live" (*Republic* 352D). The Kantian argument is not as obvious. Friendly, as well as not-so-friendly, readers of Kant often vehemently reject the assertion that Kantian ethics is primarily about the perfection of oneself rather than doing things for other people, in spite of the fact that he states his position very bluntly. Presumably, this is because of the tremendous amount of scholarly attention given to the Kantian doctrine of the categorical imperative and the emphasis within this doctrine on willing one's maxims as universal law for all rational agents. What is his argument for the claim that our duties to ourselves are "the most important of all"?

Briefly, Kant's position is that without duties to oneself there could be no moral duties at all; for a moral duty (rather than, say, a legal obligation, performance of which can be externally coerced) is by definition a voluntary undertaking performed from a certain specified motivational structure. The agent must perform the act not out of fear of external sticks or in the hope of external carrots or even from internal nonrational urges and impulses but rather *from duty*, that is, out of respect for the idea of moral law itself, as created by free, rational agents. The condition of all moral action (and for Kant, the *only* unqualified good in the universe) is the good will, a will that consistently acts from the motive of duty. As he proclaims in the powerful but cryptic opening

*For pagination, see Abbreviations.

of the *Grounding,* "There is no possibility of thinking of anything at all in the world, or even out of it, which can be regarded as good without qualification, except a *good will*" (IV 393/7). But only *we*—as individuals who are trying to live a certain way—can bring it about that we act consistently from this requisite motivational structure. The subjects of moral action are always self-obligating, in the sense that their own practical reason must move them to act. And so, at bottom, the central idea behind the Kantian doctrine of duties to oneself is that each of us has a fundamental duty to care for his or her own character, to develop and educate it so that certain traits rather than others consistently become the basis for our actions. We need to educate our emotions and desires so that we act consistently on the basis of reason. All morality is ultimately "a matter of self-dedication . . . to the ideal defined by the moral law,"[8] since only we ourselves can bring ourselves to act from the requisite motivational structure.

The Kantian commitment to self-control under the guidance of reason is also one of the clearest points of contact between Kant and the Greeks. As Aristotle notes, "The good man ought [*dei*] to be a lover of self [*philauton*]" (*NE* 1169a11–12, cf. 1169b1), though he emphasizes that he is not advocating the usual sense of "self-love." The true lover of self is not the one who assigns to himself the greater share of wealth, honors, and physical pleasure but he who is obedient to the voice of reason within himself; for reason is "the man himself" (1168b35, 1169a1–2), or at least the "the authoritative and better part of him" (1178a2–3). When a man "gratifies the most authoritative element in himself and in all things obeys this" (1168b30–31), he is a true lover of self as well as a good man.

Egoism, Narcissism, Prudence

The claim that morality is primarily self-regarding raises multiple specters of self-centeredness. Some people, Dewey notes, "become engrossed in spiritual egotism. They are preoccupied with the state of their character, concerned for the purity of their motives and the goodness of their souls. The exaltation of conceit which sometimes accompanies this absorption can produce a corrosive inhumanity which exceeds the possibilities of any other known form of selfishness."[9] Are moral agents who care for their souls simply ethical egoists who always act so as to best serve their own interests? Are they narcissists who take an excessive interest in themselves and who reveal a lack of concern for others? Or are they merely prudential deliberators who possess a knack for playing it safe and for looking out for number one? What is the difference between care of soul and spiritual egotism? I believe that the doctrine of moral self-perfection, properly understood, is quite different from these and other "self-centered" views about human motivation. In what follows, I shall try briefly to differentiate moral self-perfection from other self-regarding doctrines to which it bears only a superficial resemblance.

Consider first ethical egoism, the doctrine that agents always ought to act so as to best serve their own self-interests. When an ethical egoist's own personal interests conflict with another person's interests—"even when this other person is his wife, child, mother, or friend"[10]—he is always morally obligated, on this view, to pursue his own well-being at the other person's expense. However, moral agents who care for their souls in the sense here intended reject this doctrine; that is, it does not follow at all from the claim that morality is primarily self-regarding that moral agents ought always to maximize their own self-interests. People who obey "the authoritative and better part of themselves" do so not because they seek to maximize their own self-interests but because they see that morally right actions and attitudes are not possible unless they acquire, through their own efforts, the requisite intentions and dispositions. Additionally, moral agents whose fundamental commitment is care of soul frequently do act for the sake of other people's interests. They do not merely view others as means toward their own goals but recognize that the goods of others do, in and by themselves, provide morally compelling reasons for action. It is frequently the case that the authoritative and better part of ourselves (reason) will order us to take less for ourselves so that others may benefit.[11]

Second, consider the charge of narcissism, or what Dewey calls "spiritual egotism." Unlike ethical egoism, narcissism is not usually put forward as a normative view about how people ought to act (the heavy emphasis on self-fulfillment in certain popular psychology circles being one notable exception). It is intended rather as a descriptive, psychological claim about how people do act, or perhaps as a claim intended to have both descriptive *and* normative force. ("People *do* act in this manner, and it is *disgusting* that they do.")

At any rate, the assertion that in ethics self-regarding concerns are more fundamental than other-regarding concerns should not be construed either as an endorsement of narcissism or as an attempt to deflate the significance of our duties to others. Granted, there is a real danger that moral agents who do undertake to follow the authoritative and better part of themselves will become mere "image burnishers," moral show-offs who seek simply to embellish their own characters in this or that way when the right situation presents itself.[12] Dewey's warning is well taken: spiritual egotism is morally repugnant. But the motivational structure of people who believe that their primary moral obligation is to care for their souls is radically different from that of spiritual egotists. Again, people who successfully seek to realize a state of virtue in their own characters as the basis for all their acts do so because they see that this is what morality demands. They do it for the sake of a moral ideal, not because they desire to polish up their own images. Moral self-perfection is not narcissism for the simple reason that an overriding commitment to develop one's moral character is not identical with—and clearly will often conflict with—an overriding interest in one's own personal image. The narcissist and the person who seeks to strengthen his or her moral character are, so to speak, developing different selves.

The doctrine of moral self-perfection is, for three reasons, not an attempt to deflate the significance of our duties to others. First, our moral commitments to self and to others possess a logically different status. The subjects of moral action are always self-obligating, for only their practical reason can provide them with the requisite motivational structure to live and act morally. This is part of Kant's point concerning the priority of duties to ourselves over duties to others. A moral duty to others always presupposes a duty to oneself as well, for one must first *motivate oneself* to carry out such a duty to others in the proper spirit. But to claim that morality is self-regarding in this specific sense is in no way to deny that the *objects* of our moral concern are frequently the needs and claims of others. Nor is it to deny the obvious truth that moral acts are often intended to benefit others rather than oneself.[13]

Second, the moral duty to promote others's welfare is itself entailed by the commitment to oneself to develop one's character; for it is the special capacities of *humanity within oneself* that one is fostering when one undertakes such a commitment, and along with acceptance of this commitment goes a recognition that one is also obligated to promote similar capacities in others as well:

> While we should make ourselves a fixed center of our principles, we should regard the circle thus drawn around us as one that also forms a part of the all-inclusive circle of those who, in their attitude, are citizens of the world. (*DV* VI 473/145)

> Our duties toward ourselves consist ... in guarding, each in our own person, the dignity of mankind. A man will only reproach himself if he has the idea of mankind before his eyes. In this idea he finds an original, with which he compares himself. (*Ed.* IX 489/103)

In seeking to develop those essential capacities of humanity within themselves on which morality depends (e.g., the power to set goals for oneself, the ability to act according to principles), moral agents realize that they are morally obligated to create an environment in which everyone is in a position to develop his or her own capacities of humanity. In other words, our self-regarding duties point directly to active social duties. The man "who wills to develop his own talents wills that everyone develop his talents; he wills not only the cultural facilitation of his own moral improvement but cultural progress in general as a step toward the moral improvement of humanity and the corresponding happiness."[14]

Third, the realization that we have a duty to promote the happiness of others "follows from the fact that our self-love cannot be divorced from our need of being loved by others (i.e. of receiving help from them when we are in need), so that we make ourselves an end for others" (*DV* VI 392/53; cf. *G* IV 423/32). Selfishness cannot be willed a universal law, at least not by people who value their own happiness. A rational agent could not consistently will personal happiness and then refuse to accept the aid of others, for there may be times when his or her continued existence will depend upon the aid of others. Realization of this contradiction in willing must lead a rational agent to accept the rational necessity of a duty to help others.

By accepting the challenge to dedicate ourselves to a moral ideal and to educate our characters accordingly, we are not thereby given warrant to ignore the sufferings of rest of the world. On the contrary, we are placed in a better position to see what needs doing and then to do something about it. Nor should moral commitment be viewed as a rationalization for self-worship. Pure practical reason "strikes self-conceit [*Eigendünkel*] down, since all claims of self-esteem which precede conformity to the moral law are null and void" (C2 V 73/76).

Finally, modern critics have turned repeatedly to the sphere of prudence in their attempts to dismiss self-regarding concerns from ethics. Self-regarding concerns are not properly a part (much less the most important part) of ethics, according to such critics, because agents are already naturally disposed to care for themselves. Since it is prudent and expedient for people to care for themselves, any moral ought in this case is totally redundant. But as W. D. Falk points out, "Not everything done for oneself is done for reasons of prudence."[15] It is prudent to get into the housing market if a person has the funds to do so and knows that real estate prices will soon jump. But it is not prudent (though it may still be the thing to do, all things considered) for an AIDS patient to take a dangerous experimental drug in the hope of prolonging his life. Prudence "is only one way of looking after oneself. To act prudently is to play safe, for near-certain gains at small risks. But some good things one cannot get in this way. To get them at all one has to gamble."[16]

People do things for themselves not only for prudential reasons (when they are playing safe) but for a variety of other reasons, as well, including recklessness (when they ought to play safe but do not) or timidity (when it is in their own best interests to show courage but they fail to do so). Also, there are clearly cases where people do things to themselves in which the concept of prudence is much too weak to explain the agent's motives. "To call a self-made derelict, having progressed from folly through various stages of degradation to utter depravity, not immoral but only imprudent or misguided is to put an intolerable strain upon our language: it is to maintain a thesis at all costs."[17]

Moral and Nonmoral Selves

> In praising culture, we have never denied that conduct, not culture, is three-fourths of human life. Only it certainly appears, when the thing is examined, that conduct comes to have relations of a very close kind with culture.
>
> MATTHEW ARNOLD, *Literature and Dogma*

Once we accept the claim that morality ought to be construed as fundamentally self-regarding rather than other-regarding in the manner described, we are not given carte blanche for all of our personal projects. For it is the *moral* self and its *moral* traits of character that are placed at center stage by the care-of-soul doctrine, not the nonmoral self and its nonmoral traits of character. If someone is really convinced that, say, refining his backhand in tennis is a more important life goal than becoming a person of moral integrity who seeks justice in the world, none of these mental exertions can make a difference. Or can they?

It is no secret that the demarcation line between moral and nonmoral traits has been drawn very differently by different theorists. Aristotle argues that quick wit or urbanity (*eutrapelia*) and cleverness (*epidexiotēs*) are important moral virtues (*NE* IV.8); few if any modern moral theorists would do so. Surprisingly, three-fourths of the ancient cardinal virtues (wisdom, courage, self-control) have been deprived of moral status in the hands of some modern theorists, including Kant. Only justice appears immune from challenge—although Bentham tried to demote it, as well, in declaring justice to be "but a portion of benevolence in disguise."[18]

Faced with such extreme cultural variations, some contemporary writers have eschewed the moral/nonmoral distinction altogether, opting instead to "work with a network of more concrete and informal distinctions" within the broad sphere of the practical.[19] Such skepticism seems unwarranted. The terms *morality* and *ethics* are thrown about in our culture as never before, and it seems highly unlikely that people are ready to give them up.[20] Though a formal definition of morality (one consisting of a neat list of necessary and sufficient properties of what is being defined) is not possible,[21] more attention needs to be paid to what is meant by the concept. First and foremost, I have argued, morality is to be identified with a certain understanding of self-regarding values concerning how to live and act. This usage is in opposition with the modern tendency to use the word *morality* to refer exclusively to other-regarding values of justice and beneficence, and it owes strong debts to the Socratic doctrine that care of one's soul is the most important moral obligation.

Second, I believe that morality has ultimate importance in human life—that it is more important (in a sense and for reasons that I shall articulate in chapter 4) than all other areas of human life. Moral considerations have ultimate importance not (as many philosophers have argued) because they form a tightly packaged set of interests that can be shown to logically "override" all other competing sets of interests but rather because they concern values to which the pursuit of any and all interests, including scientific and technical ones, must answer. Morality is not just one narrow point of view competing against others.

Third, (and related to ultimate importance) is *pervasiveness*.[22] Moral considerations literally appear able to pervade or permeate into more areas and aspects of human life and action (and once they gain entry, to have, somehow, the final word) than do any other kinds of considerations. Part of the explanation for morality's pervasive reach in human life lies in the traditional identification between morality and the voluntary. Whatever is within our control is (subject to the usual excusing conditions) a possible object of moral assessment. My natural eye color is not a fact for moral assessment; my diffidence may well be. Even the most innocent or trivial-sounding voluntary act (e.g., to paint the kitchen floorboards turquoise or avocado) may, depending on the contextual circumstances, call—or even scream—for moral assessment. (For instance, suppose that I decide I want to paint the floorboards avocado but that it is a commonly known fact that the only brand of avocado paint available is one manufactured by a firm that has racist and sexist hiring policies and continually flaunts environmental regulations in its production processes.) But in recent years a number of writers have argued that morality's reach extends even further than the voluntary. In real life we often morally appraise emotions, desires, and attitudes in others, as well as in ourselves, that are not directly within our control. Someone may "not be able to help" feeling angry with, or jealous of, another person; yet we may continue to feel, with justification, that such a state of mind is nevertheless morally objectionable.[23] The claim that many involuntary states of mind are appropriate objects of moral appraisal is clearly more controversial than the tamer thesis that morality's reach stops at the boundary of what is within our control, but it is also one that appears to receive strong support from ordinary moral judgment and practice.

These and other properties of morality will be identified and explored in greater detail in later chapters. Suffice it to say for now that the moral/nonmoral distinction, difficult as it is to demarcate precisely in a hard-and-fast manner, continues to serve numerous important purposes and ought not to be jettisoned. I assume that truthfulness, justice, and beneficence are unquestionably moral and that hair color and musical talent in most circumstances are not. My immediate aim now is to show that moral agents are obliged to cultivate not only their directly moral traits but their indirectly moral traits, as well, and that doing so will make them more effective moral agents. The precise breakdown of traits into moral and nonmoral becomes less pressing once they are viewed within the larger perspective of overall character development.

As noted earlier, Aristotle seems to place under the rubric *moral* several traits that most moderns would label nonmoral.[24] Perhaps because the scope of his investigation into *ēthikē aretai* is much wider than what most moderns would regard as moral virtues, the possibility of a conflict between one's self-regarding moral concerns and one's self-regarding nonmoral concerns does not often arise.[25] But I shall try to show now that even for Kant, who supposedly did make a radical distinction between moral and nonmoral concerns and who claimed that moral concerns always override nonmoral ones, the likelihood of conflict between one's moral and nonmoral self-regarding projects is vastly overrated.

Kant divides our imperfect duties to ourselves into two categories: duties of *natural perfection* and duties of *moral perfection*. Natural perfection consists in the development of the powers that belong to us as rational animals. As Kant writes: "Man has a duty to himself of cultivating [*cultura*] his natural powers [*Naturkräfte*] (powers of mind, soul, and body), which are the means to all sorts of rational ends.—Man owes it to himself (as a rational being) not to leave idle, and as it were, rusting away the natural dispositions and powers that his reason can in any way use" (*DV* VI 444/110–11). Powers of mind (*Geisteskräfte*) include the capacities of understanding, judgment, and reason, particularly the sort of abstract deductive reasoning needed in mathematics and logic. Powers of soul (*Seelenkräfte*) include "memory, imagination and the like"— capacities that aid the understanding in interpreting experience. Finally, under powers of body (*Leibeskräfte*) comes the general command to look after "the basic stuff (the matter) in man, without which he could not realize his ends"— physical education and gymnastics (*DV* VI 445/111–12).

Which of our various *Naturkräfte* should we try to develop, and to what degree should we develop those we have chosen? Here the distinction between imperfect and perfect duties is critical. The duty to develop one's natural powers is an imperfect, as opposed to a perfect, duty. We cannot lay down an exact metric concerning its extent, focus, and degree but must leave such matters to individual discretion: "As to which of these natural perfections should take *precedence* among our ends and in what *proportion* to one another we should make them our ends in keeping with our duty to ourselves, it remains for us to choose, according to our rational deliberation about what sort of life we should like to lead and whether we have the powers necessary for that way of life" (*DV* VI 445/112).[26] The question is not whether cultivation of one's natural powers does or does not possess moral worth. (It does, though *only indirectly*. A good will is the only unqualified good, but a good will that has developed its natural powers will be able to realize moral goals more effectively. An agent's voluntary nonmoral capacities are often "conducive to this good will itself and can facilitate its work" [*G* IV 393/7].) Rather, the question is whether an agent who takes the moral life seriously must, as antimorality critics claim, deny his or her nonmoral self, suppress whatever artistic, scientific, or athletic talents he or she may possess in the name of higher moral concerns. And clearly the answer is *no*. The good will of an agent who is also physically strong and agile will sometimes be in a better position to realize certain moral ends than will one who lacks these nonmoral traits; the good will of an agent who has developed *Geisteskräfte* will often be able to carry out moral projects more successfully than will an ignoramus.[27]

In sum, since each of the natural powers can at various times serve as an enabling, or second-order, virtue that can serve to enhance the use and development of the moral virtues and since agents have a moral duty to develop the natural powers that will best help them in their chosen life plan, the possibility of conflict between moral and nonmoral self-development is greatly diminished.[28] Williams's "Gauguin problem"—the issue of how to reconcile the importance of artistic and scientific development with everyday moral commitments—is severely overblown. Yes, we need to decide what to do with our lives, but the idea that there is some simplistic either/or to agonize over ("Shall I choose art or morality?") is a false dilemma. People do not succeed in escaping from morality when they choose to focus exclusively on some of their natural powers. Nor do moral agents succeed in escaping from the significant claims of scientific truth and artistic beauty in human life by promoting moral projects. Both sides need each other.

However, perhaps we have missed the point, since the antimorality critic's decisive claim is not so much that the person who strives for virtue cannot become a great artist as that the morally good person is simply boring. Wolf, for instance, complains that a moral saint "will have to be very, very nice. It is important that he not be offensive. The worry is that, as a result, he will have to be dull-witted or humorless or bland."[29] If the real charge against morality is that its cultivation will result in uninteresting personalities, we may well have to admit defeat. For it is not possible to require of people that they develop interesting personalities. Once it is determined (if indeed it ever can be) which precise list of traits (in which precise amounts) constitutes an "interesting" personality (say, for starters, one-third athletic ability, one-third artistic appreciation, and one-third wittiness?),[30] it will definitely be the case that not everyone is in a position to develop such traits in their requisite amounts. Such matters are not substantially under everyone's control, and the dictum " 'ought' implies 'can' " applies here. However, it is by no means clear that those who do not place moral concerns among their highest priorities in life are in any better position to become interesting personalities than are those who do. Certainly, academics have no monopoly on interesting personalities. So the interesting personality argument is ultimately a nonstarter. Morality has no special hold on the property of an interesting personality; but neither does nonmorality. Still, given the duty to develop our indirectly moral powers, we *should* try to become interesting people, assuming we can ever figure out what the word *interesting* means.

Friends

Without friends no one would choose to live, though he had all other goods.

ARISTOTLE, *Nicomachean Ethics*

Friendship is . . . an ideal of emotional and practical concern [*ein Ideal der Teilnehmung und Mitteilung*] which each of the friends united through a morally good will takes in each other's welfare; and even if friendship does not produce the complete happiness of life, the adoption of this ideal in men's attitude to one another contains their worthiness to be happy. Hence men have a duty of friendship.

KANT, *The Doctrine of Virtue*

Finally, a few words about others—"significant others" about whom we care deeply. Related to the charge that morality severely downgrades personal concerns is the additional accusation that it "cannot allow for love, friendship, affection, fellow feeling, and community."[31] Just as morality does not allow us to value ourselves and our personal projects, critics claim, neither does it allow us to care deeply for, or to develop special attachments toward, other persons whom we value as persons rather than as producers or possessors of moral value. Morality is thus a severe form of double jeopardy, for it not only alienates us from ourselves and our own personal projects but also from our friends and their concerns.

The charge that the moral point of view cannot account for (and, even worse, is in unreconcilable conflict with) the value of friendship stems directly from the claim that impartiality is definitive of the moral point of view. If being committed to impartiality means according no special privilege and adopting no special attitude toward any person, thing, or situation and if taking up the moral point of view requires that we make impartiality our central value, it does follow that a commitment to morality will often alienate us from our friends. How can we act consistently on our deep concern with the good of our friends for their own sake if morality obligates us to give "equal time" to the legitimate moral claims of all, including total strangers?

Fortunately, the first half of this antecedent is false, so the argument itself fails. Being committed to impartiality does *not* mean according no special privilege and adopting no special attitude toward any person, thing, or situation. As John Rawls and Adrian Piper have noted, this equation fails to distinguish between *impartiality* and *impersonality.* According to the *Oxford English Dictionary, impartial* means "unbiased, unprejudiced, just, fair, or equitable." *Impersonal,* on the other hand, means "having no personal reference or connection." One may strive successfully to be impartial (strive, that is, to be just and fair) without being impersonal (being completely indifferent to others), and vice versa.[32] But a second fundamental error occurs when critics assume that impartiality (much less impersonality or indifference) is "definitive" of the moral point of view for Kantians.[33] Impartiality (understood here not as impersonality but as a commitment to fairness and justice) is an extremely important virtue in Kantian ethics, but it is certainly not the only one. As I shall try to show, friendship is also a virtue for Kant.

Aristotle, in the *Nicomachean Ethics,* devotes more space (all of books VIII–IX) to the analysis of friendship than he does to any other virtue; and when contemporary critics say that morality has no place for friendship they clearly are not thinking of Aristotelian ethics.[34] Rather, their intended targets are utilitarians and Kantians. Lawrence Blum, for instance, asserts that friendship stands "morally condemned" on "the Kantian view."[35] I shall not be concerned to defend utilitarian conceptions of morality against the charge that they condemn friendship (I think they do); but I do believe that Kant can be easily acquitted. Friendship *is* an important virtue within Kant's moral outlook; and as we have seen already, he states explicitly that "men have a duty of friendship" (*DV* VI 469/140).[36] In calling friendship "an ideal of practical and emotional concern," Kant indicates to readers that it is an ideal of humanity both in action or willing (*humanitas practica*) as well as in feeling (*humanitas aesthetica*). This double characteristic is definitive of human beings, for they are "animals endowed with reason" and not mere rational beings as such.[37] Far from denying that emotional attachment to others has a rightful place in human morality, Kant explicitly advocates its necessary place. Emotional love is (for human beings only, not for rational beings in general) a natural predisposition for the concept of practical love as a duty.[38] Humanly speaking, emotional love is a subjectively necessary condition without which we would be incapable of acting according to practical reason.

Kant also recognizes (as utilitarians do not) that friendship "is not universal; it is a particular association of specific persons [*eine besondere Vereinigung gewisser Personen*]" (*LE* 262/207). Yet despite Kant's supposed monolithic commitment to the values of universality and impartiality, he defends the rightful role of particularistic friendships within human communities. An association of nonhuman purely rational beings ("holy wills," in Kant's terminology) would not feel the need (or be obligated) to form strong, exclusive friendships with one another, so that ordinary friendship would not likely exist in such a community. They would be "friends" to everyone (in so far as it makes sense to talk of friendship in this watered-down manner) and bear good will toward everyone without exception. But for the vast majority of humans this is not desirable or even possible: "To be the friend of everybody is impossible, for friendship is a particular relationship, and he who is a friend to everyone has no particular friend. . . . As a rule, men are inclined to form particular relationships because this is a natural impulse and also because we all start with the particular and then proceed to the general" (*LE* 265/209).[39]

Clearly, the natural impulse within humans to form close friendships with others is not something Kant's ethics seeks to suppress. Rather, the idea is to build on it, to promote moral community through friendship. Still, the critic may reply, is this not a distortion of moral common sense, one that severely underrates friendship? In seeking to build upon friendship in order to produce the true, "universal" morality, does Kant not demote friendship to a merely instrumental status? And does friendship not have a more-than-instrumental value within our own lives?[40]

Admittedly, Kant does appear to assign a merely instrumental value to what he calls the minor "virtues of social intercourse." In a brief appendix to the account of friendship offered in *The Doctrine of Virtue,* he writes:

> Affability, sociability, courtesy, hospitality, and gentleness (in disagreeing without quarreling) are, indeed, only small change [*nur Scheidemünze*]; yet they promote the feeling for virtue itself by [arousing] a striving to bring this illusion as near as possible to the truth. All of these, like the mere manners of social intercourse, manifest what is obligatory and also bind others to it; and in so doing they work toward a virtuous attitude in so far as they at least bring virtue into vogue [*beliebt machen*]. (*DV* VI 473–74/146)

Similarly, Kant states that social intercourse "is in itself a cultivator of virtue and a preparation for its surer practice" (*LE* 251/198). But the virtues of friendship are, on his view, deeper than this: they are not tacked on as a brief appendix. Kant does not advocate that humans seek to transcend friendship or to merely use it as a stepping-stone to an allegedly higher moral good: "A man without friends is entirely isolated" (*LE* 265/209), and human beings cannot flourish in isolation. The human condition requires that we cultivate the virtues of friendship. Not to do so would be to sacrifice our humanity, and nowhere does Kant advise us to attempt such a sacrifice.

In conclusion, Kantians can (and should) seek friendship, and Kant's view is that each of us has a duty to do so. Kant's moral cosmopolitanism is too pervasive to ignore, and the gradual creation of a universal ethical community where all people are treated with equal respect and dignity is, for him, the central moral task. However, the Kantian universal ethical community is certainly not one where all agents speak Esperanto and local traditions and ties of friendship have been obliterated. This is much too crude a rendering of the kingdom of ends.

At the same time, we must not pretend that the values of friendship and justice will never pull in different directions or that moral theorists will always have a magic wand to wave at them (when they do pull in different directions) to make conflict disappear. Not all moral disputes are resolvable; not all tragedies are avoidable.

2

Morality, Lives, and Acts

For you see, don't you, that our discussion is about this—and what would anyone with the slightest intelligence be more seriously concerned about than this? I mean—the way we ought [*chrē*] to live.

PLATO, *Gorgias*

Morality is character, character is that which is engraved [*kharassoō*]; but the sand and the sea have no character and neither has abstract intelligence, for character is really inwardness.

KIERKEGAARD, *The Present Age*

The Return of Virtue

Perhaps the liveliest debate within recent ethical theory concerns the question whether morality's primary evaluative focus should be on the acts that agents perform or on the agents themselves—who and what they are as persons in some deeper way that is not merely derivative upon a tallying up of judgments concerning the rightness of the deeds they have performed or of the value of the consequences of their acts.[1] If we focus on acts, we seem naturally led to the task of formulating rules and principles of right conduct[2] and then inevitably to the additional task of constructing a decision procedure to handle cases where the rules or principles conflict with one another.[3] On the other hand, if we focus on agents, the quest for rules and decision procedures is never seriously entertained, being replaced by the even more ambitious project of articulating an ideal of human flourishing and then locating the virtues within this larger depiction of human life.[4]

The acts-versus-agents (or doing-versus-being) debate is usually said to have begun in 1958 with Elizabeth Anscombe's advice to "do ethics without" the notion of a "moral ought." Without the belief in a divine lawgiver to back them up, she argued, notions such as "moral obligation" and "morally ought" lack intelligibility. Secular moralists should thus take their cue from Aristotle and "look for 'norms' in human virtues: ... perhaps the species *man*, regarded ... from the point of view of the activity of thought and choice in regard to the various departments of life—powers and faculties and use of things needed— 'has' such and such virtues: and this 'man' with the complete set of virtues is the 'norm'."[5] Shortly thereafter, the philosophical marketplace began to be flooded with warnings that modern moral theorists had "neglected virtue" and that this neglect was the chief cause of the moribund state of academic ethics.[6] Since then, the virtue ethics literature has swelled enormously; and it now seems safe to say that the genre has not only established itself as a settled paradigm within ethics but is on the verge of achieving hegemony as the outlook of choice among younger writers in ethics.[7] Today one finds fewer and fewer theorists engaging in efforts to construct viable utilitarian or deontological systems: Aristotle has replaced Mill and Kant as the classical moral philosopher most likely to inspire allegiance.

Stating precisely and in detail what an ethics of virtue is is a difficult if not impossible task; for, as one reviewer notes, a "plethora of issues, charges, claims, and counter-claims [are present] in recent work on the virtues."[8] However, all concerned parties should agree with the simple claim that an ethics of virtue holds that judgments about the character of persons, independent of an assessment of either the rightness of their actions or the value of the consequences of their actions, is what is most fundamental in moral evaluation. This does not necessarily mean that an ethics of virtue must reject the claim that acts and/or consequences of acts are also sometimes important, for it can still assign a secondary or derivative status to them. It merely means that judgments about persons, in some strong and nonderivative sense, come first. This character-first conception of virtue ethics is a very minimal definition within which we can both locate the common ground shared by all virtue theorists and avoid the more internecine definitional squabbles that have marked much of the debate.

My aim in the present chapter is to articulate and defend the underlying conception of morality implicit in the commitment to the character-first thesis of virtue ethics.[9] How does our understanding of what morality is change once we give up the claim that moral evaluation should focus first on discrete acts or consequences of acts in favor of the view that it is persons and their lives that count most? Why is this alternative conception of morality a stronger, richer moral conception, one that is much better able to withstand the attacks of antimorality skeptics and to provide us with an ideal that is worthy of our allegiance? Finally, how does acceptance of this alternative moral conception bring us closer into agreement with previous insights into the nature of the moral life, both ancient as well as modern?

Why Being Is Better

Briefly, I believe that a moral conception which gives priority to being over doing is superior for six reasons:

1. It is a bigger conception.
2. It puts mere do-gooders in their place.
3. It is integrating, not alienating.

4. It emphasizes the need for moral salience and judgment.
5. It leaves scope for aspiration.
6. It is a richer conception.

A Bigger Morality

The first point that becomes apparent when one adopts a virtue ethics perspective is that morality is suddenly much bigger. Under the act conception, moral questions arise only when one is trying to figure out the right thing to do in certain problematic situations. Defining what, exactly, constitutes a "moral problem" in a manner that will satisfy all act and rule theorists is difficult, since, as Edmund Pincoffs notes, the question What is the right thing to do in a morally problematic situation? fails to distinguish "between queries concerning what is the morally *correct* (rule-required, expected, proper, appropriate, fitting) thing to do and queries concerning the morally *useful* (fruitful, helpful, practical, optimum) thing to do."[10] Nevertheless, in spite of the deep disagreement that exists between deontologists and consequentialists concerning the identifying features of a moral problem, both sides share the assumption that moral problems (however defined) are only occasional phenomena within one's life. Moral problems do not permeate every moment of our existence: occasionally, we are unsure about what to do (e.g., whether to tell the truth, when doing so may bring irreparable damage to our career and economic hardship upon our family); but thankfully, such quandaries are the exception rather than the norm in day-to-day life. However, if the primary moral question is not What is the right thing to do in a problematic situation? but What is a good life for a human being? morality suddenly seems to invade all corners of life. As David Norton remarks:

> For classical [virtue] ethics nothing in human experience is without moral meaning, and "the moral situation" is the life of each person in its entirety. . . . If morality is coterminous with human life and unrestrictedly pervasive within it, then individuals are afforded no non-moral domain of refuge, and no human institution, practice, or discipline can claim exemption from morality's ultimate concern—the good life for human beings.[11]

While it is true that bigger is not always better, in the case of morality I believe that bigger generally *is* better. The act conception of morality insulates too many important aspects of human life from morality's reach, aspects that have a deep and lasting impact not only on how we turn out as persons but also on how we act. Focusing on an adult's occasional moral quandaries is often too little too late, in the sense that who and what the person is is, for the most part, already determinate when the quandary hits. On the other hand, if we can bring ourselves to step back and inquire into the character of the agent who is now faced with a moral problem, we will often be in a better position to know why he or she is in such a position in the first place. Properly applied, the agent perspective functions as an effective preventive medicine.

Unadmirable Do-gooders

Moral conceptions that give priority to the evaluation of acts have the paradoxical implication that the persons who perform the greatest number of right acts are sometimes those whom we admire least. An adequate moral conception ought not to have such an implication and needs to embrace more inspiring ideals if it is to gain our allegiance. In articulating the disillusionment with act theories that has fueled the interest in virtue ethics, Sarah Conly writes:

> We are all familiar with the picture of nasty do-gooders whom we hardly admire, do not want to emulate, and whose company we avoid, even while admitting the merit of their actions. In contrast to this we have the picture of those whose concerns do not lead to a life of perfect fulfillment of duty but who attract us by the strength, purity, and sensitivity of their characters.[12]

The most obvious problem with unadmirable do-gooders lies in their emotional makeup. They are able consistently to do the right thing by overcoming or suppressing contrary desires, but they have not succeeded in educating their desires properly. They have not trained themselves to *want* to follow reason, but through sheer strength of will they manage to do so anyway. There is thus a fundamental lack of harmony between the affective and cognitive dimensions of their character. As a result, they tend to be too leaden and solemn and are often unable to appreciate humor or irony.

But their emotional coldness is itself a clue to a deeper problem: they somehow miss the point. They always try to *do* the right thing; but they fail to see that morally admirable doing must flow more directly out of being, out of a settled character whose various internal aspects are at peace with one another rather than constantly at war. It doesn't matter how many morally right acts a person performs if the acts in question are not characteristic manifestations of a settled personality in which the emotions have been properly educated to want what reason enjoins. On the other hand, people who believe that moral evaluation is primarily about the question of how to live will not make this mistake. They will see that the issue of what kind of person one is must always be at the forefront of moral evaluation.

Integrity and Alienation

A related issue concerns the frequent tendency of people who subscribe to act conceptions of morality to view moral demands as externally imposed constraints, constraints, that, if followed, will alienate them from their own deepest projects and commitments. Conly writes:

> It is a fact of common experience that attention to moral duty can be felt as an intrusion in one's life, taking time and attention away from one's more heartfelt concerns and subordinating them to the stern impartial demands of moral law.

Moral goodness, then, is held to by some to be bought at the price of internal harmony and wholeness. The proponent of the ethics of virtue, on the contrary, hopes to bring about a rapprochement of meaning and morality. A virtue is generally held to be a part of one's character, and thus something within the person. The possession of a virtue thus provides an internal impetus to action which is not at odds with the general orientation of the person.[13]

One primary reason why morality is felt to be alienating is that morality, on the act view, is often held to be a set of "side constraints" on our projects. We do what we will, and for the most part what we do is nobody else's business—until we stray into some area over which a moral rule exercises authority. At that point (if our commitment to doing the morally right thing prevails), we have to alter our project accordingly. On the other hand, if the moral question is how to live, what to make of ourselves as persons, morality itself becomes our ground project and the possibility of being alienated by morality's demands lessens considerably (*lessens* rather than *vanishes,* since the prospect of conflict between moral and nonmoral concerns is an ineliminable fact of life).

Moral Salience and Judgment

It has long been recognized that rules for right action require judicious interpretation in order to be effective and that there are no rules for applying rules. How do we know whether and how a given rule applies to an act under consideration? Ironically, Kant (the virtue theorists' favorite example of morality by rules for action) insists repeatedly that moral laws require "a power of judgment [*Urteilskraft*] sharpened by experience, partly in order to distinguish in what cases they are applicable, and partly to gain for them access to the human will as well as influence for putting them into practice" (*G* IV 389/3). Furthermore, knowledge of rules and formal instruction alone are no guarantee of good judgment, since possession of *Urteilskraft* is "a peculiar talent which can be practiced only, and cannot be taught. It is the specific quality of so-called mother-wit; and its lack no school can make good" (*Cl* A 133/B 172; cf. *TP* VIII 273/61 and *A* VII 68–73/196–201). The "peculiar talent" of good judgment is of course a trait of character, a disposition that can be strengthened through experience and exposure to examples but never simply reduced to an algorithmic package deal. But rule theorists, since they place insufficient weight on the concept of character, leave agents in the awkward position of being unable to apply their theories effectively.

Related to judgment is the even more fundamental ability to pick out morally salient features in the environment. How do people come to know which aspects of their proposed actions call for moral attention?[14] Here, too, the requisite perceptual skills are character traits that are developed and refined over a long period of time. They cannot be assumed at the outset or handed over to someone as a list of rules.

The main point to emphasize here is that rule conceptions of morality are guilty of putting the cart before the horse. Action-guiding rules are useless and/ or dangerous when placed in the hands of persons who lack good character. As Joel Kupperman writes:

> Good character is required for reliably correct ethical choice. This is not only the obvious point that one must have a good will as well as the knowledge of what is right. Someone who lacks an adequate set of perceptions, concerns, and commitments cannot be relied upon to know what is right. Sometimes he or she can get the correct ethical answer as it were by luck; but in many cases the correct answer will disappear into the huge, unmediated gap between theory and particular case.[15]

Ironically, rule conceptions of morality often stand little chance of providing efficacious guidance to practice; for rules require character for effective application, but such approaches do not take character formation seriously. An agent conception of morality is in a better position to address the fundamental questions of judgment and salience and hence to guide practice effectively.

Space for Aspiration

Because act conceptions of morality focus on discrete time-slices in the here and now (What is the right thing to do, in the face of this quandary that looms before me at this moment?), they have little room for long-term ideals and projects that guide human development. But it is a truism that we cannot seriously understand a person's present actions unless we also know what the person is aiming at. Action is structured by intentions, and significant actions are generally expressions of persistent, underlying, long-term goals. These underlying goals are in turn tied to basic hopes and concerns for the future. David Norton writes:

> The effect of modern moral minimalism is to afford moral life little space for aspiration; it is a small room with a low ceiling and not much of a view.... By contrast to modern ethics, classical [virtue] ethics gives a central place to ideals, and it is characteristic of ideals that they are capable of enlisting the full measure of human aspiration. The function of ideals in classical ethical theory and moral life is to guide moral development, transforming random changes in the lives of individuals and societies into directed change that deserves to be called moral growth.[16]

Ethics ought to provide space for aspiration, for it is impossible to achieve any detailed understanding of human action unless we grasp how and in what ways present conduct is meant to further underlying goals. But if acts themselves can only be understood well once their relations to long-term goals are grasped, it appears that act ethics must seek conceptual resources outside of its own narrow sphere (i.e., within the domain of agent ethics) in order to evaluate acts. Paradoxically, act ethics is forced to seek aid from agent ethics in order to carry out its own project.

A Richer Morality

Finally, the virtue ethics conception of morality is superior because it is richer in content. Once persons, rather than acts, are placed at the center of the moral stage, it becomes much harder to compartmentalize moral assessment. In making moral judgments, we are now free to draw upon *all* aspects of a person's life that directly, as well as indirectly, concern voluntary processes. Athletic and intellectual abilities, aesthetic and religious concerns—all qualities of persons over which at least some individual control is exercisable now become at least indirectly relevant to the moral project of choosing a way of life. This is not to claim that the distinction between the moral and the nonmoral vanishes (e.g., that justice is no more a moral virtue than poise). A family of core virtues must remain at the center of a viable moral conception. But we are now free to enlist a wide variety of other traits to support or activate the directly moral virtues. Physical strength and agility can often help further the ends of courage; wit and an appreciation for the ironic can often help promote the aims of justice. Any trait that can help people better to promote moral ends will have an indirect moral worth.[17]

The richness of a character conception of morality is evident in several other ways as well. First, a greater potential exists for grasping the underlying connections between morality and many areas of culture such as art, religion, and language. A person's own moral conception—not to mention the dominant morality of the society in which he or she lives—is influenced by such factors in innumerable ways. However, theorists who confine their sense of the moral to patterns of action and to the imperatives that enjoin them are often not in a good position to detect these cultural influences. We are most likely to discern the enormous impact of culture upon morality not in explicit rule-governed acts but in more subtle states of mind, attitudes, and emotions. Second, with the notion of flourishing that seems to be built into the concept of a virtue, connections are drawn between morality and medicine (particularly psychiatry and psychotherapy) and, indeed, between morality and all of the life sciences. Moral theory is not the only discipline that concerns itself with questions about living creatures' modes of life and of the circumstances most favorable for them.[18]

A large part of the antimoralists' objection to morality can be seen to stem from the narrowness of the act conception that they implicitly assume in making their criticisms of moral commitment. Wolf, for instance, is worried that the moral virtues will somehow crowd out the nonmoral virtues within the personality of a would-be moral saint, the result being that we will be left with a maximal do-gooder whose nonmoral personality is empty; while Williams is critical of the earnest husband who, in deliberating whether he should save his drowning wife, has "one thought too many." Such criticisms lose their force when an act conception is replaced by a broader agent conception; for the latter requires us to ask how a person's life in general and overall is going. Someone whose nonmoral personality is empty or who typically carries around excessive cognitive baggage in situations that will not tolerate it cannot be said to have a good life, for such a person is going to fail morally in too many cases.

Ancients Versus Moderns: How Large a Gulf?

A stock-in-trade pronouncement found in much recent ethical theory that concerns itself with the history of ethics is that Aristotle has no concept of moral ought, obligation, or duty.[19] Elizabeth Anscombe, as we saw earlier, encourages contemporary moral theorists to drop the notion "morally ought," claiming that we can "do ethics without it, as is shown by the example of Aristotle."[20] And Bernard Williams asserts in *Ethics and the Limits of Philosophy* that there "is no ancient Greek word for duty."[21]

Many classicists have also argued that a concept of moral duty or obligation is nowhere to be found in Aristotle. Alexander Grant, for instance, in his commentary on the *Nicomachean Ethics,* writes, in a note on the Greek phrase *tou deontos* at *NE* 1094a24, "Not 'our duty' in the modern sense, this concept not having been as yet developed."[22] And D. J. Allan, in *The Philosophy of Aristotle,* concludes his discussion of Aristotle's ethics by stating that Aristotle "takes little or no account of the motive of moral obligation; he does not speak in terms of rules of conduct which apply equally to all men."[23]

A companion claim that frequently works its way into such discussions is that "modern" ethics neglects virtue concepts and is exclusively concerned with formulating rules for right action. Alasdair MacIntyre, for instance, states in *After Virtue* that in Kant's moral writings

> we have reached a point at which the notion that morality is anything other than obedience to rules has almost, if not quite, disappeared from sight. And so the central problems of moral philosophy come to cluster around the question "How do we know *which* rules to follow?" Virtue-concepts become as marginal to the moral philosopher as they are to the morality of the society which he inhabits.[24]

But are the differences between ancient and modern ethics on these fundamental issues of obligation and virtue really so enormous? How could someone reflect critically about ethics without employing concepts of both character and right action?[25] I shall now argue that recent critics have seriously exaggerated two alleged differences between ancient and modern ethics: Aristotle does, indeed, employ a concept of moral obligation; and virtue concepts are not marginal to modern ethics.[26]

Aristotle's Moral Ought

Surprisingly, several of the critics who assert that there is no concept of a moral ought in Aristotle decline to state what they mean by a moral ought. Furthermore, some of those who do discuss the idea make highly controversial claims on its behalf.[27] But before we decide whether Aristotle does or does not employ a concept of moral ought, we need some initial agreement concerning the meaning of the concept. As a means toward this end, I shall start by trying to articulate what I believe are the basic features of this concept present in ordinary contemporary usage. I hope that what follows is plain and ordinary enough that competing parties can agree that it captures the minimum content of what most people today mean by the idea of a moral ought.

Let us start with the common distinction between role-related versus non-role-related duties. Role-related duties concern jobs which people are expected to perform in virtue of the fact that they occupy an office or station within a social organization. Thus, a father has certain role-related duties to his daughters, a professor to her students, and so on. This concept of role-related duties is an extremely modest one that exists in all cultures and that Aristotle noncontroversially recognizes. As W. F. Hardie notes, the detailed discussions of justice and friendship in the *Nicomachean Ethics* (books V, VIII, and IX) "tell us about the duties which fall on judges and jurymen, on soldiers and on voters, on husbands and wives and parents and children; on men as members of clubs and fraternities, as business partners, even as belonging to a parish or local community."[28]

It is the stronger, non-role-related sense of duty that critics generally have in mind when they claim that Aristotle has no concept of moral ought or duty; and I agree that this is what we must find if we are to prove our case. Roughly, this stronger sense of moral duty or ought has the following four features:

1. Performance is not tied to fulfillment of a specific social role but is simply something that one recognizes, all things considered, that one must do. It is potentially tied to the fulfillment of every social role.
2. Moral oughts and obligations concern actions that are in our power—we are not obligated to do things that it is physically impossible for us to do.[29]
3. Failure to perform, without a recognized excuse, reflects poorly on the agent's character.[30]
4. The requirement is viewed as being not just one of prudence or convenience[31] but as stemming from an all-things-considered assessment of what ought to be done. The potentially competing claims of prudence, convenience, etiquette, custom, law, and so on must all be included in considerations of what morally ought to be done; but *how* important each factor is in a particular case depends on a whole range of things that cannot be laid down in advance. Morality considers *all* claims upon our behavior; but each claim has the status of a *prima facie* demand until we decide what, all things considered, we must do.[32]

Although I cannot argue the case further at present, I submit that this list captures the basic minimum content of what is normally meant today by a sense of moral ought or obligation. To my knowledge, there is nothing in it to which moral philosophers need object.[33] I turn next to some passages from the *Nicomachean Ethics*, in an attempt to show that Aristotle does indeed discuss deliberative contexts in which these four features are present.

I am in agreement with the following observation of Hardie's: "If we ask in what shapes the experience or fact of obligation came into [Aristotle's] view we should discuss his use of 'ought' [*dei*] and of 'right' [*dikaion*] but also what he calls the 'noble' [*kalon*]."[34] To this trio I would add the frequently occurring phrase "according to correct reason" (*kata ton orthon logon*). Although much has been written about the use of each of these four terms in Aristotle, it is my hope that the following brief analysis can add to the discussion by focusing attention on an Aristotelian use of *ought* that is (or so I shall argue) clearly moral by contemporary standards.

Dei, usually translated as "one must" or "one ought," has many different senses in Greek, as is also true of the word *ought* in English. According to Gauthier, "Aristotle, in the *Nicomachean Ethics* alone, employs [*dei*] about 170 times in a sense which is uncontestably moral."[35] Typical passages include 1119b17–18 ("The temperate man craves for the things he ought, as he ought, and when he ought; and this is what reason [*logos*] directs [*tattei*]") and 1115b12–13, where Aristotle notes that the brave man faces fearful things "as he ought and as reason directs [*hupomenei*], for the sake of the noble [*tou kalou heneka*]; for this is the end [*telos*] of virtue." In the last clause of this second passage we are told that *all* virtues involve acting and feeling as one ought and as reason directs and for the sake of the noble. I infer from this that each of these three Aristotelian terms is roughly synonymous (in the sense that they direct us to the same act or same feeling) when used in the context of discussion concerning how humans should act and feel.

Another representative passage from the *Nichomachaean Ethics* in which a moral sense of *dei* occurs is 1121a1–4, where the virtue of liberality is discussed. If the liberal man spends in a manner "contrary to what is *to deon* and *to kalon,* he will be pained, but moderately and as he ought [*hōs dei*]; for it is the mark of virtue both to be pleased and to be pained at the right [*dei*] objects and as one ought [*hōs dei*]." Here again, as we saw a moment ago at 1115b12–13, the implication is that *all* the virtues concern acting and/or feeling as one ought. At 1118b20, where the vice of self-indulgence is analyzed, Aristotle criticizes the gluttons who fill their bellies "beyond what is right" (*para ton deon*); and at 1123a20 the vulgar man is identified as he who spends *para ton deon.*

Granted that on Aristotle's view, someone who responds to a situation as he ought is not usually following a specific rule of action. However, the concept of action-guiding rules is noticeably absent from our earlier list, and it is my contention that this idea does not from a necessary part of what most people today mean by a moral ought. On my view, what makes Aristotle's use of *dei* a *moral* use (in the contexts where it is arguably so) is simply that it satisfies the four conditions. In other words, when Aristotle's temperate man "craves for things he ought, as he ought, and when he ought," it seems to be the case that (1) he is not merely fulfilling a social role, (2) he is concerned with things that are in his power, (3) failure to express the appropriate desires will reflect poorly on his character, and (4) these requirements are not merely matters of prudence or convenience but, on the contrary, constitute the agent's most serious concerns. There is no need to muddy the waters further by dragging in wild speculations as to whether such oughts exert a "mesmeric force" or are "peculiarly modern" or are a remnant of Christian theology.[36]

To kalon, translated as "the noble" in the revised Oxford translation, can also be rendered as "the fine" or "the beautiful."[37] Although the term does have a definite aesthetic use that predates its moral use, several factors suggest that it also has a clear moral sense in Aristotle. First, as we saw earlier, Aristotle occasionally uses this term in conjunction with *dei* as well as with *logos* (e.g., *NE* 1115b12), suggesting that what one ought to do and what reason directs one to do are at least sometimes synonymous with what it is noble or fine to do.[38] Second, as Irwin points out, politics is frequently defined by Aristotle as being concerned with "noble and just things" (*ta de kala kai ta dikaia*) (1094b14–15, cf. 1095b5; practical wisdom is said to have the same concerns at 1143b22 and 1144a12). Politics aims at making the citizens "to be of a certain character, viz. good and capable of noble acts" (1099b31–32). Third, Aristotle states several times that *all* virtuous actions "are noble and done for the sake of the noble" (1120a23–24; 1122b6–7). In each of these cases, the text sounds extremely odd if we assume that *kalon* is being used in a purely aesthetic sense. On the other hand, it is quite easy to convince ourselves that *to kalon,* as used in most of these contexts, does meet the four earlier-specified conditions. For instance, when Aristotle's brave man faces terrible things for the sake of the noble (1115b12–13), it seems to be the case that (1) he does so because he thinks he must, not just because it is his job to do so, (2) it is in his power to do so, (3) failure to face terrible things without a recognized excuse will reflect poorly on his character, and (4) the sense that he must face terrible things in the right way is among his most important and inescapable concerns and not a mere matter of prudence, legality, or etiquette.

However, elsewhere Aristotle states that "it is impossible, or not easy, to do noble acts without the proper equipment" (*NE* 1099a32–33, cf. 1098b26, 1101a15–16); and the equipment alluded to includes such "external goods" as riches, political power, good birth, and even good looks (*kallos,* here definitely in an aesthetic sense).[39] Clearly, then, performance of *some* noble acts does presuppose that the agent occupy a certain role in the social hierarchy. For instance, although the magnificent man spends money "for the sake of the noble; for this is common [*koinon*] to the virtues" (1122b6–7), this particular virtue concerns expenditures on a very large scale (1122a23), so that people of modest means cannot acquire it. Similarly, performance of *some* noble acts does lie outside the voluntary control of agents. For instance, the great-souled man possesses nobility and goodness of character (*kalokagathia,* 1124a4); but his characteristic deep voice and regal bearing (1125a12–13) involve dispositions that are not within many peoples' voluntary control. But again, since *all* virtuous acts are done for the sake of the noble (1115b13, 1120a24, 1122b7), there will be many noble acts that are exceptions to both of these claims. The earlier-discussed virtues of temperance and bravery, for instance, do not presuppose much at all in the way of external goods.

The third term mentioned by Hardie, *dikaion,* is usually translated as "right" or "just." The virtue of justice, *dikaiosunē,* is discussed at length in book V, and at the beginning of this discussion Aristotle states that one sense of *to dikaion* is the lawful, *to nomimon.* Justice in the sense of the lawful is complete (*teleia*) virtue, "not absolutely, but in regard to another person" (*NE* 1129b26–27). From this statement we cannot quite infer that all virtuous acts are just acts (as we could earlier with both *to kalon* and *dei*), but we can infer that all *other-*

regarding virtuous acts are just acts. As he notes at the end of chapter 1, virtue and this broader sense of justice "are the same but their being [*einai*] is not the same; what, as concerns another person, is justice is, as a certain kind of state without qualification, virtue" (1130a12–13).

Here, too, it seems evident that performance of actions that are *to dikaion* in the sense of "lawful" meet the conditions of a moral ought listed earlier; that is to say, performance of such actions is not tied to fulfillment of a social role, does concern actions that are in the agent's power to carry out, does reflect poorly on the agent's character who fails to perform them without a recognized excuse, and does stem from an overall assessment of what is best rather than an assessment based solely on the desires and goals of the actor. However, when one considers the distinction between moral and legal requirements and asks which are stronger, a potential problem arises; for since this form of justice is *identified* with the lawful, it does appear that requirements of moral justice, on Aristotle's view, will not be viewed as being stronger than potentially competing claims of law. On the contrary, he seems to make "no clear distinction between law and morality."[40] But while the sense of a "higher" moral law that stands opposed to convention is absent in Aristotle, I believe that the distinction between morally just and unjust laws is one he can easily make. Morally unjust laws (Aristotle might say) are laws created by legislators who lack practical wisdom.

Finally, the fourth phrase—*kata ton orthon logon*. In book II, Aristotle states: "Now, that we must act according to correct reason [*kata ton orthon logon*] is a common principle and must be assumed" (*NE* 1103b31–32). Similarly, he notes that "all men, when they define virtue, after naming the state of character and its objects, add 'that [state] which is *kata ton orthon logon*' " (1144b21–23). The implication is that this phrase was already commonplace among moral thinkers of his time.[41] As to what the *orthos logos* itself is, we are told at the end of book VI that it is "that which is in accordance with practical wisdom [*kata ten phronesin*]" (1144b24, cf. 1144b27), that is, the man who possesses and exhibits practical wisdom (1107a1). Here the "situational appreciation"[42] of the *phronimos* comes into play. *Orthos logos* does not present us with a specific list of rules, much less a decision procedure. But it does direct us (*tattei*, 1119b17) and command us (*prostaxē*, 1114b30) to perform certain individual acts rather than others.[43]

Here, too, acts that are done *kata ton orthon logon* appear to meet the four conditions of a moral ought discussed earlier:

1. *Logos* does not merely order certain human role-players to act. Every *anthropos* has *logos,* and *anthropos* on his view is the only animal who has the gift of *logos* (*Pol* 1253a9–10, 1332b5).[44]
2. The temperate man who educates his desires as *logos* directs (1119b20) does something within his voluntary control.
3. If he fails to so educate his desires, this will reflect poorly on his character.
4. The motivation to do so stems not just from a consideration of his own particular desires but from an all-things-considered assessment of how to

live and act. Doing what *logos* bids him to do is more important to him than anything else.[45]

In drawing attention to some contexts where I believe Aristotle is using a sense of *ought* that is fairly close to what most people today mean by a *moral* ought, I have also alluded briefly to some stark differences between current moral conceptions and the subject matter of the *Nicomachean Ethics*. For instance, on Aristotle's view, the scope of moral agency in the strict sense extends only to free adult males. He does not believe that women or natural slaves can acquire the crucial virtue of *phronēsis*. Secondly, several of the "moral virtues" (*ēthikē aretai*) Aristotle discusses (*megaloprepeia, megalopsuchia*) concern traits and actions that are beyond many people's voluntary control and presuppose a high station in social life and thus are not what most people today would regard as *moral* virtues at all.[46] Obviously, these are not merely minor differences; nor are they the only differences that exist between Aristotelian and contemporary moral views. But it seems to me that we put ourselves in a suitable position to see such differences clearly only after we first posit some common, shared beliefs between Aristotle and ourselves. Meaningful disagreement depends on some foundation in agreement.[47] One basic point of agreement, I have argued, concerns the presence of cases where people do what they feel they must do in the strong sense indicated earlier.

Benthamite Virtue

Just as we see, upon inspection, that Aristotelian ethics does indeed reveal a strong concern for morally right action, so, too, when we turn to modern utilitarian and Kantian traditions of ethical theory, we find that modern moral theorists have not in fact neglected virtue. Let us turn first to Bentham's analysis of virtue.

In an unpublished manuscript written in 1827, Bentham argues that what people really mean when they call a character trait a virtue is that (1) they approve of the trait; (2) they attach "a degree of importance not altogether inconsiderable" to it; and (3) the ground for the sentiment of approval or approbation of the trait "is its tendency to give a net increase to the aggregate quantity of happiness in all its shapes taken together."[48] The third condition contains his basic definition of virtue. Benthamite virtue is a disposition that tends to maximize utility. As one might expect, this is a straightforwardly consequentialist conception of moral virtue. Character traits are to be evaluated in terms of their results, and a trait will count as a virtue only if it tends to maximize utility.[49]

An almost identical definition of virtue can be gleaned from the earlier-written and better-known *Introduction to the Principles of Morals and Legislation* (1789). In his discussion of the evaluation of motives, Bentham writes, "If they are good or bad, it is only on account of their effects: good, on account of their tendency to produce pleasure, or avert pain: bad, on account of their tendency to produce pain, or avert pleasure."[50] And in the preface he declares that it is quite easy to generate a theory of the virtues and vices from his analysis of "the terms *pleasure, pain, motive,* and *disposition.*"[51] The latter are to serve as explanations for the former: virtues are simply the dispositions and patterns of motivation that have a tendency to produce pleasure and/or avert pain.

Because Bentham defines virtue as any pleasure-producing disposition, he tends to reduce all of the virtues to forms of benevolence. This gives him both a built-in (but rather boring) unity-of-the-virtues thesis and also an extremely nontraditional list of virtues. Justice, for Bentham, is "but a portion of benevolence in disguise"; and he notes with disapproval that in Aristotle's list of virtues, "no such virtue as benevolence or beneficence is to be found."[52] Of the traits that are traditionally called virtues, Bentham recognizes only two as virtues proper: "prudence and benevolence (or beneficence), the virtues to which all others are reducible—of which all others are but modifications. . . . All other virtues howsoever denominated are but so many modifications of prudence or benevolence or both together."[53] This is basically a classification of virtues into self-regarding and other-regarding traits. Prudence is reluctantly allowed in as a virtue because it is understood to be a trait that has a tendency to bring happiness to oneself, although, as we saw earlier (chap. 1, n.5), Bentham, like most modern theorists, often tends to exclude prudence and self-regarding concerns from the realm of the moral. Benevolence, of course, is unquestionably a virtue, since it is the tendency to bring happiness to others. In principle, courage, self-control, and other traditional virtues could still be counted as secondary virtues by Bentham, provided that they could pass the pleasure-production test. However, in practice this is highly unlikely: Bentham himself recognized that these traits are not primarily pleasure-producing or pain-averting traits and declared that he had no use for them.[54]

But while Bentham does indeed discuss virtue and while it is indeed possible, as recent writers have argued, to offer a systematic consequentialist account of moral character that grants priority to agents over acts, the utilitarian approach to virtue is unlikely to appeal to anyone who is not already a committed utilitarian. The reason for this is simply that its approach to the virtues is reductionist to a draconian degree: all traits are to be measured and compared on the common scale of utility, and only those traits that can be shown to maximize utility are to be counted as virtues. Most traditional, as well as contemporary, concern about the virtues cannot be captured by such a simplistic model. Utilitarianism, whether it be applied to acts or to agents, suffers from an impoverished conception of the good. Still, it remains open for a more pluralistic-minded consequentialist to reply: "Very well, let's drop the 'common scale' requirement. There is a diversity of different kinds of results we are interested in measuring, pleasure production being only one of them. We will call any trait that maximizes any of these results a virtue." I have never heard a consequentialist talk in this pluralistic manner; but theoretically, it is an option. The source of the difficulty with consequentialist analyses of virtues lies in their reductionist conception of the good rather than with anything they assert about traits per se. If their theory of the good can be somehow opened up, consequentialist analyses of the virtues might begin to show more promise.

Kantian Virtue

Bentham *did* discuss the virtues, and it is *possible* to apply utilitarianism to motives and traits; but it remains a historical fact that utilitarianism was from the beginning more concerned with the consequences of acts and events than with agents and their lives. However, when we turn to Kant, it is much easier to demonstrate that the primary evaluative focus of his ethical theory was indeed agents, rather than acts.[55] As we saw earlier, he announces at the beginning of the *Grounding:* "There is no possibility of thinking of anything at all in the world, or even out of it, that can be regarded as good without qualification, except a good will" (*GIV* 393/7). In other words, what is unqualifiedly good according to Kant is neither an end-state such as pleasure nor the performance of certain atomic acts in conformity to rules but rather a state of character. On the Kantian view, the moral worth of agents, as judged by their underlying intentions, is prior to, and definitive of, the moral rightness of acts. To answer the question Is my will good? (a question that can never be answered with any certainty, due to the fundamental opacity of human intentions), we must look beyond atomic acts and decisions and inquire into how we have lived. Have our choices and acts reflected a persistent pattern of adoption of motives fit to serve as universal practical law? Determining the moral worth of one's character amounts to limning one's entire personality, for a man cannot be "morally good in some ways and at the same time morally evil in others" (*R* VI 24/20).

Kant repeatedly defines virtue (*Tugend*) in the *Doctrine of Virtue* as "fortitude in relation to the forces opposing a moral attitude in us" (*DV* VI 380/38; cf. 390/49–50, 393/54, 398/58, 404/66, 409/71). The emphasis on inner strength and self-mastery implies a commitment to disciplining oneself so that one lives according to reason. "Pull [yourself] together," he advises at one point. Bring all of your decisions and plans under the rule of reason. Motivate yourself to act consistently out of respect for morality. Bring all of your powers and inclinations under reason's control (408/69). Kantian virtue is strength (*Stärke*) or power (*Kraft*) of will, in the sense not of an ability to accomplish one's chosen goals but rather of attaining mastery over one's inclinations and constancy of purpose.

However, attaining mastery over one's inclinations does not mean acting without feeling or emotion. Humans, as sensuously affected rational agents, are *always* influenced by their feelings: they cannot—and hence should not try to— "rise above" feeling. Rather, what is called for is emotional reform: training and educating one's feelings so that they act with, rather than against, reason. One aspect of Kantian emotional reform involves cultivating the emotions that "follow from the thought of the law" and then acting in concert with such feelings:

> In every determination of choice we go *from* the thought of the possible action to the action by way of feeling pleasure or pain and taking an interest in the action or its effect. Now in this process our *emotional* state (the way in which our inner sense is affected) is either pathological or moral feeling. *Pathological* feeling precedes

the thought of the law: *moral* feeling can only follow from the thought of the law. (*DV* VI 398/59; cf. *G* IV 460/59 and *C2* V 72–79/74–82)

Moral emotions are caused by reason, but at the same time they are "natural dispositions of the mind" that are present to some extent in all humans. In addition to respect or reverence (*Achtung*), the most frequently discussed moral emotion, others discussed by Kant include benevolence and the "power and will to share in others' feelings" (*DV* VI 462/125, 401/62).[56] The need to cultivate sympathetic joy and sorrow in the projects of others is a point stressed repeatedly by Kant: "For what one does not do gladly he does so grudgingly— even to the point of sophistical pretext to avoid duty's command—that this incentive [of duty] cannot be counted on to any great degree unless the command is accompanied by love" (*End* VIII 338/101; cf. *R* VI 23–24n./19n., *DV* VI 484/159, *A* VII 282/147). This commitment to share in others' feelings should take the form not only of an interest in those "with whom we have been brought up" but "there should also be an interest in the highest good in the world [*das Weltbeste*]. Children should be made acquainted with this interest, so that it may give warmth to their souls. They should learn to rejoice over the highest good in the world, even if it is not to their own advantage or to that of their country" (*Ed* IX 499/121).

A second, less radical aspect of Kantian emotional reform involves simply working with the natural feelings that are most likely to help humans "in *putting into practice* the laws given in a metaphysic of morals" (*DV* VI 216/14). Kantian moral emotions, it may be said, are not "ordinary" emotions, precisely because they are reason-derived. Kant may well allow space within morality for certain rationalized feelings. But what positive role, if any, do ordinary (or what Kant calls "pathological") emotions play in human moral life on his view? Here, too it is clear that Kant does not want agents to alienate themselves from their feelings:

> We have an indirect duty to cultivate the sympathetic natural (aesthetic) feelings in us and to use them as so many means to participating from moral principles and from the feeling appropriate to these principles. Thus, it is our duty: not to avoid places where we shall find the poor who lack the most basic essentials, but rather to seek them out; not to shun sick-rooms or debtors' prisons in order to avoid the painful sympathetic feelings that we cannot guard against. For this is still one of the impulses which nature has implanted in us so that we may do what the thought of duty alone would not accomplish. (*DV* VI 457/126)

Natural feelings are therefore to serve "as means to participating from moral principles and from the feeling appropriate to these principles." Sympathy, for instance, is an appropriate feeling from which to carry out to the duty to help others in need; resentment is not.[57] Sympathetic concern can also serve as an indispensable means to acting from moral principle in general, in the sense that it tends to alert one to the situations that have morally significant features. This perceptual sensitivity and awareness can then be regulated by higher-order moral principles that inform agents which acts are morally recommended, permissible, or required.[58] We see, then, that far from requiring that "we must abstract or distance ourselves from our feelings and emotions"[59] in order to be morally worthy agents, the Kantian view in fact requires us to cultivate a wide range of both moral (or rational) and natural (or pathological) emotions.

Just as Bentham's systematic approach to virtue resulted in a reduction of all virtues to forms of either benevolence or prudence, so Kant, with his emphasis on virtue as dutifulness, is often held to have reduced all of the virtues to forms of conscientiousness. And such a view, critics allege, "does not do justice to the value we place upon kindness, compassion, and generosity. We believe that however conscientious someone might be, if he were altogether lacking these virtues that are forms of benevolence, he would be seriously defective as a human being."[60] But the reductionism charge does not stick when applied to Kant; for we have seen already that he does urge us to cultivate feelings of compassion and kindness toward others and does recognize that love and benevolence are necessary emotions in the virtuous agent. To be sure, the objective determining ground of action must be reason, not feeling. But humanly speaking, because we are sensuously affected rational agents, it is subjectively necessary for us to cultivate to the best of our best abilities the feelings that will help us to advance moral interests. And while Kantian virtue does imply a subordination of the will to moral law, such obedience to law is far removed from the narrow-minded pharisaic obsession with rules that is the favored target of virtue theorists; for there is no arcane list of rules which the Kantian moral agent is expected to follow. The only "rule" given is the categorical imperative; and this is best understood, as Onora O'Neill argues, as "a fundamental strategy, not an algorithm; it is the fundamental strategy not just of morality but of all activity that counts as reasoned. The supreme principle of reason is merely the principle of thinking and acting on principles that can (not 'do'!) hold for all."[61] Kant's conception of the place of emotions in morality is in fact much closer to the classical ideal of living a life according to reason.

But, the critic may respond, even if it is the case that Kant is not guilty of reducing all of the virtues to conscientiousness, is it not true that he distorts our emotional life in a more serious way, by treating all emotions as mere instrumental means toward the goal of acting from principle? Emotions are justified only to the extent that they help to produce actions performed from the motive of duty; and their moral assessment is always couched in terms of their effectiveness as instruments in production of dutiful action. But in real life moral emotions and attitudes have intrinsic worth: the anger and compassion we feel toward others are often morally assessed regardless of whether they contribute to the omission or commission of morally required acts.

A close relative of this "instrumental status" charge was examined earlier in the analysis of Kant's views on the place of friendship in the moral life (chap. 1). To be sure, Kant does occasionally appear to attribute a merely instrumental status to natural feelings such as joy and sadness. As noted earlier, he does state in the *Tugendlehre* that such feelings are to be used "as so many means [*Mittel*] to participating from moral principles and from the feeling appropriate to these principles" (*DV* VI 457/126). But again, as "animals endowed with reason" our humanity is located in both reason *and* feeling. The presence and proper cultivation of such feelings are subjectively necessary conditions without which we would be incapable of acting according to practical reason. Purely rational beings have no such feelings and have no need to cultivate them. But such feelings do constitute a fundamental characteristic of humanity's condition; thus, their status is not merely instrumental. Nowhere does Kant advise readers to dispense with their natural emotions once they have succeeded in developing a will that acts from duty. People who lack moral feeling are "morally dead" (*sittlich tot*), and their humanity soon disappears (*DV* VI 400/60).[62]

In conclusion, though the differences between ancient and modern ethics are both numerous and significant, it is not true that Aristotle had no conception of a moral ought or, more generally, that he was not concerned with morally right action. Nor is it true that modern ethics—in either its utilitarian or Kantian forms—neglects virtue or reduces morality to obedience to action-guiding rules. The best of the ancient, as well as modern, moral theorists recognized that any adequate moral theory must assess the character of agents, as well as their discrete acts. At the same time, at least for Aristotle and Kant,[63] evaluation of character, rather than of acts or consequences of acts, is what comes first in ethics.

3

Morality and Maximization

Things have their due measure; there are ultimately
fixed limits, beyond which, or short of which,
something must be wrong.

HORACE, *Satires*

We are . . . determined by reason to promote with all our powers [*nach
allen Kraften*] the highest good in the world [*das Weltbeste*] which
consists in the combination of the greatest welfare of rational beings
with the highest condition of the good in itself, i.e., in universal
happiness conjoined with morality most accordant to law.

KANT, *Critique of Judgment*

Too Much Morality?

The next area of morality I propose to examine concerns the issue of how much
of it we should have. Should we strive to make our society as morally good as
possible, or is it better if we do not? Should we try to be as morally good as
we can be, or is it better if we do not? Susan Wolf claims that there is "a limit
to how much morality we can stand" and argues that it is not always "better
to be morally better."[1] Similarly, Robert Adams, though critical of much of
what Wolf says in her essay, concludes his response by agreeing with her underlying claim that "maximal devotion" to the interests of morality is not desirable.[2] Finally, Bernard Williams, in *Ethics and the Limits of Philosophy*, offers
an even stronger condemnation of moral aspiration when he announces that
"we would be better off without" morality.[3]

I do not believe that there can ever be too much morality. According to my
conception of what a morality is, I do not think it makes good sense to claim
that individuals or societies can be "too moral." The aim of the present chapter
is to articulate and defend this claim. My conviction that we ought to strive to
be as morally good as we can be and to make our communities as morally good
as possible commits me to a version of what is often called a "maximization"
thesis with respect to morality, since I intend to argue that as concerns morality,
more is always better than less.

The realization that I believed morality ought to be maximized was something
I resisted strongly at first. Within ethical theory, the term *maximization* is most

45

at home within the utilitarian tradition; and I have always had strong visceral reactions against any and all utilitarianisms. According to utilitarianism, we ought always to maximize or produce the highest degree possible of "utility" (defined most clearly by Bentham as pleasure but more recently as "preference satisfaction") for the greatest number of sentient (or preference-possessing?) creatures. However, I was quickly (in hindsight, too quickly) convinced by innumerable stock examples from the vast antiutilitarian literature that this deceptively simple and seductive injunction to maximize good unfortunately entails that one stand ready to commit all sorts of moral evils in the process. Punishing an innocent victim may on occasion definitely increase the overall happiness of the majority within a community; preventing five murders by committing one oneself may maximize utility; torturing the civilian daughter and grandmother of a terrorist leader in order to extract information concerning the whereabouts of a bomb planted within one's own extremely populous city will bring more happiness to a greater number; and so on. Adherence to the utilitarian formula for maximizing good, in other words, requires that one always be ready and willing to commit morally unacceptable acts of the most blatant sort.[4]

If this is what maximizing morality means, I thought, count me out. For one of the most fundamental characteristics of morally good people is that there are limits to what they will do to others or to themselves. Morally wise people discern these limits and structure their lives in accord with them, but the utilitarian literally knows no limits. And if being a morally good person means knowing and acting in accord with constraints on action, I inferred, perhaps morality ought to be maximized. Maybe morality is concerned only with respecting limits and not with maximization at all.[5] I shall elaborate on the differences between utilitarian conceptions of maximization and my own in greater detail later. For now, let me merely emphasize that though I do wish to defend a moral maximization claim, it is one that differs radically from utilitarian maximization.

A second, related point that made me reluctant to accept the claim that morality ought to be maximized came from economics and decision theory. Within this body of literature it is widely assumed that rational individuals are (by definition) always maximizers: a rational decision is simply one that maximizes the satisfaction of one's desires. This assumption has always struck me as highly implausible. The people we normally regard as rational are not boundless optimizers who are always busy calculating how to achieve their greatest preference satisfaction. Rather, they possess the virtue of self-control. Two signs of their wisdom are that they know when to call it quits in pursuit of a preference and that they are not troubled by the unquenchable thirst that torments preference satisfaction maximizers.[6] Furthermore, it seems that the wise and the unwise do not even always act on the same desires. Certain acts are *unthinkable* for wise people, and the presence of such aversions is itself a manifestation of their fundamental rationality.[7] It is only the lunatic who feels no such aversions. Here, too, I felt that theorists, in their eagerness to come up with something they could measure quantitatively, were guilty of dragging in an alien sense of what it is to be rational that is at odds with traditional and common sense views—views that ought not to be jettisoned without convincing argument. Just as utilitarians could, by means of their definition of *good*, literally measure how much moral good was being brought into the world and by whom (but in a way that ran strongly counter to traditional conceptions of what moral good and evil are), so economists and decision theorists could, by means of their maximization axiom, determine with precision who was and who was not acting rationally (but in a way that ran strongly counter to traditional senses of what it means to be rational).

I shall also examine in greater detail the question of when and under what circumstances it is rational to try to maximize. Here let me merely assert that I do not regard maximization to be a necessary part of the definition of rationality: rational people, on my view, only occasionally seek to maximize satisfaction of their preferences.

But now an additional doubt arose concerning moral maximization. If the connection between rationality and maximization is in fact much weaker than is often assumed and if the connection between rationality and *morality* is strong,[8] then perhaps morality is *not* a maximizing matter. The resolution of this particular dilemma, I shall argue later, is in fact simple: morality is the *only* object of human concern it is rational to maximize.

What to Maximize?

As one might suspect, Bentham appears to have introduced the term *maximization* into ethics. Phrases such as "the maximization of the happiness of the greatest number" and "the maximization of the aggregate of good" are occasional stand-ins for the more familiar "principle of utility."[9] Since Bentham first began using the term in 1802, it has become one of the favorite technical terms of utilitarians, economists, and rational choice theorists. In this section I shall examine several aspects of Benthamite maximization in order to prepare the way for an alternative account of moral maximizing.

Aristotle, at the beginning of the *Nicomachean Ethics,* notes that "a certain difference is found among ends; some are activities [*energeiai*], others are products [*erga*] apart from the activities that produce them" (1094a3–5). Following Aristotle, let us mark a distinction between *activity-ends,* or goals that can only be achieved in and through our own action, and *product-ends,* or goals that bear no necessary connection to action. My desire to play Corelli's violin sonatas well is an activity-end. If it is ever going to happen, it will only happen as a result of my doing it. But my desire to hear some uplifting sounds in the morning as I make breakfast is a product-end. I do not particularly care who or what creates the sounds, I just want to experience them. So rather than drag out my fiddle, I simply turn on the radio. Aristotle goes on to argue that the end of ethics, *eudaimonia,* or flourishing, must be an activity-end as opposed to a product-end. Specifically, *eudaimonia* is "activity of soul exhibiting virtue" (*psuchēs energeia ginetai kat' aretēn*) (1098a16–17). If we are ever to achieve this goal, it will only come about by our living our lives in a certain way and by our training our souls in a certain way.[10]

When Bentham defines the principle of utility as "that principle which approves or disapproves of every action whatsoever, according to the tendency which it appears to have to augment or diminish the happiness of the party whose interest is in question: or, what is the same thing in other words, to promote or oppose that happiness,"[11] he is clearly describing a product-end. It does not matter who or what augments the happiness (defined later by Bentham to mean "pleasure") "of the party whose interest is in question" or even how the augmentation is achieved. The important thing is just that it happen. Now, humans are sentient creatures; and the fact that someone is experiencing unwanted pain is often of crucial importance in moral deliberations. If I am witness to a motorcycle accident on a back road where someone is injured and am in a position to render aid, obviously, I ought to do so. Bentham's principle of utility was a very progressive force at first, particularly in the area of penal reform, where torture and flogging were still accepted practices within English law. But humans are also agents who want to *live* and *act* by their own lights, and I believe that the end to be sought in ethics must reflect this fact. Ethics concerns how we shape our lives through our own voluntary efforts. The primary end to be sought must therefore be something achievable only in and through our own actions. It cannot simply be a pleasing set of sensations that we experience passively.

According to the product-end conception, a world where people experience the sensation of sexual orgasm only by plugging into an orgasmatron machine (such as that portrayed in Woody Allen's *Sleeper*) would be preferable to the one most of us inhabit, where one can achieve the goal only by doing certain things and where there is no guarantee of a pleasurable outcome at any point along the way. Similarly, the product-end conception would favor a world where "half-gramme holidays" produced by the drug soma (as portrayed in Aldous Huxley's *Brave New World*) are the order of the day over the world most of us inhabit, where taking a holiday requires that one do many things and the prospect of pleasurable sensations is never guaranteed. But most people would not want to live in such worlds, given the choice; and this fact suggests strongly that what matters most to us are not simply experiences. As Robert Nozick notes: "What does matter to us in addition to our experiences? First, we want to *do* certain things, and not just have the experience of doing them. . . . [Second,] we want to *be* a certain way, to be a certain sort of person."[12]

So one fundamental error in Benthamite maximization is that the proposed object of maximization—the experience of pleasure—does not accurately reflect our own sense of what is most important to us as persons.[13] The proper arena in which to look for a suitable candidate for moral maximization efforts must lie only in what we can achieve through our own voluntary efforts. The directive to inhabit a world where pleasurable sensations are maximized, without regard to who or what produces such experiences, should not be the fundamental goal in ethics.

Let us, then, set aside the fictional metaphysics of producing good states of affairs and restrict our purview to the realm of human action. Perhaps what moral agents should maximize are simply acts that contain a certain specified value. Wolf, for instance, sets up her case against moral commitment by defining the moral saint as "a person whose every action is as morally good as possible"[14] The image of a calculative, obsessive do-gooder who spends as much time as possible producing as much moral good as possible is admittedly not very inviting; but it is also by no means clear that those whom we regard as morally outstanding individuals do in fact live and act in this manner. Adams, in his reply to Wolf, remarks:

> The idea that only a morally imperfect person would spend half an hour doing something morally indifferent, like taking a nap, when she could have done something morally praiseworthy instead, like spending the time in moral self-examination, is at odds with our usual judgments and ought not to be assumed at the outset. The assumption that the perfection of a person, in at least the moral type of value, depends on the maximization of that type of value in every single action of the person lies behind much that is unattractive in Wolf's picture of moral sainthood; but I believe it is a fundamental error.[15]

One basic problem with the "every action as morally good as possible" scenario lies in what may be called its *commensurability assumption*. In order to know who is winning the moral saints game, we must have a standard unit of measurement by means of which we can gauge how much value is being produced by each contestant's acts. For Bentham, of course, the unit of measurement was utility—defined very concretely by him as pleasure—which could then be measured objectively in terms of intensity, duration, certainty, and so on.[16] On the classical utilitarian model, all moral interests and ideals are thus reduced to a common dimension for purposes of measurement. But this reduction strategy (not to mention the hedonist bias, which I will not bother to discuss here) is extremely artificial and does not reflect accurately what lies behind our own judgments concerning who is, and who is not, a morally outstanding individual. Real-life moral exemplars promote a variety of different values in their actions, values that are not viewed as being commensurable on any single scale of measurement.[17] Some exhibit great courage in life-threatening situations, others work tirelessly for social justice. Some are seemingly endless sources of generosity and charity, others are stern models of integrity and honesty. It is ridiculous to assume that there exists a common underlying value that is being maximized in each of their acts. There is no standard production model for moral exemplars.

Though die-hard utility maximizers and perhaps a few others continue to hold onto the commensurability assumption, the claim that all moral values can be realistically measured and ranked on a single scale finds fewer and fewer advocates today. But suppose we take a further step toward reality and grant that there exists an irreducible plurality of moral values. There are acts of courage, friendship, kindness, and justice; and they do not all bring the same kind of value into the world. Why not say that moral exemplars are simply those who successfully maximize a certain specified mix and amount of *irreducible* values—

x percent courage, y percent justice, and so on?[18] This particular maximization conception is definitely an improvement over its reductionist predecessor; for the recognition that not all moral values are commensurable is built into it. And it does seem to be the case that there exists a family of core virtues that all moral exemplars exhibit to a strong degree. It is difficult to imagine that someone who knew nothing of the virtues of justice and beneficence but who exhibited more minor virtues such as gratefulness or a sense of humor to a strong degree, could qualify as a moral exemplar. So the assumption of a *core family* of values to be maximized is at least arguable, so long as the family members are described in relatively innocuous terms such as *justice, beneficence,* and *honesty*. But the additional assumption that there exists some uniform mix and amount of values to be maximized must again be rejected as overly simplistic. Some morally outstanding individuals are more courageous than others, some are kinder than others, and so on. It is simply not the case that all morally outstanding individuals produce the same specified mix and amount of values in their actions. Moral exemplars are not all stamped from the same mold.[19]

The Measure of a Moral Person

I have argued so far that several familiar candidates for moral maximization are all unsatisfactory. First, maximizing a state of affairs, whether it be the simple sensation of pleasure or the more nebulous satisfaction of "preferences," does not make good sense morally; for it bears no necessary connection to our own voluntary efforts. Second, the assumption that there is a single moral value to be maximized in action must be rejected; for it is not the case that moral considerations are reducible to one single value. Third, the assumption of a specified mix and amount of different values to be maximized in action, though a marked improvement over the other two candidates, must also be rejected; for our judgments concerning moral exemplars reveal a much stronger tolerance for diversity of character types than this assumption allows for. Finally, a common feature shared by each of the three models that does not hold up under scrutiny is the calculative, compulsive mentality implied in the image of someone who seeks to maximize values in either states of affairs or actions. Those whom we regard as morally outstanding individuals do not possess this trait.

So where does this leave us with respect to the thesis that morality *is* a maximizing matter? If our ideal of the morally good person does not translate into the agent who maximizes either a single value or a plurality of values in either states of affairs or actions, what options remain? What is it that the moral person maximizes if not values in events and actions? Must we accept the conclusion that maximization in ethics is "mistaken, irrelevant, and parasitic"?[20]

Instead of construing morally excellent individuals as maximizers of values in events and actions, I suggest rather that we understand them to be those who are disposed to live according to principles and ideals which they reflectively accept. We recognize morally excellent individuals as being those people who are more strongly disposed than the rest of us to stand fast by their reflectively chosen principles and ideals when tempted by considerations that are morally irrelevant. As Bradley remarked: "Who is the most moral man? ...The most moral man is the man who tries most to act up to what his light tells him is best. But in that we must remember is included the getting the best light which, up to his light, he can."[21] I submit that this maximizing conception not only squares better with common sense and with the views of many[22] classical moral theorists (e.g, the Aristotelian *phronimos*, whose virtue is determined "according to reason" [*kata ton logon*]; the Kantian good will who thinks and acts according to principles that can be adopted by all) but that it also represents a much more laudable goal than other maximizing conceptions.

But *which* principles and ideals do morally excellent individuals live by? What *constraints* must be placed on the content of their chosen principles and ideals in order that they be recognizable as distinctively moral in character rather than, say, simply aesthetic or rational? These are notoriously difficult questions, particularly for me, since one of my primary concerns is to show that morality needs to be understood in a much broader and more multidimensional sense than is often done. Again, I reject the claim that there exists a standard model of moral excellence. A viable concept of moral excellence must be generous enough to allow room for the extremely wide range of role models that is available to us within our present culture and realistic enough to recognize the obvious fact that we do not all share the same list of moral heroes. Whatever constraints we place upon the choice of ideals and principles, we need to ensure that there remains plenty of room for a rich and intriguing diversity of character types. Also, in attempting to articulate some basic constraints on the content of moral ideals and principles, we need to avoid the reductionist assumption that all moral concerns can be derived neatly from a core group of abstract categories.

Without attempting a detailed, exhaustive definition of *morality* (my aim in part I being merely to explore certain *select areas* within the broad territory of morality, nor do I believe it possible to state all the necessary and sufficient properties of morality), three general points should help to establish some central parameters within which we can better locate the ideals and principles of morally excellent individuals.

First, as argued in chapter 1, morally excellent individuals care for their souls and view morality as a fundamentally self-regarding project. However, as we saw, proper care of soul in the moral sense must not be confused with narcissism or other objectionable forms of self-centeredness. Our self-regarding duties point directly to active social duties. Thus, one distinguishing mark of morally excellent individuals is that they are committed to maximizing their own human powers, as well as the human capacities of all other persons. Again, the various means by which this overarching cultural prerogative may be advanced are infinite. Since no two individuals possess the same exact mix of talents and interests, each individual will necessarily undertake this aspect of the moral maximization project in his or her own unique way.

Second, another basic constraint that must be placed on the choice of principles and ideals, if they are to count as moral, concerns the duty of beneficence.

Morally excellent individuals are committed to promoting the well-being of all other persons. As Kant states in the second epigraph for this chapter, we have a moral duty "to promote with all our powers the highest good in the world." Literally speaking, this involves a commitment to create a new moral order, one where all persons seek to promote one another's ends and where people seek to make each other happy. The virtuous person takes satisfaction in others' achieving the well-being they seek and helps them further their ends.[23] Here, too, the ways in which this end can be promoted are infinite, so there is ample space for a wide diversity of character types. For instance, some will choose to focus their efforts on local problems within their own communities; others will work for world peace.

Third, a final fundamental constraint that must be placed on the choice of principles and ideals, if they are to count as moral, concerns duties of justice and respect. Morally excellent individuals respect all persons (including themselves); and this commitment sets strict limits to what they will allow themselves to do to others, as well as to themselves, in pursuing their ends. The opening epigraph from Horace is relevant here. There are fixed limits in the moral sphere, and virtuous people sense that something has gone wrong when these limits are transgressed. Innocent persons ought not to be punished in order to make a majority happy; we ought not to commit a murder when told to either shoot one person or let five die.

This third family of constraints also sets limits on what we may and may not do in carrying out the two previously mentioned maximizing projects of developing human powers and making people happy; for here we are generally talking about specific acts that are either morally forbidden or morally required (e.g., do not murder, do not steal, tell the truth), rather than broad goals that may be advanced in a number of different ways. Contra consequentialist conceptions of the good, the highest good that morally excellent individuals strive to realize contains built-in deontological constraints; for it consists in "universal happiness conjoined with morality most accordant to law." In our desire to bring forth a better world, we must not violate important ground-level constraints of justice and respect.[24]

Much more can be, and has been, said about each of these three constraints; but it is not necessary to do so here. Let us now examine how well this maximizing conception fares against the critic's complaint that morality is not a suitable object of maximal devotion.

Consider first the most prevalent objection, that moral maximizers lead lopsided lives and develop lopsided personalities. Because they are committed exclusively and compulsively to realizing moral projects, they have no time for anything else. Because the traits they choose to develop and refine are narrow moral traits, any nonmoral talents and skills they may possess lie dormant and eventually wither away due to lack of exercise. To be blunt, they are boring and lead boring lives.

Several aspects of this objection were addressed earlier (chap. 1), but the points bear repeating. The moral project, properly construed, is not narrow but extremely broad-ranging. Each of our natural powers can, in the right circumstances, serve as an enabling, or second-order, virtue that can enhance the effectiveness of the first-order virtues. The focal point in chapter 1 concerned the self-realization of moral powers; but the same connection between directly and indirectly moral traits holds when we turn to the duties of beneficence. Someone who wants to help others and who is also intelligent and strong will often be better able to do so than one who is ignorant and weak. As for the boringness charge, we have already seen that it generates more heat than light for a variety of reasons. People and things that some people find boring are a source of endless fascination for others; and, as Mill pointed out in *On Liberty,* societies are intellectually and spiritually richer because of such diversity. Also, even were we to reach agreement concerning who and what is interesting, it is by no means evident that we would find more interesting people outside of the moral camp than within it. Morality has no monopoly on interesting personalities; but neither does art or philosophy or any other area of life. Finally, the quest for an interesting personality has more than a grain of futility in it, since the elements that in many people's eyes constitute such a personality are often beyond a person's control. Katherine Hepburn's grace and Paul Newman's cool are not live options for many of us who presently lack such traits.[25]

Second, consider the related charge that moral maximizers are dangerous fanatics or zealots.[26] Mere reflective acceptance of one's chosen ideals and principles cannot rule out fanaticism, for some fanatics are extremely reflective. Hitler was reflectively committed to morally abhorrent ideals; and if the degree or quality of his reflection is a problem, we can always point to his supporters among the German professoriate. Also, not all morally excellent individuals are themselves given to intense reflection, so we ought not to crank up the reflection criterion too highly. Here the three constraints on the choice of principles and ideals that were summarized earlier must be summoned to rule such reflective fanatics out of court. Such persons are simply beyond the pale of morality, and no philosopher's rescue kit can pull them back in.

But what about the *moral* fanatic—the person who, say, is exclusively and obsessively committed to alleviating poverty, whose life is devoted to this and no other goal? Here, too, the earlier-discussed trio of constraints needs to be invoked. Such a person is not thereby ruled out of the moral court entirely (he or she is after all a *moral* fanatic), but it can be quickly shown that such a person fails to appreciate the scope and depth of the moral project. If one's devotion to the goal of alleviating poverty is so exclusive that, for example, important duties of justice are violated, then such devotion is morally wrong.

Blind devotion to a narrow cause is clearly not something to which a human life should be dedicated, for such devotion prevents one from appreciating important avenues that make a life fully human. People who seek without reflection to maximize an objectionably *narrow* conception of morality are zealots; and they may be dull-witted, humorless, and bland as well. However, the problem lies not with those who take morality seriously but rather in the objectionably narrow construal of morality assumed by critics. We ought not to conclude that our choice must be either blind devotion to a narrow cause or the abandonment of all serious commitment to ideals on the other. There are other alternatives.

The trick is to cultivate a more critical, more imaginative commitment to something that is broad enough and rich enough sufficiently to challenge a human being's multiple talents and interests. I do not see how devotion to a profession, career, family, avocation, hobby, or the like could fulfill this requirement. Nor, contra Adams, do I see how religion necessarily constitutes a more suitable object of maximal devotion than does morality. Religion, according to Adams,

> is richer than morality, because its divine object is so rich. [God] is not too narrow to be a suitable object of maximal devotion. Since He is a lover of beauty...as well as commander of morals, maximal submission of one's life to Him may in some cases...encompass an intense pursuit of artistic excellence in a way that maximal devotion to the interests of morality, narrowly construed, cannot.[27]

Morality needs all the friends it can get, and I have no wish to wage a quarrel with religion. But there is no need to do so. Nothing I have said so far concerning the nature of morality need rule out a theistic interpretation of the moral life. As should be evident, this is not the interpretation I have chosen to give it; but that is irrelevant. Many of our central moral concepts, as Adams and others have noted, were developed in a religious tradition; and for some this tradition remains a live option. Reflective commitment to one's own chosen ideals and principles may well lead to the view that there is more to life than the merely human and that humans are children of a Creator. Some of our strongest images of justice and beneficence do come from religious traditions. But it should be obvious that reflective commitment to *moral* ideals and principles may also in many cases "encompass an intense pursuit of artistic excellence." Again, there is more than one way to promote a moral project; and the arguments of chapters 1 and 2 have hopefully shown by now that religion certainly has no monopoly on richness.

My view is that all reflective choices about what to believe—when the beliefs in question are known strongly to influence their subscribers's practical life—are ultimately moral choices. (I leave aside here the religious commitments that are not based on reflective choice. Much real-life religious commitment does appear to be unreflective; I do have a quarrel with *it*.) The reflective commitment to lead a religious life, in other words, is itself a moral commitment, one that will in turn shape a person's own future moral conception in distinctive ways.

When Is It Rational to Maximize?

I noted earlier the widespread assumption within economics and rational choice theory that to be rational is *necessarily* to maximize. As David Gauthier remarks, practical rationality "in the most general sense is identified with maximization."[28]

Even revisionists within this tradition (such as Herbert Simon, with his notion of "satisficing," or, more recently, Gauthier himself, with his theory of "constrained maximization") do not question the root assumption that the *norm* is maximization, since their views each depend on the articulation of *special situations* where maximization is not rational.[29] My view is the opposite. I believe that maximization makes good sense in only one area of life and that in all other situations the norm should not be maximization. On my view, morality is the only area of life in which maximization efforts are rational. Morality, in other words, is the only thing of which it is true that there is "no limit to how much of it we can stand." My primary aim in the present section is to try to justify this claim. Before proceeding to the argument, I shall make several brief remarks concerning the relationship between rationality and maximization. One caveat: in what follows I make no attempt to offer any sustained analysis of rationality. To do so would take us too far beyond the bounds of our immediate concerns.

Vulgar maximizers equate rationality with maximizing the satisfaction of any and all desires, but it should be obvious that this will not do. First of all, we need to insist that whatever wants are to be maximized first pass some minimal tests for logical and factual consistency. Maximizing satisfaction of raw, unreflected-upon desires is asking for trouble. The lunatic whose overriding desire is to cut off people's thumbs and take them home to add to his collection is, according to this definition, conceivably more rational than the scientist whose overriding aim is to find a cure for AIDS. The victor in the "Who is more rational?" contest would be decided simply by determining which contestant chose the most effective means toward his or her desired end. Given the present lack of solid immunological knowledge concerning AIDS and the multiplicity of sure-fire ways to detach other people's thumbs, the lunatic is a cinch to win. Some preferences simply are crazy, and others are not. A conception of rationality that refuses to come to grips with this truism is just not facing facts.

Increasingly, many utilitarians and rational choice theorists do seem ready to concede this mundane point, as evidenced by their various attempts to let in only "perfectly prudent" or "autonomous" preferences.[30] However, the doctoring-up effort to deny entry to certain actual preferences seems ultimately to be merely a strategy for holding onto a thesis at all costs. Rather than admit that not all preferences ought to be maximized, they simply declare that some of our actual preferences are not "true" preferences.

So one fundamental constraint that must be placed on any desires whose satisfaction is to be maximized is that said desires must first survive rational criticism. However, even if we allow only reflected-upon desires into the maximization formula—desires that have survived "maximal criticism and correction by facts and logic"[31]—its seems obvious that we are still a long way from capturing even a rough sense of what is ordinarily meant by rational action. First of all, not all nonmaximizing acts are necessarily irrational acts.[32] Over the course of a day, most rational people undertake numerous actions (e.g., tying shoes, reading newspapers, driving to work) that normally do not involve an attempt to maximize anything. Unless it can be shown that in undertaking such everyday actions one is trying, say, to kill or disable oneself, it is difficult to see how or why such actions could be declared irrational. And it is even more difficult to see how or why they could be held to involve the maximization of any desire. (What is being maximized when rational people tie their shoes on a Monday morning? In most cases, nothing.) Rationality simply does not always require maximizing behavior. There is no necessary connection between rationality and maximization.

But even the person who only *occasionally* maximizes the preferences that have survived "correction by facts and logic" falls far short of an ideal that most people would wish to emulate; for we need to keep in mind that the sense of *rational* assumed in such discussions is a strictly instrumental one. Gauthier writes:

> The theory of rational choice . . . treats practical reason as strictly instrumental. . . . In identifying rationality with the maximization of a measure of preference, the theory of rational choice disclaims all concern with the ends of action. Ends may be inferred from individual preferences; if the relationships among these preferences, and the manner in which they are held, satisfy the conditions of rational choice, then the theory accepts whatever ends they imply.[33]

On my view, if we are going to try to produce as much as possible of what we seek and if we are going to call this endeavor rational in any serious sense, we need to place constraints on the ends of action, as well as on the means by which we seek to attain our ends. The purely instrumental conception of rationality that is typically assumed in maximization circles needs to be replaced by a substantive conception. The traditional value-laden view that practical reason includes not only the ability to select efficient means but also the power to determine ends and to discern among them needs to be reinvoked; for again, the wise and the unwise do not always pursue the same goals. It is the wisdom of a *phronimos* rather than the instrumental reasoning of a bureaucrat that needs to be summoned. Not all things that are instrumentally rational to want are good to want.

To sum up our discussion so far:

1. Rationality does not always require maximization. Some rational acts are nonmaximizing acts.
2. Not all preferences should be maximized, though perhaps some that survive rational criticism should be.
3. Not all preferences that are pursued in an instrumentally rational manner should be maximized, though perhaps some that also promote substantively good ends should be.

Clearly, even if one accepts each of these claims, there still remains considerable room for maximization efforts to play a significant role in human life. Why should we not simply select from among our instrumentally rational preferences and seek to maximize the ones that contribute to substantively good ends?

If it is true there is "a limit to how much morality we can stand," then, obviously, we should not try to maximize morality. On the other hand, if, upon inspection, we see that there is not a limit to how much morality we can stand, then we should try to maximize morality; for more will always be preferable to less. I shall now attempt to show, by means of a process of elimination, that the alternative conception of morality defended herein is in fact the only good thing of which there is no limit to how much we can stand, thereby proving my thesis that morality is indeed the only thing it is rational to maximize. Two noncontroversial provisos should be noted. First, in attempting to answer questions of the form Is there a limit to how much x we can stand? we need to view them "from the inside," in a first-person motivational sense. We need, in other words to ask, What kind of person would I be if my life were dominated by the project of increasing *x* to the highest possible degree? Second, we should remind ourselves that to maximize means not just to produce a little or even a lot of *x* but the highest possible amount of *x*.

Let us start with health. Is there a limit to how much health we can stand? Clearly, health is a major human benefit, and it is nearly always in our interests to want more of it. If we were healthier, we and our insurance companies and governments would not have to spend as much money on medical care, and we might even enjoy life more and live longer as well. How could someone be too healthy? But again, the question needs to be rephrased: Will someone whose life is dominated exclusively by the desire to maximize his or her health be living an admirable life? I submit that the answer to this latter question is *no*, for consider what extreme lengths our hypothetical health fanatic would have to be prepared to go in the quest for better health. Other people's health might not matter much to such a person; and if, say, a runner's heart were known to be in better shape than the one our health maximizer was unfortunately born with, the health maximizer would necessarily have to try to take it. Also, human life presents many opportunities: there are places to go and people to meet. But the true health maximizer would have to decline to go anywhere or meet anyone unless first having good reason to believe that doing so would, when compared to other options, such as staying home with some orange juice and a soloflex machine, maximize his or her health.

For a second example, consider art. Is there a limit to how much art we can stand? Here, too, I take it as noncontroversial that art (understood here not merely as museum art but as a broad concern for beauty in all areas of human life) is a major human benefit and that it is something we all could use more of in our lives. The total environment in which we live clearly plays a strong causal role in who and what we and our children become. How could our surroundings ever be too beautiful? Again, the important question is not whether our environment could ever be too beautiful but whether the person whose life is exclusively dominated by the aim of producing or acquiring as many beautiful objects as possible is leading an admirable life. And I think the answer is *no*. True art maximizers will have to be prepared to ignore traditional moral constraints of justice in their quest for more beauty. And their obsession with producing or acquiring as much beauty as possible will soon cut them off from family, friends, and society at large. They will simply not take an interest in many aspects of life that those of us who are not beauty maximizers regard as fundamentally important.

Further examples will fall prey to the same objection: nearly all good things, when pursued in excess, have a way of turning bad. But why should morality remain an exception to this truism? Admittedly, not all moral conceptions are exceptions to it; but I contend that the specific conception of morality being advocated here is. First of all, this moral conception contains built-in deontological constraints that prevent the attempt to maximize its presence in the world from getting out of hand. Moral maximizers, as I understand them, will never trample over the rights of others in seeking to bring more morality into the world. Such an option is ruled out from the start. The same cannot be said of health or art maximizers, or indeed, of any other type of maximizer. Second, only the kind of moral conception being advocated here is broad enough and rich enough sufficiently to challenge a human being's multiple talents and interests and to ward off "narrow obsession" rebuttals. The single-minded pursuit of most ideals does soon become a stultifying affair. However, properly construed, maximal devotion to moral interests does not suffer from this defect, since the kind of devotion that morality calls for is not "single-minded" at all but, rather, multifaceted. There is no one correct way to promote morality. In some cases, the best way for a given individual to promote morality may well be to develop his or her considerable artistic talents—not, à la the philosophy professor's fictionalized Gauguin, to the total exclusion of everything else that is important in life but certainly in a manner and to a degree that is consistent with exceptional professional accomplishment. But the road to success in the arts and sciences is much more narrow. For instance, a person who wants to become a great astrophysicist should not assume that the best way to attain this goal is to practice piano four hours daily and do weekly volunteer work at a homeless shelter.

Not-quite-perfectionism

The conception of moral maximization here invoked is one that draws its inspiration primarily from the Aristotelian notion of human flourishing, the teleological side of Kantian ethics, and, more generally, what is often called "perfectionism" in ethical theory literature.[34] I have never been comfortable with the term *perfectionism,* however. In this final section I wish to summarize briefly four objections to using this term for the kind of moral-maximizing project advocated in the present chapter. In articulating these reservations concerning perfectionism, my own contrasting view will also be further clarified.

First, perfectionism implies (on some interpretations) that it is our duty to become perfect. Critics naturally reply that such a view is ridiculous, for perfection is unattainable for finite human creatures. We can not be obligated to do the impossible. Similarly, perfectionism also implies (again, on some interpretations) that we need only concern ourselves with pictures of ideal behavior—

images of the very best, as opposed to the Lake Wobegonian well-above-average or the clearly mediocre. Critics naturally reply that such a view makes moral reflection irrelevant to the vast majority of people by restricting its scope to a concern for rare luxuries rather than common necessities. The employment of such high-end ideals tends to be confined to "the imaginatively restless and materially cosy"; but this is not the life most of us live.[35] While I do not think that most so-called perfectionists in ethics have actually advocated either of these views, there may nevertheless be something about the word *perfectionism* that unfortunately lends itself to such interpretations.[36] At any rate, the conception of moral maximization presently under consideration does not suffer from either of these defects. In saying with Kant that we have a moral duty to promote the highest good (an imperfect duty, one that requires each agent to use personal inclinations and personal circumstances to decide how best to promote it in a personal way), we are not guilty of a conceptual faux pas that orders imperfect creatures to become perfect, nor are we saying that the only moral categories worth our attention are high-end ones.

Second, perfectionism sometimes connotes a brand of cultural elitism that has nothing to do with what I take to be the project of maximizing morality. Rawls, for instance, begins his discussion of "the principle of perfection" by asserting that one of its two primary variants is the view that it is our duty "to maximize the achievement of human excellence in art, science, and culture."[37] Perhaps the most unabashed version of this view is found in Nietzsche's proposition that all of us " 'must work continually at the production of individual great men—that and nothing else is the task'. . . . For the question is this: how can your life, the individual life, receive the highest values, the deepest significance? . . . Only by your living for the good of the rarest and most valuable exemplars."[38] But this is clearly a call for cultural, as opposed to moral, maximizing; so Rawls's criticism of it is irrelevant to the conception of moral endeavor defended here. It is not artistic or scientific achievement that we are to maximize but moral striving, construed broadly and multidimensionally so that the arts and sciences are themselves reinterpreted as instruments for moral purposes. Individuals do differ greatly in the distribution of artistic and scientific talents and abilities, but all individuals "share the moral vocation and destiny common to all humanity—a good will."[39]

Third, liberal critics often assume that perfectionism implies standards that are too narrow and/or too arbitrary, standards to which members of pluralistic, secular societies cannot and should not be forced to adhere. Thus, Rawls's major objection to perfectionism is that moral agents "do not share a conception of the good by reference to which the fruition of their powers or even the satisfaction of their desires can be evaluated. They do not have an agreed upon criterion of perfection that can be used as a principle for choosing between institutions."[40] But the conception of moral maximizing that I am advocating is neither narrow nor arbitrary. It is not narrow because, as I have stressed repeatedly, *all* aspects of human life over which we exercise at least some degree of voluntary control have indirect moral relevance and can be enlisted to further moral projects. Each individual can and must choose how best to make the world more moral, based on an accurate assessment of his or her own talents and inclinations. No single, preferred pattern of moral excellence is being advocated here; indeed, no single preferred pattern *could* be seriously advocated once we understand some rudimentary facts about human life. Granted, I argued earlier that there exist three fundamental constraints that must be placed on the choice of ideals and principles if said ideals and principles are to count as moral. But it is hard to see how anyone could call them arbitrary. What is so arbitrary about proper self-development, beneficence, and justice? As Edmund Pincoffs notes, it would seem that the burden of proof lies with those who would call such standards arbitrary rather than with those who advocate them.[41]

Finally, to some people perfectionism connotes an extreme form of self-absorption, a repugnant narcissism. This particular criticism is often aimed at the forms of perfectionism that stress "self-realization" as the end of ethics.[42] Self-realization *is* integral to my conception of morality, since I argued at length in chapter 1 that morality is best understood as self-regarding rather than other-regarding. However, moral self-development, properly understood, is not a form of narcissism, for several reasons. First, agents often feel no inclination to develop their moral powers and must overcome an aversion to doing so. We have a duty to maximize our moral powers, but the narcissist refuses to recognize this duty. Second, the self that morality urges us to realize and the self with which the narcissist is obsessed are simply not the same self. Different capacities and powers are being realized in each case. Third, and most importantly, our duties to ourselves point directly to active social duties. It is humanity within oneself that the virtuous agent seeks to develop; and the virtuous agent who wills to develop his or her own talents wills that all agents develop their talents. The aim is to help *all* people make the best of themselves. Moral endeavor must include not only individual character development but broad-scale institutional reform, for a moral society is not possible without just institutions and favorable socioeconomic conditions for all citizens.

Ultimately, when all is said and done, it is not the specific label invoked to denote the moral maximization project that is important but, rather, what the label points to.[43] For reasons indicated, I prefer not to use the term *perfectionism* even though my own view owes much to this school of ethical thought. My primary aim in this chapter has been simply to demonstrate that we cannot have too much morality, properly understood, and that the world and its inhabitants can use as much morality as possible. The specific words one uses to refer to the project of making the world moral are not what matters most.

4

Morality and Importance

A man's life, we take it, can not . . . be cut in pieces. You can not say, "In this part the man is a moral being, and in that part he is not." . . . Whatever has been brought under the control of the will, it is not too much to say, has been brought into the sphere of morality; in our eating, our drinking, our sleeping, we from childhood have not been left to ourselves; and the habits, formed in us by the morality outside of us, now hold of the moral will which in a manner has been their issue. And so in our lightest moments the element of control and regulation is not wanting; it is part of the business of education to see that it is there, and its absence, wherever it is seen to be absent, pains us. . . . Character shows itself in every trifling detail of life; we can not go in to amuse ourselves while we leave it outside the door with our dog.

F. H. B R A D L E Y, *Ethical Studies*

Morality is concerned with what a man or group think most important for the guidance of their lives, with their master-concerns.

N E I L C O O P E R, *The Diversity of Moral Thinking*

When people argue for or against the claim that morality is important, it is (to put it mildly) not always clear what they are arguing about. First of all, the term *morality,* as we have seen, has no simple, univocal meaning. Second, the vague word *important* brings its own problems. Important in what sense? And in what degree? The second question is easier to answer than the first, for my thesis is that morality is supremely important in human life. Moral considerations are, in senses I have yet to articulate, the most important considerations humans face. But the first question—the senses of *importance* assumed by both defenders and critics of morality—is much harder to pin down. Let us begin by reviewing a particular sense of importance prominent in recent philosophical debate about morality.

Overridingness

Contemporary philosophical discussion of morality's importance has tended to focus on the so-called overridingness thesis, which holds, as Michael Slote puts

61

it, "that morality automatically overrides all opposing considerations—more precisely, that there cannot be any (overall) justification for doing what is morally wrong."[1] Surprisingly, not much attention has been given within this literature to what exactly is meant by *overridingness;* but we may fairly assume something like the following: X is overriding if it takes precedence, or prevails, or dominates over all other considerations. *Overridingness* thus connotes a relationship between or among considerations and, as such, presupposes the existence of at least two different sets of considerations. Note, first, the underlying image of competing sets of considerations assumed here. There must be at least two different entities if one is to override the other. The basic idea seems to be that these competing considerations will eventually and inevitably bump into one another in combat and that when they do, only one (the moral) will emerge as victor. This picture of what makes morality important is problematic for three reasons.

First, it misconstrues moral considerations as simply one more set of narrowly circumscribed interests on a par with interests drawn from other departments of life, such as the legal or scientific. But when people talk of morality's being important (and more important than, say, law or science), what is usually meant is that it is "bigger" than these other areas of life—bigger not in a literal, spatial sense, but in the sense that it surfaces in our deliberations much more frequently and more powerfully than do other considerations. D. Z. Phillips captures at least part of this sense of bigness when he writes:

> Moral considerations do not constitute an interest, but values to which the pursuit of any interest is answerable. For the same reason paying heed to moral considerations in one's life cannot be called an occupation. Moral values are not characteristics which belong to any distinctive interest or occupation, but may arise in any interest or occupation men engage in. They are not relative to an activity, but [are] an absolute measure to which any activity is said to be answerable.[2]

Similarly, Lawrence Becker, in defending what he calls the general, as opposed to the special, conception of morality, asks, "If morality is just one point of view among many, why should we give it any more weight than any other?"[3] Thus, one fundamental problem with the overridingness thesis is that it assumes moral considerations to be simply another set of narrowly defined interests to be placed alongside others. This assumption is false; at least, it contradicts what is normally assumed in discussions regarding morality's place in life. Morality is commonly held to be important in life precisely because it is felt to be not just one more point of view but, rather, something to which all points of view must answer.

Second, there is an ambiguity in the way the term *override* is used. To claim that moral considerations override, say, aesthetic ones might mean, on the one hand, that someone who weighs up moral considerations against aesthetic ones in deciding what to do will always *as a matter of fact* choose the moral ones. On this "conventional" reading of what overridingness means, it becomes impossible to account for the well-documented fact that people often do not, as a matter of fact, follow moral considerations in doing what they do. A more sensible reading would be to interpret overridingness in a normative sense: the person who weighs up moral considerations against aesthetic ones believes that he or she always *ought* to choose the moral ones. Though this second reading does constitute an advance over the first, it still fails to account for another well-documented fact, namely, that a fair number of people occasionally believe, upon consideration, that they ought to choose nonmoral values over moral ones. Michael Slote, for instance, describes the case of a father who deliberately misleads police

> about his son's whereabouts, even knowing that the son has committed a serious crime and even while acknowledging the validity of the local system of justice. He may feel he mustn't let the police find his son, but must, instead, do everything in his power to help him get to a place of safety, even though he is also willing to admit that there can be no *moral* justification for what he is doing.[4]

While the example itself probably raises more questions than it answers (Why does opting to help one's son in this context necessarily lack moral justification? Does the father believe he is justified or merely excused in acting in this manner?), it seems we must at least grant that there do exist intelligent people who, upon reflection, are not convinced that moral considerations ought to override others.

Finally, the overridingness thesis lacks explanatory force in articulating the importance of morality. We want to understand *why* morality is supremely important in human life. To assert in answer to this question that it "ought to override other considerations" is not very satisfactory. Philosophy (even moral philosophy) ought to be able to do better. I am thus in sympathy with Philippa Foot's charge that moral theorists are guilty of "relying on an illusion, as if trying to give the moral 'ought' a magic force," at least in so far as their frequent invocations of the word *overridingness* do not appear to have explained much.[5] If we are to make a convincing case for morality's importance, we had best look elsewhere.

Pervasiveness

The claim that overridingness talk is flawed by the dubious assumption that moral interests are simply one more set of neatly defined interests to be placed alongside others in combat suggests that the property of *pervasiveness* is a better way to capture at least part of what people mean when they assert that morality is important. Moral considerations appear to possess the ability to permeate or diffuse themselves into nearly all arenas of human life. The battlefield, the board-room, the bedroom, the scientist's laboratory, the artist's studio, and the author's study can all on occasion find themselves unexpectedly but justifiably invaded by moral assessments.

The epigraph from Bradley cited at the beginning of the chapter is a classic statement of morality's pervasiveness: "Whatever has been brought under the control of the will, it is not too much to say, has been brought into the sphere of morality." Bradley, in other words, construes morality to be at least potentially coextensive with what is within our voluntary control. On this view, there is nevertheless a fixed limit to morality's extensive reach: moral considerations do not spread into those aspects of life over which we exercise no voluntary control.[6]

This identification of the moral with the voluntary has been made by numerous philosophers. Aristotle, at the beginning of his discussion of the voluntary (*to hekousion*) in book III of the *Nicomachean Ethics,* announces that it is necessary to distinguish the voluntary and the involuntary for those who are studying virtue (1109b32–34), since the virtues are "in our power and are voluntary" (1114b29). Stuart Hampshire, in *Thought and Action,* echoes this Aristotelian claim when he states that one of the two thoughts traditionally associated with a moral trait is that it is "a human excellence that can in fact be attained by persons who try to attain it."[7] And Samuel Scheffler, in articulating the idea that morality is pervasive, states that "no voluntary human action is in principle resistant to moral assessment (although of course one or another of the familiar excusing conditions may apply)."[8]

Recently, however, some writers have tried to extend morality's reach even further, beyond the limits of the voluntary and into the involuntary. For instance, as we saw earlier (chap. 1, n.23), Robert Adams has argued that many involuntary states of mind are legitimate objects of ethical appraisal and censure in their own right. Part of the motivation behind such arguments is a commitment to the general view that moral considerations ought not to be construed as things we need listen to only occasionally in assessing our intentional, discrete acts but rather that the proper scope of their concern extends over much of the fabric of our lives. Our emotions, attitudes, gestures, and even our unconscious motives are all in their own right proper objects for moral assessment, regardless of whether they lead to observable acts. Though I share this fundamental rejection of moral conceptions that limit themselves to act assessment (see chap. 2), I do not think the strategy of extending morality's reach beyond the voluntary and into the involuntary is sound. What is needed are finer-grained distinctions within the broad realm of the voluntary rather than a simple dichotomy of voluntary/involuntary.

To begin with, a distinction between the *directly* and *indirectly* voluntary should be made. Roughly, something is directly voluntary if the time, place, and manner of its occurrence depends directly on my choosing. On the other hand, something is indirectly voluntary if, though I am unable to always choose the exact time, place, and manner of its occurrence, I am nevertheless able to undertake some voluntary efforts to control it. Thus, my desire to congratulate a professional colleague on her accomplishment would in most cases (assuming I am not on drugs, brainwashed, or the like) be a directly voluntary act. But the slight tinge of jealously in my voice as I speak to her (she's just had an article accepted for publication in the premier journal *Micrologos,* which has sent me only rejection slips) may be only indirectly voluntary. I try hard not to be jealous upon hearing the news, but jealous I am. Still, even though in this instance I seem unable to control the feeling of jealousy rising within myself, there are steps I can take in the future to control it. (I could, as they say, "work on it" through self-analysis or perhaps by seeking professional counseling.) Also, no doubt, there are past events over which I did exercise some control that have contributed causally to this current manifestation of jealously over which I unfortunately lack control. (Perhaps I began making invidious comparisons at an early age. It was open at the beginning for me not to become a jealous man, but now the habit is too deeply etched within me to shake off easily.) Ultimately, I am responsible for my character as the dispositional source of my feelings, even though I now lack direct control over the specific occurrences of some of my feelings.[9]

Within the category of the indirectly voluntary, a further distinction should be made between indirectly voluntary states of mind and indirectly voluntary physiological conditions. The earlier-mentioned case of jealousy is an instance of the former; many forms of obesity are examples of the latter. We can take voluntary steps to control both jealousy as well as obesity, but it seems that indirectly voluntary states of mind are often more fitting objects of moral assessment than are indirectly voluntary physiological conditions. Morality is more concerned with our cognitive life than with our physiological life, though physical conditions that can be changed through cognitive efforts may nevertheless be appropriate objects of moral assessment in the right circumstances.

Finally, within the category of indirectly voluntary states of mind, a further distinction should be noted between those with an intentional object and those without. My jealousy is directed at a specific person; my occasional free-floating depression is not. Here, too, it seems that moral assessment is more appropriately concerned with the former than with the latter. Morally speaking, the feelings we have toward other people and things are more fitting objects of appraisal than feelings that are not directed at any person or object.

No doubt, further distinctions are called for, as well. My point is simply that there is no need to drag in the sledgehammer category of the involuntary in order to articulate the claim that many of our emotions are proper objects of moral assessment. Invoking the unqualified concept of the involuntary is liable to mislead; for there are clearly many types of involuntary states (e.g., skin color, bone structure) that are not proper objects of moral assessment.[10]

Let us then interpret the pervasiveness thesis broadly, so that it encompasses not only directly voluntary processes but also many types of indirectly voluntary ones as well, while recognizing that it nevertheless respects definite limits and does not seek to make moral assessment of completely involuntary states. But perhaps moral concerns are not the only pervasive concerns in human life. May not, say, art or politics or religion possess equally legitimate claims to having a pervasive reach in many people's lives? In response, I do not deny that many things in addition to morality possess the property of pervasiveness. Aesthetic considerations, for instance, also appear to possess the ability to permeate themselves into many areas of human life. Indeed, aesthetic considerations have an even wider scope than do moral ones, for they are not restricted to voluntary actions and attitudes in the way that moral considerations are. Voluntariness is not even a necessary condition for aesthetic assessment. People often make aesthetic assessments of natural objects that are not voluntary productions of any human agent (e.g., when they admire the sunset from their porch at the end of the day).

However, when we restrict our judgments to voluntary attitudes and acts broadly construed, it does seem that moral considerations are generally more fitting than others, however pervasive these others may be. Suppose a man has just murdered several innocent children and elderly adults and has displayed great skill and style in doing so. His hair was perfect, his clothes impeccable, his grace with a gun most admirable. I submit that even the most jaded among us would have to admit that such aesthetic judgments are out of place here, given the gravity of his moral offense. Granted, one could *try* to make an aesthetic assessment of the situation ("Just how great was his hair?"); but to hold onto such a judgment in light of what has occurred would simply not work. Within the context of judgments concerning who we are and what we should do, moral considerations generally do seem to have the final say over other pervasive considerations.[11]

Three objections have been raised against the claim that morality possesses the property of pervasiveness. Each one stems, I think, from an underlying fear that in calling morality pervasive, we are liable to become intolerably moralistic by searching in every conceivable nook and cranny for something upon which to place a moral judgment.

First, there is the *ubiquity charge*. Amélie Rorty writes: "If the dominance of morality is a function of its comprehensiveness, then it is ubiquitous. Embarrassingly, then, the wise man and the fool, the villain and the saint can have the same general ends, and sometimes even the same understanding of those ends."[12] The second sentence does not follow. The villain and the saint cannot be judged to have the same ends, much less the same understanding of those ends; for it is precisely in virtue of the ends people pursue (and the way in which they pursue them) that they become villains or saints. Morality does permeate into the lives of both the villain and the saint; but there is nothing embarrassing about this, for the judgments made on its behalf with respect to the villain and the saint are radically different. Simply put: one person is evil, the other good.

Second, there is the *triviality charge*. Some voluntary acts and attitudes, it is often said, are too trivial or unimportant to warrant moral assessment. Thus, the alleged pervasiveness of the moral is now limited not only by what is within our indirect control but also by a second factor, that of triviality. On the surface, it does indeed seem to be the case that many voluntary acts and attitudes are too trivial to warrant moral assessment. Scratching one's left ear lobe and uttering a sigh of relief upon completion of said act do not seem to be anything to get excited about, morally speaking. But, of course, there is scratching, and there is scratching. Perhaps the scratcher is a member of a white supremacist group, and this particular act of scratching is a signal to his partner that he should now plant a bomb in the previously agreed-on location of a government complex where numerous civilians work, while the concomitant sigh of relief expresses his genuine feeling about the affair after sensing that his partner has correctly interpreted the signal and is about to carry out the act of destruction. Or (more realistically) perhaps the scratcher is merely trying to put a new dinner guest at ease, by implying a certain informality. In other words, as Scheffler notes: "The judgment that a particular act is too trivial to warrant moral evaluation always depends on an assessment of the act and its context.... For any given act that is said to be too trivial, we can imagine a change of context that would render it suitable for moral evaluation."[13] In daily life many things, thankfully, are too trivial to get heated up about morally. But we should never rule out the possibility that there is more to some situations than meets the eye. Morality often has a way of seeping into many seemingly innocuous situations, precisely because it turns out that they are not so innocuous.

Finally, there is the *beyond justification charge*. Some acts and attitudes, it is claimed, lie beyond moral justification. Take the favorite case of a shipwreck where a number of people are drowning and in which a man can save the life of either but not both of two people, one of whom happens to be his wife. Now suppose he does save his wife. Bernard Williams asserts that it would be wrong to claim that the man is morally justified in saving his wife on the ground that she is his wife. Instead, Williams claims, we should see this case "as being a reminder that some situations lie beyond justification."[14] Williams does not reject the claim that the man ought to save his wife. Rather, what he objects to is the kind of convoluted reasoning which he believes the man who is committed to morality will have to go through in such a situation. Williams's view is that the man will reason as follows: "Morality dictates that I must be impartial and not show favoritism. There are a number of people drowning here, and if I choose to save my wife, won't I be guilty of showing partiality? However, given that I can only save one person, and given that she is an innocent victim who could use my help, it at least appears to be morally permissible for me to save her." Williams accuses such a man of having "one thought too many"; and his wife (no doubt) and others (hopefully) would agree: he should save her because he loves her,[15] not because he has reached a decision that it is morally permissible to save a loved one in cases where an agent can only save one person and must choose between saving a stranger and a loved one.

But while I agree with Williams that such a man does, unfortunately, have one thought too many, I do not see why morality dictates that the husband must reason in the manner described, nor do I see why the act itself is "beyond justification." He should save her out of love, and in many cases that is moral reason enough. Morality may at some point have to step in and inform him that the motive of saving a loved one because she is a loved one is not *always* morally acceptable (e.g., suppose he had to throw three innocent children overboard first in order to reach her); but that is another story.[16] Certainly, an event is beyond moral justification if we cannot confidently locate any agents within its boundaries who have played some (directly or indirectly) voluntary role in determining how things turned out. Situations of this sort (e.g., natural catastrophes) are indeed beyond moral justification. But whenever we can locate actors who have played at least indirectly voluntary roles in the way things turn out, the issue of moral assessment is in principle appropriate. Even here, however, as noted earlier, "one or another of the familiar excusing conditions may apply."

Each of these three efforts to stake out areas of voluntary acts and attitudes that are immune to morality's reach therefore fails. This point, when considered in conjunction with the commonsense observation that moral considerations do exhibit ways of sprouting up repeatedly and unexpectedly in numerous areas of human life, lends considerable weight to the claim that morality is indeed pervasive. Nevertheless, there is an obvious problem with the pervasiveness thesis when it is used to support the claim that morality is supremely important: the fact that something is pervasive does not necessarily make it important. Tiny particles of dust pervade my study, but I do not regard them as being particularly important. Weeds pervade my lawn, but they are not terribly important to me (one reason they are there). Pervasiveness itself gives us no direct pipeline to importance. Still, the mere fact that something is nearly ubiquitous may, in the right circumstances, give it one leg up on the competition in deciding what is most important. The fact that moral assessment is in principle appropriate in such a wide variety of situations (and, unlike dust and weeds, presses questions of justification upon us) means, if nothing else, that we need to consider it often. Because morality is pervasive, it, so to speak, has its foot in the door of our deliberations much more often than nonpervasive concerns. If we can now show, once it gets in, that it possesses additional importance-granting properties, we are getting somewhere.

Architectonic Status

Moral considerations, I have argued, permeate our judgments concerning voluntary acts and attitudes much more often than other sorts of consider-ations. But once they are in there, so to speak, what is it about them that enables them to win out over other sorts of considerations? Why do we tend to attend to them more than to other sorts of considerations? In other words, what importance-granting property does morality possess in addition to sheer pervasiveness?

I shall argue now that morality possesses, in addition to pervasiveness, the property of *architectonic status*. The classic statement of this view is found near the beginning of Aristotle's *Nicomachean Ethics,* when he is discussing the human good:

> We must try, in outline at least, to determine what [the human good] is, and of which of the sciences or capacities it is the subject. It would seem to belong to the most authoritative [*kuriōtatēs*] and most architectonic [*malista architektonikēs*] sci-ence, and politics appears to be of this nature; for it is this that ordains which of the sciences should be studied in a *polis,* and which each class of citizens should learn and up to what point they should learn them; and we see even the most highly esteemed of capacities to fall under this, e.g., strategy, economics, rhetoric; now, since politics uses the rest of the sciences, and since, again, it legislates as to what

we are to do and what we are to abstain from, the end of this science must embrace [*periechoi*] those of the others, so that this end must be the human good. (1094a25–b7; cf. 1094a14, 1152b2, 1141b22, 1141b25, and *Pol* 1252a5–7)

Before turning to the term *architectonic*, it is necessary to describe briefly Aristotle's conception of the relationship between ethics and politics; for even though this passage occurs in his *Nicomachean Ethics,* Aristotle specifically says that it is politics or the political (*hē politikē*) that is architectonic, rather than ethics per se. In one sense, the modern distinction between the ethical and the political is not even one that Aristotle chooses to make: politics, as he understands it, is a normative, practical discipline that investigates "noble and just things" (*kala kai ta dikaia,* 1094b14 and 1095b5). His *Politics* (which is, in a sense, the second half of the *Nicomachean Ethics,* for the latter concludes with a discussion of the need for good laws, as well as a brief summary of the contents of the *Politics*) is essentially a guidebook for prospective statesmen and deals with such matters as which type of political arrangement is best and why and how citizens should be educated. Since normative concerns are at the center of Aristotle's discussion of politics, the once-popular modern notion of a "value-free" political science is quite distant from his conception of politics.

The political thus overlaps with the moral for Aristotle, since both are concerned with how humans ought to live and act. At the same time, he occasionally suggests that ethics can be distinguished from politics in so far as ethics is primarily concerned with how *individuals* can flourish and politics, with how *communities* can flourish. Thus, in the same chapter of the *Ethics* from which the quoted passage is taken, Aristotle goes on to state:

> For even if the end is the same for a single person and for a *polis,* that of the *polis* appears at all events something greater and more complete [*telioteron*] whether to attain or to preserve; though it is worth while to attain the end merely for an individual, it is nobler and more divine to attain it for a group [*ethnos*] or for communities. These, then, are the ends at which our inquiry aims, since it is politics, in one sense of that term [*politikē tis ousa*]. (1094b7–11)

Similarly, in the *Rhetoric,* when Aristotle is defining the nature of rhetoric, he states that it appears to be "an offshoot of dialectic and also of ethics [*ēthē*], which may fairly [*dikaion*] be called *politikē*" (1356a25–26).

Ethics and politics are thus closely connected for Aristotle; but the ends of the latter do encompass—and thus have a higher status than—the ends of the former. A human individual is by nature a political animal (*politikon zōon, Pol* 1253a2) and can flourish only within a polis. Ethics and politics deal with the same broad subject (i.e., the human good and how to achieve it), but from different points of view. The point of view of ethics in the strict sense is more individualistic, that of politics, more communal. I follow Aristotle in choosing not to make a strong distinction between the moral and the political. Most[17] political problems are moral problems; and most moral problems—particularly those that concern real persons situated in specific societies rather than those of the solitary, decontextualized individual favored in ethics textbooks—are also political problems. However, in the following analysis I shall generally refer to morality or ethics rather than politics as possessing architectonic status. Since the primary focus of Aristotle's inquiry is unmistakably normative and practical (How ought we to live and act?) and since modern conceptions of politics are too often shaped by narrow concerns about power, interest groups, and allegedly value-free scientific pursuits, the term *moral* rather than *political* captures more of the spirit of his investigation.

I turn now to the term *architectonic*. What does Aristotle mean when he calls morality architectonic? The English word *architectonic* comes from the Greek compound noun, *architektonikos*. *Archi* comes from the verb *archein*, "to begin or lead." Thus, an *archos* is a leader, chief, or commander; and an *archē* is a beginning or first cause. A *tektōn*, on the other hand, is a carpenter or builder. Accordingly, an *architektōn* is a master builder. Calling a set of human concerns architectonic means, in the first sense, that it rules or has authority over other concerns. Architectonic concerns are master concerns. Just as an architect organizes and directs the skills and insights of roofers, electricians, plumbers, and others toward the end of creating a beautiful home, so morality, on Aristotle's view, regulates the skills and insights of the other arts and sciences toward the goal of achieving *eudaimonia* within the polis. How does Aristotle support this claim? Three short arguments are presented.

First, it is politics "which ordains which of the sciences should be studied in a *polis*, and which each class of citizens should learn and up to what point they should learn them" (*NE* 1094a29–b1). The earlier analogy (1094a10–16) to bridlemaking and the more architectonic art of equestrianism is relevant here. The ends of the former are subordinate to those of the latter. The art of riding ultimately rules over the art of bridlemaking; for equestrianism is concerned with the larger issue of how best to ride horses, and bridlemaking concerns only a means toward this end. Similarly, we study the various arts and sciences in order that human beings may flourish; but it is up to politics, as the master art concerned with the human good, to regulate which amounts and combinations of which of the arts and sciences will best enable us to flourish. Politics has authority over all other subjects because the goals of all other subjects are desirable for the sake of the final end studied by politics.

Second, "politics uses the rest of the sciences" (1094b4–5).[18] Thus, a statesman will commonly employ economic, military, and scientific advisors in his administration, using their expert advice as he sees fit, in order to promote the common good. Just as a conductor employs the skills of the various musicians in an orchestra with the aim of creating beautiful music, so politics uses the insights of the arts and sciences and regulates their presence to promote the human good.

Finally, Aristotle reminds his audience that politics "legislates as to what we are to do and what we are to abstain from" (*NE* 1094b6–7). Legislation, or *nomothetikē*, is only one branch of politics; but it is a vital branch, since "it is difficult to get from youth up a right training for virtue if one has not been brought up under right laws; for to live temperately and hardily is not pleasant to most people, especially when they are young" (1179b31–34). Legislation exerts a tremendous influence on all citizens regardless of occupation; and it plays an architectonic role, since who and what each of us becomes is partly a factor of the laws and conventions that we follow from youth onward.

Although Aristotle's doctrine of the architectonic status of ethics and politics is not without its own problems,[19] I do believe that his basic position captures an essential part of the claim that morality is supremely important in human life. Once the scope of morality's concern is construed broadly so that it encompasses the question How should we live and act?, it does make good sense to assert that the end of morality embraces or includes all other ends. For the proper degree to which other activities are to be pursued is a matter to be determined by looking at this larger question. The question of how to live and act does set limits on all other activities, since it is literally a larger, more inclusive question, into which all others fit.[20] Morality in this sense is architectonic in our lives; and the issue of how to live and act does function as an organizing principle in all areas of life, setting conditions on both the means, as well as the ends, of all other human activities.

However, it is important to note that the sense of importance of morality that issues from its architectonic status concerns not the ability to *override* decisions in other spheres of life but, rather, to embrace or encompass them. The correct picture here is not one of competing sets of narrow considerations engaged on a collision course with each another, with one sole victor emerging on top of all the losers. Rather, it is one of a broader set of interests being able to embrace narrower ones. It is morality's breadth of concern, as revealed in its focus on the all-things-considered question of how to live and act, that enables it to embrace or include all other considerations.

Before moving on to an additional importance-granting property of morality, it may be worthwhile to comment briefly on Kant's slightly different use of the term *architectonic*. In a general sense, *architectonic* for Kant refers to a grand systematization effort involving all of the various branches of knowledge, an attempt to order all of them under one alleged megaprinciple. Readers of Kant, particularly of the first *Critique,* often voice legitimate complaints regarding the "highly elaborate, and extremely artificial"[21] arrangement of topics and arguments that is one unfortunate consequence of such a strong commitment to the systematic unity of knowledge. It is not my intent here to defend this particular aspect of Kantian architectonic, for I do not believe that all branches of knowledge can be squeezed into one overarching system. But I am concerned with how Kantian architectonic hooks into the doctrine of the *primacy of the practical* and with whether any of the arguments used by Kant and others to defend this latter doctrine can then be adopted to support my own thesis concerning the supreme importance of morality.

Basically, what drives Kantian architectonic is a doctrine of essential ends of human nature. These ends are then ranked hierarchically, some essential ends being subordinated to others. According to Kant, human reason's demand for "complete systematic unity" entails that one, and only one, essential goal properly be called the ultimate end, or *Endzweck:* "Essential ends are not as such the highest ends; in view of the demand of reason for complete systematic unity, only one of them can be so described. Essential ends are therefore either the *Endzweck* or subordinate ends which are necessarily connected with the former as means" (*C1* A 840/B 868). And what is the one *Endzweck* to which all other goals are subordinate? According to Kant, it is

> no other than the whole destiny of man [*die ganze Bestimmung des Menschen*], and the philosophy which deals with it is entitled moral philosophy. On account of this priority [*Vorzug*] which moral philosophy has over all other occupations of reason, the ancients in their use of the term "philosopher" always meant, more especially, the *moralist;* and even at present we are led by a certain analogy to entitle anyone a philosopher who appears to exhibit self-control under the guidance of reason, however limited his knowledge may be. (*C1* A 840/B 868)

In other words, Kantian architectonic is itself shaped by, and presupposed by, the doctrine of the primacy of practical interests. Among other things, this makes Kant's own conception of the architectonic status of morality much more radical and unequivocal than Aristotle's: *theōria* itself is now unequivocally subordinated to moral praxis. The following passage from Kant's *Logic* brings this out clearly:

> Everything terminates ultimately in the practical [*Alles läuft zuletzt auf das Praktische hinaus*]; and in this tendency of everything theoretical and everything speculative in respect of its use, consists the practical value of our cognition. This value, however, is an unconditioned value only if the end to which the practical use of cognition is directed is an unconditioned end. The only unconditioned and final [*letzte*] end [ultimate end (*Endzweck*)] to which all practical use of our cognition must ultimately refer is morality, which for that reason we also call the plainly or absolutely practical. (*L* IX 87/94–95)

I turn next to Kant's doctrine of the primacy of the practical. Why do practical interests have primacy over all others, and how does this doctrine enable us further to support the claim that morality is supremely important?

Primacy of the Practical

> Every interest is ultimately practical, even that of speculative reason being only conditional and reaching perfection only in practical use.
> KANT, *Critique of Practical Reason*

We noted earlier that most recent philosophical discussions of morality's importance have focused on the property of overridingness. It is ironic within this literature that Kant's doctrine of the categorical imperative is used again and again as a scapegoat to demonstrate that morality can not always be overriding but that no mention is ever made of his doctrine concerning the primacy of the practical. And it is perhaps even more ironic that within the contemporary secondary literature on Kant's ethics, few topics "have been discussed so infrequently as the primacy of practical reason."[22] On my view, Kant's doctrine of the primacy of the practical is a much more fruitful source for understanding the ultimate importance of morality than are his narrower remarks concerning the formal structure of categorical, as opposed to hypothetical, oughts.

The following account does not aim at a detailed analysis of Kant's views concerning the primacy of the practical in part because, like many critics, I find some aspects of the doctrine to be philosophically unpersuasive.[23] I shall focus on the questions What does it mean for reason to have "interests"? How do theoretical and practical interests differ? What does *primacy* mean in this context? What are some of the implications of asserting that the practical has primacy over the theoretical? What arguments does Kant offer on behalf of the claim that the practical has primacy over all other interests? Which of his arguments (if any) can still be employed today to defend persuasively the thesis of this chapter, namely, that moral concerns are our most important concerns?

For Kant, reason is construed as a system of interests, which means both that each different aspect of reason can be seen to have its own defining aim, and that these interests can be hierarchically related to one another. Kant's not-terribly-helpful definition of *interest* is "a principle which contains the condition under which alone its exercise is advanced" (*C2* V 119/124).[24] Essentially, an interest of reason, for Kant, is a fundamental goal that defines what that aspect of reason seeks to accomplish. As Yirmiahu Yovel notes, for Kant, reason's "basic feature is *teleological* activity, pursuing its own 'essential ends' or immanent tasks."[25]

Mention of practical versus theoretical interests may appear to imply that there exist two different faculties of reason or two completely different entities. However, Kant states several times that this is not the case: "In the final analysis there can be only one and the same reason, which is to be differentiated solely in its application [*bloss in der Anwendung*]" (*G* IV 391/4; cf. *C2* V 89/121, 92/125 and *DV* VI 207/3). Kant states in the second *Critique* that the fundamental interest of theoretical reason "consists in the knowledge of objects up to the highest a priori principles" (see n. 24). More generally, the task of theoretical reason is to give us knowledge of the world we experience by contributing the conceptual structure by which the human mind organizes experience and to see that knowledge does not transgress its limits. On the other hand, the practical interest of reason is said by Kant to lie "in the determination of the will with respect to the final and perfect end" (*C2* V 120/124). Practical reason's task is to determine the will, that is, to lead agents to act not on the basis of desire but on rational grounds. But there is also a definite goal toward which this action of free wills aims: the final end, or *Endzweck*. As we have seen, in the *Critique of Judgment* Kant states that the *Endzweck* toward which the moral law obliges us to strive is "the highest good in the world possible through freedom" (*C3* V 450/118).[26]

The moral obligation to promote the highest good is crucial but often underappreciated aspect of Kant's conception of practical reason. Practical reason's task is not only to get agents to act but to implant within them the desire to realize a truly moral society where all people are treated as ends in themselves. This obligation to seek to realize the highest good is the generating force behind the primacy of the practical. As Lucien Goldmann remarks, for Kant, the fundamental category of existence is "the task of creating a world."[27]

What does it mean for practical interests to have "primacy" over others? Kant's own definition of *primacy* (*Primat*) runs as follows:

> By primacy between two or more things connected by reason, I understand the priority [*Vorzug*] of one by virtue of which it is the primary determining ground of combination [*erste Bestimmungsgrund der Verbindung*] with all the others. In a narrower practical sense it refers to the priority of the interest of one so far as the interest of the others is subordinated [*untergeordnet*] to it and it is not itself inferior to any other. (*C2* V 119/124)

Primacy in a narrower sense refers to the subordination of one interest to another. *Primacy of the practical* in this narrower sense means that practical interests are always preeminent over other interests in cases of conflict. However, *primacy* in this narrower sense is not something that Kant generally emphasizes. As he notes later, "It is not a question of which must yield, for one does not necessarily conflict with the other" (*C2* V 120/125). Again, ultimately there is "only one and the same reason, which is to be differentiated solely in its application."

Primacy in a broader and more fundamental sense refers to one interest's being the primary determining ground of combination with all others. *Primacy of the practical* in this broader and more fundamental sense means that the determining ground of all theoretical activities must always be located in the field of the practical and not vice versa. The ultimate justification and very possibility of any and all theoretical pursuits comes from practical sources. In other words, on Kant's view, all scientific and theoretical endeavors are conceptually dependent on, as well as normatively constrained by, moral categories. Science and technology—and indeed, all forms of critical thought—are both conceptually dependent on, and normatively constrained by, ethics. As we shall see shortly, this is the most powerful idea to be gleaned from Kant's doctrine of the primacy of the practical; and it is a prominent theme among many post-Kantian writers as well.

Finally, what arguments does Kant offer in defense of his claim that the practical has primacy? A number of very different sorts of arguments are put forward, not all of which need concern us here. In the following account three modified Kantian arguments for the primacy of the practical are summarized and then deployed to support the thesis of this chapter.

Theoretical Reason's Dependence on Moral Values

The most compelling argument in defense of the claim that the practical has primacy is that theoretical reason is necessarily dependent on moral values to carry out its own interest, values that are beyond its own justificatory capacities.

Practical reason "has of itself original a priori principles with which certain theoretical positions are inseparably bound but which are beyond any possible insight of the speculative reason" (*C2* V 120/125). The regulative norms Kant refers to most often in this context are the ambitious ideas of freedom, soul or self-consciousness persisting through time, nature as a purposive unity, and God.

Kant's argument here—that theoretical reason cannot pursue its own interest without employing these regulative ideas—has failed to convince many readers, in large part because it appears to be a disingenuous way for a supposedly critical theory to drag in tired metaphysical notions that have already been the subject of its own critique. But I believe that Kant's perceived failure has more to do with the specific norms on which he tends to focus (and the heavy-handed way in which he introduces them) than with his general claim that theoretical reason is dependent upon regulative norms. The underlying claim is, I submit, true and has received support from a variety of post-Kantian sources. Hilary Putnam, for instance, has in recent years defended the view that

> any choice of a conceptual scheme presupposes values, and the choice of a scheme for describing ordinary interpersonal relations and social facts, not to mention thinking about one's own life plan, involves, among other things, one's *moral* values. One cannot choose a scheme which simply "copies" the facts, because *no* conceptual scheme is a mere "copy" of the world. The notion of truth itself depends for its content on our standards of rational acceptability, and these in turn rest on and presuppose our values. . . . Theory of truth presupposes theory of rationality which in turn presupposes our theory of the good.[28]

To assert that "any choice of a conceptual scheme presupposes values" is not quite to assert that any choice of a conceptual scheme presupposes *moral* values; for, of course, there are many different kinds of values. Not all values are moral values, so that even if it can be shown that our choice of a conceptual scheme presupposes (some kind of) values, such values might not turn out to be moral values. Similarly, one might believe that our choice of conceptual scheme presupposes a variety of different types of value (say, aesthetic as well as moral), without having a view as to whether one of these types of value is the primary determining ground of combination with all other interests. In order to support the claim that morality has primacy, we need to show both that our choice of conceptual scheme presupposes specifically moral values and that such values themselves are the primary determining ground of combination with all other interests.

A variety of arguments from earlier pragmatist writings can be employed to meet this need. For it is well known that all of the classical American pragmatists held that logic and knowledge in general are dependent upon ethics. Knowing, on the pragmatist account, is a fundamentally evaluative activity. Charles Sanders Peirce, for instance, writes, "If, as pragmatism teaches us, what we think is to be interpreted in terms of what we are prepared to do, then surely *logic* or the doctrine of what we ought to think, must be an application of the doctrine of what we deliberately choose to do, which is Ethics."[29] Truth itself is assigned a moral basis in William James's pronouncement that "truth is *one species of good*, and not, as is usually supposed, a category distinct from good, and co-ordinate with it."[30] This commitment to the priority of the moral continues in the later writings of John Dewey and C. I. Lewis. Dewey, for instance, in his 1929 Gifford Lectures, *The Quest for Certainty*, discusses briefly the logical positivists' attempt to exorcise values from the field of philosophy. According to this school of thought, which was rapidly gaining in popularity when Dewey's lectures were first delivered, all value judgments are subjective expressions of emotion; and values thus have no proper place in any discipline that seeks to give an objective, critical account of reality. Dewey counters with the claim that "to say that the object of philosophy is truth is to make a moral statement. . . . To assert that contemplation of truth for its own sake is the highest ideal is to make a judgment concerning authoritative value."[31] In what way does a commitment to truth presuppose moral values? Regardless of what specific theory of truth we adhere to, we are committing ourselves in advance to following certain fundamental norms of argument and to following them fairly and impartially. Adherence to such norms requires self-control, as well as the identification of one's own interests with those of the community of inquirers. Critical thinking itself is a normative activity, for our basic concern is not just random thoughts but what is *right* or correct in the way of believing. Moral norms are necessary presuppositions for all scientific and critical thought.

The necessary underlying moral character of all knowledge is also a pervasive theme in Lewis's work. He states: " 'Knowledge' is itself a normative word. Cognition which is not valid is not knowledge but error or baseless fancy. . . . [Scientific conclusions] necessarily reflect ways of coming to conclusions which satisfy the norms of consistency and cogency. . . . An exclusive descriptivism and repudiation of the normative digs a pit for its own feet."[32] The assertion that knowledge is normative is not quite the assertion that knowledge presupposes moral norms; for, again, not all norms are moral norms. But Lewis explicitly embraces the latter claim a few pages later when he states: "The normative character of thinking, concluding, and believing, like the normative in general, relates directly to the right and represents a nonrepudiable demand. . . . Conforming our empirical conclusions to what is most fully supported by all the evidence, consistently and cogently considered, is such a nonrepudiable imperative for our thinking."[33] Unavoidable deontic constraints are operative in any conceptual framework, and such constraints regarding what is right and wrong in the way of belief are fundamentally moral constraints. Indeed, the ethics of belief and of action are two parts of a larger whole; for morality concerns much more than our discrete acts: "Right thinking and right doing are simply the two major subdivisions of our self-directed activities—decisions as to fact and decisions as to bring about [*sic*]"[34] Furthermore, these constraints are not subordinate to other values; for they are necessary presuppositions of *every* type of critical thought. It is not just scientific and mathematical thought that presuppose moral norms concerning what is right, but for example, reflective criticism in art and religion, as well. Admittedly, these deontic constraints of right and wrong are highly abstract; and they certainly do not represent the whole of morality. But they do form a central and uneliminable aspect of any adequate moral outlook.

Lewis's efforts centered on an attempt to show that the normative character of all critical thinking presupposes a commitment to what ethical theorists call "the right." But the contrasting moral value of the good is presupposed by our choice of conceptual schemes as well. Charles Taylor argues, in *Sources of the Self*, that "in order to make minimal sense of our lives, in order to have an identity, we need an orientation to the good, which means some sense of qualitative discrimination, of the incomparably higher. . . . This sense of the good has to be woven into my understanding of my life as an unfolding story."[35] Humans are goal-oriented creatures who necessarily make qualitative discriminations; and we cannot begin to say who or what we are without indicating where we have been and where we think we are headed: "To know who you are is to be oriented in moral space, a space in which questions arise about what is good or bad, what is worth doing and what not, what has meaning and importance for you and what is trivial and secondary."[36] However, it is not just our choice of a scheme for describing personal and interpersonal relations that presupposes an orientation to the good. Scientific inquiry, too, in seeking to arrive at "the *best* account we can give at any give time" (my emphasis), necessarily presupposes an orientation to the good. The language of scientific assessment presupposes the ability to make discriminations between what is good and what is bad; and "the terms we use to decide what is best are very much the same as those we use to judge others' actions."[37] Moral presuppositions are inescapable, even when the focus of inquiry does not include people.

The claim that all conceptual schemes presuppose and employ moral values seems to me to be the irrefutable core of truth in the Kantian doctrine of the primacy of the practical. Again, the moral values on which knowledge depends—the right and the good—are terribly abstract. But in this particular instance abstractness is a virtue rather than a vice, for their very abstractness virtually ensures that they will be interpreted and applied somewhat differently by different thinkers. Furthermore, the specific content of these values within a given culture is itself subject to revision as knowledge increases and worldviews change.[38] In other words, we should not leap from the claim that all conceptual schemes necessarily presuppose and employ moral values to the wild assertion that morality somehow dictates the form and content of every thought we are allowed to entertain; for there is no single, morally correct conceptual scheme at any detailed level. Furthermore, our moral values are themselves subject to revision as we acquire better information about ourselves. Morality does not perpetually police thought or set up round-the-clock surveillance programs to spy on it. Rather, moral values make thought possible.

Moral Constraints on Theoretical Pursuits

All conceptual schemes presuppose moral values at the initial choice stage; but once a particular framework is chosen and employed in the carrying out of, say, scientific pursuits, moral values continue to serve as ultimate criteria of acceptability for such activities. These constraints do not take the form of perpetual policing or constant surveillance monitoring, but they do set fundamental limits on what can and cannot be done in pursuing an interest. All scientific ambitions—and, indeed, all nonpractical interests, whether scientific or not—must ultimately be subordinated to, and guided by, moral considerations. Kant clearly rejects the dogma of knowledge for knowledge's sake. The ultimate value and justification of any and all knowledge lies in the manner in which it is used and the ends to which it is directed; for "science [*Wissenschaft*] has a true inner value only as an organ of wisdom [*Weisheit*]" (*L* IX 26/30).

Science itself is thus a moral enterprise, and its practice must be constrained (but not determined) by basic moral considerations. In the *Anthropology,* as well as in the third *Critique* and the *Logic,* Kant offers the following three "unalterable commands" meant to guide the practice of all researchers: "(1) to think *for ourselves,* (2) to think ourselves into the place *of every other man*..., (3) always to think *consistently with ourselves*" (*A* VII 228/96–97; cf. *C3* V 294/152 and *L* IX 57/63). As Roger Sullivan notes, "It turns out that these rules are simply a restatement of the purely formal but supremely powerful Categorical Imperative, the law of autonomy, universality, and consistency."[39] The legitimacy of the scientific enterprise, for instance, requires of scientists that they think for themselves rather than plagiarize the research of others or blindly follow dying paradigms; that their experiments be conducted from the "standpoint of everyone," so that anyone anywhere with the right training and equipment can in principle reproduce the results; and that they think consistently, which is a defining characteristic of objective rationality.

It is important to note that these moral constraints serve a double function in that they serve to protect the legitimate interests of a field of activity both from within and without. For instance, practicing researchers are morally forbidden from fabricating data or tampering with evidence (protection from within); but external political or religious groups are also morally forbidden from interfering with research efforts in an attempt to make them serve their own ideological agendas.[40]

An additional moral constraint on theoretical pursuits can be gleaned from the third version of the categorical imperative, which holds that we must always act so that we treat other humans, as well as ourselves, as ends and never simply as means. Any and all uses of human beings in scientific experiments are subject to this constraint. Science must respect our worth as moral agents.

Finally, Kant states in the *Logic* that we "must concede to the [moral] will an influence on the use of the understanding and thus, indirectly, on conviction itself," since the will may legitimately impel the understanding "to explore a truth or restrain it therein" (*L* IX 74/82). The search for truth in science and elsewhere is justified, as well as constrained, by respect for the good will, the only "good without qualification." Because moral interests have primacy over nonmoral interests, it is up to them to set limits on both which subjects may be investigated and by what means.

Moral Community Is the Endzweck

For Kant, "the highest ends are those of morality" (*C1* A 816/B 844); and the ultimate source of value and meaning in the world lies in moral praxis rather than theoretical contemplation. As he writes in the third *Critique:*

> Without human beings the whole creation would be a mere waste, in vain, and without final purpose [*ohne Endzweck*]. But it is not in reference to man's cognitive faculty (theoretical reason) that the being of everything else in the world gets its worth; he is not there merely that there may be someone to *contemplate* the world. For if the contemplation of the world only afforded a representation of things without any final purpose, no worth could accrue to its being from the mere fact that it is known; we must presuppose for it a final purpose, in reference to which its contemplation itself has worth.... It is that worth which [man] alone can give to himself and which consists in what he does, how and according to what principles he acts, and that not as a link in nature's chain but in the *freedom* of his faculty of desire. That is, a good will is that whereby alone his being can have an absolute worth and in reference to which the being of the world can have a final purpose. (*C3* V 442–43/108–9)[41]

Kant announces at the opening of the *Grounding* that the only unqualified good in the universe is the good will. Here we see the thought repeated. All other goods have a merely derivative value: without the good will, nothing else would have any value at all. Of crucial importance is the fact that the ancient Greek ideal of *theōria* is specifically singled out for criticism in this passage. A fundamental difference between Aristotle's and Kant's understanding of the architectonic role of morality now emerges. For Aristotle, morality's architectonic status is ultimately compromised by the fact that the life of moral praxis is an inferior, all-too-human life when compared to that of the godly *bios theōrētikos*.[42] For Kant, the moral life retains supremacy over (and again, makes possible) the theoretical life. Theoretical contemplation cannot be what is most valuable because there must first be something of value in the world if it is to be worth contemplating. This value is found only in moral agents striving to realize the highest good.

The unabashed anthropocentrism in Kant's vision of the final end of creation is unlikely to win over many contemporary readers. But strictly speaking, it is not human-centered in any "speciesist" sense. What gives humans ultimate worth on Kant's view is their capacity to live their lives in accordance with freely chosen moral ideals that accord with standards of reason. It is "only as a moral being that we acknowledge man to be the end of creation" (*C3* V 444/110). Other nonhuman rational agents elsewhere who possess this same capacity (should any exist) would logically be due the same exalted status.[43] And while he does dogmatically proclaim that "animals are not self-conscious and exist merely as means; but man exists as an end" (*LE* 302/239; cf. *G* IV 428/35–36), this is in part an empirical question. If it could be shown that some animals do in fact possess self-consciousness, then they, too, would warrant moral status in their own right according to Kant's own definition. But even when properly qualified in this manner, Kant's "ratiocentrist" outlook still does not go far enough. I believe that any acceptable moral scheme must grant at least a degree of direct moral consideration to all living things. Bentham's hedonist retort ("The question is not, Can they *reason* nor, Can they *talk?* but, Can they *suffer?*") is equally simplistic;[44] but the capacity to suffer clearly ought to count for something. Even if nonhuman animals do not quite qualify as ends in themselves, we ought not to infer that the only remaining option is to treat them as mere means.

Morality is important for many reasons, but the most significant of these reasons have received scant attention in recent literature. I have argued that morality's pervasive reach and breadth of concern (as expressed in the question of how to live and act) enable it to embrace and include narrower interests, thus giving it an architectonic status in human life. Additionally, I have argued that the choice of any conceptual scheme necessarily presupposes fundamental moral values; that the scope, focus, and methodology of all research activities must be ultimately constrained by basic moral considerations; and that moral community itself is the sole source of unconditioned value in the world.

Each of these arguments serves also to reinforce our earlier suspicion that morality's supreme importance is not well articulated by the overridingness thesis. For we see now that morality's fundamental importance stems not from its "standing above" everything else but rather from the fact that it literally surrounds everything else, lies underneath everything else, and is continually embedded in everything else. Admittedly, this way of defending morality's importance does not allow us the luxury of issuing an authoritative decision procedure that can declare who is victor whenever interests clash. But the "battle of the interests" picture itself presupposes that moral, as well as nonmoral, interests can always be narrowly and neatly defined; and we have seen that this presupposition is false. Furthermore, the dependence claims that I have been making here show much more graphically what is at stake in contemporary efforts to dismiss moral concern. The attempt to convince us that we would be "better off without morality" is no mere effort to erase a small and superficial corner of life. Rather, as Lewis saw, the attempt to repudiate the moral "digs a pit for its own feet"—indeed, for everyone's feet.

Enough has now been said, I hope, to show how and where our moral conception needs overhauling. I do not pretend to have offered an exhaustive definition of morality: my goal has been the more modest one of reappraising certain key aspects of morality and of then urging the substitution of this particular alternative moral conception for that assumed by contemporary antimorality critics. In each of the four chapters of part I, the basic strategy has been not to rebut directly the arguments of critics but to shift the grounds of debate by invoking alternative considerations, thereby defusing their criticisms. Thus, in chapter 1, I argued that morality should be viewed as fundamentally self-regarding rather than other-regarding, thereby undercutting the criticism that morality downgrades personal concerns and alienates moral agents from their own deepest projects and convictions. In chapter 2, I urged that morality be understood as something much broader and richer than is normally the case at present—as a force for assessing the fabric of our entire lives rather than simply our discrete acts. Here, the narrowness charge was undercut by showing that morality, properly understood, is anything but narrow. In chapter 3, I argued against the claim that there is a limit to how much morality we can stand, presenting an alternative account of what moral maximization means. Finally, in chapter 4, I have defended the claim that morality is supremely important in human life, presenting an alternative account of what it is that makes morality important. In each case, I contend, skeptical attacks against morality lose much of their force once the alternative conception of a key aspect of what a morality *is* is adopted. Morality is thus reaffirmed when reappraised in the ways here indicated. Furthermore, as I have stressed repeatedly, the alternative moral conception defended herein has direct ties to certain aspects of Aristotelian, as well as Kantian, ethics: it is not a mere product of conceptual jugglery but something that has vital roots in our not-always-remembered past. The same claim cannot be made accurately on behalf of the truncated moral conception assumed by contemporary critics.

But still (a by-no-means-unfriendly reader might protest), even if all of these claims made on behalf of a broader, richer, more important morality are accepted, why do we need to cloud our practical insights with *theories* of morality? Are not the mounting pretensions and illusions of moral theories chiefly to blame for morality's gradual fall from grace? Are not the recent arguments against academic moral theorizing indeed compelling ones that friends of morality ought to embrace, rather than reject? Do we need moral theories at all? I turn next to these questions.

II
MORAL THEORY

When Leon the tyrant of Phlius asked Pythagoras who he was, he said, "A philosopher," and he compared life to the public festivals, where some went to compete for a prize and others went with things to sell, but the best as observers [*theatai*]; for similarly, in life, some grow up with servile natures, greedy for fame and gain, but philosophers seek the truth.

Diogenes Laertius

If human flourishing [*eudaimonia*] is activity in accordance with virtue, it is reasonable that it should be in accordance with the best [*tēn kratistēn*] virtue; and this will be that of the best thing in us.... That this activity is theoretical [*theōretikē*] we have already said.

Aristotle, *Nichomachean Ethics*

5

What Do Antitheorists Mean by *Theory?*

I shall argue that philosophy should not try to produce ethical theory.
BERNARD WILLIAMS,
Ethics and the Limits of Philosophy

I want to attack the whole idea of a moral "theory" which systematizes
and extends a body of judgements.
ANNETTE BAIER, *Postures of the Mind*

Ethical theory is essentially a modern invention.... I will argue that
the structures known as ethical theories are more threats to moral
sanity and balance than instruments for their attainment.
EDMUND PINCOFFS, *Quandaries and Virtues*

Origins: *Theōria*

Our word *theory* comes from the Greek *theōria*, an abstract noun based on the verb *theōrein*, "to look at, view, behold." In ancient Greece, *theōroi*, "observers," was a word "originally applied to sight-seeing travellers and to the attendants at festivals of distant cities." In time, it became "an official title given to a city's representatives at another city's festivals."[1] Oedipus weeps when he considers what the future holds for his children: "What gatherings will you go to, what festivals, without returning home in tears, instead of viewing the ceremonies [*tēs theōrias*]?" (*Oedipus the King* 1489–91). Herodotus observes that Hippocrates, "who held no public office, was a *theōros* at the Olympic games" (I.59). Alcibiades, friend and pupil of Socrates, boasts in a speech recorded by Thucydides of "the magnificence" with which he represented Athens as "a *theōros* at the Olympic games" (VI.16). Socrates, Plato informs us at the beginning of the *Phaedo*, could not be legally executed for several months after his trial, because the Athenians had just sent a mission or group of envoys (*theōria*) to Delos; and the law held that "as soon as this *theōria* begins the *polis* must be kept pure, and no public executions may take place until the ship has reached Delos and returned again" (58B; cf. Xenophon, *Memorabilia* IV.8.2). Similarly, Creon informs Oedipus that his father Laius, king of Thebes, was killed while

85

on a journey as a *theōros* to consult with the oracle at Delphi (*Oedipus the King* 114).

The early *theōroi* were thus "summoned on special occasions to attest the occurence of some event, to witness its happenstance, and to then verbally certify its having taken place.... In other words, their function was one of see-and-tell."[2] Eventually the *theōroi* became official government functionaries, and *theōros* became a term simply for one of the lesser magistrate offices as well as for the discharge of one's official duties in this office. Thucydides, for instance, records the details of an alliance between the Athenians, Argives, Manitineans, and Eleans in which it is stated that an oath shall be taken at Manitinea "by the Demiurgi, the Senate, and the other magistrates, the *Theōroi* and Polemarchs administering it" (V.47).

Pythagoras, in the famous story recorded by Diogenes Laertius, compares philosophers to *theōroi* at the public games who go not to compete or do business but simply to observe what is happening; and at this point a connection between philosophy and theory is asserted. Once the link to philosophy is made, *theōria* gradually loses its earlier sense of ordinary visual observation and acquires new shades of meaning: contemplation, reflection, speculation. Still, the garden-variety observational sense of *theōria* remains common even in the writings of Plato and Aristotle. Socrates asks whether men who are to be warriors should first "observe [*theorein*] war as boys" (*Republic* 467C). Aristotle, arguing against Plato's communal utopia states, "We see [*theōroumen*] that there is much more quarrelling among those who have all things in common" (*Pol* 1263b25–26). In the *History of Animals,* he notes that the laying of infertile eggs by birds "has been observed [*tetheōretai*] especially in the case of pigeons" (562a23, cf. 540b20).

Gradually, however, *theōria* as ordinary visual perception does gives way to *theōria* as a mental gazing at, contemplating, or studying. In Plato's *Laws,* the Athenian stranger states that "without contemplation and inquiry" (*aneu ... tēs theōrias kai zdeteseōs*) into the nature of good and bad character traits, no design for a *polis* can be complete (951C). In the famous simile of the cave in the *Republic,* Socrates asks, "Do you think it at all strange ... if a man, returning from divine contemplations [*theion ... theōrion*] to the petty miseries of men cuts a sorry figure and appears most ridiculous?" (517D) Aristotle, in the *Nicomachean Ethics,* announces at the beginning of his discussion of *phronēsis,* "We shall get at the truth by considering [*theōresantes*] who are the persons we credit with it" (1140a24–25). Similarly, in the *Generation of Animals,* he states that in order to find out more about the differences between hornets and wasps, "the records given in the *History* [*of Animals*] should be studied [*theōrein*]" (761a11).

Finally, we begin to detect a more familiar use of *theōria* by these authors as well. Aristotle states that "it is the function of the philosopher to be able to theorize about all things [*peri panton dunasthai theōrein*]" (*Meta* 1004a35–b1). He notes that an "accurate theorist [*akribos theōrousin*] would not deem a society lacking a communal space [*koinonia topou*] a true *polis*" (*Pol* 1280b28–30). Though the often asserted etymological connection between *theos* (God) and *theōrein* is false, Aristotle is speaking for many Greeks when he announces at the end of the *Nicomachean Ethics* that the *bios theōrētikos* is a divine life and that we must "strain every nerve to live in accordance with the best thing in us [i.e., reason, *nous*]; for even if it be small in bulk, much more does it in power and worth surpass everything" (1177b32–78a2).

Executions today are not postponed if a theorist happens to be out sailing; and while many contemporary theorists do enjoy observing sports events, they are not usually ordered to do so by their governments. Today theorists not only proliferate within the field of ethics but in all of the arts and sciences, as well as in numerous professions and applied fields.[3] At the same time, as the epigraphs for this chapter illustrate, increasing numbers of philosophers have recently begun to assert that we should not try to produce new moral theories, much less consort with theories that already exist. Similar antitheory attacks are also being waged within the disciplines of literature, aesthetics, and law.[4]

But what exactly do antitheorists in ethics mean by *theory*? My aim in the present chapter is to answer this question. For the most part I shall work at a descriptive level, allowing ample opportunity for antitheorists to speak in their own words about the nature of moral theory. I regard the conceptual issue of what is meant by a moral theory as crucially important, for, as should be clear by now, *theory* has had different meanings in different times and places and continues to be used in wildly different ways even by those who profess to be theorists. Before one decides whether one is for or against moral theory, it is necessary to consider (*theōrein*) what is meant by moral theory.

In the remaining sections of this chapter, I shall highlight the key features of moral theory, as conceived by contemporary antitheorists in ethics. Two cautionary notes are in order. First, the antitheoretical camp is far from unified; and it is not the case that one always finds a standard, shared use of (moral) *theory* among these writers once one leaves generalities behind and heads for the details. In the following account I attempt to locate the common ground shared by antitheorists in ethics as regards their use of the *T* word. However, I do not intend to examine all of the disagreements that exist among them concerning the meaning of *theory*. Some antitheorists may reject the following account if the highlighted features are construed too narrowly as constituting necessary and jointly sufficient properties of moral theory. Nevertheless, I am confident that a less rigoristic interpretation of these conditions (i.e., one that views moral theory as any intellectual project that satisfies a simple majority of the conditions, without treating any of them as strictly necessary properties) will gain their assent. Second, as indicated earlier, my own strategy in later chapters will be not so much to rebut antitheorist arguments against moral theory directly as to argue for a different conception of moral theory, one that does not suffer the defect of "making everything theory"[5] and that also reflects more accurately (or so I shall argue) what two of the best moral philosophers of the past were trying to do. For this reason, the following account focuses chiefly on what antitheorists mean by moral theory rather than on an assessment of the various arguments they offer against moral theory.[6] Ultimately, I regard many of their arguments against moral theory as being not so much strong or weak arguments as simply irrelevant arguments that are based on highly questionable assumptions. At bottom, I believe the following antitheorist conception of theory is close to a red herring—albeit an extremely influential and widely accepted one and one whose underlying assumptions are seldom spelled out clearly.

Particularism Versus Universal Principles

First of all, antitheorists assume that a moral theory consists of an abstract principle or set of principles that all agents are expected to use to guide their own moral behavior and thought as well as to evaluate the moral behavior and thought of others. Annette Baier, for instance, defines a "normative theory" as "a system of moral principles in which the less general are derived from the more general" and then proceeds to chastise all of "today's moral theorists" for "their prejudice in favor of formulated general rules."[7] Similarly, John Mc-Dowell, begins with the claim that whereas most philosophers conceive moral theory to be "a discipline which seeks to formulate acceptable principles of conduct," he himself, following what he takes to be Aristotle's position, believes that morality is "uncodifiable" and that "one knows what to do (if one does) not by applying universal principles but by being a certain sort of person: one who sees situations in a certain distinctive way."[8] Stuart Hampshire, in *Morality and Conflict,* characterizes one of the book's major themes as an "insistence on the particular and on the limits of rational argument, . . . [a recognition of] the multiplicity and diversity of the local and historical attachments that give sense to a normal person's life."[9] Martha Nussbaum argues for the priority of perceptions over rules, claiming that "to confine ourselves to the universal is a recipe for obtuseness."[10]

This same preference for particular perceptions and local practices[11] over abstract rules and principles is also evident in the antitheory writings of literary critics. Steven Knapp and Walter Benn Michaels characterize theory as "the name for all the ways people have tried to stand outside practice in order to govern practice from without."[12] The theorist, by means of employing highly general principles, attempts to govern practice by standing outside of practice, looking down on it from a transcendent vantage point. Similarly, Stanley Fish writes:

> The argument *against* theory is simply that this substitution of the general for the local has never been and will never be achieved. Theory is an impossible project which will never succeed. It will never succeed simply because the primary data and formal laws necessary to its success will always be spied or picked out from within the contextual circumstances of which they are supposedly independent. The objective facts and rules of calculation that are to ground interpretation and render it principled are themselves interpretive products.[13]

Thus, one thing that antitheorists mean by *theory* is an intellectual project that is preoccupied with highly abstract, universal rules and principles, one that, as a result, fails to take seriously both the particular perceptions of individual moral agents and the local practices of moral communities. Beneath the general heading of particularism lie a number of subsidiary theses, which, while not strict entailments of an "insistence on the particular," are often viewed as such by antitheorists. For example, a strong particularist in ethics might claim that substantive universal moral principles simply do not exist, that moral deliberation always ought to be a matter of seeing rather than of deductive reasoning, or that we ought not to try to stand outside of local practices. Finally, as we saw in chapter 1, the debate concerning impartiality is also relevant here. Bernard Williams states that for both Kantians and utilitarians,

> the moral point of view is specially characterized by its impartiality and its indif-
> ference to any particular relations to particular persons, and that moral thought
> requires abstraction from particular circumstances and particular characteristics of
> the parties, including the agent, except in so far as these can be treated as universal
> features of any morally similar situation; and the motivations of a moral agent,
> correspondingly, involve a rational application of impartial principle and are thus
> different in kind from the sorts of motivations that he might have for treating some
> particular persons . . . differently because he happened to have some particular in-
> terest towards them.[14]

According to antitheorists, a defensible morality does not need to be grounded in the values of either universality or impartiality. But, antitheorists allege, all moral theorists subscribe to the opposite view—that is, that the only defensible morality is one that is grounded in the values of universality and impartiality. Accordingly, any approach to moral reflection that does not aspire to universality and impartiality is simply not a moral theory.

Plural Values Versus Reductionism

A second shared assumption among antitheorists is that moral theory is a severely reductive enterprise. Moral theorists, antitheorists assert, assume that the moral field is unitary and that all moral values are commensurable with respect to a single standard. Williams, in *Ethics and the Limits of Philosophy,* claims that "the desire to reduce all *ethical* considerations to one pattern" is one of the central aims of ethical theory; and because he believes that "in ethics the reductive enterprise has no justification and should disappear," he is logically led to the position that we ought to stop constructing ethical theories.[15] Similarly, Cheryl Noble writes:

> An unavoidable assumption for the moral theorist is that there is some coherence
> or unity among all moral standards—unavoidable because as a moral theorist his
> goal is to reduce the apparently endless diversity of particular moral judgements to
> some order, absolute or relative. He will attempt to do so by finding the basic or
> underlying principles which, when combined with a certain spirit of judgment and

knowledge of fact, would lead to the acceptance of these particular moral judgments.[16]

Nussbaum wages a lengthy "argument against Singleness," concluding that "there is no one standard in terms of which all goods are commensurable *qua* goods."[17] Charles Taylor devotes the bulk of an essay to a defense of the claim that "the ethical is not a homogeneous domain, with a single kind of good, based on a single kind of consideration. . . . The goods we recognize as moral . . . are therefore diverse."[18] Edmund Pincoffs, in *Quandaries and Virtues,* announces that "the cardinal sin of ethical theories is that they are reductive. . . . They eliminate by fiat what is morally relevant and legislate the form of moral reflection."[19] Finally, Thomas Nagel argues against the claim that "the source of value is unitary—displaying apparent multiplicity only in its application to the world. I believe that value has fundamentally different kinds of sources, and that they are reflected in the classification of values into types. Not all values represent the pursuit of some single good in a variety of settings." The goal of constructing "a general and complete theory of right and wrong," Nagel continues, is a fundamental mistake. "There will never be such a theory, in my view, since the role of judgment in resolving conflicts and applying disparate claims and considerations to real life is indispensable."[20]

The assumption that all theorists must subscribe to a "unity thesis" also pervades antitheory writings in literary criticism. W. J. T. Mitchell offers the following summary: "Theory is monotheistic, in love with simplicity, scope, and coherence. It aspires to explain the many in terms of the one, and the greater the gap between the unitary simplicity of the theory and the infinite multiplicity of things in its domain, the more powerful the theory. Theory is thus to thought what power is to politics."[21]

Irresolvable Conflicts

Related to the issues of both particularism and the plurality of moral values is a third debate: Are there irresolvable conflicts within morality? Antitheorists assume that moral theorists must deny the possibility of such conflicts. Hampshire writes:

> My claim [is that] there must always be moral conflicts which cannot, given the nature of morality, be resolved by any constant and generally acknowledged method of reasoning. My claim is that morality has its sources in conflict, in the divided soul and between contrary claims, and that there is no rational path that leads from these conflicts to harmony and to an assured solution.[22]

Moral philosophy, Hampshire notes a few pages later, whether "Aristotelian, Kantian, Humean, or utilitarian,"

> can do harm when it implies that there ought to be, and that there can be, fundamental agreement on, or even a convergence in, moral ideals—the harm is that

the reality of conflict, both within individuals and within societies, is disguised by the myth of humanity as a consistent moral unit across time and space. There is a false blandness in the myth, an aversion from reality.[23]

Similarly, Charles Larmore, in *Patterns of Moral Complexity,* argues against "the monistic assumption" of moral theory and claims that sometimes "we know that . . . conflict is irresolvable":

Only when we suspend the monistic assumption underlying so much of moral theory, only when we acknowledge that not everything is good or right to the extent that it is commensurable with respect to any single standard, will we be able to recognize that even our understanding of what *the moral viewpoint* enjoins upon us in particular situations can call for the exercise of judgment. . . . [But] in many cases . . . judgment will be powerless to settle the conflict.[24]

The plurality-of-values thesis is often held logically to entail the irresolvable conflict thesis,[25] but it is important to distinguish the two for several reasons. In many cases, someone who does believe that all moral values are commensurable with respect to a single standard will also believe that all moral conflicts are resolvable; after all, resolving such conflicts is what the single standard is for. But someone who believes in the existence of a plurality of irreducible moral values is not necessarily forced to embrace the additional claim that irresolvable moral conflicts are inevitable. First of all, it could be the case that though various types of irreducible moral value do exist, the various types simply do not ever come into conflict with one another (a sort of "preestablished harmony" position). Second, nothing prevents a theorist from granting the reality of an irreducible plurality of moral values on the one hand but then constructing a weighting scheme or set of priority rules to decide conflicts among values on the other. For instance, conceivably, one could hold that there exist three irreducible types of moral value but that in situations where types 1 and 2 are both present, type 1 wins out; and so forth. Finally, in certain situations it seems possible for even a single moral value to conflict with itself. If this is the case, we can have irresolvable conflicts without even letting go of the monistic assumption. For instance, a person may believe that innocent lives are to be saved but may one day face a situation where it is possible to save the life of one innocent person or of another but not of both. Or a person may believe that promises must be kept only to face the awkward situation of having made a promise to two different parties, only one of which can be kept.[26] Thus, strictly speaking, the plurality-of-values thesis does not entail the irresolvable conflict thesis. Nevertheless, most antitheorists who subscribe to the first thesis also subscribe to the second.

Similarly, the earlier-discussed commitment to particularism bears no logically necessary connection to the irresolvable conflict thesis. Conceivably, someone could subscribe to a strong version of ethical particularism (e.g., "Moral principles do not exist; and all moral decisions must be made on a case-by-case basis, without the comforting illusion of general principles") and yet reject the claim that there are unresolvable moral dilemmas, simply asserting that in every particular situation calling for judgment, the practically wise person correctly sees what needs to be done. I am not aware of any contemporary antitheorists who subscribe to this position, but it should be kept open as a possibility.[27]

However, it might be thought that a commitment to particularism in the sense of a recognition of the primacy of local practices does entail that irresolvable moral dilemmas exist. This is Hampshire's position. On his view, moral conflicts arise not at the level of species-wide norms that exist largely in virtue of our common biological nature but, rather, at the level of convention, which is always underdetermined by human nature. Morality is both natural *and* conventional; but because humans in different times and places have adopted different conventions, the possibility of irresolvable moral conflict looms large: "Just as there is no ideally rational arrangement of a garden, and no ideally rational clothing, so there is no ideally rational way of ordering sexuality and there is no ideally rational way of ordering family and kinship relations."[28] Even here, however, nothing prevents a person from accepting the claim that there is no one right way, say, to regulate sexual activity and yet maintaining that where there are apparently conflicting claims on how one ought to act with respect to questions of sexuality, there are either (1) ways of drawing on the features of a given situation, including whatever conventions are in place on that occasion, to determine one way of acting in preference to all the others or (2) rational means of determining that at a certain level it makes no moral difference which of certain alternatives one takes. In either case, the possibility of irresolvable moral dilemmas is ruled out. Thus, even a commitment to the claim that different conventions may be equally good in different situations is compatible with the claim that apparent conflicts concerning how one should behave with respect to such conventions are always resolvable. Of course, such conflicts will not be resolved by appealing to a single correct convention; but that is not the only thing one could appeal to in such cases.[29] So again, particularism (whether understood as an epistemological thesis about moral judgments or as an anthropological thesis concerning moral practices) does not logically entail the irresolvable conflict thesis.

Decision Procedures and Formalism

One of the favorite terms of abuse among antitheorists is *decision procedure*. Moral theorists, antitheorists claim, assume that for every moral problem there exists a correct decision procedure or algorithmic set of rules that rational moral agents must turn to in deciding what to do. One of the key aims of moral theory, according to antitheorists, is to produce decision procedures. Thus, Williams, in critiquing the "rationalistic assumptions" of ethical theory, argues that theorists unfortunately do not rest content after arriving at a set of discursively stated principles but continue onward in an attempt to meet the further requirement "that there should also be a rationalistic decision procedure, a method for resolving conflicts that can itself be discursively laid out. It is this requirement that issues in an ethical theory in the fullest sense."[30] Baier warns readers to beware of theorists "who try to sell us any ready reckoner or decision-making machine."[31] And Larmore, in *Patterns of Moral Complexity,* announces that "the two dominant traditions of modern moral philosophy, Kantianism and utilitarianism, have been at one in seeking a fully explicit decision procedure for settling moral questions. As a result, they have missed the central role of moral judgment."[32] Stanley Clarke and Evan Simpson, in *Anti-Theory in Ethics and Moral Conservatism,* accuse contemporary "theory builders" such as Richard Brandt, David Gauthier, Alan Gewirth, R. M. Hare, and Thomas Nagel of seeking to articulate normative theories that "can guide our behavior by systematizing and extending our moral judgments. These judgments, they think, can be thought of as consequences of applying abstract principles to moral problems in an almost computational way, giving a procedure for deducing the morally correct answer in any given circumstances."[33] Pincoffs, while not using the explicit jargon of computational decision procedures, achieves similar rhetorical results in arguing against moral rules and formulas:

> There are mutually irreducible types of moral consideration.... There is no hierarchy—with the king consideration at ease on the apex—no one-principle system that incorporates all of the moral rules.... To decide rationally is to compare the joint strength of one set of considerations to the joint strength of alternative sets. There is no formula for such comparisons.[34]

Most antitheorists assume that the quest for a decision procedure is a perverse dream of modern Enlightenment intellectuals; but Nussbaum, in *The Fragility of Goodness,* argues that it can be traced back at least as far as the discussion of Socrates and Protagoras concerning the need for a science of practical reasoning (*hē metrikē technē*). Socrates asks Protagoras:

> Haven't we seen that the power of appearance leads us astray and throws us into confusion, so that in our actions and our choices between things both great and small we are constantly accepting and rejecting the same things, whereas the *technē* of measurement [*metrikē*] would have cancelled the effect of the appearance, and by revealing the truth would have caused the soul to live in peace and quiet abiding in the truth, thus saving our life? Faced with these considerations, would human beings agree that it is the *technē* of measurement that saves our lives, or some other *technē*?
> Measurement, he agreed.[35]

As one might expect, the assumption that theory necessarily entails a commitment to decision procedures is also evident in the antitheory polemics of literary critics. Fish, for instance, assents to E. D. Hirsch's maxim that the only aspect of interpretation "that has earned the right to be named a 'theory'" is one that employs formal rules rather than mere rules of thumb and distinguishes these two types of rule as follows:

> A rule is formalizable: it can be programmed on a computer and, therefore, can be followed by anyone who has been equipped with explicit (noncircular) definitions

and equally explicit directions for carrying out a procedure. A rule of thumb, on the other hand, cannot be formalized, because the conditions of its application vary with the contextual circumstances of an ongoing practice; as those circumstances change, the very meaning of the rule...changes too.[36]

But, as we saw earlier (p. 88), Fish's own position is that "this substitution of the general for the local has never been and will never be achieved. Theory is an impossible project which will never succeed." According to Fish, all rules are inevitably local interpretive products and are never entirely context-free. A true formal decision procedure can never be constructed for any cultural practice. As he notes, "Rules *are* texts. They are in need of interpretation and cannot themselves serve as constraints on interpretation."[37]

Related to the assumption of a decision procedure quest are the larger issues of formalism and rationalism. Antitheorists assume that a true moral theory must abstract from all empirical data in order to achieve its aim of a universal, rational grasp of moral practices. But morality itself, antitheorists argue, is conventional to the core, so that the rationalist pretensions of moral theorists necessarily prevent them from achieving an accurate understanding of morality. Thus, Noble claims that "recent attempts to develop ethical theories entirely apart from empirical inquiries into the historical and social origins of the ethical ideas that are defended can only fail."[38] And Baier, in summarizing her antitheory essays, says that "they argue in support of those moral philosophers who did not rest everything on arguments, who looked to psychology and history to find out what sort of good we have any chances of successfully attaining, creating, preserving, and recognizing as our own."[39]

Governing Practice

Antitheorists assume that the primary aim of moral theory is not to describe or explain existing moral phenomena but, rather, to issue normative pronouncements concerning what ought to be. Moral theories, on this view, are designed to tell people what to think, what to do, and how to live.[40] Thus, Williams, in his formal definition of ethical theory, states, "An ethical theory is a theoretical account of what ethical thought and practice are, which account implies either a general test for the correctness of basic ethical beliefs and principles or else implies that there cannot be such a test."[41] Williams's own view, however, is that such tests, while not always an intellectual's pipe dream, are severely limited in scope and applicability: "There may be tests in some cultural circumstances and not in others." And because he is skeptical about transcultural moral belief tests, he is led to the conclusion "that philosophy can do little to determine how we should [think in ethics]."[42]

Baier also makes much of the distinction between descriptive and normative theory, and it is clear that most of her wrath is reserved for normative moral theories. On her view, Hume's way involves descriptive psychological and political–economic theories but "no *normative* theory" (see n. 39). As she sees it, moral philosophy should be a kind of descriptive anthropology, aspiring to be "simply an account of our customs and styles of justification, criticism, protest, revolt, conversion, and resolution."[43] Once moral philosophy moves beyond the descriptive level and tries to articulate and enforce its normative pretensions, it "will tend to merge with moral action," thus losing its claim to objectivity and neutrality, as well as its theoretical status.[44] Baier acknowledges the need for descriptive theories but is extremely skeptical when it comes to normative theories: "We need psychological theories and social theories, and, if we are intent on political change, theories about political power and its working, and about economics. But do we need *normative* theories, theories to tell us what to do, in addition to theories that present to us the world in which we are to try to do it?"[45]

Here, too, the assumption that theory entails an illegitimate attempt to guide practice is evident in the antitheory writings of literary critics. Knapp and Michaels, as we saw earlier (p. 88), define theory as "the name for all the ways people have tried to stand outside practice in order to govern practice from without"; and Fish sees theory as an attempt to govern practice in two senses: "(1) it is an attempt to *guide* practice from a position above or outside it, . . . and (2) it is an attempt to *reform* practice by neutralizing interest, by substituting for the parochial perspective of some local or partisan point of view the perspective of a general rationality to which the individual subordinates his contextually conditioned opinions and beliefs."[46]

The goal of governing practice can, of course, come in many different sizes and shapes. In its most extreme rationalistic guise, the governing of practice would allegedly take the form of an all-purpose decision procedure, designed to tell agents what to do in every instance. Moving a bit closer to reality, a normative moral theory might merely claim to be "action-guiding," where *guiding* does not have the authoritarian connotations implied by a set of computational instructions that assumes that there is one (and only one) objectively correct answer waiting to be determined. As we saw in chapter 2, many ethical theorists deny that the primary job of ethics is to evaluate discrete acts, arguing, instead, that the evaluation of agency and of character is what comes first. Thus, the commitment to governing practice in this instance would focus primarily on character development rather than on specific acts. The precise focus, as well as the intensity of the normative assumption, may vary from theory to theory; but antitheorists would presumably reject it in any and all of its manifestations. Philosophy and theory, in their view, are simply not powerful enough to tell us how to think, act, or live—to any degree whatsoever.

Moral Experts and Puzzle Solvers

If moral theories in the sense described exist—that is, if an axiomatic hierarchy of context-free moral rules and principles exists, with solutions to problems waiting to be churned out by correct application of a decision procedure—then it follows that there also exist, at least potentially,[47] moral experts who can arrive at correct answers to moral problems in virtue of their superior knowledge and logical acumen. Just as some people are much better at constructing mathematical proofs than others, so should some be much better at solving moral problems than others. Pincoffs writes, "There would be moral experts if the claims of ethical theory were true. There would be people who knew something the rest of us do not know. They would know what the formula is by which we determine the difference between right and wrong, and they would know how best to apply it to cases that arise."[48]

A similar animus against the idea of moral expertise is expressed by Noble. Here she criticizes the recent migration of moral philosophers into applied and professional ethics work, arguing that the numerous conflicting ethical theories produced by philosophers are of no help in resolving concrete moral problems and that professional moral philosophers as a group possess no better claim to expertise in solving ethical issues than do other groups of professionals or laypeople. Speculating that the real underlying motive behind the applied turn in ethics is economic, she hypothesizes that in "a time of declining enrollments and scarce jobs, the temptation to entice students with 'pop' courses is hard to resist. Courses in applied ethics draw students and seem to enable philosophers to make themselves useful."[49]

The antitheorist attack on moral expertise appears to incorporate four related claims. First, they claim that moral theories are useless, at least in so far as they are not pertinent to the understanding of actual moral problems. The rule model of decision making employed by alleged moral experts does not always, or even usually, illuminate what is at stake in most moral situations. Second, they assume that moral knowledge (if indeed *knowledge* is the right word), unlike, say, knowledge of physics, is simply not theoretical knowledge. A person who is totally ignorant of the laws of thermodynamics could not be said to have much knowledge of physics, but someone could be morally wise without having been exposed to any moral theorist's favorite principle. One does not need a theory of ethics to possess moral knowledge. Third, they reject the analogies often tacitly made by moral theorists between mathematical and moral problems, namely that moral problems always admit of one right solution (even if the answer is not yet at hand), that a proof procedure exists for reaching the correct answers, and that the problems are discrete and self-contained in the way that, say, a child's puzzle awaits someone to put it back together.[50] Finally, they seem also to rely on the argument that since alleged moral experts disagree strongly with one another on the basic issue of theory choice, there cannot be true expertise in this area. As Barry Hoffmaster remarks: "One would think the failure of the [moral theory] program would be more disconcerting. Despite the extensive and extended discussion that philosophical moral theories have received, there remains no uniformly accepted moral theory.... Every philosopher has his or her own favorite moral theory."[51]

A moral theory, according to antitheorists, is a project that involves the following assumptions and aims:

1. Correct moral judgments and practices must be deducible from a hierarchy of timeless, universal principles. The moral theorist's task is to articulate such principles and to police their proper application.
2. Behind the apparent diversity of moral values lies a hidden unity, which theory must uncover. All moral values are commensurable with respect to a single standard.
3. All moral disagreements and conflicts are rationally resolvable. There is one right answer to every moral conflict, and it can only be reached through ratiocination. Theory's job is to articulate the techniques by means of which such answers are to be found.
4. The ideal method for reaching right answers in ethics takes the form of a computational decision procedure. Moral theory aims at providing all agents with such a tool.
5. Moral theory is fundamentally prescriptive rather than descriptive. It professes to dictate to all people in all places how they must think, act, and live; but it does not concern itself with descriptive analyses of existing moral phenomena.
6. Difficult moral problems can be solved best by moral experts who understand ethical theories well and who know how to apply them to specific cases. Severe exposure to moral theory, when combined with native puzzle-solving ability, is the best guarantor of moral expertise.

As noted earlier, antitheorists in ethics do not always speak in a single, unified voice; and the above six-point summary is not intended to hide the sometimes substantial disagreements that exist among them. However, I do believe that there exists solid agreement among antitheorists with regard to these six core areas of concern. I have tried to document such agreement by citing their own statements repeatedly. Again, I do not think the antitheorist position in ethics can be summarized fairly as saying that moral theory consists simply in the conjunction of the above six aims and assumptions in the strong sense that each of the six represents a necessary condition and that when added together we have jointly sufficient conditions. But I do take the basic target of the antitheorists to be any intellectual activity that satisfies a simple majority of the six conditions, without treating any one condition as being absolutely necessary for moral theorizing.

It is perhaps worth restating that my primary aim in this chapter has been simply to describe the underlying conception of moral theory assumed by antitheorists. For the most part, I have purposively avoided criticizing their views or even presenting the arguments they offer in defense of their views. A favorite strategy of moral theorists is to accuse antitheorists of two types of tu quoque fallacy along the lines of "Antitheorists urge us not to engage in moral theorizing, yet their own criticisms of moral theory often presuppose and employ theoretic elements. Similarly, many antitheorists continue to employ theoretic notions in their own reflections about ethics after they have chastised others for doing so. Antitheorists thus do not practice what they preach." For instance, to a Fish who criticizes moral theory as an illegitimate attempt to guide practice from a position outside or above it, one might respond that this criticism itself is an attempt to guide the practice of moral theory from a position outside or above that of traditional moral theory. Fish wants to substitute for the viewpoint of moral theory a more general antitheoretic perspective from which we can and should see that the viewpoint of moral theory is illegitimate; but such a criticism, if correct, undercuts itself and need not be taken seriously. Or to a Williams who criticizes ethical theorists for seeking justificatory principles capable of critiquing existing practices and institutions, one might point out that William's own occasional forays into social and moral criticism presuppose and require precisely such principles. His criticisms of ethical theory have not left him with enough resources to do the tasks of criticism he regards as necessary; thus, it is little wonder that he does not follow his own advice.[52]

For the most part, I myself do not believe that a carefully formulated antitheorist position in ethics has much to fear from the tu quoque charge; but detailed examination of such intricacies will not be undertaken here. A variety of antitheoretic arguments will be assessed in detail in chapter 8; but again, the indirectness of my own strategy should be continually kept in mind. It is not so much that the arguments used to defend the antitheoretist conception of moral theory are bad arguments as that they simply miss the mark. Historically speaking, the enterprise of moral theory has not usually been understood in such a constricted manner. I shall try to substantiate this latter claim in the next chapter, when I inqure to what extent Aristotle and Kant produced moral "theories." Similarly, if, after considering the conjunction of six assumptions and aims, the reader is inclined to protest that it represents an objectionably narrow sense of moral theory and to insist that so-and-so, a card-carrying moral theorist, certainly does not hold that, for instance, moral theorists should aspire to a universal decision procedure, then my point has already been made for me. The best moral philosophers have always had something quite different in mind when they set out to theorize about morality. By reappraising how two of them understood moral theory in light of current antitheory polemics, we can, I hope, arrive at a more fruitful and realistic understanding of what a moral theory ought to be.

6

Did Aristotle and Kant Produce Moral "Theories"?

Now since the present treatise does not aim at theory [*ou thēorias heneka*] like the others (for we are inquiring not to know what virtue is, but in order to become good, since otherwise our inquiry would have been of no use)....

ARISTOTLE, *Nichomachean Ethics*

All that is practical, so far as it contains motives [*Triebfedern*], relates to feelings [*Gefühle*], and these belong to the empirical sources of knowledge.

KANT, *Critique of Pure Reason*

Morality ... requires [*bedarf*] anthropology in order to be applied to humans.

KANT, *Grounding for the Metaphysics of Morals*

I propose now to turn to some of Aristotle's and Kant's remarks about the nature of their own work in ethics, in order to try to show that their conceptions of moral theory differ strongly from the idea of moral theory that is assumed by contemporary antitheorists. The issue is particularly complicated in the case of Aristotle. Antitheorists stand united in their conviction that Kant's work in ethics represents a paradigm case of the worst possible sort of moral "theory,"[1] but we find no such unanimity when we turn to their interpretations of Aristotle. Some antitheorists claim that Aristotle had no moral theory. Annette Baier, for instance, insists that "we find nothing analogous to [a normative theory]" in Aristotle; and as we saw in chapter 5, the idea of a normative, as opposed to descriptive, enterprise is essential to Baier's own definition of moral theory.[2] One can also infer from remarks made by Edmund Pincoffs and John McDowell that they, too, believe that Aristotle had no moral theory.[3] However, Martha Nussbaum, in *The Fragility of Goodness,* states, "The conception of ethical theory on which I rely ... is, roughly, an Aristotelian one."[4] Stuart Hampshire and Bernard Williams also clearly regard Aristotle as having produced a moral theory, and (unlike Nussbaum) they criticize him accordingly.[5]

Because far more antitheorist artillery is aimed at Kant than at Aristotle, in what follows I shall devote significantly more space to an attempt to exonerate Kant from the crimes of moral theory than Aristotle, whose guilt is more open to doubt among antitheorists. At the same time, in order to support further my earlier claim that their moral views share more in common with each other than is usually acknowledged, both authors' views will be compared on a variety of issues. As we shall see, one implication of this more-in-common thesis is that Kant is somewhat less of a moral theorist (in the antitheorist sense) than antitheorists presume, and Aristotle, somewhat more of one.

However, my central claim is that Aristotle and Kant both produced moral theories, but not in the antitheorist sense. In what follows, I shall try to show that they are not guilty of the crimes that antitheorists assert all moral theorists necessarily commit. In attempting to show that antitheorists misconstrue the nature of both Aristotle's and Kant's work in ethics, my underlying motive is to generate doubt concerning the whole antitheory conception of what constitutes a moral theory. Any conception of moral theory that does not reflect accurately what Aristotle and Kant were up to is a faulty conception; for even people who are not enthusiasts of either Aristotles or Kant's approaches to ethics (including, of course, many antitheorists themselves) acknowledge that they were two of the most influential practitioners of moral theory.

An additional reason for turning to Aristotle's and Kant's conceptions of moral theory is to enable us to begin to frame an alternative conception of what a moral theory ought to be, one that owes strong debts to some of the best work in classical moral philosophy (without seeking to imitate it on every point of detail). This alternative conception of moral theory will be spelled out more fully in the next chapter, but its roots lie here. The aim is not to propose a conception of moral theory de novo but, rather, to find one that coheres better with previous outstanding efforts in this field and then to develop it so that it better meets present needs and concerns. It is not my intent here, however, to engage in an exhaustive, comparative analysis of the moral theories of Aristotle and Kant. That is a task for another book. Rather, my strategy is the more modest and manageable one of inquiring where each of them stands with respect to the six foci discussed in chapter 5. The earlier-enunciated aims and assumptions of moral theory so-called will be now be employed as an aid in helping to determine whether or not Aristotle and Kant are guilty of moral theorizing.

Ethics for Humans

The first set of issues examined in our earlier exploration of theory-according-to-antitheorists was that of particularism versus universal principles. Theorists are said to hold that correct moral judgments and practices are always deducible from a hierarchy of universal, timeless principles. Accordingly, a central aspect of their mission is to articulate such principles and police their proper application. Kant's infamous categorical imperative is the most obvious target in much of this discussion, so let us begin with it.

As is well known, Kant regards the categorical imperative as "the supreme principle of morality"; and his primary aim in writing the *Grounding* is "to seek out and establish" this principle (IV 392/5). What does not appear to be as well known is that Kant views this search-and-establish mission as being only one aspect (albeit a fundamentally important one) of the larger project of moral theory. Kant views himself, in both the *Grounding* and the later *Critique of Practical Reason,* as engaging in "pure practical philosophy." He is attempting to uncover an a priori proposition that is "free from everything empirical" and hence owes nothing to the experience of any particular human being. "Moral principles," he states—or at least, we might add, the *kind* of moral principles with which he is there concerned—"are not grounded on the peculiarities of human nature, but must . . . be derivable [*abgeleitet*] for every rational nature" (*G* IV 410n./22, n. 1; cf. 388/2, 410/22, 412/23). However, as the second epigraph for this chapter indicates and as Kant states repeatedly, whenever human beings attempt to use such a priori principles to help them determine how to live and act, they must employ "anthropology"—empirical generalizations concerning the cognitive and appetitive powers of human nature *as a species* (*G* IV 388/2, 389/3, 410/22, 412/23; cf. *A* VII 119–22/3–5).

The task of *grounding* this supreme principle of morality is an a priori venture and must be "wholly cleared of everything which can only be empirical and can only belong to anthropology" (*G* IV 389/2). Such a principle holds (at least in Kant's view) universally and necessarily for all rational beings, and we cannot derive the concepts of universality and necessity from experience.[6] Additionally, every empirical example of morality must "first be judged according to [a priori] principles of morality in order to see whether it is fit to serve as . . . a model" (*G* IV 408/20). Our own reason, not examples or personal exemplars drawn from experience, shows us what we have to do (*DV* VI 481/154). But the task of *applying* the supreme principle of morality to the human situation[7] is most definitely something that requires extensive empirical knowledge.

It is crucial that each of these two aspects of Kant's ethics (i.e., the *grounding* and *applying* aspects) be kept separate from each other, but it is also important that each aspect be given its due. As Kant writes in the *Doctrine of Virtue:*

> A metaphysic of morals cannot dispense [*nicht können mangeln lassen*] with principles of application; and we shall often have to take as our object the particular [*besondere*] nature of man, which is known only by experience, to show in it the implications of the universal moral principles. But by this we in no way detract from the purity of these principles or cast doubt on their *a priori* source. This is to say, in effect, that a metaphysic of morals cannot be based on anthropology but can be applied to it. (*DV* VI 216–17/14)

And even if moral theory "cannot be based on" anthropology, Kant insists elsewhere that it "cannot subsist without" anthropology:

> Practical philosophy (that is, the science of how man ought to behave) and anthropology (that is, the science of man's actual behavior) are closely connected [*hängen sehr zusammen*], and the former cannot subsist without [*ohne . . . nicht bestehen*] the latter: for we cannot tell whether the subject to which our consideration

applies is capable of what is demanded of him unless we have knowledge of that subject. It is true that we can pursue the study of practical philosophy without anthropology, that is, without the knowledge of the subject. But our philosophy is then merely speculative, and an Idea. We therefore must [*müßen*] make at least some study of man. (*LE* 2–3/2–3)

So far, I have emphasized the necessity of species-specific empirical knowledge in applying Kant's moral theory to human life. But what about particular moral issues that concern not merely "men as such to one another" but "men to one another with regard to their *circumstances*"? (*DV* VI 468/139). Here, a second level of empirical knowledge must enter into the picture, one dealing not merely with generalizations that hold true across the entire species *Homo sapiens* but, rather, one that concerns itself with generalizations that hold true among only certain relevant groups or classes of individuals and (where possible) with the unique situations of individuals themselves. In *The Doctrine of Virtue*, Kant speaks briefly of a projected applied part of his ethics that would apply "the pure principles of duty to cases of experience, would schematize these principles, as it were, and present them as ready for morally-practical use. How should one behave, for example, to men who are morally pure or depraved? to the cultivated or the crude?" (VI 468/139). Intended as a necessary segment of "the complete exposition of the system" (VI 469/140), this projected applied part was never completed. But we can see that it is nevertheless an integral aspect of Kant's ethics by reviewing his position concerning the necessary place of judgment in moral deliberation.

As we saw earlier (chapter 2), Kant holds that every particular moral decision concerning what to do in a specific set of circumstances requires the exercise of judgment. But judgment, on his view, is "a peculiar talent, which cannot be taught." Because judgment cannot be formally taught, Kant believes, there is not much that a theorist can say about it. Judgment is a pragmatic skill "sharpened by experience"; but some people (particularly those who have "done well in school") unfortunately never acquire it (*G* IV 389/3; cf. *C1* A 133/B 172, *TP* VIII 275/61, *C2* V 67/70, *A* VII 145/25 and 196–202/69–73). The task of moral judgment is always to ascertain how a particular way of acting or thinking does or does not fall under principles that one already accepts. But since principles and rules are never self-deploying (there are "no general rules by which we could decide whether or not something is an instance of the rule" [*A* VII 199/71]), it simply cannot be the case that the categorical imperative ever "tells us what to do." In most cases, as Roger Sullivan notes, "the Categorical Imperative plays only a background role in our everyday moral life."[8] The categorical imperative is designed to help us see whether a proposed course of thought or action is universalizable and thus morally permissible, but this is a long way from telling us what to do in any concrete detail.

It is no secret that Kant was obsessed with "keeping philosophy pure."[9] But I hope I have now established that moral theory, in Kant's own view, has both pure as well as impure parts and that both are necessary and important whenever we try to apply moral theory to human life. When contemporary antitheorists criticize Kant for his alleged prejudice in favor of universal rules and for his alleged belief in the complete codifiability of moral conduct, they are guilty of taking remarks he makes concerning the pure part of moral theory out of context and of then trying to apply them to the impure realm of human practice.

To summarize Kant's position with respect to the first set of issues, nowhere does he assert that human beings can simply deduce correct moral judgments from universal, timeless principles. Empirical or "anthropological" knowledge is always needed when we apply moral theory to human life; and in many cases not only "species-specific" but also "circumstances-specific" empirical knowledge is also needed. Kant acknowledges repeatedly that principles and rules are never self-deploying and that non-rule-driven judgment is needed in ethics whenever we deliberate about specific cases. Moral principles, in his view, cannot simply tell us what to do.[10]

Aristotelian ethics, of course, is anthropologically infiltrated from the start. Aristotle seeks to ascertain "the function of man [*to ergon tou anthrōpou*]" (*NE* 1097b24–25) and is not interested in a pure practical philosophy. Here, the issue of a theory's not being intended solely for human beings does not arise. Instead, a problem comes up from the opposite side: To what extent do the culturally specific Greek ideals that saturate his ethical writings render the theory inapplicable to human communities in other times and places?[11] Is Aristotelian ethics too culturally specific?

The gulf between abstract principles and particular judgments is also not as severe in Aristotle, since he is more skeptical about the contribution that universal principles bring to our understanding of morality. In recent years, a great deal of scholarly attention has focused on Aristotelian practical particularism, and several contemporary writers associated with the antitheory movement (e.g., McDowell and Nussbaum) are strongly influenced by this interpretive tendency. I agree with these writers in holding that particularism is the dominant feature of Aristotle's moral epistemology, and have so argued in previous work.[12] Moral judgment, on Aristotle's analysis, rests with perception (*aisthēsis*) of particulars; and universal principles are not of much help in capturing the requisite details of the situation (*NE* 1109b20–23, 1126b4, 1147a26). At the same time, as we saw earlier (chap. 2), it is incorrect to argue that principles have no significant role to play in Aristotelian moral deliberation. All the moral virtues involve acting and feeling "as correct reason prescribes" (*ho orthos logos protaxē*, 1114b29–30) and "as one ought" (*hōs dei*, 1121a4). All virtuous actions "are noble and done for the sake of the noble [*tou kalou heneka*]" (1120a23–24). And justice as a concern for what is lawful or right (*nomimon*) is "complete virtue in its fullest sense" when viewed from the perspective of our relations toward others (1129b30, 1130a12). Aristotle's repeated efforts to understand the moral virtues in terms of what reason prescribes, of how one ought to think and feel, of what nobility requires, and of what is just are clear signs that he believes that principles and higher-order considerations are necessary and important in morality. Granted, his analysis of these higher-order considerations is not spelled out in as detailed a manner as is Kant's analysis of the categorical imperative; nor does he wish to claim that they are quite universal or timeless. The kind of reasoning

that virtue brings to Aristotelian moral choice must always be understood contextually, in terms of the habits of thought embodied by the *phronimos* or *spou-
daios* (good man) (1107a2, 1099a23, 1113a22–23, 1166a12–13). Learning
how to deliberate well thus becomes a matter more of seeking out moral exemplars within one's community and learning to deliberate similarly (allowing
for the fact that what is appropriate for one is not always appropriate for another;
cf. 1106a32) than of learning a set of rules or (as Kant would advocate) constructing an a priori norm of reason by means of which to evaluate specific
phronimoi. However, here, too, there is at least some agreement: both Aristotle
and Kant share a fundamental interest in the question of what basic constraints
reason sets on the moral life of human beings, but neither of them is interested
in giving us cookbook formulas that tell us what to do.

In regard to the first issue, then, neither Kant nor Aristotle ever asserts that
human beings can simply deduce correct moral judgments from universal principles. Both of them recognize the obvious necessity of informed empirical
knowledge in human practical reasoning. At the same time, each theorist is
deeply concerned with the issue of what limits general rational considerations
place on morality. However, in neither case does this latter interest take the
form of issuing step-by-step rules that tell people what to do.

Virtue and Happiness

The second issue explored in chapter 5 was the so-called unity assumption.
Moral theorists, antitheorists allege, assume that there exists a unity and coherence among all moral standards. Theorists believe that all moral values are
commensurable with respect to a single standard; and the reductionist aim of
squeezing all moral considerations into one tidy pattern is a hallmark of their
work in ethics. The question I wish to address now is Do Aristotle and Kant
subscribe to the unity assumption? Do they assert that all moral values can be
compared on a common scale?

In recent years a number of Aristotelian scholars have argued vigorously in
defense of the claim that Aristotle was an opponent of value commensurability.
David Wiggins, for instance, writes that Aristotle

> states explicity at *Politics* 1283a3 that the very idea of universal commensurability
> is absurd. And in the *Eudemian Ethics* he denies that knowledge and money have
> a common measure (1243b22–23). . . . There are no signs in the *Nicomachean Ethics*
> of Aristotle's supposing that there is a common measure to assess exhaustively the
> values of the noble, the useful, and the pleasurable.[13]

Similar claims have been put forward by Myles Burnyeat, Nussbaum, and Michael Stocker.[14]

According to this view, Aristotle clearly rejects the unity assumption. The
values of courage, friendship, justice, and so on are all distinct moral values that
cannot be compared in terms of a common denominator. Rather, each is to be

valued for its own sake as an intrinsic good. As he states in book I of the *Nicomachean Ethics*, "Honor, pleasure, reason, and every virtue we choose indeed for themselves (for if nothing resulted from them we should still choose each of them)" (1097b2–4).[15]

However, I believe several points speak against such a strong incommensurability reading of Aristotle. Consider, first, his famous doctrine concerning the unity of the virtues. At the end of book VI of the *Nicomachean Ethics* Aristotle states that "with the presence of the one quality, practical wisdom, will be given all the virtues" (1145a1–2). Aquinas, citing not only "the Philosopher" on this issue but also Ambrose, Gregory, and Cicero, puts the point even more plainly: "The virtues are connected."[16] Someone who believes in the unity of the virtues via *phronēsis* would also seem to be logically committed to the claim that all moral values are commensurable, at least in the sense that they will be viewed as such by the *phronimos* (who is supposed to serve as an exemplar for the rest of us). For *phronēsis*, like all of the other intellectual virtues, is a state "by which we possess truth and are never deceived" (*NE* 1141a3–4). *Phronēsis*, at least as Aristotle understands it, is infallible: it cannot be wrong. And the *phronimos*, the man who possesses practical wisdom, is the one "who is able in his calculation to reach [*stochastikos kata ton logismon*] the best for man of things attainable by action" (1141b13–14).[17] If the *phronimos* is always able to calculate what is best for himself, as well as for men in general (1140b8–9), it would seem that he himself does compare conflicting values with respect to a single standard.

Second, consider Aristotle's frequent remarks concerning the need for human beings always to act for the sake of *eudaimonia*. At the beginning of the *Eudemian Ethics*, for instance, he announces, "We must enjoin every one that has the power to live according to his own choice to set up for himself some goal [*tina skopon*] for the noble life [*tou kalōs zdēn*] to aim at . . . with reference to which he will then do all his acts [*pasas tas praxeis*], since not to have one's life organized in view of some end is a mark of much folly" (1214b7–11; cf. *NE* 1094a18–25). And even in the "Honor, pleasure, reason" passage, which is often used as evidence that Aristotle asserts the incommensurability of the various virtues, he goes on to say, "But we choose them also for the sake of *eudaimonia*, judging that through them we shall be happy" (1097b4–5). Aristotle clearly does urge humans to choose everything with *eudaimonia* in mind. And in so far as different values and traits are all to be evaluated in terms of their tendency to contribute to happiness, *eudaimonia* itself appears to be the common denominator by which we appraise different values. If a value or character trait does not contribute to one's *eudaimonia*, one ought not to pursue it. *Eudaimonia* is *the* end to be sought, and the various values that go into a good life are means that help to produce this end.[18]

Aristotle's views on *eudaimonia* and its role in human deliberation continue to be one of the most debated topics among commentators, and it is not my intent to enter into the numerous details of this debate here.[19] But with respect to its bearing on the commensurability issue, I think it is true that for Aristotle *eudaimonia* does represent, at least in one sense, a common measure across values. At the theoretical level, the good "is not something answering to one idea [*idean*]" (*NE* 1096b25–26), and here the Platonists are wrong. But at the practical level, the life of *eudaimonia* does integrate otherwise incommensurable values. Commensurability of value, we might say, is a practical achievement, not a theoretical datum.[20] To say this is not to say that agents do not deliberate about the nature of *eudaimonia*, that their views concerning *eudaimonia* may not change in significant ways over time and space, or that they are simply out to maximize *eudaimonia* in every act. Nor is it even to say that on Aristotle's view *eudaimonia* (assuming for a moment that it is a common denominator across values) is itself *one* thing, separable from the activities that constitute it. For Aristotle specifically states that we regard *eudaimonia* as "most desirable of all things, without being counted as one good among others" (1097b17–19; cf. *MM* 1184a18–19). It is simply to assert that on Aristotle's view, it is always possible to ask how various values do or do not contribute to human flourishing, and that the person who does flourish is the one who has achieved an integration of otherwise incommensurable values. All values that are important to human beings can be subsumed under the general goal of *eudaimonia*, or, as the medievals later called it, the summum bonum. The practically wise man who deliberates with an eye to *eudaimonia* does compare values with respect to a single standard.

Now it is precisely on this issue of whether all values can be subsumed under the summun bonum that an important contrast between Aristotle and Kant occurs. For Kant, who is viewed by contemporary antitheorists as being a much more obvious paradigm of value commensurability than Aristotle, explicitly denies that all moral values can be subsumed under the summum bonum. In the *Lectures on Ethics*, he states, "One must note that ethics and happiness [*Glückseligkeit*] are two elements of the highest good, that they differ in kind, and that they therefore must be kept distinct [*unterschieden*]" (*LE* 97/77). And in his later discussion of the concept of the highest good in the second *Critique*, he specifically singles out ancient Greek moralists for committing the reductionist error of treating morality and happiness as analytically identical notions. Kant's own opposing view is that "the maxims of virtue and those of one's own happiness are wholly heterogeneous and far removed from being at one in respect to their supreme practical principle" (*C2* V 113/117).[21]

One might be inclined to dismiss this point by replying that happiness, or concern for one's well-being, is not even an intrinsic good on Kant's view and therefore does not (or at least ought not to) enter into moral deliberation proper. However, this "opponent of happiness" position, while often attributed to Kant, is not in fact his view. In the *Religion* he states: "Natural inclinations, *considered in themselves*, are *good*, that is, not a matter of reproach, and it is not only futile to want to extirpate them but to do so would be harmful and blameworthy. Rather, let them be tamed and instead of clashing with one another they can be brought into harmony in a wholeness which is called happiness" (*R* VI 58/ 51; cf. *C1* A 800/B 828). Given our human nature as finite, sensuous rational beings, we cannot give up our concern for our own well-being; consequently, no moral theory ought to ask us to try to do so: "Man is not...expected to *renounce* his natural aim of attaining happiness as soon as the question of following his duty arises; for like any finite rational being, he simply cannot do so" (*TP* VIII 278/64).[22] Practical reason in its pragmatic aspect helps human beings bring about happiness as a harmony of ends.

True, Kant also holds that the good will is the only unqualified good in the universe and that good moral character therefore constitutes "the indispensable condition of being even worthy of happiness" (*G* IV 393/7; cf. *C2* V 110/114). Also, his theory of moral motivation requires that the determining ground of our acts always be respect for the moral law rather than garden-variety natural inclinations. (However, this does not at all mean that natural inclinations are supposed to be repressed, for the strategy is one of emotional reform; see chap. 2.) But neither of these points in any way diminishes the claim that happiness constitutes an intrinsic good for human beings on Kant's view—a good that is different *in kind* from moral virtue.

Since Kant regards both virtue and happiness as intrinsic goods that "differ in kind" and that "therefore must be kept distinct," it appears to follow that he does not in fact regard all values as commensurable. If so, he is not an adherent of the reductionist approach to value—as antitheorists accuse him of being— even though (ironically) he himself asserts that all the ancient Greek moralists are guilty of conflating qualitatively different kinds of value.

But perhaps we have merely shown that Kant denies that all values are com- mensurable without showing that he denies that all *moral* values are commen- surable; for while happiness and the duty to promote the highest good play a much larger role in his ethics than is often acknowledged, Kant insists that we are not to allow this overarching goal to serve as a norm of moral judgment: "Though the highest good may be the entire *object* of a pure practical reason, i.e., of a pure will, it is still not to be taken as the *determining ground* of the pure will: the moral law alone must be seen as the ground for making the highest good and its realization or promotion the object of the pure will" (*C2* V 109/ 113; cf. *Rel* VI 5/5). Furthermore, in his discussion of the highest good in the second *Critique* and elsewhere, Kant argues that there must be a necessary unity between virtue and happiness (*C2* V 113/117; *LE* 97/78; *C3* V 453/122). In his desire to show that reason presents us with the idea of the highest good as an ultimate end that comprehends "the totality of all ends within a single prin- ciple" (*TP* VIII 280 n./65 n.; cf. *C2* V 108/112), the architectonic philosopher ultimately may have succumbed to a different kind of reductionism.[23]

Both of these challenges raise a number of issues that cannot be pursued in sufficient detail here. But I do wish to make two brief points by way of reply. First, most antitheorists who accuse Kant of trying to reduce all ethical consid- erations to one pattern are themselves presupposing a larger Aristotelian sense of the practical in making their criticism. This larger sense of the practical includes both happiness and virtue as central components. When Kant's own position on value commensurability is viewed from this larger perspective, he does not appear to be as reductionistic as one might have supposed. Second, Although I do regard Kantian architectonic as objectionably reductionistic in its assumption that all forms of knowledge can be squeezed into one overarching system, I do not believe that the practical drive toward totalization associated with this architectonic commitment is itself objectionably reductionistic. As Yirmiahu Yovel notes, totalization refers to the need to transform the empirical order to fit moral demands,[24] and this seems to me to be qualitatively different from the kind of value reductionism that worries antitheorists; for in appealing to this sense of totalization, Kant is not asserting or implying that there is only one type of moral value or that moral values can always be compared on a common scale. He is articulating our duty to realize moral community in the world and reminding us that acceptable performance of this duty requires on-going social transformation.

Although the verdict on this second issue is mixed, I am not convinced that Kant is quite as guilty of the sort of crude value reductionism of which anti-theorists accuse him. Here, too, I detect a surprising similarity between Aristotle and Kant: both Aristotle (by means of his doctrine of *eudaimonia*) and Kant (through his concept of the highest good) are committed to the claim that commensurability of values is achievable from a *practical* point of view within our own lives.

"Collisions Between *Bestimmungsgründe*"

The third feature of moral theory so-called explored in chapter 6 was irresolvable conflict. Moral theorists, antitheorists charge, must deny the reality of irresolv-able moral conflicts. Whatever moral precepts a theorist comes up with (and however he or she comes up with them), it must be the case, if the theory in question is to be a contender, that the precepts do not offer contradictory advice when applied to the same case. Granted, the *appearance* of moral conflict is often undeniable (even to rationalist eyes); but underneath the appearances—or so theorists tell us—all is harmonious.

The question I wish to address now is Where do Kant and Aristotle stand on the issue of irresolvable moral conflict? Is it the case, as antitheorists allege, that they deny that moral conflict is ever rationally irresolvable? Or do they in fact allow for the possibility that there may be genuine moral dilemmas?

Of all the issues to be examined in this chapter, the denial-of-moral-conflict charge is the most difficult one from which to exonerate classical moral philos-ophers. Particularly in the case of Kant, the prudent thing to do would probably be to throw in the towel at the start; for as critics never tire of pointing out, he explicitly states that "a collision [*Kollision*] of duties and obligations is in-conceivable [*nicht denkbar*]" (*DV* VI 224/23).[25] The full text reads as follows:

> A collision of duties and obligations is inconceivable. For the concepts of duty and obligation as such express the objective practical necessity of certain actions, and two conflicting rules [*zwei einander entgegengesetze Regeln*] cannot both be necessary at the same time: if it is our duty to act according to one of these rules, then to act according to the opposite one is not our duty and is even contrary to our duty. But there can, it is true, be two grounds [*Gründe*] of obligation (*rationes obligandi*)

both present in one agent and in the rule he lays down for himself. In this case one or the other of these grounds is not sufficient to oblige him (*rationes obligandi non obligantes*) and is therefore not a duty. When two such grounds conflict with each other [*einander widerstreiten*], practical philosophy says, not that the stronger obligation holds the upper hand [*die Oberhand behalte*] (*fortior obligatio vincit*), but that the stronger ground of obligation holds the field [*behält den Platz*] (*fortior obligandi ratio vincit*). (VI 224/23)[26]

Partly because of the current intense interest in moral dilemmas and partly because this passage is unfortunately Kant's most detailed statement about conflicts of duties, a number of writers have commented extensively on it.[27] Although I cannot examine all of the issues raised, in what follows I shall try to show that Kant's position on conflicts of duty is not nearly as dogmatic as most people have made it out to be. He does, indeed, recognize the reality of irresolvable moral conflict.

In the passage quoted, Kant makes a distinction between conflicts of duty and conflicts between *grounds* of duty (*Verpflichtungsgründe*). Although he declares the first to be inconceivable, he readily acknowledges the reality of the second. However, when two grounds of duty conflict, Kant holds that one of the grounds is not sufficient to oblige us. Unfortunately, he says nothing regarding how we are to determine *which* of the two grounds of obligation is sufficient and why. Instead, he concludes merely by noting that we should say the stronger ground does not "hold the upper hand" but rather "holds the field."

What does it mean for one ground of obligation to "hold the field" over another? Alan Donagan, Nussbaum, and Christopher Gowans all interpret this phrase to mean that the weaker ground "simply vacates" or "quits the field; it no longer exerts any claim at all," the result being that there was "only one actual obligation" all along.[28] Their remarks should be understood, I believe, within the context of William's influential comment that many ethical theories (including Kant's) "do not do justice to the facts of regret and related considerations: basically because they eliminate from the scene the *ought* that is not acted upon."[29] In Williams's language, all three writers interpret Kant as holding that in a case of conflicting grounds of obligation, the ought that is not acted upon is simply eliminated from the scene. One (and only one) ground of obligation holds the field; and the Kantian agent feels no regret about the ought which was not acted upon, since it was not a real ought to begin with.

I do not think this is the most reasonable interpretation of Kant's remarks. Nowhere does he assert that the ground of obligation that fails to hold the field is eliminated or revealed to be illusory. In a case of conflicting grounds of obligation, only one ground of obligation can be acted on *at the time of decision*. But this leaves open the possibility that the ground of obligation not acted on at the initial time of decision must be acted on *in the future*. If the ground not acted on at the time of decision is a legitimate one (and it would have to be, in order for true conflict between two grounds to exist), the agent who is aware of this will feel regret over not having acted on it initially, and will try to set things straight when circumstances permit. As Barbara Herman notes:

If the moral feature remains, it may still require attention—not as a residue, but as a moral feature of the circumstances in which the agent now stands. So if I cannot at once help and tell the truth, a judgment that truth telling is required does not free me from a requirement to help, if it is still possible to do that, or to do something else (explain myself, say) if the time to help is past.[30]

When grounds of duty conflict (such that only one of them can be acted upon at the time of decision), the one that is not acted on remains as a moral feature that must, whenever possible, be attended to in the future. The fact that we sometimes "cannot at once help and tell the truth" *is* cause for regret, and nothing in Kant's ethics frees us from the obligation to try to set right what we have left undone. Overridden oughts frequently *do* continue to have moral force even after they are overridden; thus, they may still require our attention.

If this is indeed Kant's position, the critic might respond, why does not he himself say it? Does Kant ever come out and state unequivocally that irresolvable moral conflicts exist? I think he does. In one of the "casuistical questions" raised later in *The Doctrine of Virtue,* Kant asks readers to consider whether there may sometimes exist "a permissive law of morally practical reason, which in the collision of its determining grounds [*der Kollision ihrer Bestimmungsgründe*] makes permissible something that is in itself not permitted . . . in order to prevent a still greater transgression?" (*DV* VI 426/89). Note that the same German terms *Kollision* and *Gründe* that were used earlier (*DV* VI 224/23) now appear again. Here we find textual support for the claim that Kant recognizes the existence of cases of moral conflict in which agents must choose the lesser of two evils. Not to do so, as he goes on to say, would be a "purism," "a pedantry in the observance of duty" (VI 426/89).[31]

It is odd that so little reference has been made to the various "casuistical questions" sections of *The Doctrine of Virtue* in discussing Kant's views on conflicts of duty;[32] for casuistry deals with contingent circumstances in which individual agents find themselves. It is precisely at this level of radical contingency (rather than, say, at the level of "men considered merely as men," with which the *Metaphysics of Morals* is primarily concerned, or the even more abstract level of "rational beings in general," with which the *Grounding* is concerned) that we should expect to find moral conflicts. Casuistry for Kant "is neither a science nor a part of a science" and is added to ethics "only as scholia to the system" (*DV* VI 411/74, cf. 469/140). But precisely because the casuistical level deals with contingent circumstances, it is much more representative of the real life deliberations that we all face.

I realize that I am in danger here of placing much too philosophical weight on a small batch of words, and I do not want to belabor the issue. Kant does not pay much attention to conflicts between rules, in part because, as Sullivan suggests,[33] he tended to be preoccupied with conflicts between reason and desire and because he also believed that conflicts between rules, which are most likely to occur at the level of contingent circumstances where judgment is required, are simply not things concerning which a theorist can offer much enlightenment. Such judgments, as we have seen, cannot be reduced to schematized procedures but depend on *Mutterwitz*. Also, we need to remind ourselves that Kant himself, even in *The Doctrine of Virtue*, tries to set strict limits on the kinds of empirical knowledge that is admissible in a metaphysic of morals. Because he is trying to apply moral theory to "men as such to one another," he can only bring in empirical knowledge of what belongs essentially to human nature as such. But again, it is precisely at the more contingent level of unique individual circumstances that moral conflicts usually arise. Mary Gregor writes:

> We must remember that the prohibitions he formulates are intended to be valid for "men considered merely as men," and that the nature of the work prevents him from considering special cases in which we might assert a moral title to perform a generally prohibited action on the ground that failure to perform the action would involve a violation of another duty. Kant recognizes a distinction between arbitrary and morally necessary exceptions to the laws of a metaphysic of morals, but the scope of the work prevents him from considering the circumstances in which a "collision of grounds of obligation" might occur.[34]

The above argument is text-based. The following non-text-based argument gives additional support for the claim that Kant can, at least in principle, allow room for genuine moral dilemmas.[35] Suppose a man is told to participate in an act of arson under threat of serious harm to his family upon refusal. In such a situation, Kant asks us to determine whether the maxims "Do A" (i.e., commit arson) and "Do not do A" can either one be willed as universal law. If "Do A" can, and "Do not do A" cannot, be so willed, then we ought to do A. If "Do not do A" can, and "Do A" cannot, be so willed, then we ought not to do A. If both "Do A" and "Do not do A" can be willed to be universal law, then it is morally permissible to do either action. Finally, if neither "Do A" nor "Do not do A" can be willed to be universal law, then we are faced with a genuine dilemma. Since neither doing A nor not doing A can be willed to be universal law, neither kind of action is morally permissible. But in this instance there are no other alternatives: either he participates in arson or he does not; and if he does not, serious harm will come to his family.

In this particular case, it seems that neither doing A nor not doing A can be willed as universal law. If the man does A, he is willing the universalization of acts of arson in all similarly relevant situations. If he does not do A, he is willing the universalization of serious harms to family members in all similarly relevant situations. Neither maxim can be universalized without severe undeserved evils resulting.

Granted, it is possible that Kant himself believed human beings would simply never face circumstances where none of their available maxims could be universalized. Perhaps his faith in reason was so severe that he assumed that we would always have a universalizable maxim available, whatever the circumstances. Nevertheless, in theory this possibility (i.e., that sometimes none of our available maxims can be universalized) clearly exists; and I could easily construct additional examples to illustrate it. So there is in principle *room* for Kant to acknowledge genuine moral dilemmas even if he never actually did so.

When we turn to Aristotle's views about moral conflict, contemporary antitheorist opinions are much more mixed. Larmore, for instance, claims that
"Aristotle showed little awareness of moral conflict"; and Hampshire holds that
an Aristotelian *phronimos* might face "difficult decisions" but not "deep ultimate
moral conflicts."[36] On the other hand, McDowell, Nussbaum, and Michael
Stocker all read Aristotle as asserting that irresolvable moral conflicts are an
inescapable feature of human life.[37]

I accept the claim that Aristotle believes irresolvable moral conflicts are real,
and I think Stocker is right to refer to Aristotle's discussion of mixed acts in
Nicomachaean Ethics book 3 as textual support for this claim.[38] Thus, there is
no need to belabor the issue. But our earlier comments on *phronēsis* and *eudaimonia* need to be kept in mind here as well. The man of practical wisdom, as
Aristotle understands him, is infallible and always chooses what is best. This is
not to say that regret and anguish are necessarily foreign to him (when faced
with deeply conflicting demands, he undoubtedly will experience these emotions). However, it *is* to say that the life of the *phronimos* represents, as a practical
achievement, an integration of otherwise conflicting values and that such integration is absent in the lives of those who fail to flourish.

Also, as we saw earlier, Aristotle's doctrine of the unity of the virtues implies
that the virtues cannot conflict with one another (*NE* 1144b30–1145a2). The
possibility of conflict between virtues is explicitly denied in the following passage
from the *Magna Moralia*:

> One virtue does not contradict [*enantiōsetai*] another virtue, since the nature of
> virtue is to obey reason [*upeikein tō logō*], so that it inclines to that which reason
> leads. For it is this which chooses the better. For the other virtues do not come
> into existence without *phronēsis*, nor is *phronēsis* perfect without the other virtues,
> but they work together [*sunergousi*] with one another, following [*epakolouthousai*]
> *phronēsis*. (1200a5–11)

A conflict of virtues would be a situation that seems to call for the display of
two different traits (say, bravery and justice) but in which it is only humanly
possible to exhibit one of them (cf. *MM* 1199b36–37). In such a situation,
ought one to perform a brave act or a just act, and why? Though the author
of the *Magna Moralia* does not answer this particular *aporia* (i.e., he does not
tell us whether we are to perform a brave act or a just act), he does assert that
(1) the virtues always cooperate with, and listen to, reason and (2) reason always
chooses the better. Nevertheless, while conflicts of virtue are ruled out, a moral
dilemma of the sort described earlier in my discussion of Kant is not; for Aristotle
himself mentions a case quite similar to the arson case when he asks what one
ought to do "if a tyrant were to order one to do something base [*aischron*],
having one's parents and children in his power, and if one did the action they
were to be saved, but otherwise would be put to death" (*NE* 1110a5–7). Here
it is not a question of determining whether one should do the just act or the
brave act when both are called for but only one can be performed but rather
of determining, in light of contingent and special circumstances, whether either

alternative is morally permissible. Aristotle, like Kant, suggests that in such tragic situations reason cannot always give us a solid answer.[39]

In conclusion, neither Aristotelian nor Kantian ethical theory need deny the possibility of irresolvable moral conflict. Kant admittedly does not discuss the issue in much detail (though, as we saw, he has good reasons for not doing so); but he clearly does hold that overridden oughts can still retain moral force, and nothing in his general theory of the categorical imperative rules out the possibility of genuine moral dilemmas. Finally, while both authors reveal a strong faith in reason's ability to choose what is morally best, each of them also acknowledges that reason sometimes underdetermines moral choice in tragic situations.

"The Shackles of a Permanent Immaturity"

The fourth assumption of moral theory so-called concerns decision procedures and formalism. Moral theorists, according to antitheorists, are united in their effort to construct a computational decision procedure that can provide a definitive solution for every moral problem. Such a procedure is only possible if the rules and principles from which decisions are to be derived are themselves deprived of all empirical content. One must abstract completely from substantive matters of history, psychology, ethnography, and so forth in order to satisfy the requirement of formalization. So the next question is Did Kant and Aristotle seek to produce a moral decision procedure?

It should be admitted at the start that the rule or law model of morality is a pervasive metaphor in Kant's writings on ethics. He often assumes a strong analogy between laws of nature on the one hand and moral laws or laws of freedom on the other and (like Hume) viewed himself as extending the Newtonian quest for universal laws from the field of inanimate nature to the field of human nature (*C2* V 162/166; *G* IV 412–13/23–24). Furthermore, in several notorious passages he appears to assert that the "carrying out of rules" is our "sole concern" in ethics. Two of these rule-obsessed declarations occur in the *Critique of Pure Reason:*

> In the practical employment of understanding, our sole concern is with the carrying out of rules [*Ausübung nach Regeln*]. . . . We must be able, in every possible case, in accordance with a rule [*der Regel nach*], to know what is right and what is wrong, since this concerns our obligation, and we have no obligation to that which we cannot know. (*C1* A 328/B 385, A 476/B 504)[40]

It is also true that even sympathetic and perceptive readers of Kant have occasionally construed his project in ethics as being a quest for a decision procedure. Onora O'Neill, in her early work, *Acting on Principle: An Essay on Kantian Ethics,* writes:

> The Categorical Imperative is to provide in the first place a decision procedure for maxims of duty, and as a second step a decision procedure for the moral status of

acts. It is not merely to differentiate those maxims and acts which are morally acceptable from those which are not. It is a precision instrument to test whether an act is obligatory, forbidden, or permissible, and also whether it is morally worthy, morally unworthy, or lacking in moral worth.[41]

However, all such rule-fixated readings of Kant's ethics fly in the face of his core thesis concerning autonomy (self-legislation) and the need to think for oneself. He begins his essay on enlightenment by exclaiming, "*Sapere aude!* Have courage to use your own understanding! That is the motto of enlightenment" (*E* VIII 35/41). It is inconceivable that such a fervent believer in the absolute necessity for each person to think for him or herself rather than to kowtow before authority would set out to construct a mechanical formula that would tell agents what to do. As Kant explicitly states, "Rules and formulas [*Satzungen und Formeln*], those mechanical aids to the rational use, or rather misuse, of one's natural gifts, are the shackles of a permanent immaturity" (*E* VIII 36/41). The "natural gifts" in question are of course one's power of judgment (*Urteilskraft*). As I have stressed repeatedly, Kant subscribed to the sensible view that there can be no algorithms for judging and hence no formal instruction in this matter. Judgment is a talent that can be sharpened through experience via reflective exposure to hypothetical cases and to moral exemplars; but many people—particularly academics—remain defective in this area throughout their lives. Furthermore, this need to use our own understanding is viewed by Kant as being the most consequential change in the human condition:

> The most important revolution [*wichtigste Revolution*] within man is "leaving the tutelage for which he himself is responsible." Before this revolution others did his thinking for him, and he merely imitated them or let them lead him by guide ropes. Now he risks walking forward with his own feet on the ground of experience, even if he wobbles along. (*A* VII 229/97)

Granted, there is no inconsistency in "following" a rule such as the categorical imperative and yet acting autonomously; for the rule can still "be one's own" if it is consulted in a reflective manner and not adhered to blindly. Also, moral agents can learn about a rule from parents or teachers and still *make* it their own in the appropriate sense by independently scrutinizing its merits rather than simply accepting it out of obedience to authority. Following a rule—even one that has been learned from others—does not necessarily require the abandonment of autonomy. But while autonomous agents who test their maxims by the categorical imperative are "following a rule," they are not applying a moral decision procedure that can issue a definitive solution to any specific moral problem. For insightful application of the categorical imperative always requires judgment at a variety of levels. First of all, in deciding whether or not a rule is applicable to the case at hand, agents must select out certain details as being more significant than others; and no rule-governed procedure can make such selections for them. Second, they must imaginatively weigh similarities and differences between the case at hand and previous cases to which the rule was declared relevant; and this skill of weighing cannot be usefully formalized. Nor is it simply the necessity of judgment that prevents the categorical imperative from becoming a decision procedure. The categorical imperative merely helps us to determine the basic moral status of maxims or underlying policies of action. Ascertaining that a maxim is, for example, morally permissible or morally forbidden is not the same as giving agents a determinate step-by-step formula that purports to tell them exactly what to do.[42]

The alleged attempt on the part of moral theorists to force agents to apply the formula of some alleged moral expert to their own life situation is therefore completely foreign to Kant's antiauthoritarian outlook. As the teacher informs a student in *The Doctrine of Virtue:* "The rule and instruction [*die Regel und Anweisung*] in this lies in your reason alone. This means that you need not learn this *Regel* for your conduct from experience or be taught it by other men. Your own reason teaches you what you have to do and directly commands it" (*DV* VI 481/154–55; cf. *Ed* IX 475/77).

When we turn to Aristotle, the problem is again, in a sense, the reverse. No one accuses him of the crime of decision procedure, since he repeatedly registers objections to the claim that universal rules and principles can serve as arbiters of ethical correctness. The most famous passage occurs at the end of book II of the *Nicomachean Ethics:*

> The man who diverges only slightly from the correct is not blameworthy, whether he errs in the direction of the more or the less; but the man who diverges more is blamed; for this is evident. But to say to what point and how much someone is blameworthy is not easy to determine by a principle [*to logō aphorisai*], any more than anything else that is perceived by the senses. For things of this sort are among the particulars, and the discrimination [*krisis*] lies in perception [*aisthēsis*]. (1109b18–23; cf. 1126b4, 1147a26–28).

But we ought not to infer from such passages that Aristotle believes there are no rules or principles that we ought to consult in living our lives. The *phronimos* does have knowledge of important general principles; and the fact that the *Nicomachean Ethics* is a preliminary to the lectures on *Politics* and leg-islation (*nomothetikē*) is a clear indication that Aristotle subscribes to the view that human relationships and activities need to be guided by general principles. As he states at the conclusion of the *Ethics:* "If a man does wish to become master of an art or science he must go to the universal [*to katholou*], and come to know it as well as possible. . . . And surely he who wants to make men, whether many or few, better by his care must try to become capable of legislating, if it is through laws that we can become good" (1180b20–25). Aristotelian ethics is action-guiding, and rules and principles do form a necessary and important part of the effort to guide human practice: "It is difficult to get from youth up a right training for virtue if one has not been brought up under right laws [*nomois*]" (1179b31–32). The end aimed at in his lectures on ethics is "not knowledge but action" (*ou gnōsis alla praxis,* 1095a5–6). And we study ethics not in order to obtain a theoretical account of the essence of virtue "but in order to become good people [*agathoi genōmetha*]" (1103b28).

In sum, neither Kant nor Aristotle subscribes to the myth of a moral decision procedure. Each of them stresses the importance of rules and principles in practical deliberation, but neither pretends that such rules and principles can ever obviate the necessity of non-rule-governed judgment and interpretation.

Gemeine Menschenvernunft and Ta Endoxa

The fifth topic explored in chapter 6 concerned the distinction between *describing* and *governing* moral practices. Moral theorists, according to antitheorists, seek to govern practice, that is, to determine how we should think, act, and live. Moral theory is an attempt to lay down dicta concerning what ought to be the case rather than what is the case. If moral theorists were smart, antitheorists imply, they would stick to description. Descriptive accounts of moral practices are sometimes useful; normative theories are not.

Perhaps the most fundamental misunderstanding of what classical moral theorists have tried to do occurs right here, in the antitheorists's simplistic dichotomy between descriptive and normative undertakings. I shall now try to show that both Aristotle and Kant agree that moral theory is a fundamentally *descriptive* project—albeit one that, if conducted correctly, has definite normative implications for how humans should live and act. Essentially, they both agree that one of the moral theorist's primary tasks is to clarify what people really do think about moral issues. However, this attempt to clarify, if carried out properly, is simultaneously both descriptive and normative, simply because we are not always aware of what we really do think about moral issues. Moral theory confronts us with norms that might otherwise remain subconscious or inarticulate and thus less forceful. But these norms are not dragged in from above or from outside of practice. Rather, they are arrived at through a descriptive analysis of ordinary moral beliefs. I shall start, once again, with Kant, since there exists a much stronger consensus among antitheorists that he commits the sin of normative theorizing than is the case with Aristotle.

Kant announces repeatedly in his ethical writings that the principles he puts forward and the justifications he offers on their behalves are reached through a descriptive analysis of what "common human reason" (*die gemeine Menschenvernunft*) holds to be true. In the *Grounding,* the reality of a pure moral philosophy is declared to be "self-evident from the common idea [*gemeinen Idee*] of duty and moral laws" (IV 389/2). Similarly, the concept of the good will is said to "dwell already in the natural sound understanding," so that it "needs not so much to be taught as merely to be brought to light [*aufgeklärt*]" (IV 397/9). And when the principle of the categorical imperative is first mentioned, Kant is quick to state that "*Gemeine Menschenvernunft* in its practical judgments agrees completely with this and has this principle constantly in view" (IV 402/14). His fundamental aim in section 1 of the *Grounding,* to uncover the supreme principle of morality, is reached (*gelangt*) "within the moral knowledge of *gemeine Menschenvernunft*" (IV 403/15). Similar appeals to common human reason and to the necessity of moral theory's pronouncements being constrained by it, are made in numerous other Kantian texts (e.g., *C1* A 807/B 835, A 831/B 859; *C2* V 87/90, 91–92/95, 105/109; *DV* VI 376/33; *TP* VIII 286/70).

Kant's frequent appeals to common human reason are important for three reasons. First and foremost, they serve to indicate that moral theory, as he construes it, is primarily a descriptive, phenomenological undertaking. The primary task of the moral theorist is to provide an accurate map of ordinary moral consciousness.[43] If the theorist fails in this initial project, he or she will necessarily fail in any and all further theoretical undertakings (including the justification of moral principles and the application of principles to practice), simply because the initial data that must constrain the larger project are skewed from the start. As Sullivan remarks, "Kant believed that the main task for a moral philosopher is to clarify what everyone already knows, if only in a confused way."[44] At the same time, the *normative* implications of moral theory are apparent in the last clause of Sullivan's statement. Often, in real life, when difficult moral decisions must be made, there is no time to reflect before choosing. And even in those rare cases where we can afford the luxury of meditation, our cognitive capacities are often temporarily distorted by, for instance, self-deception or anger, so that any reflective efforts undertaken will prove ineffective. In such cases, we "do not know" what we really think, that is, we are unable to articulate what our cooler, more reflective self would say about the matter. This, for Kant, indicates one of the basic reasons why moral theories are humanly necessary: in real life, there "arises a natural dialectic, i.e., a propensity to quibble" with what we know to be morally right, to rationalize our choices in order to make them compatible with our wishes and inclinations. Moral theory is needed to disabuse us of such rationalizations; thus, we are compelled "to seek help in philosophy" (*G* IV 405/17).

Second, Kant's persistent appeal to ordinary thought provides an opening through which moderate skeptics (who, like myself, do not reject totally Kant's aims and assumptions in ethics but believe he does not always describe ordinary moral convictions accurately) can enter into fruitful dialogue with him. Since Kant claims again and again to be constrained by *gemeine Menschenvernunft*, readers are always free to challenge him in this area. Is it really the case, for instance, that common human reason agrees that action done out of respect for duty is "the sole genuine moral feeling" (*C2* V 85/88)? Critics who do not dismiss Kant's methods tout court are always free to challenge him by asserting that he has not correctly described ordinary people's moral convictions and/or by producing evidence to show that such convictions are subject to conceptual change (cf. n.43).

Finally, the appeal to common reason reveals Kant's own antiaristocratic, egalitarian sympathies. He does not believe that philosophers can legitimately lay claim "to higher and fuller insight in a matter of universal human concern than that which is equally within the reach of the great mass of men (ever to be held by us in the highest esteem)" (*C1* B xxxiii).

To be sure, Kant's method of moral analysis, while descriptive, is not empirical. He believes that our ordinary moral judgments have an a priori element within them, and it is this that he is usually after.[45] He is not merely attempting to give sociological or psychological generalizations of a community's moral practices. But the fact remains that he is adamantly opposed to any attempt by moral theorists to "govern practice" from on high by imposing foreign normative principles on people. The principles he is trying to elucidate are ones that we already use *before* the theorist tells us about them. But these descriptions necessarily *become normative,* so the idea that one can engage in the appropriate sort of moral phenomenology without also accepting the inherent normative implications of so doing is a fundamental mistake.

Turning now to Aristotle's method of moral analysis, we see that there are obvious similarities, as well as differences, between it and the Kantian model. As is well known, Aristotle's method of ethics begins with a sorting through of the intuitions and beliefs people already have about the subject at hand, combined with an attempt to preserve the beliefs that are internally consistent:

> We must, as in all other cases, set down the appearances [*ta phainomena*], and after first working through the puzzles, go on to prove, if possible, the truth of all the common beliefs [*panta ta endoxa*] about these experiences or, if this is not possible, of the greatest number and the most authoritative [*ta pleista kai kuriōtata*]. For if we both resolve the difficulties and leave the *endoxa* undisturbed, we will have proved the case sufficiently. (*NE* 1145b2–7; cf. *EE* 1235b12–18)

Sometimes, in his scientific writings, Aristotle uses the term *ta phainomena* to refer to perceptual data; but in the ethical treatises it is clear that the "phenomena" in question are commonly held opinions (*endoxa*) about matters and "the things said" (*ta legomena*) about them (see, e.g., *NE* 1145b20).[46]

Like Kant, Aristotle asserts that moral theorists can only get off to a proper start if they pay close attention to peoples' ordinary moral beliefs. As Nussbaum notes, Aristotelian theory "must remain committed to the ways human beings live, act, see—to the *pragmata,* broadly construed."[47] However, there is one clear difference. As I shall demonstrate, Kant gives much more weight to the moral beliefs of uneducated peasants and laborers than he does to intellectuals or aristocrats. Aristotle, on the other hand, grants no privileged status to the moral beliefs of the hoi polloi. Whenever some moral opinions contradict others, he sides with "the most authoritative ones" (*ta kuriōtata*). And for Aristotle, the most authoritative beliefs will always be the beliefs of the educated male elite within the polis. For instance, in the *Topics* Aristotle refers to the beliefs of the *sophoi* as being the most notable and reputable (100b21–23; cf. *NE* 1145b6).[48]

The existence of a strong descriptive dimension in Aristotelian moral theory is a widely shared *endoxa* even among contemporary antitheorists. But what about a normative dimension? As we have seen, Baier insists that Aristotle had no normative moral theory. However, the Aristotelian epigraph for our present chapter would seem to be a clear refutation of her claim: "We are enquiring not in order to know what virtue is, but in order to become good" (*NE* 1103b26–27). As Myles Burnyeat notes, "The goal of the study of ethics is action, not merely knowledge: to become fully virtuous rather than simply to know what virtue requires."[49] The chief aim of Aristotelian moral theory is to serve as a guide to human action and living; indeed, this is why he declares that his approach to ethics does not aim at theory (*ou theōrias heneka*)—in the special Greek sense of contemplation of necessary and unchanging objects. Aristotle's approach clearly does aim at theory in the more ordinary sense of a desire to give a general account of the nature of ethics. Aristotle is not interested in a coolly dispassionate understanding of morality: he wants us to change our lives. The aim of his lectures on ethics is "not knowledge but action" (*ou gnōsis alla praxis,* 1095a5–6).

Now, one might accept each of these assertions concerning the presence of both descriptive and normative dimensions within Aristotelian and Kantian moral theory and yet still insist that there nevertheless exists a fundamental difference between the respective evaluative focal points of their theories; for it is normally claimed that Aristotle's strategy for guiding moral practice is more prospective than Kant's: he is much more interested in moral education and in character development than he is in moral argumentation. Kant, on the other hand, supposedly focuses more on "the logic of moral argument," with an eye toward helping autonomous adults in modern, pluralistic societies make moral decisions. Kantian ethics, in other words, is basically action-guiding; while Aristotelian ethics is character-guiding. As Sullivan remarks, in a brief comparison of Aristotelian and Kantian models of moral philosophy:

> The main point of doing moral philosophy has been taken [by Kantians] to be the clarification of moral terms and an examination of the various justifications offered for morality in general and particular substantive rules in general. . . . By contrast, in his *Ethics* Aristotle . . . considered moral education to be an initiation into a kind of life rather than as learning the logic of moral argumentation.[50]

I disagree. Kant, too, was profoundly interested in moral education and in character development. (He was after all the author of both the *Education* and *The Doctrine of Virtue*). The claim that he is only concerned with rationalistic adults who themselves are obsessed with pharisaic distinctions between moral rules is simply false. As he states in the *Education:* "Man can only become man through education [*Erziehung*]. He is nothing but what education makes of him" (IX 443/6). And as we saw earlier (chap. 2), the primary evaluative focus of Kant's moral theory is, in fact, the underlying character of agents rather than their discrete acts. Indeed, his core thesis concerning the unqualified goodness of the good will presupposes this view.

Similarly, it is false to suppose that Aristotle was a moral educator concerned exclusively with the training of impressionable youth. At the beginning of the *Nicomachean Ethics,* he informs us that his lectures on ethics are aimed at an "adults only" audience: "A young man is not a proper hearer of lectures on politics; for he is inexperienced in the actions that occur in life; but its discussions start from these; and, further, since he tends to follow his passions, his study will be vain and unprofitable" (1095a2–5). It is true that Aristotle is less optimistic than Kant when it comes to the power of abstract principle to elucidate and resolve moral conflicts. But it does not follow from this that he is concerned to evaluate character only and not action or that the intent of Kant's theory is exclusively action-guiding.

In conclusion, both Kant and Aristotle constructed normative moral theories; but the normative dimension of their respective theories is a necessary outcome of detailed, descriptive accounts of ordinary moral beliefs. Neither of them sought to guide moral practice "from a position above or outside it."

Still, how do these arguments serve to rebut the antitheorist charge of governing practice? Antitheorists, recall, believe that it is a mistake to engage in normative enterprises when reflecting about moral practices. How does showing that what Aristotle and Kant are doing is both descriptive and normative get them off the hook? Perhaps we have only got them into deeper trouble by admitting that they are doing something antitheorists say they should not be doing (i.e., normative theorizing) and by leaving them open to attack by positivist-influenced critics who may feel they have confused the factual with the normative. I shall defend the necessity of normative ethical theory in chapters 7 and 8. My aim here has been simply to show that the normative aspect of Aristotelian and Kantian ethics has been radically misunderstood. Their goal is not to govern practice from above but rather to influence it from within.

Phronimoi and Collegia Pietatis

Finally, the issue of moral expertise. Moral theories, according to antitheorists, presuppose the possibility that there exist moral experts. Such experts would know which formulas apply to which problems and their superior knowledge and logical acumen would enable them to solve moral problems more efficiently than those who lack moral expertise. Nonexperts, on the other hand, would either not know what rule to apply to a given problem or would make logical errors in their reasoning or both. I shall now try to show that neither Aristotle nor Kant is committed to the thesis of moral expertise, at least as the term *moral expertise* is understood by antitheorists.

The antitheorist conception of moral expertise is what might be called a *technocratic* model. According to the technocratic model, moral expertise is both character-free and experience-free. Anyone who knows the right formulas and has sufficient logical skill can hang his or her shingle on the door. Indeed, this is a large part of the attractiveness of the technocratic model. Because technocratic expertise is character-free and experience-free, reasonably intelligent people may acquire it simply by attending the right course of instruction at a certified school. According to this view, neither a corrupt moral character nor a lack of practical experience are necessarily impediments to acquiring moral expertise. On the other hand, a diploma testifying that one has mastered a certain body of formal instruction is a necessary (and, in cases where the student also possesses satisfactory logical acumen, a jointly sufficient) condition for moral expertise.[51] Finally, as noted in chapter 5, this particular notion of moral expertise incorporates several subsidiary assumptions as well—for example, that moral problems are discrete and self-contained puzzles that admit of one right solution and that moral knowledge is formal knowledge of universal laws and principles.

An alternative conception of moral expertise—one that will be relied on heavily in the following analysis—is what might be called a *wisdom* model. The wisdom model is neither character-free nor experience-free. On the contrary, it is, so to speak, character-embedded and experience-embedded. According to this view, good moral character and extensive life experience are both necessary preconditions for the possession of moral expertise. Also, the wisdom model rejects the assumption that formal academic training can ever be a guarantee of moral expertise. Formal education may (and probably will if the student has first had a good upbringing) help one attain moral wisdom, but there is no necessary connection between moral wisdom and formal education. It is definitely possible to attain this sort of moral expertise outside of academia, through careful and extensive reflection on real-life problems. And, of course, if the academic institutions are themselves morally corrupt, the odds become even stronger that anyone who is fortunate enough to possesses such wisdom will have acquired it in spite of, rather than because of, schools and universities.[52] The wisdom model also rejects the subsidiary assumptions associated with the technocratic model. Moral knowledge, according to this model, is not to be equated simply with theoretical knowledge of universal laws and principles; and moral problems are not to be equated simply with discrete and self-contained puzzles.

Like most dichotomies, this distinction between the technocratic and wisdom models of moral expertise is somewhat simplistic. At the same time, like Weberian ideal types, it can serve to orient our thinking on a difficult issue precisely because it abstracts from the welter of specific qualifying issues that would inevitably complicate any detailed examination of alleged experts in a given field of knowledge. In what follows, I shall argue that Aristotle and Kant both reject the technocratic model of moral expertise, but that they each embrace versions—albeit mutually conflicting versions—of the wisdom model.

Aristotle's conception of moral expertise is captured in the Greek term *phronēsis*, "practical wisdom," and in the person who possesses this intellectual virtue, the *phronimos*. He begins his discussion of *phronēsis* in book VI of the *Nicomachean Ethics* by remarking that we shall get at the truth regarding it "by considering who are the persons we call practically wise" (1140a24–25). Who are his nominees for the title of *phronimos?* "We think Pericles and others like him have *phronēsis*, viz. because they can see [*theorein*] what is good for themselves and what is good for men in general; we consider that those can do this who are good at managing households or states" (1140b7–11).

We have seen already that Aristotelian *phronimoi* are indeed experts of a very high order. For *phronēsis*, like the other intellectual virtues, is a state "by which we possess truth and are never deceived [*mēdepote diaopseudometha*]" (*NE* 1141a3–4). The *phronimos*, in other words, is infallible; and his judgment is an unerring guide to action. Aristotle's understanding of moral expertise is part of a larger view concerning the nature of knowledge and of claims to knowledge. Any claim to know something must be open to assessment by the relevant group of qualified judges; and if the knowledge claim is to be meaningful, there must also be some way to distinguish between competent and incompetent judges. In each field of knowledge there exist established conventions and practices in which we can locate standards for resolving disagreements. As Nussbaum notes, "Aristotle asks us to look at our practices, seeing, in the different areas, what sorts of judges we do, in fact, trust. The judgment about whom to trust and when seems to come ... from us. ... The expert, and our reasons for choosing him, are not behind our practices; they are inside them. And yet such experts do, in fact, help us to unravel puzzles."[53]

Aristotle, therefore, does subscribe to a conception of moral expertise, but it is one that differs radically from the technocratic model assumed by antitheorists. Among other things, this means that on his view professional philosophers and other intellectuals who theorize about morality are in most cases not going to be promising candidates for moral expertise. Aristotle's *phronimoi* are men of action; intellectuals who aspire to the *bios theōrētikos* are not generally going to be a strong source of wisdom concerning matters relating to praxis. At the same time, Aristotelian *phronimoi* are definitely not uncultured workers: they will be members of an educated male elite who have leisure time (*scholē*) and appreciation for at least the less esoteric branches of philosophy (e.g., Aristotle's own lectures on ethics and politics).

When we turn to Kant's views concerning moral expertise, we see both similarities to, and divergences from, the Aristotelian model. First, as noted earlier, Kant believes that the primary task of moral theory is to elucidate the moral norms and beliefs that are already inherent in ordinary human reason. Second, as noted earlier, he explicitly asserts that philosophers and intellectuals must be brought to recognize that they can never lay claim "to higher and fuller insight in a matter of universal human concern than that which is equally within the reach of the great mass of men (ever to be held by us in the highest esteem)." Kantian moral theory, whatever virtues it may prove to possess, is not a tool that gives its possessors any secret access to moral wisdom. Third, despite Kant's more-than-occasional lapses into a rule model of morality, his considered view is that autonomous agents must always think for themselves and that to follow the formula of an alleged moral expert in deciding what to do constitutes a violation of the ground of the dignity of one's humanity. Autonomous agents are to obey only the laws that they give to themselves (*G* IV 435–36/41). Fourth, as we have stated repeatedly, Kant holds that the capacity of judgment, while necessary for all human moral decision making, is not something that can be taught in formal academic settings. On his view, judgment

> cannot be *instructed;* it can only be *exercised.* ... To instruct is to impart rules, and if judgment could be taught there would have to be general rules by which we could decide whether or not something is an instance of the rule; and this would involve a further inquiry to infinity. So judgment is, as we say, the understanding that comes only with age. (*A* VII 199/71)

Judgment is a natural power that can be sharpened by experience but whose lack "no school can make good."

Like Aristotle, Kant clearly rejects the technocratic model of moral expertise. It is not part of his aim to offer a ready-reckoner to agents who, regardless of character formation and moral enculturation, will churn out correct solutions to moral puzzles. And Kant also agrees with Aristotle in favoring a version of the wisdom model of moral expertise, for he obviously recognizes that some people possess more moral insight than others and that we can and should try to learn from such people. Kantian moral education, in its earliest stages, involves the attempt to imitate the behavior of exemplary individuals. As he states in *The Doctrine of Virtue:*

> The experimental (technical) means to the formation of virtue is good example on the part of the teacher (his exemplary conduct) and cautionary example in others. For, as to the as yet unformed human being, imitation is what first determines him to embrace the maxims that he afterwards makes his own. (*DV* VI 479/152; cf. *LE* 136–38/109–11; *G* IV 408–9/20–21; *C2* V 159/162; *Ed* IX 475/77)

However, when we ask Aristotle and Kant who, in their view, is most likely to possess moral wisdom, a clear difference emerges. Aristotle, we saw, points to "Pericles and men like him" as being paradigmatic *phronimoi.* Such men were members of an educated, aristocratic elite; and it is inconceivable that Aristotle would allow for the possibility that an uneducated, poor person who did not participate in civic life might yet qualify as a *phronimos.* But Kant, whose father was a harnessmaker and whose parents were devout Pietists,[54] did not place nearly as much trust in people of leisured backgrounds. It is far more likely that his preferred candidates for morally wise people would have come from within the informal *collegia pietatis* (associations of piety) that met together in private homes for the mutual enrichment of Christian faith. The members of these intimate religious communities were usually not well-connected civic leaders who had benefited from a university education (or its Aristotelian equivalent): they were often social nobodies. As we have seen, when Kant discusses the need for good judgment, he frequently singles out academics and university-trained people as sorely lacking in it (e.g., *C1* A 134/B 173; *TP* VIII 275/61); and it is clear that he felt ordinary, uneducated working people were often superior moral judges. As he wrote in a well-known note penciled into his copy of the early work, *Observations on the Feeling of the Beautiful and the Sublime* (1763): "There was a time when I despised the masses. . . . Rousseau has set me right. This blind prejudice disappears; I learn to honor men" (XX 44).

I have tried to show that neither Aristotle nor Kant is in most cases guilty of doing what antitheorists claim all moral theorists do. If, upon inspection, the antitheorist conception of moral theory turns out to be one that fundamentally fails to reflect accurately what two of the most outstanding practitioners in the field of theoretical ethics were attempting to do, prudence would suggest that there is something radically wrong with the antitheorist notion of what constitutes a moral theory. What is therefore needed is an alternative conception of moral theory, an alternative that seeks not to reinvent the wheel or to dazzle with unrestrained conceptual jugglery but to take its cue from the best efforts of the past and then to locate itself within present needs and concerns. In chapter 7 I shall draw the basic features of this alternative picture of moral theory.

7

What Should Moral Theory Be?

Moral theory . . . does not offer a table of commandments in a catechism in which the answers are as definite as are the questions which
are asked. It can render personal choice more intelligent, but it cannot
take the place of personal decision, which must be made in every case
of moral perplexity. . . . The student who expects more from moral
theory will be disappointed.

JOHN DEWEY AND JAMES H. TUFTS, *Ethics*

We must conclude that no philosophy of ethics is possible in the old-
fashioned absolute sense of the term. Everywhere the ethical philosopher must wait on facts. The thinkers who create the ideals come
he knows not whence, their sensibilities are evolved he knows not
how; and the question as to which of two conflicting ideals will give
the best universe then and there, can be answered by him only through
the aid of the experience of other men.

WILLIAM JAMES, *The Will to Believe and
Other Essays in Popular Philosophy*

I have argued that the antitheory conception of moral theory is objectionably
narrow, and that is does not reflect accurately the nature and aims of two of
the most outstanding past efforts in moral theory. At the same time, several
of the antitheory criticisms are well taken: moral theorists should not always
do what anti-theorists say all moral theorists always do. If a would-be moral
theorist can do nothing but offer society yet another abstract program that
claims to have reduced all ethical considerations to one tidy pattern, to have
provided a "solution" to all moral "problems" by means of a computational
decision procedure, and so on, then he or she ought to find some other line
of work.

The aim of this chapter is to develop an alternative conception of moral
theory, one whose final shape is guided by two constraints: (1) a desire to follow
the spirit (if not always the precise letter) of both Aristotelian and Kantian ethics
and (2) a qualified appreciation for at least some antitheory criticisms regarding
the shallowness and sterility of certain moral theory programs. Obviously, some
critics will protest immediately that such an alternative has no chance of success,
since (to their eyes) the two guiding constraints are themselves mutually con-

tradictory. However, in chapter 6 I argued at length against precisely this assumption. Aristotelian ethics and, to a lesser extent, even Kantian ethics can
and do survive the antitheory onslaught relatively intact. Two qualifications
should be noted with respect to the claim of an alternative conception of moral
theory.

First, in what follows I am not trying to construct or defend a *specific, normative*
moral theory. As should be clear by now, my own preferences in this area lie
in the direction of a mixed aretaic–deontic effort. However, I see little hope of
such a theory's winning the day in the foreseeable future and would even be a
little saddened if (mirabile dictu) one were somehow to do so. I am a pluralist
in ethics in two senses: I believe (1) that any satisfactory normative ethical
theory must reject the monistic assumption of textbook utilitarianisms and
deontologisms and, instead, incorporate a variety of irreducibly plural types of
moral value into its basic structure and (2) that the existence of conflicting types
of normative ethical theories is both intellectually healthy and close-to-inevitable.
The desirability of gradual convergence upon a single theoretical model within
a given domain of knowledge has been overplayed, and, at least within ethics
(but elsewhere too?), it is neither feasible nor desirable. Obviously, there do
need to be mutually acceptable grounds for ruling out *some* alternatives, but this
requirement can be met easily without succumbing to the boring ideal of a
single winner-take-all theory. Theorists in all domains need to get used to the
idea of unending competition, for knowledge ceases to grow when theoretical
competition stops.

Second, what I *am* trying to do is elucidate and justify some basic features
and aims that *any* acceptable moral theory ought to have, regardless of its
specific character or special normative commitments. At the same time, I am
sympathetic to the common complaint that moral theorists tend to be con-
stitutionally disposed toward overly schematic and highly general accounts
whose usefulness is a very open question, a particular body of literature it is
not my intent to contribute further to.[1] But the current skeptical tone of
philosophical discussion about moral theory necessitates a willingness on the
part of moral theorists to once again raise second-order questions concerning
the nature and aims of moral theory. Granted, a theorist ought not to reside
forever within second-level districts: eventually, a specific, developed moral
theory should be put forth and applied to some real issues. However, such
tasks will not be undertaken here.

In order to keep the investigation within manageable proportions, I shall
once again follow a strategy adopted in chapter 6. The six focal areas originally
analyzed in chapter 5 will now be used to structure my discussion of the nature
and aims of moral theory. My primary goal is thus to present and defend some
fairly specific features and aims of moral theory that relate directly to the six
earlier-enunciated areas of antitheorist concern. Needless to say, the resulting
list of features and aims is by no means intended to be exhaustive. At the
conclusion of the chapter, I shall also offer some more general remarks about
moral theory that are intended to help unify the earlier discussion.

Empirically Informed Theories

If moral theories are to be of any real help in an increasingly complex and changing world, they must become more empirically informed. The philosopher's quest for universal principles should not be dismissed entirely but it needs to combine forces with a genuine conviction that a wide variety of historical, psychological, and cultural forces are clearly relevant to any critical understanding of human morality. American pragmatists such as William James and John Dewey preached this message to academic moral philosophers a hundred years ago; antitheorists are doing so again today. Not all moral theorists convert upon hearing the message, but there are clear signs that it is finally beginning to have a definite impact on the direction of recent theoretical efforts in moral philosophy. Moral psychology is currently one of the biggest growth fields within contemporary ethical theory.[2] Some moral theorists are starting to devote serious attention to history.[3] Finally, within the enormous surge of applied and professional ethics work since the late 1960s there exists abundant evidence that some moral theorists are beginning to take empirical matters seriously. No one who proposes to do meaningful work in applied or professional ethics can do so without first acquiring extensive empirical knowledge of the area being studied; for what is always needed is "a firsthand knowledge of the values, organization, and practices of the groups or communities under investigation."[4]

The demand that moral theory become more empirically informed should not be confused with the request that it become either "less philosophical" or "merely" sociological, historical, psychological, or the like; for these are not equivalent claims. Theoretical and conceptual issues often dominate even the most applied areas of research. How should such-and-such a term be defined? What particular research strategy is likely to be most helpful in addressing the issue at hand? The normative intent of empirically informed moral theories also ensures that they stay sufficiently philosophical.

But again, the quest for universal principles still ought to have an important place within future theoretical efforts. The inability of all previous moral theorists to win broad acceptance for their chosen principles should encourage future theorists to be more humble in making any claims to have finally uncovered the True Principle, but the principle hunt nevertheless remains important for three reasons.

First, effective moral criticism is not possible without careful reflection on local standards. Such reflection, in my view, does not necessarily entail emotional detachment from, or intellectual disinterestedness regarding, local mores; but it does require that the would-be critic stand back and ask: "What about my community's normative standards? Are these the right ones by which to judge ourselves?" Asking such second-order questions about local standards will be aided by, and also often leads to the formulation of, more general principles of evaluation. ("How would a more just society evaluate its actions? What principles have other communities in other times and places employed that might be of benefit to us?")[5] Granted, a moral critic who wishes to have some impact on his or her own society is well advised, whenever possible, to appeal to local traditions and to connect the criticisms to defensible aspects of local culture.[6] But attempts to "speak with the natives" are in no way inconsistent with reflecting on the nature of the natives' moral principles. The kind of moral criticism referred to so far is limited to criticism within *one* moral community—criticism of individual or group activities within the community, of the community as a whole, or of oneself as a member of a specific moral community who has been morally educated in a certain way. But what about moral criticism of people outside of one's own *Gemeinschaft*? How can meaningful moral criticism of practices outside of one's local community be made without appealing to principles that carry a more-than-merely-parochial weight? Common, shared ground needs to be found for rational discussion to occur; and unless members of both cultures are willing to step back a bit to look for it, it is not likely to be found. Granted, the track record of moral theorists and other intellectuals in resolving international disputes peacefully is dismal (though recent events in Czechoslovakia and elsewhere in Eastern Europe give some cause for hope). Here, too, humility is called for. But at the same time, intercultural moral criticism is sometimes effective at more modest levels; and its effectiveness often depends on a willingness to look for general principles that both sides can accept.

Second, the search for general moral principles is defensible on a variety of heuristic grounds. People do not need to reinvent the wheel each time they engage in an act of moral deliberation. Sometimes, someone before them in a relevantly similar situation made a wise choice about the matter at hand. Historically informed theorists could save people a great deal of time and energy by developing moral principles that transmit in economical form the normative force of good decisions of wise persons from other times and places. More generally, in demonstrating concern for both particulars and principles, moral theorists can help people place their specific moral concerns within a larger (and more rationally justifiable) context by (1) generalizing different types of relevant moral conflicts for which historical records exist; (2) indicating, in encapsulated form, how such conflicts were addressed previously, by both the wise and the ignorant; (3) advocating better alternatives that might otherwise be overlooked; and (4) rendering judgments more consistent.[7]

Finally, we should not infer from the claim that moral theories need to become more empirically informed that the a priori part of moral theories is eliminable or inconsequential. In any moral theory—in any *theory*—there will always be important questions about the meanings of the terms employed and the purposes we have for them. Certain things will or will not follow, depending on how these terms and their purposes are understood. But the answers to these questions, if and when they come, cannot come entirely from empirical observations. Granted, meanings and purposes change; and such changes are often due to changes in our understanding of matters of fact. Even our most abstract theories are like "a field of force whose boundary conditions are experience."[8] But a priori bashing is a self-destructive enterprise. While its substantive results are more meager than many philosophers have assumed, the a priori part of moral theory remains a necessary and important one.

Nonreductionist Theories

Antitheorists, we have seen, claim that the chief motivation behind moral theory is reductionism. Ethical theorists, Bernard Williams charges, desire to reduce all ethical considerations to one pattern. But *why* must moral theory be reductionist? Unfortunately, antitheorists (Williams included) do not address this question. The possibility of a nonreductionist moral theory is ruled out from the start without argument. The closest thing to an antitheorist answer that I have been able to find is the following previously quoted remark of Cheryl Noble's: "An unavoidable assumption for the moral theorist is that there is some coherence or unity among all moral standards—unavoidable because as a moral theorist his goal is to reduce the apparently endless diversity of particular moral judgments to some order, absolute or relative."[9] Here we find the familiar sentiment that theory's chief task is to bring order to the phenomena by selecting out general laws which can explain some aspect of their behavior. On this view, the goal of seeking order is what gives rise to reductionism. Note, first, that this charge applies to *all* theories. Neurological and astrophysical theories, along with ethical theories, are being charged with reductionist motives. But the implication seems to be that reductionism in neurology and astrophysics is acceptable, that it is only objectionable in the field of ethics.

We should acknowledge at the start that *all* of our cognitive constructs— including not only theories but more informal belief systems, as well as natural languages—are highly selective. They enable us to attend to some aspects of the world and discourage us from attending to others. But since it is impossible for finite rational beings to attend to all available information, the built-in selectivity of our all-too-human cognitive constructs is in most cases something for which we should be grateful; for it is in virtue of their selectivity that our inquiries are able to proceed at all. A theory can be faulted for being too selective, but it does not make sense to plead for a theory that is nonselective. All theories select out some aspects of the world at the expense of others; hence, a nonselective theory is a contradiction in terms. Selectivity is only a vice if it can be shown (by another competing selective theory!) that some of the things the first theory is ignoring ought not to be ignored.[10]

But perhaps "selectivity"—focusing on certain aspects of experience at the expense of others—is not what antitheorists mean by *reductionism*. Perhaps the sense of reductionism they have in mind occurs when a theorist says, "I know that there are several irreducibly different types of pattern before me; but to make things easier, I will simply tell people that there is really only one pattern." If this is what is meant by reductionism in ethics, then it is indeed indefensible; for it is intellectually dishonest. The theorist knows that different types of moral value exist but for the sake of convenience chooses not to acknowledge them.

On the other hand, in the more typical sort of case, a theory is faulted for being overly selective and/or reductionistic because (according to the critic) the theorist lacks the requisite concepts to make the sorts of distinctions that need to be made within the theory's domain. A better theory is therefore needed, one that will enable the theorist to make distinctions that are fine-grained enough.

But regardless of how one interprets the reductionism charge, the bald claim that all moral theorists have adopted a reductionist attitude is demonstrably false. As we have seen, some theorists begin their efforts by seeking to describe accurately how ordinary people actually think about moral issues and then use the results of their analysis of ordinary moral consciousness as a continual check upon their own work. Those who believe that the primary task of moral theory is to elucidate ordinary peoples' actual moral views are clearly opposed to any reductionism that denies what people already know. If there is a coherence and unity in ordinary moral valuations, such theorists, of course, hope to explicate it. But if there is not, they cannot simply announce that there is without violating their own methodological constraint.

I argued in chapter 6 that both Aristotle and Kant in fact subscribe to just such a view. While Kant may be faulted for not always doing an accurate reporting job concerning ordinary people's moral convictions, the fact remains that he is on record as always trying to do so and that he believes his own theoretical constructions are consistent with such data. Any moral theorist who believes that his or her first responsibility is to explicate what ordinary peoples' actual moral views are, and who believes also that any subsequent theoretical principles, justifications, and applications must cohere with such explication is explicitly rejecting a reductionist approach that denies what is known.

Even if one asserts that (contrary to my claim) Aristotle or (more likely) Kant is motivated by reductionism, there exist numerous counterexamples to the claim that all moral theory must be reductionist within contemporary ethical theory. Some consequentialists are beginning to endorse hybrid conceptions that recognize the validity of certain traditional deontological or "agent-relative" permissions. According to these theorists, one is always permitted—though not always required—to seek to maximize the best overall state of affairs.[11] Two irreducibly different types of value—a consequentialist conception of the good and a nonconsequentialist limitation on what can be required of agents—are thus incorporated into the basic structure. Other writers sympathetic to consequentialism have defended "goal right systems," in which fulfillment and non-realization of rights are included among the goals to be realized.[12] Here, too, a pluralist theory that incorporates fundamentally different types of values is being advocated. Additional pluralist efforts to bridge the stalemate between consequentialist and agent-relative moral theories include Thomas Scanlon's defense of a "two-tier view: one that gives an important role to consequences in the justification and interpretation of rights but which takes rights seriously as placing limits on consequentialist reasoning at the level of casuistry."[13]

Rights theorists in recent years have also revealed a much greater awareness of the need for irreducibly plural categorial schemes in ethics. For a while, Ronald Dworkin and John Mackie's project of a "right-based" moral theory, in which basic statements about rights are taken "as capturing what gives point to the whole moral theory," was pursued in earnest.[14] Today such monistic fervor finds few supporters, and in its place is the growing recognition that a theory of rights "is not capable of standing on its own. It needs to be complemented by a general theory of virtue or moral action to guide the conduct of the rights-bearers in the exercise of their rights."[15]

Finally, pluralistic models have also been advocated in recent years by theorists who work in the virtue ethics tradition. Gregory Trianosky did argue that judgments of virtue and vice frequently have a life of their own, independent from that of deontic judgments concerning right and wrong action. But he also concluded by stating, "I do not here suggest, as some have, that an ethic of virtue can operate with full autonomy, entirely independent of a theory of right."[16] And I have elsewhere stated that "we need to begin efforts to coordinate irreducible or strong notions of virtue along with irreducible or strong conceptions of the various act notions into our conceptual scheme of morality."[17]

In short, there is currently a pronounced trend toward nonreductionist ethical theorizing, one that is being played out on both consequentialist and nonconsequentialist sides of the fence. One may protest that such efforts are themselves not fine-grained enough—that what is needed are not moral theories that incorporate, say, two or three highly abstract types of value into their conceptual schemes but theories whose ears are open to the stronger, more varied multiplicity of nonreducible ethical considerations that we encounter in real life and whose authors stand ready to offer an account of *why* such considerations are in fact irreducibly plural. I myself am sympathetic to such criticisms but remain convinced that the situation with respect to value reductionism has improved immensely in recent years. It seems to me that most contemporary ethical theorists in fact agree with Williams when he writes:

> If there is such a thing as the truth about the subject matter of ethics, . . . why is there any expectation that it should be simple? In particular, why should it be conceptually simple, using only one or two ethical concepts, such as *duty* or *good state of affairs,* rather than many? Perhaps we need as many concepts to describe it as we find we need, and no fewer.[18]

Conflict-recognizing Theories

Moral conflict is a fact of life, and sometimes there is no morally right course of action to be had. When confronted with a divisive moral issue, intelligent and sensitive people sometimes have to agree to disagree with one another, for morality, as Michael Walzer notes, "is something we have to argue about. The argument implies common possession, but common possession does not imply agreement."[19] Moral theorists need to begin to accept these truisms, but some of them have done so all along (see chap. 6).

It may be objected here that would-be moral theorists will be putting themselves out of work once they embrace moral conflicts, for instead of proceeding with their usual labors of providing "solutions" to moral "problems," they will now have to throw their hands up and announce that there is no single, objectively correct answer to be discovered or constructed. But this objection is itself a product of the simplistic dichotomy ("one objectively right answer or . . . no theory") that pervades much of the antitheory literature. Human beings must still make choices when they are confronted with irresolvable conflicts, and a good moral theory should be able to offer us four different kinds of help.

First, conflict-recognizing theories can simply *point out* the presence of moral conflict. It should not be supposed that everyone (even those who have not suffered severe exposure to moral theory) is easily able to recognize moral conflicts. Because we often do not see all of the relevant factors when we are engaged in difficult moral deliberations, we are liable to gloss over or even ignore many points that ought to be included in any critical appraisal of a situation.

Second, conflict-recognizing theories can help explain *why* there is a moral conflict in a particular situation. The basic structure of such explanations would involve three moves: (1) pointing to the different types of moral value that are present in the case at hand, (2) offering a convincing account that shows why they cannot be reduced to a common denominator, and (3) showing the equal importance of each type of value, in order to support the claim that there is no single right answer in this particular case.

Third, conflict-recognizing theories can construct relevant choice models for agents to consider. Such models will often prove most fruitful when they are the products of informed historical research involving similar conflicts to the one currently under consideration. ("In a relevantly similar case, the agent did *x,* based on considerations *y* and *z;* and this is what happened.") Though the kind of help being offered here is primarily descriptive rather than prescriptive (the theorist is not dictating an answer), such choice models can acquire additional prescriptive weight if further arguments are offered that establish that the actor in the story is morally exemplary. But in either case we ourselves should be able to make more informed decisions by considering how other people faced with similar dilemmas arrived at their own decisions, as well as by learning of the consequences of such decisions.

Finally, conflict-recognizing theories can serve to remind us of "the ought not acted upon" and of its continued moral bearing after the deed is done. ("In this particular case, you cannot at once help and tell the truth; and we agree that both are equally important. If you decide to tell the truth, remember that you are not thereby freed from the moral requirement to help if it is still possible to do so in the future. And if the time for help is past, you must be prepared to explain your actions to those who ask.")

Deliberative Strategies and Moral Catechisms

The goal of an all-purpose, formalized moral decision procedure is a false ideal, one that suffers severe epistemological, as well as moral, defects. However, at least within the history of ethics, it is also something of a red herring; for it is not clear that any major moral theorists have subscribed to it wholeheartedly.[20] But there is still plenty of work for moral theorists to do once the universal decision procedure quest is renounced. Again, we ought not to assume that there are only two options available: formulate a decision procedure or abandon moral theory.

First of all, it is important to distinguish between a full-fledged decision procedure (that literally tells people how to deliberate and make moral decisions in every instance by providing them with a list of easy-to-follow rules) and an attempt to formulate general criteria for determining which acts are morally right (or which agents morally good).[21] Moral theorists of all persuasions have traditionally engaged in the latter pursuit, and I believe they should continue to do so. The need for critical standards of appraisal in ethics and elsewhere is obvious, and the articulation and defense of such standards is an appropriate task for theorists. Granted, we have still not achieved much solid consensus concerning *which* criteria of moral assessment are the correct ones and why; and this mediocre track record should give future theorists pause. Lack of consensus does not necessarily indicate the presence of a tragic flaw in a theoretical enterprise (some disagreement is unavoidable, and life would be boring without it); but when it is as deeply etched into the terrain as is presently the case with discourse concerning ethics, I think it is a sign that something has gone wrong with our efforts to formulate standards of appraisal.

If my earlier claim that moral theorists must recognize the reality of irresolvable conflicts is accepted, it follows that the effort to provide general criteria for moral assessment will often be less than total: in situations where a variety of competing values are present, it may not be possible to determine which act is morally right or which person is more admirable morally. Still, in the more usual sort of case, it is often possible to offer rationally justifiable criteria of moral assessment. People deliberating about what to do and how to live have often found such criteria to be helpful, and I believe that moral theorists ought not to give up on their efforts in this area. Such efforts should be more empirically informed and sensitive to the possibility of irresolvable conflict than has sometimes been the case in the recent past; but simply to urge that we stop formulating criteria of appraisal is impossible advice. Humans are "strong evaluators" who have always employed vocabularies of worth; and along with this ingrained predisposition to weigh things in qualitative ways comes the need not only to try to justify our qualitative evaluations but also to reflect continuously on the meaning of the terms within these vocabularies.[22]

Supplying agents with a list of properties in virtue of which objects of moral assessment are deemed right (or good or evil or cowardly or brave)[23] does not go terribly far in the direction of telling people what to do; for, as we have seen, agents must always interpret these criteria in light of their own experience and knowledge; and judgments must be made as to whether and how the concepts actually apply to the case at hand. I do not believe that moral theorists *ought* to take too many steps in the direction of telling people what to do, for (like Kant) I believe that people are autonomous agents who must think for themselves. However, in cases where moral deliberators either have not yet learned how to think for themselves (e.g., children) or feel a need for advice or at least information and resources that will enable them to improve their own deliberative capacities, there are several additional efforts that theorists can and should take. These additional efforts fall somewhere between the offering of criteria of moral assessment on the one hand and that of authoritarian decision procedures on the other.

One such effort may be termed *deliberative strategies*.[24] Adults who are faced with difficult moral choices may wish to know how competent moral judges in the past deliberated when confronted with similar issues. Which features of the situation did they believe called for particular attention? What did they think were the most relevant alternatives to consider? Theorists who have analyzed the actual deliberative processes of competent moral judges on the relevant issue(s) and who have determined which aspects of such processes can be accurately codified could make the results of their researches available to other interested parties.[25] The resultant formalized reasoning processes could then be used by those who are looking for strategies to help them decide what to do. Judgment would still need to be employed at a variety of levels, and no one should suppose that he or she is being given a ready-reckoner for all occasions. But the more modest aim of developing quasi "diagnostic prompting systems" in ethics, that is, empirically based choice models that, while not seeking to replace human judgment, serve to encourage agents to consider relevant alternatives and not to jump to conclusions, is well worth investigating.[26] Work of this sort is going on in many different areas at present, and it is odd that (to my knowledge) no one has yet tried it in ethics.

A second type of effort, to be used with children, is what Kant called the method of *moral catechism*. It is actually a much more open-ended affair than the term *catechism* often connotes, for Kant did not advocate that specific determinate judgments be taken as constitutive of the moral life. (On this point, Kant agrees with Dewey: moral theory "does not offer a table of commandments in a catechism in which the answers are as definite as are the questions which are asked.") Rather, Kant's moral catechism is a method of questioning by which teachers develop their students' thinking about moral issues: "The teacher, by his questions, guides the pupil's thinking merely by presenting him with situations in which his disposition for certain concepts will develop (the teacher is the midwife of the pupil's thought)" (*DV* VI 478/150). The teacher alone does the questioning at this early stage of moral development (though at a later stage two-way dialogue must step in to replace it); and the answers elicited from the student are to be written down "and preserved in precise terms which cannot easily be altered, and so be committed to the pupil's memory" (VI 479/151). Like most Socratics, the Kantian moral teacher also occasionally gives the pupils's thoughts a definite push in one direction rather than in another: "Should the pupil sometimes not know how to answer the question, the teacher, guiding his reason, suggests an answer" (VI 480/153).

Kant does not develop any detailed examples of moral catechisms in his writings (he offers only a single "fragment" [*Bruchstück*] of one in *The Doctrine of Virtue*); but he clearly thought they were extremely important in moral education: "For the still untrained pupil the first and most essential doctrinal instrument of the theory of virtue is a moral catechism" (*DV* VI 478/151). Moral theorists today do not generally go in for this sort of thing, but perhaps they should. The Kantian moral catechism represents a sensible middle path that attempts to offer more determinate guidance to moral deliberation (at an early and critical stage of cognitive development) than the mere formulating of general criteria of moral assessment (which children are not usually in a position to apply wisely), but it is also consistent with agents' autonomy and thus miles away from mechanical aids, which are "shackles of a permanent immaturity." An additional benefit to be gained from such pursuits lies in the cross-fertilization between normative theory and psychological work in cognitive development that would necessarily occur.

Normative Theories

Theories are not always cut from the same cloth. Some aim primarily at empirical explanation and prediction, others at conceptual explanation, others are primarily semantic in nature, and still others focus on normative justification. But while it is not written in stone anywhere that all moral theories *must* place normative justification above all other concerns, it is the case that the best moral theories of the past have all had strong normative dimensions. Most people expect a moral theory to be able to offer some sort of guidance concerning what to do and how to live, not an unreasonable expectation. Thus, while we ought to allow room for different kinds of moral theories, not all of which need be concerned solely with normative justification, past precedent suggests that most moral theorists will continue to express strong interests in normative justification and that it is appropriate for them to do so.

I argued earlier (chap. 6) that the antitheorist division between descriptive and normative moral theories is a false dichotomy that reveals a fundamental misunderstanding of both Aristotelian and Kantian ethics. Aristotle and Kant both sought in their respective moral theories first to describe accurately how people actually think about moral issues and then to use the results of this analysis for normative purposes. The air of paradox in this strategy disappears once we remind ourselves of the simple fact that people are not always aware (for a variety of reasons) what their considered moral views are. But once we do become aware of our considered moral views, we can then use this information to help us deliberate concerning future courses of action. Similarly, Aristotle and Kant designed their respective moral theories to be both descriptive and normative, though the descriptive component precedes the normative and acts as a continual constraint on it. The normative component is intended to grow out of, and be consistent with, the implications of the descriptive component. However, since ordinary moral views are themselves not always internally consistent, theorists who adopt this approach must decide which descriptions shall count more and which less in cases of conflict. Aristotle, we saw, prefers the views of the educated elite to the hoi polloi, while Kant makes the opposite choice.

In my view, the best approach to normative moral justification is via just this sort of descriptive account of moral agent's actual moral views. Such an approach anchors normative concerns in existing moral practices and attitudes, so that the theorist does not suddenly appear from nowhere to "tell us what to do." But isn't this approach too conservative? By attempting to anchor moral oughts in existing *is*es, are we not unfairly tying theorists' hands? Not necessarily. The *is*es in question are not simply sociological generalizations about existing moral attitudes within a community (though these may be relevant). Rather, they are descriptions of considered moral judgments concerning what is good and evil— morally worthy and unworthy—and thus *already have* a normative force within them. And because they already have a normative force, they will often have implications concerning not what already exists but what morally ought to exist.[27]

Still, suppose a moral theorist wants to examine the normative justifiability of a *radically new* social practice, one concerning which people do not yet have any relevant considered judgments. Here the descriptive element appears to be missing. Is the theorist therefore forbidden to take a normative stance? No; but he or she should proceed with caution and should try, wherever possible, to offer new justificatory principles that are consistent with more, rather than fewer, existing judgments.

Generally speaking, normative moral theories may be divided into those that are primarily action-guiding and those that are primarily character-guiding. Ideally, normative moral theories should seek to be both; for persons of good character do not always know what to do in particular situations (and hence might benefit from the action-guiding aspect of a theory), and people who do deliberate effectively about what to do in particular situations may nevertheless be less knowledgeable in matters of moral education and character formation. However, as I argued in chapter 2, the character-guiding aspect of a moral theory is more fundamental than the action-guiding aspect for a variety of reasons. Restricting attention to the moral quandaries of adults (and trying to offer normative advice about them) is often too little too late; for a person's character is by this stage fairly determinate, and fundamental change is difficult. Also, a theory whose normative thrust is devoted exclusively to guiding the discrete acts of adults is putting the cart before the horse and stands little chance of success. Knowing what to do in any serious sense requires good character; for the agent must have developed certain abilities of judgment and perception over time, and the exercise of these abilities is precisely what we mean by good character. Handing over a set of action-guiding rules to persons who lack good character is a recipe for disaster.

As virtue theorists never tire of pointing out, contemporary normative moral theories have, at least until quite recently, been exclusively action-guiding rather than character-guiding. Fortunately, this is now beginning to change. Moral theorists of all normative persuasions are now paying much more attention to issues of character formation. The normative advice that comes out of a character-guiding theory is apt to be better anchored in existing moral practices and attitudes (and hence not so alienating or foreign-sounding) than is that of a strictly action-guiding theory, for it is advice that has better stood the test of time, coming as it does from a concern with how people should live their lives over the long term rather than with how they should decide what to do in discrete situations.

Moral Expert Systems

There is much of value in the antitheory critique of moral expertise. Moral problems are not usually like mathematical puzzles: they do not always admit of one objectively correct answer, they cannot always be "solved" by applying a logical proof procedure, and people who are good moral deliberators do not owe their effectiveness primarily to highly abstract reasoning abilities and formal instruction. At the same time, we have seen (chap. 6) that neither Aristotle nor Kant ever assumed that moral experts in this peculiar technocratic sense could ever exist. On the contrary, each of them specifically rejects this notion of moral expertise. Thus, the antitheorist declaration that "there would be moral experts if the claims of ethical theory were true" is false when applied to their moral theories.

However, Aristotle and Kant did presuppose the existence of a different kind of moral expertise, one that we called the *wisdom* model. According to the wisdom model of moral expertise, moral experts are persons of good moral character who, through experience, upbringing, exposure to older exemplars, and continuous reflection, have developed the requisite practical skills to know how to deliberate well about what is good for themselves and for their communities.[28] Must such persons also be able readily to explain to others *how* they arrive at their decisions? Not necessarily, for it is often the case that people who are good decision makers are unable to articulate how they arrive at their decisions. Must such persons always know what other people ought to do, in the sense of being able to help them see what they have good moral reasons for doing? Not necessarily, since, again, they may not always be aware of what their own reasoning processes are. While Aristotle and Kant both insist repeatedly that such persons ought to serve as moral exemplars for the rest of us, they nowhere assert that morally wise persons must also be instructors of moral decision making who are in a position to tell people how to deliberate and act (see, e.g., *NE* 1113a26–28, 1107a2, 1140a24; *DV* VI 479/152; VI 48/44).

In recent years much has been written about so-called expert systems—computer programs that embody human reasoning processes employed by leading experts in domains such as medicine, business, science, and law.[29] The first step in the construction of such programs involves extensive interviewing with acknowledged experts in the domain under investigation in order to find out how they make the judgments that are at the core of their area of expertise. The next step "is to codify that knowledge so computers can make similar decisions by emulating human inferential reasoning."[30] To my knowledge, no one has yet tried to construct an expert system for any aspect of moral decision making. But if there are moral experts, why could such systems not be built?

Clearly, one major reason why moral expert systems have not yet been attempted is that many people remain suspicious of the very notion of moral expertise. *Who* will be the "domain experts" in this project if the RAND Corporation or the Massachusetts Institute of Technology decides to give it a shot, and what criteria will be used for selecting them out of the general population? We noted earlier that even though both Aristotle and Kant endorse the same basic definition of moral expertise as practical wisdom, they part ways when asked to identify the most likely possessors of such wisdom—Aristotle siding with aristocratic, leisured males of the ruling class, Kant, with modest Pietists who are far removed from centers of political and cultural power. In more wildly pluralistic societies such as our own, there is likely to be even less consensus concerning the question of who is morally wise.

A second factor that may help explain the reluctance to construct moral expert systems is widespread skepticism as to whether moral deliberation processes are *codifiable* in more than a primitive and highly schematic way. Here I suspect that it is not only antitheorists such as John McDowell who subscribe to an uncodifiability thesis in ethics (see chap. 5). Most "knowledge engineers" probably do, as well, though perhaps for different reasons.

While both of these objections are serious, I do not think either one constitutes a knockdown argument against the possibility of moral expert systems. Yes, there is suspicion concerning the concept of moral expertise; and some of it is well founded. However, all that is needed is the modest admission that "some people really are more insightful and sensitive, morally speaking, than others, and that these people may possibly be ahead of the majority in their grasp of the morality of a particular kind of action."[31] And most people are, in fact, more than willing to grant this. Yes, there may often be irresolvable disagreements concerning who really is more insightful and sensitive, morally speaking, in his or her grasp of the morality of a particular kind of action. But do not people also occasionally disagree as to who is the more competent legal or medical expert? (Think of opposing legal teams at trial, each dragging in their favorite expert witness to testify before the jury.) In cases where agreement cannot be reached, the moral knowledge engineers should interview all of the contenders and look for some common ground. Finally, of course, moral deliberative processes are not entirely codifiable. No computer program can generate all of the morally wise person's perceptions. But the same is also true in other deliberative domains (such as law and medicine), where judgment and intuition are often required. In no such area is the goal of a programmable decision maker that could duplicate all of the domain expert's judgments and discernments attainable; for not all of the requisite thought processes are rule-governed. Still, such systems have already been shown to produce clear benefits elsewhere (e.g., when used as tutorials for medical students), particularly when the programs are constrained to the subfields of the domain that are fairly routine in nature. And some subfields of the moral domain are fairly routine.

I conclude that the possibility of moral expert systems in this modest sense is definitely worth exploring. A traditional concern of moral theory has been the logic of good moral deliberation. Recent developments in knowledge engineering should allow moral theorists finally to take a more empirical approach to the topic. Expert systems will never be the panacea that software manufacturers advertise them as being, but the general strategy of trying to map out at least some of the patterns of reasoning that competent moral judges employ is one that more theorists ought to undertake.

Theory Versus Nontheory

I have argued for an alternative conception of moral theory. More empirically informed and less reductionistic than current conceptions, it recognizes the reality of irresolvable conflicts and its interest in guiding practical deliberation is not underwritten by an extremist faith in a universal decision procedure; yet it also reflects more accurately some of the most outstanding past efforts in moral theory. Does this defense of a less rationalistic, more pragmatic conception of moral theory in fact *trivialize* moral theory by, in effect, turning nearly *everything* into moral theory? How can moral theory efforts be distinguished from nontheoretical approaches to morality, once this alternative understanding of what constitutes a moral theory is adopted? Stanley Fish, in several of his antitheory polemics, voices precisely this fear: "The effect of such a liberal definition would be to blur the distinction between theory and everything that is not theory, . . . but nothing whatsoever will have been gained, and we will have lost any sense that theory is special."[32]

I sympathize with Fish's fear, at least to the extent that I believe it is important to know what distinguishes a moral theory from something that is not a moral theory. Presumably, theoretical efforts outside the domain of the moral are in no danger of being misidentified as moral theories, regardless of how liberally one construes moral theory. (A theory of thermodynamics is not, and never will be, a moral theory.) But once we restrict our scope to reflective projects within the moral domain, the question of what is moral theory and what is not does become more problematic. Fish, for instance, claims that one result of adopting a more liberal understanding of what constitutes a theory is that reflective projects that are *not* theories (e.g., high-order empirical generalizations of moral practices, strong declarations of basis moral beliefs, and detailed descriptions of a culture's underlying moral assumptions) suddenly become theories, through the miracle of linguistic legislation.[33] Do these sorts of projects constitute moral theories on my view, or not?

Drawing a convincing line between theory and nontheory within any intellectual domain is proving increasingly difficult, in part because of the perceived success many contemporary philosophers of science have enjoyed in their dismantling of the theory–observation distinction. Slogans such as "All facts are theory-laden" and "All terms are theoretical terms" are part of our common intellectual culture by now; and while they have helped to rout out simplistic positivist programs in science, they have also contributed to a certain ennui regarding definitional questions about theory.[34] Without attempting the fruitless task of striving for the final word on what constitutes a moral theory (for, thankfully, our ideas about moral theories are not static),[35] the following brief remarks should at least help to give a clearer sense of what I mean by *moral theory*. Additionally, I hope they will serve to allay the fear that we stand in danger of turning everything into moral theory once we let go of a stern, rationalist model of what constitutes moral theory.

By *moral theory*, I mean, at the simplest level, any sustained attempt to give an account of how moral agents[36] ought to live and act. Such an attempt necessarily involves an effort both to *define* what is meant by, for example *morality* and *moral agents* and to *justify* the way of life that is being advocated.[37] As far as I am concerned, the legitimate ways in which this attempt can be carried out are infinite, for which we should be grateful. Wide as this conception of moral theory is, it still enables us to show that three types of reflective projects in ethics will not count as moral theories.

First, moral theories are not simply high-order empirical generalizations about moral practices. Granted, I have tried to defend the claim that moral theories should be more empirically informed than is often the case at present; but empirically informed moral theories are not the same as empirical generalizations about moral practices. Moral theories that are to be applied to human life need to be empirically informed for at least two reasons:

1. Human life may not be the only kind of rational life, but species-specific knowledge about human life can only be acquired empirically.
2. Many moral issues faced by group and individual members of the human species involve empirical facts regarding special circumstances. Here, empirical knowledge that is not merely species-specific but rather group- or even individual-specific is needed.

However, the *normative* stance of a moral theory will always clearly separate it from any project that is only concerned with empirical generalization. The person who is committed only to making empirical generalizations about practices can never move beyond these practices: the project must remain descriptive. On the other hand, the person who is committed not only to understanding the relevant history, psychology, politics, and so on of moral practices but also to *taking a stand* either for them or against them does move beyond the empirical level. But "beyond the empirical" does not mean in outer space: the effort to guide practice must be made *from within* practice, at least in the sense that it presupposes an intimate knowledge of the relevant empirical features of the practice that it seeks to guide.

Second, the conception of moral theory defended here clearly differs from a collection of declarations of basic moral beliefs. Fish writes, "Someone who declares himself committed to the promotion of individual freedom does not have a theory; he has a belief."[38] I agree. But if this same someone then proceeds to *present reasons* to support the view that we should promote individual freedom rather than some other moral value and if the reasons offered in turn are tied to a larger story about human nature and human societies, then the person does indeed have at least the beginnings of a moral theory. In short, declarations of basic moral beliefs start to figure in moral theories once a broad-scale effort is made to justify them and to situate them within an account of how human beings should live and act. And these are precisely the conceptual and normative topics to which philosophical discussion pushes us when we assert such beliefs. Furthermore, such beliefs do inevitably reflect a range of theoretical biases and assumptions in and of themselves—biases and assumptions about which we will necessarily remain forever ignorant if we forswear theory.[39] My reference to reasons that "tie into a larger story" about human nature and human societies signals a further difference between moral theory and nontheoretical approaches to morality. *Theōria* involves taking in a *larger* view of things, and adopting this perspective requires abstraction. Moral theory, like other kinds of theory, involves levels of abstraction that are not readily available to common sense. Theorists employ abstract concepts and general principles that are often intended to have reference far beyond their initial domains of application. At the same time, while moral theory does share with other forms of theory a fundamental impulse toward abstraction that sets it apart from nontheoretical endeavors, it is my view that this impulse needs to be continually checked. Moral theories cannot realistically aspire to the same generality of scope as can, say, astrophysical theories, simply because the role of culture is immensely significant in the former domain and comparatively insignificant in the latter. Moral theorists should not shy away from highly abstract concepts and general principles, for theory requires them. But in consorting with such abstractions, moral theorists always need to ask whether they are needed to illuminate the issues under investigation and whether they can illuminate moral issues in other times and places—and if so, *why*.

Finally, the conception of moral theory advocated here is not to be equated with a set of detailed descriptions of a culture's underlying moral assumptions and attitudes. As argued earlier (chap. 6), the task of carefully excavating a community's considered moral assumptions and attitudes is an essential first step in moral theorizing. But the necessary second step is to employ these data as constraints on the construction of principles and on any deliberative strategies that are intended to help people decide what to do and how to live. Here again, the normative dimension of moral theory serves to distinguish it clearly from all purely descriptive undertakings.

It is ironic that so many antitheory writings are dubbed as being the product of a "new pragmatism."[40] The classic American pragmatists were enemies of ahistorical, noncontextual theories; but they certainly were not out to kill theory. Rather, their aim was to make theory more relevant by narrowing the gap between theory and practice. As James noted, "Pragmatism unstiffens all our theories, limbers them up and sets each one at work."[41] Or as Dewey put it, in an important early essay:

> What then is moral theory? It is all one with moral *insight,* and moral insight is the recognition of the relationships in hand. This is a very tame and prosaic conception. It makes moral insight, and therefore moral theory, consist simply in the

every-day workings of the same ordinary intelligence that measures dry-goods, drives nails, sells wheat, and invents the telephone.[42]

This concern to bring moral theory and practice into closer proximity should not be equated with a desire to diminish theory's role. Moral theories still can and should be bold and imaginative; the emphasis on practice is not an endorsement of the status quo. This is not what being practical means. The basic aim is to ensure that reflections and criticisms concerning how to live and act have a proper footing in who and where we are and in what we are doing at present, rather than floating aimlessly above or beyond actual practices. In Dewey's words, moral theory "is the analytic perception of the conditions and relations in hand in a given act, it is the action *in idea*. It is the construction of the act in thought against its outward construction. *It is, therefore, the doing— the act itself, in its emerging.*"[43]

I began part II by noting that theorists were originally simply people who tried to take in a larger view of things from a distance. Pythagoras sensed that it was usually philosophers who, more than other people, felt compelled to take a larger view of things; thus, the identification between philosophy and *theōria* began. Taking a large view about ethics is something that many people (both philosophers and nonphilosophers) continue to feel compelled to do, but (despite antitheory polemics) to perform this activity well does not entail that one be ignorant of human history, psychology, and anthropology; nor does it presuppose the extreme view that all moral values can be weighed on a single scale, that all moral conflicts can be rationally resolved, or that theory can and should tell people what to do in every situation. The best moral theorists of the past were never burdened by these illusory aims and assumptions. It is time that we drop them, as well.

8
Why We Need Moral Theories

There is a Tory contention that theorizing leads to violence, and there
is a liberal contention that theories are obscurantist and blinding. Now
on the contrary it is the absence of theory which renders us blind . . . ;
and as for violence, the absence of civilized theorizing can also lead
in that direction. It is dangerous to starve the moral imagination of
the young. A more ambitious conceptual picture . . . would give us
what Shelley called the power to imagine what we know. . . . We need
. . . a framework, a house of theory.

> IRIS MURDOCH, "A House of Theory"

Great musicians are like great fighters. They have a higher sense of
theory going on in their heads.

> MILES DAVIS, *Miles: The Autobiography*

I have argued that moral theories need not be the simplistic, ahistorical constructions that antitheorists say they must be and that two of the best moral
theories of the past do not in fact possess most of the defects that antitheorists
say all moral theories must possess. But what are moral theories good for? Do
they fulfill any genuine and indispensable human needs, needs that would remain
unsatisfied in the absence of moral theories? What can moral theories help us
to accomplish in life that we would otherwise be unable to accomplish? The
aim of this last chapter is to show that there are indeed five indispensable human
needs that only moral theories can satisfy adequately: explanation, conceptual
exploration, criticism, imagination, and human curiosity.

Explanation

For many people, the single most important feature of theories is that they
enable us to *explain* natural phenomena. "What was the cause of Foucault's
death? He died of AIDS." "What caused the walls of Bookshop Santa Cruz to
collapse? The city of Santa Cruz, California, was quite near the epicenter of the
1989 earthquake, and the buildings in the center of town were older and less
able to withstand the tremors." Inquiring minds want to know, and theories

can often help satisfy this aim by showing that the event to be explained can be deduced from statements of scientific laws and statements describing antecedently known empirical facts. An additional bonus is that if such explanations are made before the events occur, they can also serve as predictions, thus giving humans the ability to foresee changes in the world and possibly use this knowledge to their advantage.[1]

But what about *moral* theories? Do they possess any significant explanatory and predictive powers? In recent years skeptics have charged moral theories with "explanatory impotence," claiming that they do not contribute to our best explanations of our experiences.[2] However, as many authors have noted, explanations involving moral concepts that actually do contribute to our best explanations of our experiences seem to abound in daily life. One typical kind of moral explanation occurs when we refer to an aspect of a man's moral character to explain why he acted as he did. Nicholas Sturgeon cites the following example from Bernard De Voto's *Year of Decision: 1846,* in which the author describes some of the efforts to rescue the Donner party in California. Passed Midshipman Selim Woodworth, described earlier in the book as "a great busybody and ambitious of taking a command," directed one such effort; but the results were disastrous. Woodworth

> not only failed to lead rescue parties into the mountains himself, where other rescuers were counting on him (leaving children to be picked up by him, for example), but had to be "shamed, threatened, and bullied" even into organizing the efforts of others willing to take the risk; he spent time arranging comforts for himself in camp, preening himself on the importance of his position; and as a predictable result of his cowardice and his exercises in vainglory, many died who might have been saved, including four known still to be alive when he turned back for the last time in mid-March. De Voto concludes: "Passed Midshipman Woodworth was just no damned good."[3]

Sturgeon regards De Voto's conclusion as being an inference to the best explanation. Alternative explanations (e.g., that Woodworth was basically a decent person who could not quite rise to the occasion) simply do not square as well with the facts of the case.

A second common type of moral explanation occurs when we refer to a moral norm to explain why a social event occurred or will occur. Joshua Cohen, in *The Moral Arc of the Universe,* cites the case of William Williams, a slave from Salisbury, North Carolina, who escaped to Canada in 1849, where he was later interviewed by the American abolitionist Samuel Gridley Howe in 1863. The Civil War had begun two years earlier, and Williams offered the following prediction concerning its outcome: "I think the North will whip the South, because I believe they are in the right."[4] Cohen argues that moral explanations of this sort actually help to explain and predict (as opposed to, say, merely appraise or evaluate) social events. On his view, unjust institutions have a limited viability within human societies; and in correctly calling the institution of slavery unjust, speakers are conveying genuine explanatory information about its nature.

In both of these examples, moral properties are invoked to identify characteristics of people or institutions that are allegedly uncapturable with differently structured categories or concepts that do not refer to moral properties. Moral explanations, on this view, "allow us to isolate what it is about a person or an action or an institution that leads to its having the effects it does."[5]

The radical skeptic (e.g., a Gilbert Harman or a John L. Mackie) who charges moral theory with complete explanatory impotency is what antitheorists call a *negative* theorist. Such a person is still a moral theorist in the sense that he or she claims to have a systematic account of what morality is, albeit one holding that moral facts and moral knowledge are both illusory and that positive moral theories play no explanatory role whatsoever. Negative theorists, as we noted earlier, share with positive theorists a strong belief in the power of theory and philosophy to stand back and render an accurate verdict on the nature of morality.[6] Antitheorists, on the other hand, do not believe that theory and philosophy are as powerful as this, at least within the moral domain. As a result, they are more agnostic when it comes to the global pronouncements of theorists concerning ways to determine which moral beliefs are true and which false. The antitheorist position "*leaves open* the question whether there could be such [general belief] tests" and reserves the right to assert that there might be an occasional *local* belief test, without succumbing to the hope of a *universal* moral belief test.[7]

Presumably, negative theorists would respond to the examples cited by Sturgeon and Cohen by denying that moral concepts are in fact necessary to pick out any properties of people or of institutions that would play a role in our best explanations. Otherwise, they would have to forfeit their root claim that moral theories are explanatorily impotent. I do not intend to analyze such responses here, since they, too, are "theoretical" and share with me the belief that philosophically informed theories are necessary for any critical understanding of morality. On the other hand, most antitheorists would presumably not deny the validity of at least certain mundane kinds of moral explanations. They would be prepared to grant that at least *some* moral terms (i.e., "thick" ones such as *treacherous* or *cowardly* as opposed to "thin" ones such as *right* or *ought*) have explanatory and predictive force when properly employed. But they would then quickly add that we *do not need* any moral theories in addition to, or on top of, such garden-variety moral terms. We can explain and predict important moral facts about human character and social institutions by correctly using thick moral terms, but we need not invoke the higher-level abstractions of philosophical theories about morality. To do so adds nothing of any real value and serves only to obscure matters.

But it is naive to assume that we can fruitfully employ moral terms in their explanatory and predictive roles without striving for a more systematic account of them. At the least, we need to do two things. First, we need a convincing account of what such terms mean when they are employed in their normal manners and what (if anything) they refer to. Second, if we do come to believe that moral terms in fact refer to real characteristics (albeit not necessarily physical properties) of people and institutions that we want to see remain in our best explanations, then we need, additionally, an account of why such characteristics are, or are not, worth cultivating in human life. To undertake either of these efforts requires moral theory; for now we are presupposing a more general and systematic understanding of moral language, as well as a justification of certain moral values over others. The specific moral theory appealed to may look quite different from the conception of moral theory assumed in antitheory arguments; but this does not alter the fact that *some* kind of moral theory is eventually needed even when we restrict ourselves to thick moral terms.

The urge to explain and predict what is going on in the world, as well as within and among ourselves, lies very deep within the human psyche; and the ability of theoretical models to satisfy this particular urge better than other strategies is by now noncontroversial. The moral domain is in this regard much like other fields of inquiry where theories are constantly called upon to help make sense out of what is happening. Of course, the explanatory and predictive powers of human theories are often feeble; and this is notoriously true of existing moral theories. Also, we ought not to assume (as positivist philosophers of science assumed) either that the only legitimate type of explanation derives a description of the event-to-be-explained from a general law and a statement of initial conditions or that explanation and prediction must always have the same logical structure. A person who announces that he or she "has a theory" concerning some real-life phenomenon is not necessarily always proposing a causal explanation of an event in terms of universal laws. Intellectuals need to pay more attention to the variety of different but legitimate ways in which actual theories seek to explain phenomena. In many cases where the object of investigation is some aspect of human behavior, what are being offered are perhaps better described as *interpretations,* attempts to unpack meanings and to understand the *reasons* why people do what they do rather than the alleged physical causes of their behavior. Furthermore, it would seem that even scientific investigations that do not concern human behavior as their object of inquiry nevertheless contain ineliminable interpretive elements, since the interests and intentions of the human investigators will always form part of the larger knowledge equation.[8]

Both in ethics and elsewhere, there exist different kinds of explanations; and good theories will be sensitive to this fact. Obviously, different theorists have favored, and will continue to favor, different kinds of explanations over others. However, progress in this area can be achieved only through the development of new and better theories. The abandonment of theory is no answer.

Conceptual Exploration

Theories are useful in explaining events and in interpreting phenomena; but— at least since Kant—it is also a commonplace that events and phenomena are never presented to us in a neutral manner but are always conceptualized in one way or another. The human mind does not read passively from the book of nature (much less culture); rather, it actively structures experience to fall into line with its own categories and concepts. Since Kant first performed his Copernican *Gedankenexperiment*—in which he asked what would happen if we assumed that objects of experience conform to our "faculty of intuition" rather than vice versa (*C1* B xvii)—it has also been a commonplace that one of the primary tasks of philosophers and theorists is to uncover the basic categories and concepts that structure our thinking in different areas of life. The post-Kantian theorist's first task, in other words, is not to explain the facts but rather to bring to light the fundamental patterns in which the facts present themselves. Questions of ontology (What is there?) are thus forced to take a back seat to questions of epistemology (What conceptual schemes do we employ in thinking about what is there?).

Kant, of course, believed that the most important categories and concepts that people use to structure experience are a priori—"prior to," or independent of, experience but, more importantly, identical for all human beings and not subject to change. The alleged universality and necessity of these patterns of thought ensure the possibility of rational communication. On this point, more and more post-Kantians have chosen to adopt Hegel's historical sense "that nothing, including an *a priori* concept, is immune from cultural development."[9] The suspicion that our concepts are subject to cultural change has been particularly influential in fields such as ethics and politics (as opposed to, say, mathematics), where an enormous act of will is required to deny the obvious influence of specific historical and cultural traditions on our thinking.[10]

Accordingly, a second fundamental reason as to why moral theories are needed lies in the necessity of bringing to light the various models, metaphors, and categorical frameworks that govern the moral outlooks of human beings in different times and places. Isaiah Berlin, in an influential essay, singled out this activity as the most fundamental and enduring theoretical task:

> The first step to the understanding of men is the bringing to consciousness of the model or models that dominate and penetrate their thought and action. Like all attempts to make men aware of the categories in which they think, it is a difficult and sometimes painful activity, likely to produce deeply disquieting results. The second task is to analyse the model itself, and this commits the analyst to accepting or modifying or rejecting it, and, in the last case, to providing a more adequate one in its stead.[11]

This effort, he continued, cannot be carried out within the confines of either empirical observation or formal deduction, and is thus irreducibly theoretical and philosophical in nature:

> If we examine the models, paradigms, conceptual structures that govern various outlooks whether consciously or not, and compare the various concepts and categories involved with respect, for example, to their internal consistency or their explanatory force, then what we are engaged upon is not psychology or sociology or logic or epistemology, but moral or social or political theory, or all these at once, depending on whether we confine ourselves to individuals, or to groups, or to the particular types of human arrangements that are classified as political, or deal with them all at once.[12]

Human beings seek understanding of themselves and their actions, and they will never achieve more than minor and fragmented success in this effort unless they seek first to uncover the basic categories and metaphors in terms of which they define themselves and their activities. But to advocate an important place for moral theory within this general effort at conceptual exploration is not necessarily to endorse ahistorical or reductionistic system building. If some of our fundamental moral categories have changed over time or if some of the concepts in terms of which we at present understand ourselves differ radically from the concepts other cultures employ, moral theorists should point this out. Similarly, if conceptual excavation reveals our moral categories to be irreducibly plural in nature and somewhat less than internally consistent, moral theorists should give us an accurate report of their findings.

Criticism

A third basic function of theories, particularly within the humanities and social sciences, is that of criticism. Theories are used not only to explain what-is-the-case and to uncover the categories by means of which we interpret what-is-the-case but also to argue that what-is-the-case morally ought not to be the case. Moral theories, on this view, are necessary in order to critically evaluate existing social practices and attitudes—to reveal through argument what is wrong with them and to show how and why they need to be changed. The potential scope of moral criticism is extremely wide. It may be directed toward the practices and attitudes of moral agents in other times and places, the practices and attitudes of people within the theorist's own society, and the theorist's own practices and attitudes. Finally, at least as the term is used here, *criticism* is not the exclusive property of any political or normative outlook. Conservatives and radicals are both free to engage in moral criticism.

Effective criticism of social practices and attitudes eventually *requires* moral theory for the fundamental reason that criticism that hopes to convince must eventually step back from particular moral practices and attitudes and ask what (if anything) *justifies* them. This search for justification is ineliminably theoretical, since it presupposes some general standards of evaluation that will be used either to defend or reject existing practices and attitudes. Regardless of whether the standards employed are viewed as foundational or antifoundational, effort must be made to answer the question Why these standards and not some others? To engage in this effort in any serious way is to engage in theory. Because moral theory involves the all-things-considered articulation and justification of certain ways of living and acting over others, all sustained attempts to criticize ways of living and acting must eventually consort with moral theory.

Regardless of whether the critic is engaged in pointing out inconsistencies among a culture's accepted practices and ideals, arguing against these ideals, or trying to put forward new ones in their place, the project of criticism itself presupposes a willingness to define and justify a way of life. Though the specific forms that this effort to define and justify a way of life may assume are infinite, all of them at bottom involve moral theory; for criticism, in the words of antitheorist Michael Walzer, "is founded in hope.... The critic must believe that the conduct of his fellows can conform more closely to a moral standard than it now does or that their self-understanding can be greater than it now is or that their institutions can be more justly organized than they now are."[13] But in each case there is a fundamental norm that the critic is invoking. Regardless of which moral standard or which concept of self-understanding or justice is called up for service by the critic, it needs—if the critic is going to be taken seriously—to be defended by argument. Like it or not, the critic is thus drawn ineluctably into moral theory.

However, as noted in chapter 7, the attempt to define and justify a way of life does not necessarily entail emotional detachment from, or intellectual disinterestedness in, the local mores of one's community. Moral critics need not feign impartiality and disinterestedness: they must simply be prepared critically to evaluate the normative standards that members of their communities (including themselves) profess to live by. We need not suppose that the only standpoint that enables us to evaluate our moral practices and attitudes is an external one. The standpoint of critical evaluation can be an immanent one, and, indeed (I have argued), *was* so for Aristotle and Kant, at least when they were addressing specific moral issues confronting human beings rather than abstract points concerning rational agency as such. Classical moral theorists have sought external justifications on general points where they believed with reason that such justifications were possible, but they have not supposed that the entire theoretical edifice could or should rest solely on external supports. Here, too, the simplistic dichotomy assumed by antitheorists ("either an external standpoint, or no theory") is historically unpersuasive.

The assertion that moral criticism eventually requires moral theory should not be construed as implying either that all effective moral critics are members of the moral theory guild or that only moral theorists are in a position to be convincing moral critics. As a group, academic moral theorists tend not to be the most convincing moral critics: they often lack sufficient empirical knowledge of relevant social and economic conditions, their rhetorical powers are often weak, and their own class interests often align them with the status quo rather than with progressive forces of change. However, I do believe that all effective moral critics inevitably employ in their thinking what have been termed "theorylike elements" and that one can locate such theorylike elements through analyses of their speeches, pamphlets, novels, and so on. As Joel Kupperman remarks:

> The moral pioneers who helped change general thinking on such matters [as] slavery, the subjection of women, or the entitlements of the very poor had, at the least, theory-like elements in their thinking. They saw that all of the moral considerations that applied to whites also applied to blacks, that those which were applicable to men were applicable to women, and that the general thrust toward the prevention of misery which links many elements of familiar morality had special relevance to the plight of the very poor.... There is no plausible way in which a group of people

can begin to criticize an established morality except by means of such theory-like elements.[14]

But to say that criticism involves theorylike elements is not to make criticism "hostage to theory."[15] Again, most moral critics who make a significant impact on their societies do not come from the ranks of professional moral theorists. A critic who successfully points out inconsistencies in existing social practices or who shows what true adherence to a professed ideal really entails is not suddenly transformed into a card-carrying Kantian. (However, it may well be that "we are led by a certain analogy to entitle anyone a philosopher" who begins to raise such questions [CI A 840/B 868].) Furthermore, we need to let go of the damaging picture that there exists one totalizing Theory waiting in the wings that will force everyone to think its thoughts. All that is being asserted is that criticism points to, and presupposes, a willingness to engage in broad-based articulation and defense of its own norms. The critic may not wish to engage in this task, and friendly supporters may not wish to press it upon the critic. But the question Why these norms and not some others? needs eventually to be addressed. Criticism must eventually consort with theory.

Now if, as I have argued, moral theory is necessary for effective social criticism, it would seem that antitheorists lack sufficient resources for such criticism. However, perhaps this charge is one that they accept without regret. The title of Stanley Clarke and Evan Simpson's anthology is, after all, *Anti-Theory in Ethics and Moral Conservatism.* And while the editors assert emphatically that the antitheorist attack on moral theory is "politically neutral," it is very difficult to see what is so politically neutral about a position that claims that there are "no theoretical criteria adequate for assessing social practices" and declares human beings "unable to describe better social arrangements";[16] for if we do become convinced that there really are no theoretical criteria adequate for assessing social practices and that we are unable to envision better social arrangements, it would seem that the moral status quo must always win by default.[17]

However, at least one antitheorist has insisted that viable resources of moral criticism will remain available to us long after moral theories have disappeared. Williams, in *Ethics and the Limits of Philosophy,* writes, "Nothing that has been said should lead us to think that traditional distinctions are beyond criticism; practices that make distinctions between different groups of people may certainly demand justification, if we are not to be content with unreflective traditions which can provide paradigms of prejudice."[18] Williams calls his alternative to moral theory "reflection," and he states unequivocally that it

should basically go in a direction opposite to that encouraged by ethical theory. ... A respect for freedom and social justice and a critique of oppressive and deceitful institutions may be no easier to achieve than they have been in the past, and may well be harder, but we need not suppose that we have no ideas to give them a basis. We should not concede to abstract ethical theory its claim to provide the only intellectual surroundings for such ideas.[19]

What does Williams mean by *reflection?* Is it really the case, as he insists, that it enables us to criticize moral practices without resorting to moral theory? The concept of reflection is most at home within the critical theory movement, and Williams's own use of the term owes clear debts to the way in which critical theorists such as Jürgen Habermas employ it. Although Williams does not offer a formal definition of what he means by *reflection,* the following passage serves both to give some sense of what he means by the term and to indicate how, on his view, reflection differs from ethical theory:

> What sorts of reflection on ethical life naturally encourage theory? Not all of them do. There is reflection that asks for understanding of our motives, psychological or social insight into our ethical practices, and while that may call for some kinds of theory, ethical theory is not among them. Nor is it merely that this kind of reflection is explanatory, while that which calls for ethical theory is critical. Much explanatory reflection is itself critical, simply in revealing that certain practices or sentiments are not what they are taken to be. This is one of the most effective kinds of critical reflection. It is a different kind of critical reflection that leads to ethical theory, one that seeks *justificatory reasons.*[20]

The kind of reflection Williams has in mind occurs when agents are led to see how they have acquired their normative beliefs and attitudes. Critical theorists often speak of this as "emancipatory self-reflection" (basically, freeing oneself from hidden forms of domination and repression through a depth explanation and understanding of social processes); but Williams intends it as a more extensive strategy for promoting not only freedom but justice and other ethical concerns, as well. Williams allows that such reflection "may call for some kinds of theory" (e.g., psychoanalysis or Marxist social theory) but not ethical theory, allegedly because ethical theory seeks justificatory reasons, which simply cannot be had. The strong justificatory urge of ethical theory is impossible to fulfill, Williams holds, because it involves a wish to see our moral life as endorsable from a standpoint external to it; and many aspects of human moral life cannot stand up to such impartial rational scrutiny:

> We may be able to show how a given moral practice hangs together with other practices in a way that makes social and psychological sense. But we may not be able to find anything that will meet a demand for justification made by someone standing outside those practices. We may not be able, in any real sense, to justify it even to ourselves. A practice may be so directly related to our experience that the reason it provides will simply count as stronger than any other reason that might be advanced for it.[21]

I believe there is good sense behind Williams's conviction that many of our moral practices are all too human and that they lose the only ground they have if we try to view them from a nonhuman perspective. But it certainly does not follow from this that such practices cannot be critically evaluated or that they can somehow be criticized effectively without invoking moral norms and justifications of these norms. Granted, our justifications often turn out to be more meager than we had hoped they would be, but this does not diminish their necessity in our thinking. Critical reflection only attains its goal when agents are able to defend or dismiss social practices *on the basis of arguments.*[22] For Habermas, the search for justificatory reasons is not an esoteric practice indulged in only by ethical theorists. It is built into the structure of everyday communication. In everyday communication we are constantly making various sorts of claims, and the communication continues only when there is a background consensus that the claims could be justified. When this background consensus breaks down, then justificatory reasons must be provided or else the communication will break down. In other words, for Habermas, the capacity to provide justificatory reasons is part of the "communicative competence" that defines us as members of a linguistic community. Contrary to what Williams says, showing that certain practices "are not what they are taken to be" is merely a first step. Defending or dismissing social practices on the basis of argument always involves an appeal to moral norms that one believes are rationally justifiable, and this, in turn, necessitates the resources of moral theory. Theorists will continue to debate the precise ways in which such norms can and cannot be rationally justified; but there is no getting around the necessity of normative justification (and hence moral theory) once one decides to venture into the arena of social criticism. The character of the arguments we are inevitably forced to employ in the moral sphere need to find their place within a larger theoretical framework in order to show that our criticisms are not ad hoc.

Williams's own use of the concept "reflection" therefore not only runs counter to how Habermas intended it to be understood, but is ultimately self-defeating, as well. Reflective knowledge in the moral sphere requires the resources of normative theory. Habermas himself, in seeking "to recover the forgotten experience of reflection" in his early work *Knowledge and Human Interests,* was explicitly trying to reappropriate a crucial insight of classical Greek *theōria* that most modern theorists unfortunately have dismissed—that is, "the insight that the truth of statements is linked in the last analysis to the intention of the good and true life."[23] In doing so, he was not only expressly acknowledging that critical reflection requires the resources of normative moral theory but also drawing attention to the fact that moral norms are embedded in, and presupposed by, all forms of critical thought (see chap. 4).

Imagination

Fourth, moral theories are indispensable aids in the cultivation and enlargement of moral imagination. Moral theorists seek not only to explain and criticize existing moral phenomena and the categories in terms of which such phenomena are understood but also to project new conceptions of how moral life ought to be and what it might become through acts of imaginative vision.[24] Part of the task of moral theory (a task it shares with art) is, in R. G. Collingwood's words, "to construct possible worlds, some of which, later on, thought will find real or action will make real."[25] In constructing possible worlds, moral theorists present us with avenues for moral change and development, as well as with ideals that can be used to defend the emerging or already-existing moral practices that may be in need of further support. The classic statement of the imaginative aim of moral theory is found in the following remark of Socrates:

> Do you think that there is any difference between the blind and those who are really deprived of the knowledge of every reality, who have no clear model [*par-adeigma*] of it in their soul and cannot, as painters can, look to that which is most true, always refer to it, contemplate it as exactly as possible, and so establish here on earth lawful [*nomima*] notions about things beautiful, just and good where they need establishing, or guard and preserve them once established? (*Republic* 484C–D)

Imagination is a frequently invoked word used in many different ways. As I am using it, the term basically refers to our capacity for a type of thought that transcends our experience and present knowledge—our ability to form meaningful mental *images* (hence, *to imagine*) or concepts that are not directly derived from either sensation or standing propositions in any rule-governed manner. Imagination is the ability to think in novel ways.[26] Imagination also enters into many different areas of moral life in fundamentally distinct ways. The type of broad-scale moral imagination referred to a moment ago (envisioning a more just society or a better life for individuals) is but one kind and needs to be contrasted with a more garden-variety type of moral imagination that plays a necessary role in all but the most mechanical acts of moral deliberation. This second type of moral imagination enters into mundane moral judgments in at least four ways: (1) when we selectively highlight certain details of a situation in order to declare that a moral principle is relevant to the case at hand, (2) when we weigh similarities between the situation at hand and others where the principle has proved to be applicable, (3) when we interpret the underlying metaphors involved in the formulation of the principle (e.g., "Treat all human beings as ends in themselves"), and (4) when we tailor the metaphorically understood moral precept to *this* particular state of affairs, thus making the situation determinate in a novel way.[27] At each of these stages or moments of moral deliberation, imaginative thought processes are required in the ways indicated. Furthermore, it seems that the acts of broad-scale imaginative vision referred to earlier (envisioning morally better worlds) may occasionally stand in tension with the more commonplace applications of moral imagination that are required whenever we attempt to see a specific moral situation before us clearly. Reflecting on a new moral order may tend to interfere with one's ability to pay close attention to the moral features of the situation at hand.[28]

In claiming that moral theories are indispensable aids in the cultivation and enlargement of moral imagination, I wish to be understood as saying that moral theories can help foster both these larger and also smaller or more ordinary dimensions of moral imagination. However, the sort of help that theory can offer each dimension of moral imagination will differ. In the first case, the theorist may be projecting a new conception of how society should be organized;

and readers are thus being presented with a vast array of novel possibilities. Here the effort is one of presenting broad-scale alternatives and then seeking to justify their plausibility. In the second case (judging specific situations), the sort of help that theory can provide is in most cases limited to that of providing an account of why and where imagination is needed, in offering criteria for determining when it does and does not "hit the mark," and in developing relevant hypothetical examples and exercises for strengthening its application; for, again, the power of judgment is a talent which can be practiced and strengthened through exposure to example but whose lack "no school [or theory] can make good."

It should be clear from what has been said so far that moral imagination is something human beings cannot do without. Without the capacity to envision moral alternatives, intentional moral change, growth, reform, and revolution are impossible. Even efforts to justify *existing* moral practices or to reappropriate and defend *past* moral practices will necessarily fail, for once the basic capacity to creatively envision moral ideals is renounced, all justificatory strategies become impossible. The defense, as well as the critique, of the moral status quo presupposes the ability to envision ideals by means of which existing practices and attitudes are to be evaluated. At the concrete level of everyday judgment, moral imagination is even more obviously necessary. Without the capacities for determining which precepts are relevant to the case at hand, for knowing how they apply in the present context, and so forth, moral deliberation and judgment are impossible.

Now antitheorists do not deny that moral imagination is necessary: they deny that moral theories are of any help in cultivating and enlarging moral imagination. On their view, works of literature (e.g., the novels of Henry James or the poems of William Wordsworth) are the only appropriate vehicles to stimulate and direct moral imagination. Martha Nussbaum, for instance, endorses Henry James's remark that the task of the moral imagination is "the effort really to see and really to represent" and then asserts that "this conception of moral attention and moral vision finds in novels its most appropriate articulation."[29] Since moral imagination finds its "most appropriate articulation" in novels, the implication is that moral theories are often inappropriate vehicles for articulating and stimulating moral imagination. Novels somehow have a monopoly on this particular project. As Nussbaum states in *Love's Knowledge,* "With respect to certain elements of human life, the terms of the novelist's art are alert winged creatures, perceiving where the blunt terms of . . . abstract theoretical discourse . . . are blind, acute where they are obtuse, winged where they are dull and heavy."[30] Why are theories unable to articulate the task of moral imagination appropriately? The style in which moral theory is written—specifically, its desire always to "speak in universal terms," as well as "the hardness or plainness" of its prose—prevent it from displaying the complexity and uniqueness of moral choice adequately.[31] Also, moral theory seeks to "converse with the intellect alone," whereas the kind of perception that moral imagination requires "centrally involves emotional response."[32]

Cora Diamond and others have offered a similar defense of literature over theory as the most appropriate vehicle for enlarging moral imagination. Diamond states that argument, or theoretical discourse, "is simply one way people approach moral questions, and there are other ways of trying to convince someone of one's view of animals or foetuses or slaves or children or whatever it may be." We are urged to recognize that imaginative literature is "of the greatest importance in developing and strengthening our moral capacities, and in turning them in new directions"—the implication being that theory is not of the greatest importance in turning our moral capacities in new directions.[33] Similarly, Richard Rorty announces in *Contingency, Irony, and Solidarity* that the imaginative ability "to see other human beings as 'one of us' rather than as 'them' " is a task "not for theory but for genres such as ethnography, the journalist's report, the comic book, the docudrama, and, especially, the novel."[34] Diamond argues that moral theorists construe the moral domain too narrowly by focusing exclusively on action and choice, whereas novelists understand morality more broadly and correctly by concerning themselves with the entire "texture of being." The theorist's specification of morality in terms of action and choice is "a limited and limiting one"; the literary artist's broader conception of morality enables him or her to cultivate the reader's moral imagination more effectively by drawing attention to the universe of gestures, manners, habits, and turns of thought in human character that more truly reveals moral attitudes.[35]

In defending moral theory's role in the cultivation of our imaginative capacities, I certainly do not intend to denigrate literature. In my view, literature, and indeed, *all* of the arts[36] are indispensable aids in the enlargement of moral imagination; but so, too, are philosophical theories. Furthermore, it should not be assumed that moral imagination can be stimulated *only* by means of art and/or theory. The ways and means by which moral imagination can be cultivated are probably infinite and certainly number larger than two.[37] This particular antitheory polemic is most unfortunate; for, as I shall try to show in responding to these above arguments for the superiority of literature, the ways in which art and theory enlarge moral imagination, in fact, tend to *complement* one another. Because they help each other out in achieving a common goal, there is no need to view the matter as a turf battle in which only one side can win.

Let us turn first to the arguments concerning style. It is simply false to declare that all traditional moral theories speak exclusively "in universal terms." Nussbaum herself recognizes that Aristotelian ethical theory is an important exception to this claim; but, as we have seen (chap. 6), so is the applied aspect of Kantian ethical theory. "All morals require anthropology in order to be applied to humans," Kant reminds us in the *Grounding;* and in saying this, he is explicitly acknowledging that empirical knowledge (of either a species-specific or more contingent situation-specific sort) is always necessary whenever ethical theory is applied to human circumstances. Since both Aristotle and Kant recognize that informed moral choice always requires judgments concerning particular, non-rule-governed features of situations, the charge that traditional moral theory speaks only in universal terms is a red herring. Furthermore, many poets and novelists definitely believe that their own works speak in fundamentally universal rather than particular terms. Shelley writes: "A poet participates in the eternal, the infinite, and the one; as far as relates to his conceptions, time and place and number are not. The grammatical forms which express the moods of time, and the difference of persons, and the distinction of place, are convertible with respect to the highest poetry without injuring it as poetry."[38] Thus clearly, we need to look elsewhere if we are going to find a solid stylistic difference between moral theory and fiction.

Perhaps, then, the stylistic difference we need is to be found in the alleged "plainness or hardness" of theoretical prose, which prevents it from doing justice to the complexity and indeterminacy of moral life? Here, we need first to note that this distinction between theoretical and fictional discourse is also much too overdrawn. Not all philosophy is plain and unambiguous (e.g., Plato's *Symposium* or Hegel's *Phenomenology of Spirit*); not all fiction containing moral insights is opulent and enigmatic (e.g., Huxley's *Brave New World* or Dreiser's *Sister Carrie*). But second, insofar as the plainness charge is intended to convince us that theory cannot cope with complexity and conflict in the moral domain, the proper response is simply to point out that a theory written in even the plainest and most unambiguous prose can allow for moral conflict by positing the claim that not all moral values are commensurable. As we saw earlier (pp. 106–8, 130–31), Kant, as well as increasing numbers of contemporary ethical theorists, are more than willing to grant this claim.

Although I believe Nussbaum is correct in holding that there is an organic connection between form and content and that different styles of writing do make different statements about what is important in the world, I do not think her dichotomy between theoretical style and literary narrative survives scrutiny. Part of the reason for this is that moral theory itself is, in Derrida's words, "a kind of writing." Figurative language pervades moral theory discourse, and its central concepts frequently rest on buried metaphors. The fact that novels and moral theories are both written in natural languages such as English and German means that they are both using the same basic tools of expression.[39] But not only do theorists and novelists use the same tools, they often share the same motives and goals as well. Again, Shelley writes:

> The distinction between poets and prose writers is a vulgar error. . . . All the authors of revolutions in opinion are not only necessarily poets as they are inventors, nor even as their words unveil the permanent analogy of things by images which participate in the life of truth; but as their periods are harmonious and rhythmical, and contain in themselves the elements of verse; being the echo of the eternal music.[40]

One commonsense way to differentiate the styles of fiction and theory (though even here, it is certainly not an absolute one)[41] is simply to note that theories characteristically seek to *justify* their claims through *argument*. The imaginative insights that a novel or poem offers, on the other hand, are not typically argued for. As Hilary Putnam remarks, "No matter how profound the psychological insights of a novelist may seem to be, they cannot be called *knowledge* if they have not been tested."[42] But here is precisely where theory can help fiction. The imaginative insights into moral life that literature offers frequently do exceed the insights that a straight-laced theory is able to propose. But theory can then take hold of these insights and seek to justify them, attempt to defend them, situate them within a more systematic context. ("Ethical science arranges the elements which poetry has created.")[43] I do not mean to suggest here that the proper relationship between theory and fiction must always be a master–slave one: moral theory's role must not be confined to carrying out the imaginative biddings of fiction. Both kinds of writing can and do push their own legitimate imaginative agendas. A related point is what Richard Wollheim, in his response to Nussbaum, calls "the requirement of the commentary."[44] Challenging works of fiction require commentaries; and in the process of commenting on, and seeking to understand, the moral insights expressed in a work of fiction, we inevitably employ the theories of others or engage in theorizing efforts of our own.

As for the charge that theory only engages our intellect and that our emotions must also be engaged in moral deliberation, we have already seen that Kant, too, like Aristotle, recognizes the fundamental importance of achieving a harmony between desire and reason in the moral life. The Kantian virtuous agent seeks to educate the emotions so that they act with, rather than against, reason (see chap. 2). Thus, nothing prevents moral theorists from acknowledging a necessary role for the emotions in human moral life; indeed, good moral theorists have always done so. But it is important to distinguish here between theories that seek to justify a necessary place for emotional response in moral deliberation on the one hand and literary or rhetorical appeals to the emotions on the other. Again, the fact that theorists must seek to justify their claims through critical argument is perhaps the greatest virtue of theoretical discourse, one that should not be jettisoned under any circumstances. Emotional appeals are not the best justificatory strategy, even if one grants that they often do have a legitimate role to play in moral argument.[45] Furthermore, we ought not to pretend either that nonfiction works are incapable of moving the emotions in ways that they need to be moved or that philosophical theories are always advanced without concern for rhetorical advantage.

Diamond's claim that argumentation is just *one* approach to moral questions is well taken. However, in so far as we wish to justify our moral positions to others, as well as to ourselves, it is an absolutely necessary approach. Contrary to what antitheorists often assume, this justificatory urge runs particularly deep in humans when they reflect on practical matters and is not merely a theoretician's occupational disease. Again, though, theorists themselves have no necessary monopoly on justificatory argument; sometimes poets and novelists outperform them in this area.

As for Diamond's further claim that the theorist's conception of morality is "a limited and limiting one" because it falsely construes the moral domain as being restricted to intentional action and choice, this is definitely the weakest of the arguments on behalf of literature's imaginative superiority. Nothing prevents a moral theorist from asserting that morality ought to be concerned with "the entire texture of a person's being"; indeed, as we saw earlier (chap. 2), increasing numbers of moral theorists are doing so at present. As more and more virtue-oriented programs gain ascendancy within contemporary moral debate, this particular criticism of Diamond's loses whatever relevance it originally possessed.

Furthermore, nothing guarantees that a novelist or poet who writes about moral issues will adopt this broader conception of morality. Conceivably, a fiction writer whose works contain valuable (or not so valuable) moral insights may adopt a narrow act-conception, rather than the broader agent-conception of the moral domain that Diamond advocates. Ironically, increasing numbers of contemporary fiction writers and literary critics seem to have accepted Oscar Wilde's pronouncement that there is "no such thing as a moral or immoral book. Books are well written, or badly written. That is all."[46] On this view, moral categories are totally irrelevant to literature; and it is very difficult to make sense out of such a claim unless the moral domain is construed extremely narrowly.

In sum, we need to insist on a negotiated settlement in the battle between literature and philosophy concerning who is the rightful servant of moral imagination. Imagination is indeed "the chief instrument of the good," as Dewey, following Shelley, remarked.[47] But our imaginative capacities need all the help they can get; thus, we require the powers of both theory and fiction in order to "imagine that which we know."[48]

Human Curiosity

I have argued that moral theories are necessary in explaining and interpreting many mundane aspects of human thought and action, in uncovering the specific conceptual schemes and categories in terms of which the moral experience of any given culture presents itself, in defending the moral practices that survive rational scrutiny and criticizing ones that do not, and in presenting new moral possibilities for our consideration. I have argued, additionally, that each of these four areas concerns a basic human need that must be addressed and that will remain unfulfilled in the absence of moral theories. In this final section, I shall argue that there is a further human need that moral theories satisfy, one that runs even deeper than the others. The presence of this final need in human life is, I believe, sufficient in and of itself to drive human beings continually to moral theory even if moral theories should prove to be, as antitheorists claim, totally impotent in addressing all of the needs described earlier.

Moral theorizing is one of the key activities by means of which human beings give expression to their pervasive curiosity concerning where and how they fit into the universe: how they ought to live their lives and how, in living their lives, they ought to relate to their fellow creatures, as well as to other forms of life. As self-conscious and rational beings who live in specific, enduring communities forged upon particular traditions, human beings experience a deeply seated need to express their sense of who and what they are, both individually and collectively, in respect to everything else in their universe of discourse. A central aspect of the quest for identity involves a dialogue with previous accounts of humanity's place, accounts produced by those who have come before us. The possible forms that this expressive activity may take are numerous and perhaps infinite; but because human beings are rational creatures who are able to take very large and long-term views on matters and also feel compelled to justify their views, one specific form that it inevitably takes is that of theory.

My present claim that moral theory is an indispensable expression of human curiosity is strongly indebted to similar remarks that John Plamenatz has made on behalf of political theory. In *Man and Society,* he writes:

> When Rousseau or Hegel or Marx tells us what is involved in being a man, he is not, when what he says cannot be verified, either expressing preferences or laying down rules; he is not putting "imperatives" in the indicative mood; he is not prescribing or persuading under the illusion that he is describing. He is not doing that or else talking nonsense. It might be said that he is telling his reader how he feels about man and the human predicament; or, more adequately and more fairly, that he is expressing some of the feelings that man has about himself and his condition. But he is not describing those feelings or just giving vent to them; he is *expressing* them, and the point to notice is that this expression takes the form of a theory about man and his condition. It could not take any other form. Thus, if it is an expression of feeling, the feeling requires systematic and conceptual expression. Only a self-conscious and rational creature could have such feelings about itself and its condition.[49]

In saying that moral theory is "one of" such key activities, I mean to underscore the point that it is not the only one. For some people, religion and/or art play a similar role;[50] and of course many people are drawn to some combination of all three activities. However, as indicated earlier, the prominence of the justificatory urge is what sets theorizing apart most clearly from both religious and artistic forms of expression; for when people do seek to express their curiosity concerning humanity's place in the universe by means of moral theory, it is crucial to note that the *form* such expression takes is one that involves broad systematic concerns and argumentation. For those who either turn to, or help to create, such products, there is a sense that the expressive activity *must* take this particular form and no other—that is, the form of theory. For many people, human beings' need to give expression to their curiosity concerning their place in the universe is not satisfied unless the form such expression takes is one that seeks to establish its case through argument and broad-scale reflection. As Plamenatz notes, only "a self-conscious and rational creature could have such feelings about itself and its condition." Humans may not be the only creatures possessing such properties, and possession of such properties may also give rise to other forms of expression in addition to theory (e.g., art and religion). But because human beings are self-conscious and rational creatures, many of them feel strongly the need to theorize about how and why they should live.

The phrase "give expression to" is meant to indicate that we may indeed not always be talking about propositional knowledge. Moral theorists, like other theorists, necessarily believe that what they have to offer does constitute knowledge; for the theoretical enterprise loses its reason for being unless this belief is retained. But what a theorist believes and what is actually the case are often quite different matters; and this is (as critics remind us) probably even more true within moral theory than elsewhere. Nevertheless, since moral theory is a form of expression in which argumentation and systematic concerns play central roles, the attempt to show that the concerns being expressed constitute knowledge is always present.

At the same time, even in cases where the moral theorist's hunt for knowledge has been shown to be unsuccessful (and admittedly, the history of ethical theory is riddled with such failures), the need to theorize about ethics is in no way diminished. The inherent pleasures of the search for knowledge depend on the conviction that there is some truth to be found (or created, as the case may be), but they are not dependent on the actual locating of such truth.[51] Indeed, how else could we account for humanity's continual consorting with moral theory once we remind ourselves of the antitheorist truism that no normative ethical theory has achieved anything close to universal acceptance? Even if all parties concerned could agree that no piece of what moral theorists have yet expressed constitutes knowledge, one suspects that the activity would nevertheless continue.

In asserting that moral theorizing constitutes a vital means of expressing human curiosity, I am not saying that everyone necessarily feels the need for it. Some people feel no need for poetry, and an even greater number may feel no need for moral theory. Clearly, some people can and do live without moral theory; and while it is often claimed that antitheorists themselves are, in spite of their best efforts, merely offering us one more theory, I do acknowledge the possibility of reflective ethical projects that are not moral theories.[52] But while arguments that aim to show that human beings have no need for moral theories may convince some who are already predisposed to such an outlook, experience shows that the vast majority of people have remained unmoved by such appeals.

Finally, there is the historical dimension. The expressive activity called moral theorizing involves, to a much higher degree than theorizing in, say, the biological and physical sciences, reflection back on previous efforts within its own theoretical domain, for most peoples' sense of how they should live is strongly influenced by previous accounts, accounts offered by earlier theorists (as well as others) that have taken root gradually within social institutions and family structures. People do not generally jump up from nowhere to choose moral values: both the manner of choosing and the values themselves have long historical trails. Whether we are aware of it or not, the history of moral theory lives on in contemporary debates concerning who and what we are. Our need to give expression to our sense of place nearly always includes a dialogue with previous expressive efforts, for our present moral identity is largely constituted out of them.

Obituaries for moral theory (like obituaries for religion and philosophy) have been written before, but subsequent history has always shown that the announcements have been a little premature. I have not quite claimed (as one recent friend of theory puts it) that one "cannot 'try' or 'not try' to be a theorist.

Theory is not simply a matter of intention or will or conscious agency. It is a matter of necessity; an impulse, an appetite."[53] Most appetites can and should be curbed occasionally, and I hope we are able to "stop doing moral theory when we want to."[54] But what would be the point of banishing entirely the natural appetite for moral theory? Such extreme temperance is only a virtue if the appetite in question can be shown to be thoroughly pernicious. I have argued that it is not. Perhaps the last word should be given to someone who followed his appetite:

> I cannot forbear having a curiosity to be acquainted with the principles of moral good and evil, the nature and foundation of government, and the cause of those several passions and inclinations, which actuate and govern me. I am uneasy to think I approve of one object, and disapprove of another; call one thing beautiful, and another deform'd; decide concerning truth and falshood, reason and folly, without knowing upon what principles I proceed. I am concern'd for the condition of the learned world, which lies under such a deplorable ignorance in all these particulars. I feel an ambition to arise in me of contributing to the instruction of mankind, and of acquiring a name by my inventions and discoveries. These sentiments spring up naturally in my present disposition; and shou'd I endeavour to banish them, by attaching myself to any other business or diversion, I *feel* I shou'd be a loser in point of pleasure; and this is the origin of my philosophy.[55]

Notes

Introduction

1. Michael Slote has perhaps developed the most extensive argument (*Goods and Virtues* [Oxford: Clarendon Press, 1983], chap. 4). His position owes some strong debts to Philippa Foot's "Are Moral Considerations Overriding?" in *Virtues and Vices* (Berkeley: University of California Press, 1978) and "Morality and Art," in *Philosophy as It Is,* ed. Ted Honderich and Myles Burnyeat (New York: Penguin, 1979), as well as to Bernard Williams's *Moral Luck* (New York: Cambridge University Press, 1981), chap. 2. Other important works on this topic include Susan Wolf's "Moral Saints," in *The Virtues: Contemporary Essays on Moral Character,* ed. Robert B. Kruschwitz and Robert C. Roberts (Belmont, Calif.: Wadsworth, 1987); Michael Stocker's *Plural and Conflicting Values* (Oxford: Clarendon Press, 1990), chap. 2; Harry Frankfurt's *The Importance of What We Care About* (New York: Cambridge University Press, 1988), chap. 7; Amélie O. Rorty's *Mind in Action* (Boston: Beacon, 1988); Owen Flanagan's "Admirable Immorality and Admirable Imperfection," *Journal of Philosophy* 83 (1986): 41–60; and Marcia Baron's "On Admirable Immorality," *Ethics* 96 (1986): 557–66.
2. Cf. Flanagan, "Admirable Immorality" p. 59.
3. Bernard Williams, *Problems of the Self* (New York: Cambridge University Press, 1973), p. 227.
4. Alasdair MacIntyre, *After Virtue: A Study in Moral Theory,* 2d ed. (Notre Dame, Ind.: University of Notre Dame Press, 1984), pp. 1–2. MacIntyre goes on to advance the "disquieting suggestion" that contemporary morality is in a state of "grave disorder."
5. Primary, but not sole. Comprehensive moral evaluation, on my view, should concern not only the lives people lead but also the rightness of their acts and the consequences of their acts. These are distinct value perspectives that should not be collapsed into each other. In the concluding section of chapter 2 I argue that Aristotle and Kant both recognize that an adequate moral theory must assess the lives, as well as the discrete acts, of moral agents.
6. Wolf, in "Moral Saints," concludes that the claims of her paper "call into question the assumption that it is always better to be morally better" (p. 151).
7. Most, but not all, since some writers in this tradition have begun to explore the possibility of consequentialist accounts of moral character. Such accounts urge us not so much to *do* what maximizes utility as to develop the character traits that tend to maximize utility and are thus (unlike most consequentialist theories) agent-centered rather than act-centered. See, e.g., Robert Adams, "Motive Utilitarianism," *Journal of Philosophy* 73 (1976): 476–81; Michael Slote, "Utilitarian Virtue" and Peter Railton, "How Thinking About Character and Utilitarianism Might Lead to Rethinking the Character of Utilitarianism," both in *Midwest Studies in Philosophy*, vol. 13, *Ethical Theory: Character and Virtue,* ed. Peter A. French, Theodore E. Uehling, Jr., and Howard K. Wettstein, (Notre

Dame, Ind.: University of Notre Dame Press, 1988). For more on consequentialist approaches to character, see Chapter 2, "Benthamite Virtue."

8. Bernard Williams, *Ethics and the Limits of Philosophy* (Cambridge: Harvard University Press, 1985), p. 174. Cf. Hilary Putnam, *Realism and Reason* (New York: Cambridge University Press, 1983), p. 246.

9. Michael Walzer, *The Company of Critics* (New York: Basic Books, 1988), p. 229. Important writings here include Annette Baier's *Postures of the Mind: Essays on Mind and Morals* (Minneapolis: University of Minnesota Press, 1985), chaps. 11, 12; Williams's *Ethics and the Limits of Philosophy*; Stuart Hampshire's *Morality and Conflict* (Cambridge: Harvard University Press, 1983); Edmund L. Pincoffs's *Quandaries and Virtues* (Lawrence: University of Kansas Press, 1986); and Stanley G. Clarke's "Anti-Theory in Ethics," *American Philosophical Quarterly* 24 (1987): 237–44. The anthology *Anti-Theory in Ethics and Moral Conservatism,* ed. Stanley G. Clarke and Evan Simpson (Albany: State University of New York Press, 1989), includes selections from several of the above works as well as an extensive bibliography on the topic. For an analogous recent debate within literary criticism, see also W. J. T. Mitchell, ed., *Against Theory* (Chicago: University of Chicago Press, 1985).

10. Allan Bloom, *The Closing of the American Mind* (New York: Simon and Schuster, 1987), pp. 81, 344.

11. Pincoffs, *Quandaries and Virtues,* p. 2.

12. The preferred strategy among many philosophers is to argue that antitheorists are guilty of one or more versions of a tu quoque fallacy ("You do it too"). For instance, to the antitheorist who claims that moral theory is an illegitimate attempt to guide practice from a position outside or above it, the philosopher replies that this criticism itself is an (illegitimate) attempt to guide the practice of moral theory from a position outside or above it. The antitheorist is thus shown to be merely a theorist in disguise. For the most part, I do not believe that a carefully constructed antitheorist position need tremble before the tu quoque charge. Not all reflective projects in ethics need be theoretical ones, and the monolithic assumption that no one can escape from the clutches of moral theory is too dogmatic. I do examine and respond to a number of specific antitheorist arguments in chapters 7 and 8; but it should be noted that my major aim is not to analyze and rebut all of their numerous arguments against theory but to show that their underlying conception of theory is historically unpersuasive. Regardless of how one judges the substantive contributions of either Aristotle or Kant to ethical theory, the tremendous weight of each philosopher's influence in the history of moral theory is acknowledged by all sides. If what is meant by *moral theory* does not capture at least a good portion of what they were trying to do, there is something wrong with the particular conception of theory being assumed.

13. Like several other contemporary philosophers, I reject the view that philosophy's sole legitimate task is to present arguments to compel readers logically to adopt the author's position. (See, e.g., Robert Nozick's criticisms of "coercive philosophy" in *Philosophical Explanations* [Cambridge: Harvard University Press, 1981], pp. 4–8; Janice Moulton, "A Paradigm of Philosophy: The Adversary Method," in *Discovering Reality,* ed. Sandra Harding and Merrill B. Hintikka [Dordrecht: Reidel, 1983]; and Richard Rorty, *Contingency, Irony, and Solidarity* [New York: Cambridge University Press, 1989], p. 44.) Historically speaking, most philosophers have set themselves a much wider and more varied agenda than this, although persuasive argumentation has always had a central and necessary place in the agenda. For a related view that also ties in to some of the antitheory issues to be explored in part II see Cora Diamond, "Anything but Argument?" *Philosophical Investigations* 5 (1982): 23–41. Like Diamond, I reject the claim that "only argument can convince" a person to adopt or reject a moral position (p. 40). Poets and novelists (not to mention songwriters, filmmakers and artists working in a variety of other media)

can often do a better job than philosophers "in developing and strengthening our moral capacities, and in turning them in new directions" (p. 41). At the same time, as I shall argue in part II, there still remain distinctive contributions for philosophers and other theorists to bring to our understanding and appreciation of morality. There is plenty of work for all to do.

Chapter 1

1. Williams first leveled this charge against utilitarian moral theories (see "A Critique of Utilitarianism," in J. J. C. Smart and Bernard Williams, *Utilitarianism: For and Against* [New York: Cambridge University Press, 1973], esp. p. 116); but in later writings (e.g., *Moral Luck,* chap. 1) the charge is extended to Kantian ethical theories, as well. See also Michael Stocker, "The Schizophrenia of Modern Ethical Theories," in *The Virtues,* ed. Kruschwitz and Roberts, and Lawrence A. Blum, *Friendship, Altruism, and Morality* (London: Routledge & Kegan Paul, 1980). For a critical discussion to which I am indebted, see Adrian M. Piper, "Moral Theory and Moral Alienation," *Journal of Philosophy* 84 (1987): 102–18.

2. Wolf, "Moral Saints," pp. 138, 139.

3. Wolf, "Moral Saints," p. 141.

4. Williams, *Moral Luck,* pp. 39, 23. See also Slote's discussion in *Goods and Virtues,* chap. 3. The Gauguin case appears to have been a favorite among academics for many years. See, for example, C. K. Grant, "Akrasia and the Criteria of Assent to Practical Principles," *Mind* 65 (1956): 405. Williams begins his description of Gauguin by announcing that we should not feel "we are limited by any historical facts" (p. 22), and this is prudent on his part. The historical Gauguin separated from his wife and five children in 1885 and did not visit Tahiti until 1891. Furthermore, it is arguable that Gauguin's basic motive for visiting Tahiti was—or at least was conceived by Gauguin to be—a moral rather than a nonmoral or antimoral one. In *Noa Noa: Voyage to Tahiti,* trans. Jonathan Griffin (New York: Reynal, 1962), Gauguin's own account of his first trip to the South Seas, he repeatedly emphasizes his desire to escape the decadence of Europe and to find a life-style that is in harmony with nature. His aim was to "get back to the ancient hearth, revive the fire in the midst of all these ashes . . . to get away from the European centre" (pp. 6–7, cf. p. 14). And he concludes his account by saying that "I had to go back to Europe—imperative family duties called me back. Goodbye, hospitable soil" (p. 26).

5. *When* exactly did the other-regarding conception of morality succeed in replacing the self-regarding one? Certainly, the switch came after Kant; and utilitarianism undoubtedly had something important to do with it ("Each to count for one, and none for more than one"). However, it is interesting to note that even Bentham, in his discussion of "ethics at large," subdivides the field into duties to oneself and duties to others. Of the former, he writes, "Ethics then, in as far as it is the art of directing a man's actions in this respect, may be termed the art of discharging one's duty to one's self: and the quality which a man manifests by the discharge of this branch of duty (if duty it is to be called) is that of *prudence*" (*An Introduction to the Principles of Morals and Legislation* [New York: Hafner, 1948], p. 312). Mill also tends to dismiss duties to oneself as mere matters of prudence: "The term duty to oneself, when it means anything more than prudence, means self-respect or self-development, and for none of these is anyone accountable to his fellow creatures, because for none of them is it for the good of mankind that he be held accountable to them" (*On Liberty,* ed. Elizabeth Rapaport [Indianapolis: Hackett, 1978], p. 77). At the same time, Mill's strong emphasis on self-development in *On Liberty* is itself clearly reminiscent of the Socratic care-of-soul doctrine.

Bradley and other idealist writers offered an important counterview to the utilitarian deflation of self, but their doctrine of self-realization in ethics remained a minority view: "[A] duty which is *not* a duty to oneself can not possibly be a moral duty" (F. H. Bradley, *Ethical Studies,* 2d ed. [New York: Oxford University Press, 1962], p. 219, n. 3). The tendency to dismiss self-regarding concerns as mere prudence (and to remove prudence from the sphere of the ethical) becomes even more pronounced in twentieth-century writings. See, for example, Marcus Singer, *Generalization in Ethics* (New York: Knopf, 1961), pp. 302–319; Kurt Baier, *The Moral Point of View* (Ithaca; N.Y.: Cornell University Press, 1958), chap. 9.

6. John Burnet, *Plato's Euthyphro, Apology of Socrates and Crito* (Oxford: Clarendon Press, 1924), p. 123. See also his note on *Apology* 30A8 on p. 124. Contra Burnet, I do not think Socrates was the first Greek to place priority on care of soul. One finds a similar emphasis in Heraclitus' well-known maxims: "I searched out myself. . . . Man's character [*ēthos*] is his destiny [*daimōn*]" (Diels-Kranz 101, 119). The Delphic maxim "Know thyself" is also an important precursor of the Socratic doctrine. Other relevant lines in the *Apology* concerning care of soul are 31B5, 36C6, 39D7, and 41E4. *Alcibiades I,* though not usually regarded as being written by Plato, is another important Socratic dialogue on this topic.

7. Philip Hallie, *Lest Innocent Blood Be Shed* (New York: Harper Torchbooks, 1985), p. 278. For a detailed discussion of Kant's doctrine of duties to oneself, see Mary J. Gregor, *Laws of Freedom* (New York: Barnes & Noble, 1963), chap. 8–11. Again, my view is that most moral theorists, until quite recently, have viewed morality as primarily self-regarding. Montaigne, for instance, writes: "To compose our character is our duty, not to compose books, and to win, not battles and provinces, but order and tranquility in our conduct. Our great and glorious masterpiece is to live appropriately. All other things, ruling, hoarding, building, are only little appendages and props, at most" (*The Complete Essays of Montaigne,* trans. Donald M. Frame [Stanford: Stanford University Press, 1958], pp. 850–51; cf. pp. 613, 852).

8. Warner A. Wick, Introduction to *Ethical Philosophy,* by Immanuel Kant, trans. James W. Ellington (Indianapolis: Hackett, 1983), p. lv. See also Wick's "More About Duties to Oneself," *Ethics* 70 (1960): 158–63, where he argues that without duties to ourselves, "the moral point of view makes no sense" (p. 158). I have also benefitted from W. D. Falk's "Morality, Self, and Others," in *Morality and the Language of Conduct,* ed. Hector-Neri Castaneda and George Naknikian (Detroit: Wayne State University Press, 1963), also in W. D. Falk, *Ought, Reasons, and Morality* (Ithaca, N.Y.: Cornell University Press, 1986). Ironically, even Michel Foucault, toward the end of his career, seems also to have advocated a similar care-of-soul doctrine: "There is another side to the moral prescriptions, which most of the time is not isolated as such, but is, I think, very important: the kind of relationship you ought to have with yourself, *rapport a soi,* which I call ethics, and which determines how the individual is supposed to constitute himself as a moral subject of his own actions" (*The Foucault Reader* ed. Paul Rabinow [New York: Pantheon, 1984], p. 352; see also his injunction to "create ourselves" on p. 351).

9. John Dewey, *Human Nature and Conduct* (New York: Holt, 1922), p. 7. I am indebted here to Pincoff's *Quandaries and Virtues,* pp. 101–14. (For related discussion, see pp. 58–60.)

10. Jesse Kalin, "In Defense of Egoism," in *Morality and Rational Self-Interest,* ed. David P. Gauthier (Englewood Cliffs: Prentice–Hall, 1970), p. 65.

11. For further discussion to which I am indebted, see Richard Kraut's *Aristotle on the Human Good* (Princeton, N.J.: Princeton University Press, 1989), pp. 78–154.

12. Cf. Pincoffs, *Quandaries and Virtues,* pp. 113–14. See also Nancy Sherman's critique of Aristotle's "grand scale" virtues in "Common Sense and Uncommon Virtue," in *Ethical Theory,* ed. French, Uehling, and Wettstein.

13. At the same time, it should be clear by now that I reject the liberal assumption that the

interests of others must be at stake before a judgment is to count as moral or that only acts that harm others are proper subjects of moral criticism. (See, e.g., Mill's discussion of the harm-to-others principle in *On Liberty*, chap. 1.) A solitary individual stranded in the middle of nowhere who never comes into contact with other persons at all must still decide how to live and what to do with him- or herself. We do not escape from morality even if we do manage to escape from other people.

14. Harry van der Linden, *Kantian Ethics and Socialism* (Indianapolis: Hackett, 1988), p. 40. This book presents an excellent defense of a socially responsible Kantian ethic. See also Alan Donagan's discussion of "the principle of culture" in *The Theory of Morality* (Chicago: University of Chicago Press, 1977), pp. 80–81. In claiming that self-regarding duties point to active social duties, it should be clear that I am here speaking more from a Kantian than an Aristotelian position. However, even on Aristotle's view, proper self-love will lead us to see that we owe certain things to other people and that the rightness of such treatment does not depend on its maximizing our own self-interests. See Kraut, *Aristotle on the Human Good*, pp. 153–54.

15. Falk, "Morality, Self," p. 34.

16. Falk, "Morality, Self," p. 34.

17. Wick, "More About Duties" p. 159. Presumably, most people will allow that the self-made derelict has made some poor choices. But why insist that these poor choices are *morally wrong* choices, particularly if they do not harm other people? Are we not in danger here of obliterating useful distinctions among qualitatively different varieties of poor choice? There are indeed many different kinds of poor choice available to us; and some of the things people do to themselves are simply imprudent rather than immoral. However, as noted earlier (see n.13), many of the things we do to ourselves—even if they effect no one else but ourselves—are proper subjects of moral evaluation.

18. Jeremy Bentham, *Bentham's Political Thought*, ed. Bhikhu Parekh (New York: Barnes & Noble, 1973), p. 94. See the opening paragraph of the *Grounding*, sec. 1, for Kant's dismissal of a variety of ancient Greek moral virtues. Strictly speaking, Kant himself recognizes only one moral virtue: fortitude or "moral strength of will," a moral necessitation by one's "own legislative reason, in so far as reason constitutes itself a power executing the law" (*DV* VI 404/66). However, since Kant states that it is "inevitable" (*unvermeidlich*) that we do think of a plurality of virtues when we focus on the objects of moral concern (VI 406/67) and since one of the most important of these objects is to treat all moral agents as ends in themselves rather than as means, he does, at a more informal level, allow that not only justice but a variety of character traits are indeed moral virtues.

19. Martha C. Nussbaum, *The Fragility of Goodness* (New York: Cambridge University Press, 1986), p. 30; cf. pp. 4–5, 28–30. See also Amélie Rorty's critique of "the myth of eminent domain" in *Mind in Action*, pp. 288–94.

20. Recently some writers, following Williams, have begun to distinguish ethics from morality, claiming that the latter is a deviant and mistaken subset of the former, one that places undue emphasis on the notions of duty and obligation (Williams, *Ethics and the Limits of Philosophy*, pp. 6, 174–96). Part of the current motivation for dropping the concept "moral" can be traced to Williams's critique of it (see, e.g., Nussbaum, *Fragility of Goodness*, pp. 29–30). However, while his dichotomy does bear some resemblance to Hegel's distinction between *Sittlichkeit* (the concrete ethics of one's community) and *Moralität* (Kantian universal morality), I find it historically unpersuasive and too much of a strain on ordinary ways of speaking. As should be clear by now, I treat the terms *morality* and *ethics* as synonyms. The etymology of morality (from the Latin *mores*, "manners, customs") is virtually identical to that of ethics (from the Greek *ethos*, "custom, habit"). On this point, it is also worth recalling the title of one of Williams's own earlier works—*Morality: An Introduction to Ethics* (New York: Harper Torchbooks, 1972).

21. "Not possible" because the concept of morality is open-textured. We can list some paradigm cases and conditions under which the concept "morality" correctly applies, but we cannot list all of them. Morality is not a static entity, and unforeseeable or novel conditions under which it might apply are inevitable. Also, as noted on p. 5, at present there are *multiple* moralities vying for our attention. But regardless which one we choose to examine, the hope of a formal definition is futile; for each one that has any life left in it is open-textured. At the same time, while I reject the formal definition quest, Part 1 of this book is an attempt to put forward an alternative conception of morality, and different properties of this alternative conception are presented in nearly every section of chapters 1–4. Adding all of these properties together still does not result in an exhaustive list of necessary and sufficient properties, but I believe that it does result in a more perspicuous understanding of morality.

22. I have borrowed this concept from Samuel Scheffler, "Morality's Demands and Their Limits," *Journal of Philosophy* 83 (1986): 534–35. I explore the idea of morality's pervasiveness in more detail in chapter 4.

23. Perhaps the most radical defense of this position is Robert M. Adams's "Involuntary Sins," *Philosophical Review* 94 (1985): 3–31, in which he defends the claim that "many involuntary states of mind are objects of ethical appraisal and censure in their own right" (p. 12). More moderate positions include John Sabini and Maury Silver, "Emotions, Responsibility, and Character," in *Responsibility, Character, and the Emotions,* ed. Ferdinand Schoeman (New York: Cambridge University Press, 1989), and Edward Sankowski, "Responsibility of Persons for Their Emotions," *Canadian Journal of Philosophy* 7 (1977): 829–40. I discuss the involuntary–voluntary distinction in more detail on pp. 64–65.

24. Part of the explanation for this is that the Greek term *aretē,* usually translated as "virtue," has a much wider range than our *moral virtue.* Animals and even inanimate objects all have their own special *aretai* or characteristic excellences, relative to their own proper functions. Also, the adjective *ēthikē* ("ethical" or "moral") is used by Aristotle to distinguish qualities of character from qualities of intellect, not moral traits from nonmoral traits. (Cf. Terence Irwin, "Aristotle's Concept of Morality," in *Proceedings of the Boston Area Colloquium in Ancient Philosophy,* vol. 1, ed. John Cleary [Washington, D.C.: University Press of America 1985], p. 119).

25. However, the possibility of conflict between the moral and *intellectual* excellences is a problem that looms large in the *Nicomachean Ethics.* Aristotle states in several places that the life of ethical activity is inferior to the life of contemplation (1141a20–23, 1145a6–11, 1177a12–79a33). Williams labels this Aristotelian failure adequately to defend the claims of the moral life against those of self-development in the arts and sciences the "Gauguin problem" (*Morality,* p. 61), a problem explored more thoroughly in *Moral Luck,* chap. 2. For an attempt to show that this alleged conflict is illusory, see Kraut, *Aristotle on the Human Good.*

26. Cf. *DV* VI 392/52: "With regard to natural perfection . . . reason gives no law for actions but only a law for the maxims of actions, which runs as follows: 'Cultivate your powers of mind and body so that they are fit to realize any end you can come upon,' for it cannot be said which of these ends could, at any time, become yours."

27. Kant does claim in the *Grounding* that the good will would, "like a jewel, still shine by its own light as something which has its full value in itself" even if it were completely unable to carry out any of its moral projects (IV 394/8). This extreme claim is intended to support the anticonsequentialist position that moral worth is not contingent upon results but is solely a matter of motive. However, to hold (as I do) that in daily life effectiveness does count and to assert that an effective good will be prized over an ineffective one is not to cave in to consequentialism. The property of effectiveness is not what gives moral projects their ultimate moral worth, but it is an important secondary value that ranks high in our moral judgments of others—in part because the motive itself

cannot be seen. As Thomas Nagel remarks, "However jewel-like the good will may be in its own right, there is a morally significant difference between rescuing someone from a burning building and dropping him from a twelfth-story window while trying to rescue him" (*Mortal Questions* [New York: Cambridge University Press, 1979], p. 25).

28. I have borrowed the distinction between enabling, or second-order, virtues and first-order virtues from William Frankena. See his discussion in *Ethics,* 2d ed. (Englewood Cliffs, Prentice–Hall, 1973), pp. 63–71.

29. Wolf, "Moral Saints," p. 140.

30. The lack of any solidly intersubjective consensus as to what constitutes an interesting personality is no small problem. Will everyone agree that humorous people are necessarily interesting? How humorous is humorous enough? What sorts of humor are appropriate here?

31. Stocker, "Schizophrenia," p. 40. For similar charges, see also Blum, *Friendship, Altruism,* chaps. 3–4.

32. John Rawls, *A Theory of Justice* (Cambridge: Harvard University Press, 1971), p. 190; Piper, "Moral Theory" p. 104. Examples of instances where critics do construe *impartiality* to mean *impersonality* include Blum, *Friendship, Altruism,* p. 44, and Williams, *Moral Luck,* p. 2.

33. Blum, *Friendship, Altruism,* p. 44: "In the Kantian conception of morality, impartiality and impersonality are central notions, definitive of the moral point of view." Cf. Williams (*Moral Luck,* p. 2), where he asserts that the moral point of view is "specially characterized by its impartiality and its indifference to any particular relations to particular persons."

34. Accordingly, in what follows I am not concerned with Aristotle's view of friendship, a view which does differ from Kant's in several fundamental respects. (For instance, in *NE* IX.4 Aristotle argues that friendship derives from self-love. Kant does not understand friendship as an extension of self-love.) But I do think Aristotle and Kant agree that true friends act for the sake of each of each other's good. For further discussion of Aristotle's views on friendship, see John M. Cooper, "Aristotle on Friendship," in *Essays on Aristotle's Ethics,* ed. Amélie O. Rorty (Berkeley: University of California Press, 1980), pp. 301–40. See also Nancy Sherman, *The Fabric of Character* (Oxford: Clarendon, Press, 1989), chap. 4, which opens with a brief comparison of Aristotelian and Kantian perspectives on friendship.

35. Blum, *Friendship, Altruism,* p. 45. Kant (or at least the ubiquitous and unnamed "Kantian") is also a primary target for Michael Stocker and Bernard Williams.

36. In the following account of Kantian friendship, I am indebted to H. J. Paton, "Kant on Friendship," *Proceedings of the British Academy* 42 (1956): 45–66 and Gregor, *Laws of Freedom,* pp. 199–202. The charge that Kantian ethics has no room for friendship is an old and familiar one; and though Paton seems to me to have acquitted Kant admirably, many contemporary critics appear to be unfamiliar with his essay.

37. Kant, *DV* VI 456–57/125. Cf. Paton, "Kant on Friendship," p. 46.

38. Paton, "Kant on Friendship," p. 50. Cf. Kant's discussion of moral feeling in *DV* VI 399/59–60.

39. Kant's emphasis on friendship as a relationship of particularity, and his remark that to be the friend of everybody is humanly impossible, are reminiscent of several of Aristotle's criticisms of Plato's attempts to promote unity among citizens in the *Republic:*

> For friendship we believe to be the greatest good of states.... But the unity [Plato] commends would be like that of the lovers in the *Symposium,* who, as Aristophanes says, desire to grow together in the excess of their affection, and from being two to become one, in which case one or both would certainly perish. In a state having women and children common, love will be watery; and the father will certainly not say "my son", or the son "my father". As a little sweet wine mingled with a great deal of water is imperceptible in the mixture, so, in

this sort of community, the idea of relationship which is based upon these names will be lost. (*Pol* 1262b7–20)

40. I would like to thank Robert C. Roberts for bringing this point to my attention.

Chapter 2

1. The broad question of *how* to evaluate character leaves room for many alternative approaches. As noted in the Introduction, some theorists have begun to explore the possibility of utilitarianisms that focus not on consequences of acts or events, but on the traits of agents. Thus, we have utilitarianisms of virtue, or character utilitarianisms, which urge us not so much to *do* what maximizes utility as to *cultivate the traits* that will tend to maximize utility. However, it remains the case that most approaches to ethics that place primary evaluative focus on agents rather than acts are decidedly antiutilitarian in tone.

2. Why *naturally?* Virtue theorists nearly always assume that people who believe that morality is primarily about the evaluation of acts rather than of agents are also necessarily committed to the additional claim that moral theory must seek to develop *rules* of right action. However, there is no necessary connection between the "act" and "rule" assumptions. "Act deontologists" believe that morality's primary job is to evaluate acts, but they reject the claim that there any rules of right action. See, for example, E. F. Carritt's critique of moral rules in *Theory of Morals* (Oxford: Clarendon Press, 1928), chap. 13; Jean-Paul Sartre, "Existentialism Is a Humanism," in *Existentialism from Dostoevsky to Sartre,* ed. Walter Kaufmann (Cleveland: Meridian Books, 1956); and Frankena, *Ethics,* pp. 23–25. The recent revival of "particularist" theories of ethics is also relevant here, since particularists deny the existence of moral principles and are not necessarily committed to the agent assumption. See, example, Jonathan Dancy, "Ethical Particularism and Morally Relevant Properties," *Mind* 92 (1983): 530–47. Finally, it has also been argued that the antirule bias of contemporary virtue theorists itself embodies an impoverished, modern conception of what constitutes a moral rule. For a recent attempt to show that virtues are not only compatible with, but entail, rules (albeit rules in a broader sense), see Robert C. Roberts, "Virtues and Rules," *Philosophy and Phenomenological Research* 51 (1991): 325–43.

3. But why *inevitably?* Here, too, there appear to be two independent claims that bear no necessary connection to one another. A person might well think that the project of developing rules and principles of morally right action is important and viable but also hold that there exists an irreducible plurality of such rules with no megarule waiting in the wings to solve all conflicts of principle. W. D. Ross's pluralistic doctrine of prima facie duties remains the best example of this approach. See *The Right and the Good* (Oxford: Clarendon Press, 1930), pp. 16–34, 41–42, and related discussion in Christopher W. Gowans's anthology, *Moral Dilemmas* (New York: Oxford University Press, 1987).

4. Could one decide to focus on character without necessarily asking what the good life for human beings is? Perhaps, but it is very difficult to see what the point of such a project would be. Virtues (Latin *virtus,* "manly excellence"; Greek *aretē,* "excellence") are traits that people need in order to live well, and the traits that are deemed virtues receive their status in terms of the larger account of what constitutes living well. If one declines to undertake the normative project of articulating an ideal of flourishing, how would one determine which traits are to count as virtues? ("Excellence" with regard to what?) At the same time, the conflicting assumptions concerning the nature of the good life that one finds in various virtue ethics programs serve to underscore in a different way the earlier point (n.1) that virtue ethics come in many different sizes and shapes.

5. G. E. M. Anscombe, "Modern Moral Philosophy," in *Ethics,* ed. Judith J. Thomson and

Gerald Dworkin (New York: Harper & Row, 1968), pp. 196, 203–4. Of course, Aristotle's analysis of the virtues is not without its own theistic assumptions. One of his major arguments in support of the claim that *nous,* or "contemplative activity," is the highest virtue is that it is "divine," (*theion*). We must, "so far as we can, make ourselves immortal, and strain every nerve to live in accordance with the best thing in us" (*NE* 1177b34–35).

6. See, for example, George Henrik von Wright, *The Varieties of Goodness* (New York: Routledge & Kegan Paul, 1963), p. 136; Lawrence C. Becker, "The Neglect of Virtue," *Ethics* 85 (1975): 110–22; and Foot, *Virtues and Vices,* p. 1.

7. For a representative survey, see the essays (as well as extensive critical bibliography) in Kruschwitz and Roberts, eds., *The Virtues.* More recent collective contributions to the literature include French, Uehling, and Wettstein, eds., *Ethical Theory,* and a double-issue "Work on Virtue," *Philosophia* 20, (1990).

8. Gregory W. Trianosky, "What Is Virtue Ethics All About?" *American Philosophical Quarterly* 27 (1990): 335. Trianosky attempts to provide a "systematic guide" to the virtues literature by listing nine "neo-Kantian" claims, of which he is convinced that "nearly every writer on the virtues rejects at least one." The attempt is noble; but I am doubtful that any "systematic guide" will meet with the approval of all participants in the virtue ethics debate, due in part to strong antisystematic tendencies within the movement. For more on this theme, see my "Virtue Ethics and Anti-Theory," *Philosophia* 20 (1990): 92–102.

9. Several readers of an earlier version of this chapter have remarked that the present defense of virtue ethics seems to be inconsistent with my earlier criticisms of it in "On Some Vices of Virtue Ethics," in *The Virtues,* ed. Kruschwitz and Roberts. As Louis Pojman remarked, "It's almost as though Louden has forgotten what he's written." For what it's worth, I do not think my views on this issue have changed in any cataclysmic ways. In the earlier piece, I was criticizing strong virtue-based programs that see no need to concern themselves with the evaluation of acts and of consequences of acts. Such approaches, I argued, suffer from the same reductionist defect of their deontological and utilitarian opponents—all of them employ mononomic or single-principle strategies that falsely assume that the moral field is unitary and that all important moral concerns can be covered adequately by one master category. In this chapter I am defending a view of morality that places primary evaluative focus on character but also recognizes the need for independent conceptual resources to evaluate acts and consequences of acts. My own position—then as now—is a pluralist one. I do not think mononomic or single-principle strategies work well in ethics, since (as I stated at the conclusion of "On Some Vices") the moral field is not unitary and the values we employ in making moral judgements sometimes have fundamentally different sources. At the same time, I have always believed that assessment of character is what is most important in moral evaluation. Assessment of acts and their consequences should be assigned a secondary but still necessary role.

10. Pincoffs, *Quandaries and Virtues,* p. 19.

11. David L. Norton, "Moral Minimalism and the Development of Moral Character," in *Ethical Theory,* ed. French, Uehling, and Wettstein, pp. 183, 187. The claim that *"nothing in human experience is without moral meaning"* (my emphasis) seems to me to be an overstatement and should at least be qualified to exclude certain completely *involuntary* aspects of human experience (e.g., the fact that one is color blind) from coming under the purview of moral assessment. For further discussion, see pp. 63–68.

12. Sarah Conly, "Flourishing and the Failure of the Ethics of Virtue," in *Ethical Theory,* ed. French, Uehling, and Wettstein, p. 83.

13 Conly, "Flourishing and the Failure," p. 83. Cf. William's discussion of integrity in Smart and Williams, *Utilitarianism,* and in *Moral Luck,* chap. 1, and Stocker, "Schizophrenia."

14. Barbara Herman in her essay "The Practice of Moral Judgment," *Journal of Philosophy* 82

(1985): 414–36, discusses "rules of moral salience" in an interesting attempt to give a more realistic account of how rules might function within a Kantian theory of moral judgment. I agree with her claim that the capacity to know what is morally salient is an important but underappreciated aspect of Kant's theory of moral judgment. However, I believe her claim that Kant holds that agents acquire such salience-locating skills primarily *through rules* is false. The ability to pick out morally salient features is not learned primarily through rules. For more on this issue, see my "Go-Carts of Judgment: Exemplars in Kantian Moral Education," forthcoming in *Archiv für Geschichte der Philosophie*. See also Nancy Sherman's Aristotelian discussion of moral salience in *Fabric of Character*, pp. 28–44.

15. Joel J. Kupperman, "Character and Ethical Theory," in *Ethical Theory*, ed. French, Uehling, and Wettstein, p. 121.

16. Norton, "Moral Minimalism," pp. 184–85.

17. Morality thus appears to be an example of what George Lakoff calls a *radial category*. There are central instances of moral virtues that remain constant (e.g., self-control, justice, and beneficence), but there will also be conventional variations on the central cases that cannot be predicted by general rules. The variations cannot be logically generated from the central cases but are culturally defined and must be contextually learned. See George Lakoff, *Women, Fire, and Dangerous Things: What Categories Reveal About the Mind* (Chicago: University of Chicago Press, 1987), pp. 83–84, 91–114.

18. I would like to thank Robert C. Roberts for bringing these two points to my attention. For further discussion of links between ethics and the life sciences, see James D. Wallace, *Virtues and Vices* (Ithaca, N. Y.: Cornell University Press, 1978), pp. 18–25.

19. Unless noted otherwise, the three terms are used synonymously in the following discussion.

20. Anscombe, "Modern Moral Philosophy," p. 196.

21. Williams, *Ethics and the Limits of Philosophy*, p. 16. In an earlier piece, Williams made the even more startling claim that ancient Greek thought "lacks a concept of *morality* altogether, in the sense of a class of reasons or demands which are vitally different from other kinds of reason or demand" ("Philosophy," in *The Legacy of Greece*, ed. M. I. Finley [New York: Oxford University Press, 1981], p. 251; cf. Williams, *Ethics and the Limits of Philosophy*, p. 32). In *Ethics and the Limits of Philosophy*, "morality" is defined as "a particular development of the ethical, one that . . . emphasizes certain ethical notions rather than others, developing in particular a special notion of obligation" (p. 6).

22. Alexander Grant, *The Ethics of Aristotle*, 3d ed. (London: Longmans, Green, 1874), vol. 1, p. 422.

23. D. J. Allan, *The Philosophy of Aristotle*, 2d ed. (New York: Oxford University Press, 1970), p. 140. Cf. Arthur W. H. Adkins, *Merit and Responsibility* (Oxford: Clarendon Press, 1960): "That there should exist a society so different from our own as to render it impossible to translate 'duty' in the Kantian sense into its ethical terminology at all . . . is, despite the evidence, a very difficult idea to accept" (pp. 2–3).

24. MacIntyre, *After Virtue*, p. 236. Similarly, in his earlier work, *A Short History of Ethics* (New York: MacMillan, 1966), MacIntyre states: "In general, Greek ethics asks, What am I to do if I am to fare well? Modern ethics asks, What ought I to do if I am to do right? And it asks this question in such a way that doing right is made something quite independent of faring well" (p. 84). See also Foot, *Virtues and Vices*, p. 1; Pincoffs, *Quandaries and Virtues*, pp. 13–15; and Richard Taylor, "Ancient Wisdom and Modern Folly," in *Ethical Theory*, ed. French, Uehling, and Wettstein, p. 54.

25. Again, I am defending an approach to moral evaluation that although placing primary emphasis on the evaluation of character, also recognizes the need to assess acts and consequences of acts. Cf. n. 9.

26. By *modern* I mean chiefly eighteenth-century European views of morality. For purposes

of illustration, I shall examine Bentham's and Kant's conceptions of virtue. I do agree that much *twentieth*-century ethical theory (say, prior to the 1960s) pays scant attention to virtue concepts. My position regarding the much-heralded neglect-of-virtue charge is that it is actually a much more recent and temporary phenomenon than alleged. For a recent attempt to document the claim that virtue was not neglected during the seventeenth and eighteenth centuries, see J. B. Schneewind, "The Misfortunes of Virtue," *Ethics* 101 (1990): 42–63.

27. Grant does not say anything concerning what is meant by " 'our duty' in the modern sense"; Allan, in his reference to "the motive of moral obligation," implies only that it is to be contrasted with "self-interest, more or less enlightened." Anscombe does refer repeatedly to a special moral sense of ought throughout her essay, but the central claim she makes on its behalf (i.e., that it is a survival of "Christianity, with its *law* conception of ethics," p. 191) is termed "a mistake" by Donagan (*Theory of Morality*, p. 3). I agree with Donagan's assessment: we can talk intelligibly about moral laws without necessarily referring to divine lawgivers. Williams's discussion of moral oughts and obligations in *Ethics and the Limits of Philosophy* is more level-headed, and I believe the following analysis departs from his position only in its failure to insist that moral obligations "cannot conflict, ultimately, really, or at the end of the line" (p. 176).

28. W. F. Hardie, *Aristotle's Ethical Theory*, 2d ed. (Oxford: Clarendon Press, 1980), p. 334. MacIntyre, for instance, recognizes the concept of role-related duties in Aristotle when he characterizes ancient Greece as "a society in which the use of evaluative words is tied to the notion of the fulfillment of a socially established role" (*Short History*, p. 89).

29. Following Williams, *Ethics and the Limits of Philosophy*, p. 175. Cf. the Kantian maxim " 'Ought' implies 'can.' " The issue of what does and what does not count as being "in our power" at the moment of action as opposed to being within our power during the course of the formation of character is explored by Aristotle in *NE* III.5. Clearly, questions concerning the *scope* of acts and attitudes that are in our power are separable from the basic issue of whether or not moral oughts concern acts that are in our power, which means (among other things) that two theorists who disagree on specifics of scope may yet concur on the in-our-power issue.

30. Cf. Anscombe's remark that the moral sense of ought implies "some absolute verdict (like one of guilty/not guilty on a man)" ("Modern Moral Philosophy," p. 191) and Williams's statement that blame "is the characteristic reaction of the morality system" (*Ethics and the Limits of Philosophy*, p. 177). Here, too, the scope issue of what does and what does not count as a "recognized excuse" is separable from the basic question of whether or not failure to act as one ought without a recognized excuse reflects poorly on one's character. For instance, people sometimes fail to do what they ought to do for reasons of immaturity, but not everyone will allow that immaturity counts as a "recognized excuse."

31. However (as argued in chap. 1) moral oughts and obligations can be, and are, performed for reasons of self-interest if by *self-interest* is meant not the usual egotistic or narcissistic motives but obedience to the voice of reason within oneself. This sense of trying to educate one's desires so that they listen to reason and follow its advice (or, as Aristotle puts it, gratifying "the most authoritative element in oneself and in all things obey[ing] this," *NE* 1168b30–31) is central not only to classical Greek ethics but also to Kantian ethics. I therefore disagree with Terence Irwin's claim that "we tend to identify moral principles ... with those that refer to the welfare of those affected by them" insofar as this statement appears to equate moral principles exclusively with other-regarding principles ("Aristotle's Concept," p. 116). For instance, Irwin states that "the feature of virtue that is properly praised is its tendency to benefit others" (p. 127). See also Nancy Sherman's "Commentary on Irwin," in *Proceedings, of the Boston*, ed. Cleary, vol. 1, pp. 149–50, where she argues that the self-regarding aspect of Aristotelian ethics is stronger than

Irwin acknowledges, and Irwin's discussion in *Aristotle's First Principles* (Oxford: Clarendon Press, 1988), pp. 379–81. Here Irwin does note that on Aristotle's view the "good person has correct concern for herself, since she is concerned for herself as a rational agent" (p. 381; cf. p. 393). Again, on my view, the most important moral principles are fundamentally self-regarding in this rational-self sense, according to both ancient and modern theorists.

32. This analysis borrows some points from Richard Brandt, "The Concepts of Obligation and Duty," *Mind* 73 (1964): 374–93, and C. H. Whitely, "On Duties," in *Moral Concepts,* ed. Joel Feinberg (New York: Oxford University Press, 1970). I would also like to thank Steven Tigner for his helpful criticisms of an earlier-formulated version of this list.

33. Note that I have not claimed that this sense of ought is "the central concept of ethics." Contrast Adkins: "For any man brought up in a western democratic society the related concepts of duty and responsibility are the central concepts of ethics" (*Merit and Responsibility,* p. 2). It seems to me that most people today would say that morality involves a variety of different concepts. A sense of ought is *a* central concept in a moral scheme, but to declare it *the* central one is a reductionist error.

34. Hardie, *Aristotle's Ethical Theory,* p. 335. Many other scholars have drawn attention to these same terms. See, for example, (particularly on *dikaion* and *kalon*) Irwin, "Aristotle's Concept"; and (particularly on *kalon* and *dein*), R. A. Gauthier, "On the Nature of Aristotle's Ethics" in *Aristotle's Ethics: Issues and Interpretations,* ed. J. J. Walsh and H. L. Shapiro (Belmont, Calif.; Wadsworth, 1967), pp. 20–23.

35. R. Gauthier, "On the Nature," p. 21. I am unable to confirm Gauthier's claim of 170 appearances of a moral *dei* in the *Nicomacheon Ethics,* but the precise number is not important for my purposes. Admittedly, Gauthier says less than one would like concerning the criteria by which we are to discriminate the "uncontestably moral" sense of *dei.* On my view, the proper criteria to employ are the earlier-specified four conditions.

36. Cf. Anscombe, "Modern Moral Philosophy," pp. 186, 191, 193, 195. Other relevant passages in the *Nicomacheon Ethics* where *dei* is used in (what I believe is) a moral sense include 1094a24, 1107a4, 1121b4, 1121b12, 1122a31–33, 1122b9, 1152a21, and 1169a10. (This list is not exhaustive.)

37. Irwin opts for "the fine" as "a fairly non-committal translation of *kalon*" ("Aristotle's Concept," p. 121, n.9). See pp. 120–38 of his essay for a detailed discussion of aesthetic versus moral uses of *kalon* in Aristotle. Joseph Owens, in "The *Kalon* in Aristotelian Ethics," in *Studies in Aristotle,* ed. Dominic J. O'Meara (Washington: Catholic University of America Press, 1981), argues that "the English word 'right' seems on most occasions appropriate to translate the Greek *kalon* in the moral setting" (p. 267). I agree with Owens that acts that are *kalon* "in the moral setting" are morally right acts, but I prefer the more literal translation "noble." D. J. Allan, in "The Fine and the Good in the Eudemian Ethics," in *Untersuchungen zur Eudemischen Ethik,* ed. Paul Moraux and Dieter Harlfinger (Berlin: de Gruyter, 1971), also translates *kalon* as "the fine."

38. Cf. Owens's remark that "the Greek term *kalon* and the impersonal *dei* . . . are used interchangeably in the *Ethics*" ("*Kalon* in Aristotelian Ethics," p. 263). Owens refers readers to 1104b10–12, 1115a12, and 1120a9–21a4.

39. For a detailed discussion of Aristotle on external goods, see John Cooper's essay, "Aristotle on the Goods of Fortune," *Philosophical Review* 94 (1985): 173–96.

40. R. G. Mulgan, *Aristotle's Political Theory* (Oxford: Clarendon Press, 1977), p. 80. As Mulgan notes, the Greek word *nomos* "covers not only laws in the sense of statutes passed by legislative bodies but also any shared rule of social behaviour, such as unwritten customs and conventions" (p. 79).

41. See J. M. Rist, "An Early Dispute About *Right* Reason," and D. P. Dryer, "Aristotle's Conception of *Orthos Logos,*" in the *Monist* 66 (1983): 39–48, 106–19. Earlier articles on *orthos logos* that I have found useful are J. Cook Wilson, "On the Meaning of *Logos*

in Certain Passages in Aristotle's *Nicomachean Ethics," Classical Review* 27 (1913): 113–17; J. L. Stocks, "On the Aristotelian Use of *Logos:* A Reply," *Classical Quarterly* 8 (1914): 9–12; and J. A. Smith, "Aristotelica," *Classical Quarterly* 14 (1920): 18–22.

42. The phrase is David Wiggins's. See his "Deliberation and Practical Reason," in *Essays on Aristotle's Ethics,* ed. Rorty. See also my "Aristotle's Practical Particularism," in *Essays in Ancient Greek Philosophy,* vol. 4, ed. John P. Anton and Anthony Preus (Albany: State University of New York Press, 1991).

43. Cf. R. Gauthier's analysis of these verbs in his discussion of the imperatival sense of *logos* in "On the Nature" pp. 22–23.

44. Aristotle's notorious remark that "the slave has no deliberative faculty [*bouleutikon*] at all; the woman has, but it is without authority [*akuron*]" (*Pol* 1260a12–13) does not seem to me to be entirely consistent with his claim that all humans have the gift of *logos*. His considered view seems to be that there exists a natural hierarchy within the human species: every *anthropos* has the gift of *logos* to some minimal degree; but certain groups within the species (e.g., free men) possess the gift to a much higher degree than others (e.g., natural slaves). Since the ability to deliberate well is the defining characteristic of practical wisdom (1140a26), natural slaves and women, on Aristotle's view, can never acquire this central virtue. Nevertheless, even if we are to infer (as I think we should) that the scope of Aristotelian ethics in the strict sense extends only to free Greek males, it will still remain the case that within this group, many of the things that agents ought to do will not be a function of their social roles. For further discussion of Aristotle's views on the rationality of slaves and women, see W. W. Fortenbaugh, "Aristotle on Slaves and Women," in *Articles on Aristotle,* vol. 2, ed. Jonathan Barnes, Malcolm Schofield, and Richard Sorabji (New York: St. Martin's Press, 1977), pp. 135–39.

45. Other passages in the *Nicomacheon Ethics* where *logos* is used in discussions of what people ought to do include 1138b25, 1138b29, 1147b3, 1151a12, 1151b21, 1169a5. (This list is far from exhaustive. See the numerous entries under *logos* in Bywater's index for others.)

46. But this is not as odd as it may seem. As Irwin notes, "The term *arete* has a much wider range than morality; and the qualification implied in *ēthikē* confines us to character as opposed to intellect, not to moral as opposed to non-moral qualities" ("Aristotle's Concept," p. 119).

47. Donald Davidson, "On the Very Idea of a Conceptual Scheme," in *Inquiries into Truth and Interpretation* (Oxford: Clarendon Press, 1984), pp. 196–97. (I am grateful to Norman Dahl for insightful criticisms of an earlier version of this section.)

48. Bentham, *Bentham's Political Thought,* pp. 88–89. (One should not infer from the fact that the manuscript of *The Nature of Virtue* remained unpublished during Bentham's lifetime that it is necessarily of only minor significance. Many of Bentham's works remained unfinished, and those that he did finish he often did not bother to publish. His collected works have yet to appear in a complete edition.)

49. Bentham's "*tendency* to give a net increase" (emphasis mine), seems to support the notion that a virtuous utilitarian would not—contrary to what critics often claim—be possessed by a single-minded pattern of motivation to maximize utility in every act. It is a general, overall tendency rather than a single-minded devotion to maximize utility that Bentham is after. Cf. Henry Sidgwick: "Happiness is likely to be better attained if the extent to which we set ourselves consciously to aim at it be carefully restricted" (*The Methods of Ethics,* 7th ed., [New York: Dover, 1966], p. 405; see also Adams's discussion of this issue in "Motive Utilitarianism," p. 467).

50. Jeremy Bentham, *An Introduction to the Principles of Morals and Legislation* (New York: Hafner, 1948), p. 102. Cf. Adams, "Motive Utilitarianism," p. 468, and Slote, "Utilitarian Virtue," p. 385.

51. Bentham, *Introduction to the Principles,* p. xxv. Cf. Slote, "Utilitarian Virtue," p. 385.

52. Bentham, *Bentham's Political Thought,* p. 94. In fact, the Aristotelian virtues of liberality and magnificence, though certainly not identical to Benthamite benevolence, do overlap with it quite a bit.

53. Bentham, *Bentham's Political Thought,* pp. 93–94.

54. Bentham, *Bentham's Political Thought,* p. 94. See Slote, "Utilitarian Virtue," pp. 389–91 for one attempt to give a utilitarian account of courage. Slote suggests that courage can be counted as a utilitarian virtue if we make "the courageousness or cowardice of an appropriate act depend solely on its overall, long-term results." But the issue of whether short-term or long-term results are to be gauged is not what is fundamental. Whatever trait is to be called courage must pass an empirical test of either pleasure production or pain aversion. It seems unlikely that much of what is traditionally called "courage" will survive utilitarian analysis.

55. Some of the material in this section is taken from my "Kant's Virtue Ethics," *Philosophy* 61 (1986): 473–89. For more on Kant and virtue, see Onora O'Neill, *Constructions of Reason: Explorations of Kant's Practical Philosophy* (New York: Cambridge University Press, 1989), chap. 8, and Roger J. Sullivan, *Immanuel Kant's Moral Theory* (New York: Cambridge University Press, 1989), chaps. 9–10. See also Schneewind, "Misfortunes of Virtue," pp. 113–16.

56. See also Sullivan's examination of Kantian moral emotions in *Immanuel Kant's Moral Theory,* pp. 132–36. Additional moral emotions discussed by Sullivan include humility, pain, moral contentment, guilt, and remorse.

57. Cf. Marcia Baron's discussion in "On the Alleged Moral Repugnance of Acting from Duty," *Journal of Philosophy* 81 (1984): 179–219, esp. p. 204: "Part of what one morally ought to do is cultivate certain attitudes and dispositions, e.g., sympathy rather than resentment or repulsion for the ailing; a cheerful readiness to help and to find ways in which one can help out."

58. This is a point stressed in several of Barbara Herman's essays: "On the Value of Acting from the Motive of Duty," *Philosophical Review* 90 (1981): 359–82, esp. pp. 372–76, and "The Practice of Moral Judgment," *Journal of Philosophy* 82 (1985): 414–36, esp. pp. 424–25. See also Nancy Sherman, "The Place of Emotions in Morality" (Georgetown University, 1990, mimeographed).

59. Blum, *Friendship, Altruism,* p. 2. See his chap. 1 for a critique of (what he takes to be) the Kantian view on the place of emotions in morality.

60. Wallace, *Virtues and Vices,* p. 130.

61. O'Neill, *Constructions of Reason,* p. 59. I discuss the place of rules in Kant's ethics in more detail on pp. 113–16.

62. Clearly, the distinction between natural, or pathological, and moral, or practical, feelings is important to Kant; and it is not my intent to downplay its significance. He views the former as passive, unfree, and nonrational; the latter as active, free, and rational. Natural feelings do possess a different status than do moral feelings, but this difference is not captured by invoking the instrumental–intrinsic status distinction. Both natural and moral feelings have intrinsic worth for human beings.

63. I do not think the same is true of Bentham.

Chapter 3

1. Wolf, "Moral Saints," pp. 140, 151. See also Stocker's defense of the claim that "what is less than best may be good enough" (*Plural and Conflicting Values,* chaps. 9–10).

2. Robert Merrihew Adams, *The Virtue of Faith and Other Essays in Philosophical Theology* (New York: Oxford University Press, 1987), pp. 171–73. Cf. Wolf, "Moral Saints," p. 149.

3. Williams, *Ethics and the Limits of Philosophy,* p. 174. The intended rhetorical shock of this passage is muted considerably by Williams's own idiosyncratic usage of the terms *morality* and *ethics.* See chap. 1, n.20.

4. Needless to say, sophisticated utilitarians are well armed with replies to such examples. For instance, they might assert that punishing innocents does *not* in fact maximize utility in the long run; for citizens will eventually find out about it and will not be happy with the deceptive leadership in their community. More generally, the assertion that such-and-such horrendous act will maximize utility is denied by claiming that "utility" has been construed too narrowly and that it is some broader rather than narrower sense of utility that we must maximize. There are often good *utilitarian* reasons for adhering to traditional principles of justice; and in fact, such principles themselves are (or so say utilitarians) best justified on utilitarian grounds. Disputes as to which act really does maximize utility (and what is the preferred scope of *utility*) are endless; and no fact of the matter seems to be of much help. This is unfortunate; for the chief selling point of utilitarianism was supposed to be its ability to turn unresolvable moral questions into questions that would admit to objective, factually determinative answers. Utilitarians have not made good on this claim. Another type of reply involves the assertion that what seems morally unacceptable according to traditional moral views is not necessarily so: we ought not to grant any sacred status to the prejudices of an unenlightened past, for the only proper criterion of moral unacceptability is utility maximization.

   On my own view, what spells defeat for utilitarianism in this area is not any specific example, however colorfully illustrated it may be, or even utilitarianism's gung-ho rejection of moral tradition and considered judgments. (The stock examples cited, though they did impress me enormously on first hearing as an undergraduate, no longer do so.) Rather, it is the utilitarian's earnest assertion that we must be ready to commit any and every act that can be shown to maximize utility. To declare in effect that *everything* (except, of course, the inviolable principle of utility) is up for grabs in ethics—that nothing simply is morally permissible or impermissible—is to make morality unworkable. Whatever morality is, it cannot be infinitely malleable.

   As a final note, I should add that on my own view, consideration of consequences is often relevant in moral evaluation. If what we are about to do will produce a catastrophe, that is a good reason not to do it. But what makes acts morally right is not usually a function of their consequences. Again, the moral field is not unitary, and critical moral evaluation requires a plurality of nonreductive categories.

5. Nozick's conception of morality as a system of "side constraints" represents one recent and influential antimaximization view. The moral side constraints upon what we may do, he claims, "reflect the fact of our separate existences. They reflect the fact that no moral balancing act can take place among us; there is no moral outweighing of one of our lives by others so as to lead to a greater overall *social* good" (*Anarchy, State, and Utopia* [New York: Basic Books, 1974], p. 33). For an earlier antimaximization view, see John L. Stocks: "The claims of morality, as they operate in human life, present on the face of it a very different appearance from the claims of policy or purpose. They come as a recognized obligation to do or not to do, which is often seen to involve the temporary surrender or restriction of a desire in itself innocent, of a perfectly legitimate purpose. ...The moral attitude is essentially a concern for the rightness of action" "Is There a Moral End?" in (*Morality and Purpose,* ed. D. Z. Phillips [New York: Schocken Books, 1969], pp. 73, 77). Consequentialist theories have been placed on the defensive in recent years, due to a variety of efforts from deontological and "rights-based" corners. One unfortunate result of this tendency is that moral teleology itself has been given a bad name. But it should not be assumed that consequentialism has a monopoly on moral teleology.

6. For an extensive critique of these and other maximization assumptions, see Michael Slote,

Beyond Optimizing: A Study of Rational Choice (Cambridge: Harvard University Press, 1989).

7. For elaboration and defense of this claim, see Frankfurt, *Importance of What We Care About,* chap. 7.

8. But how strong? It seems obvious that not all rational acts (e.g., turning on a light) necessarily fall under the purview of the moral every time they are performed. But can morality ever legitimately ask us to do something that is irrational or arational? (And if it can, what should we do?) Are all morally right or morally good acts necessarily rational acts? Unlike many philosophers, I am not sure that this question should be answered in the affirmative. The values of morality may not always coincide with the values of rationality.

9. Jeremy Bentham, *Principles of Judicial Procedure,* in *The Works of Jeremy Bentham,* ed. J. Bowring (Edinburgh: William Tait, 1843), vol. 2, pp. 6, 29. ("Maximization of the happiness of the greatest number" is the first entry under *maximization* in the *Oxford English Dictionary,* but the editors incorrectly list it as occurring in chap. 6, sec. 1 of the *Principles of Judicial Procedure,* rather than chap. 7, sec. 3, where it actually occurs.)

10. Aristotle's claim that humanity's end is to develop its active powers has several important descendants within Western thought. As C. B. MacPherson notes:

> Whether [the] Western tradition is traced back to Plato or to Aristotle or to Christian natural law, it is based on the proposition that the end or purpose of man is to use and develop his uniquely human attributes or capacities. His potential use and development of these may be called his human powers. A good life is one which maximizes these powers. A good society is one which maximizes (or permits and facilitates the maximization of) these powers, and thus enables men to make the best of themselves.... When this ethical concept [of maximizing individuals powers] was reintroduced in the nineteenth century [by, e.g., T. H. Green] it contained a more specific egalitarian assumption than it had contained in its ancient and medieval forms. It assumed not only that each individual was equally entitled to the opportunity to realize his human essence, but also (as against the Greeks) that men's capacities were substantially equal, and (as against the medieval tradition) that they were entitled to equal opportunity in this world. (*Democratic Theory: Essays in Retrieval* [Oxford: Clarendon Press, 1973], pp. 8–10)

MacPherson goes on to argue that is is impossible to maximize each person's ability to use and develop his or her powers within a market economy, since market economies allow and encourage each individual "to try and maximize his power by engrossing some of the powers of others" (p. 21). I cannot pursue the economic issue at present, but my own view is that market economies have a necessary role to play in "the maximization of democracy."

11. Bentham, *Introduction to the Principles,* chap. 1, sec. 1.

12. Nozick, *Anarchy, State,* p. 43. Cf. Nozick's own description of the "experience machine" (pp. 42–45), which seems to be a generalized version of Woody Allen's orgasmatron machine (in turn, a takeoff on Wilhelm Reich's orgone energy accumulator?). At the same time, not all versions of utilitarianism are open to this particular criticism. As noted earlier (pp. 39–40), some utilitarians urge us not so much to do what maximizes utility as to cultivate the traits that will tend to maximize utility. Such "character utilitarianisms" are indeed agent-oriented rather than act-oriented and thus do take into account (albeit in an objectionably reductionistic manner) the fact that we want to *be* a certain way.

13. A similar underlying conception of personhood is present in a number of well-known contemporary criticisms of utilitarianism. For instance, Rawls holds that utilitarianism "does not take seriously the distinction between persons" (*Theory of Justice,* p. 27; cf. his

remarks concerning "bare persons" in "Social Unity and Primary Goods," in *Utilitarianism and Beyond*, ed. Amartya Sen and Bernard Williams [New York: Cambridge University Press, 1982], p. 181). Rawls's primary concern here is with the distribution of goods among individuals as opposed to the total quantity or net aggregate of good produced. Utilitarianism is only concerned with the latter; any adequate moral conception must address the former. But I think the distributive concern itself reflects an underlying conception of the importance of persons and their capacities (cf. MacPherson's remarks quoted in n.10). Second, consider Williams's criticism that utilitarianism "cannot understand integrity" (Smart and Williams, *Utilitarianism*, p. 100). The integrity criticism relies on a distinction between positive and negative responsibility—between being responsible for what one does, rather than for what others do, and being responsible for what one allows or fails to prevent (pp. 95, 99). Utilitarianism subscribes to a wide doctrine of negative responsibility; thus, it "cannot coherently describe the relations between a man's projects and his actions" (p. 100). Here, too, an underlying conception of persons as actors generates the criticism. Finally, compare Philippa Foot's argument that consequentialist talk about maximizing good states of affairs only makes sense in limited contexts where the virtue of benevolence gives them a sense—that is, where agents who possess certain traits of character or who *are* a certain way try to *do* something ("Utilitarianism and the Virtues," in *Consequentialism and Its Critics*, ed. Samuel Scheffler [New York: Oxford University Press, 1988]). Again, a root conception of persons as creatures whose voluntary efforts are of fundamental importance plays a crucial role in the argument.

14. Wolf, "Moral Saints," p. 137.

15. Adams, *Virtue of Faith*, pp. 165–66. Like Adams, I believe that "sainthood" is "an essentially religious [rather than moral] phenomenon" (p. 168) and so will normally use phrases such as "morally outstanding individual," "moral exemplar," and such, rather than "moral saint."

16. Bentham, *Introduction to the Principles*, chap. 4.

17. The view that morality consists not in a single value but rather in an irreducible plurality of potentially conflicting values is an increasingly popular theme within contemporary ethical theory literature. See, for example, Nagel, *Moral Questions*, chap. 9; Charles Taylor, "The Diversity of Goods," in *Utilitarianism and Beyond*, ed. Sen and Williams, also in *Anti-theory in Ethics*, ed. Clarke and Simpson; and Charles Larmore, *Patterns of Moral Complexity* (New York: Cambridge University Press, 1987).

18. Some authors contend that maximization only makes sense in contexts where there is a single value or end to be produced. David Gauthier, for instance, writes: "The identification of rationality with maximizing activity requires the reduction of problems about incompatible or unattainable ends to problems about a single open end, characterized in a purely formal way. That is, we suppose that there is a single measure of a man's ends, which can be applied to evaluate the contribution each of the actions possible for him in a situation makes to the overall realization of his ends" ("Reason and Maximization," *Canadian Journal of Philosophy* 4 [1975]; 414). I do not see why the assumption of a single end is necessary. Efforts at maximization can still be measured if a plurality of ends is assumed, so long as there is some weighting scheme included within the plurality. Furthermore, the plurality assumption is much more psychologically realistic than is the reductionist assumption.

19. One could perhaps continue this line of inquiry further by next specifying only a *threshold amount* of each value to be produced; for example, "At least 25 percent of a morally outstanding person's acts must be justice-producing, at least 25 percent must produce beneficent results, etc." But why bother? Here, too, the objection would be that it squeezes our judgments concerning moral excellence into an unrealistic straitjacket.

20. Stocker, *Plural and Conflicting Values*, p. 342.

21. Bradley, *Ethical Studies,* p. 237. In comparing two different individuals to determine who is more moral, Bradley argues that the concept of *acting according to one's best light* is the first of four features to examine. The remaining three are *formal energy, disposition,* and *external circumstances.* Individuals may be equal in one feature but vary in another. Ultimately, "an accurate comparison is scarcely possible, and fully ... [justifies] the saying that 'only God sees the heart'.... The data for solving the psychological problem are not accessible to us" (p. 238). Compare Kant: "The real morality of actions, their merit or guilt, even that of our own conduct, ... remains entirely hidden from us" (*C1* A 552/B 580) and "We can never, even by the strictest examination, completely plumb the depths of the secret incentives of our actions. For when moral value is being considered, the concern is not with the actions, which are seen, but with their inner principles, which no one sees" (*G* IV 407/19). Still, one should not exaggerate the difficulties of determining who is more moral than whom. In real life we do make such judgments on a daily basis, and they are not all entirely erroneous. While I do think Kant and Bradley are correct in implying that such judgments clearly rest primarily on an admittedly problematic assessment of motivational commitment rather than mere "value output," reliable indicators of moral motive do exist. ("By their acts ye shall know them.")

22. But not all. For instance, according to some interpretations, in Christianity the highest state of perfection is held to be one in which the law of God has been so thoroughly "taken to heart" through the invasion of personality by the Holy Spirit that the individual acts rightly out of sheer joy and without "moral struggle." My emphasis on self-control does not square well with this particular moral conception. We could arrive at a maximizing conception of the morally excellent individual that would work for all moralities by means of the question-begging formula: the one who exemplifies to the highest degree possible whatever traits are regarded as virtues in his or her moral community. However, it is not my aim to find a lowest common denominator across all moral traditions. (I would like to thank Robert C. Roberts for bringing this point to my attention.)

23. For further discussion of the duty of beneficence, see van der Linden, *Kantian Ethics,* pp. 21–22, 35; and Donagan, *Theory of Morality,* pp. 85–86.

24. It is important to note that the conception of moral maximization advocated throughout this chapter places much more emphasis on imperfect duties than on perfect duties. Both the duty to develop human capacities and the duty of beneficence are imperfect duties— duties that require us to adopt certain broad policies and then to use our own judgment in determining how best to achieve them in a manner that suits our own individual circumstances. (See Sullivan's discussion in *Immanuel Kant's Moral Theory,* pp. 51–54 and Kant's own discussion at *DV* VI 390–91/49–51.) On the other hand, consequentialist conceptions of moral maximization generally assume that we must always do what is morally best and interpret *best* as a perfect duty that prescribes specific acts. (See, e.g., Peter Singer's interpretation of the obligation to assist in *Practical Ethics* [New York: Cambridge University Press, 1979], chap. 8). A common and (I believe) justified criticism of such "perfect duty" interpretations of moral maximization is that they demand too much of us. By placing more emphasis on imperfect duties, we are (hopefully) able to avoid this defect.

   The third family of constraints I have summarized—duties of justice and respect— does concern perfect, as opposed to imperfect, duties. But in asserting that this group of constraints normally sets limits on how we may legitimately pursue the goals of human development and of beneficence, I do not wish to be interpreted as holding that fulfillment of perfect duties must always take precedence over fulfillment of imperfect duties. In certain situations, it seems to me that the latter are more important than the former. For instance, I do not believe that relatively trivial questions must always be answered truthfully in cases where an innocent human life could be saved by answering falsely ("Is so-and-so inside your house at the moment? I want to shoot him"). For an opposing view, see (alas) Kant's "On a Supposed Right to Lie from Altruistic Motives" (VIII 423–30), in Sissela Bok, *Lying* (New York: Vintage Books, 1979), along with his remark in the *Grounding* that perfect duties "admit of no exception in the interest of inclination" (IV 421n./30n.). On my view, we are not entitled to assert categorically that perfect duties can *never* be overridden by imperfect duties, but only that *in most cases* they cannot. Here, as elsewhere, judgment must be used to consider the particular features of the case at hand before a competent decision can be reached. H. J. Paton, in his commentary on Kant's *Grounding*, advocates a similar position (*The Categorical Imperative* [Philadelphia: University of Pennsylvania Press, 1971], p. 148). See also Donagan's discussion of this issue in *Theory of Morality*, pp. 149–57. Donagan interprets the Pauline maxim that "evil is not to be done that good may come of it" (Romans 3:8) as an alternative way of stating that perfect duties must always override imperfect duties. But here, too, I do not believe that adherence to the view that evil is not be done so that good may come of it necessarily requires us always, for example, to tell the truth and pay our debts on time. Sometimes other things are more important.

25. Wolf discusses these two examples in "Moral Saints."

26. In ethical theory circles, the topic of fanaticism is often associated with R. M. Hare's discussion in *Freedom and Reason* (New York: Oxford University Press, 1965), chap. 9. As defined by Hare, the fanatic is one who subscribes to an ideal that is made "to override all considerations of people's interests, even the holder's own in actual or hypothetical cases" (p. 176). I agree with Hare that fanatics of this sort are going to remain unshaken by any arguments that philosophers or others can muster (p. 184); but I think it also obvious (and I am sure he would concur) that such fanatics are plainly immoral rather than moral, for their choice of ideals is not limited by any of our three constraints. Moral fanatics are less abhorrent than immoral fanatics, but antimorality critics are still deeply bothered by them. The sort of unadmirable do-gooder discussed earlier in chapter 2, if sufficiently fixated on a desire to do good, can serve as a model of what is here meant by a moral fanatic. Wolf's own definition of a moral saint (a person whose life is "dominated by a commitment to improving the welfare of others or of society as a whole") can also serve as a rough definition of a moral fanatic.

27. Adams, *Virtue of Faith*, p. 172.

28. David Gauthier, *Morals by Agreement* (Oxford: Clarendon Press, 1986), p. 22. Cf. John C. Harsanyi, "Morality and the Theory of Rational Behavior," in *Utilitarianism and Beyond*, ed. Sen and Williams, p. 43: "The secondary definition of rationality is *utility maximisation*." See also Martin Hollis, *The Cunning of Reason* (New York: Cambridge University Press, 1987), chap. 8, for a general discussion.

29. *Satisficing* is the view that the rational individual will sometimes set a threshold level of fulfillment (e.g., when selling a house) and then choose the alternative that comes closest to this threshold level, rather than holding out for the maximum amount possible. See Herbert A. Simon, "A Behavioral Model of Rational Choice," *Quarterly Journal of Economics* 69 (1955): 99–118. *Constrained maximization* is the view that individuals ought to maximize expected utility in all circumstances except when engaged in certain cooperative strategies (e.g., bargaining situations) that are to the benefit of all cooperators. See D. Gauthier, *Morals by Agreement*, chap. 6.

30. For further discussion of this point, see Sen and Williams's discussion in *Utilitarianism and Beyond*, pp. 9–11.

31. Richard Brandt, *A Theory of the Right and the Good* (Oxford: Clarendon Press, 1979), p. 10. Brandt's strategy in defining rationality is another example of the doctoring-up effort referred to in the previous paragraph.

32. Cf. Bernard Gert, "Rationality, Human Nature, and Lists," *Ethics* 100 (1990): 279–300, esp. pp. 96–97. I find Gert's essay to be a forceful critique of formalist definitions of *rationality*, and I share his general conviction that any acceptable definition of *rationality*

must specify some content. However, I am wary of his Hobbes-inspired list on p. 280: "death, pain (including mental suffering), disability, loss of freedom." Furthermore, I am not convinced that the best way to ensure content is to trot out such a specific list. Gert's assumed either/or ("either a formula or a list") seems to me to be a false dichotomy.

33. D. Gauthier, *Morals by Agreement,* pp. 25–26.
34. For a recent view, see Pincoffs, *Quandaries and Virtues.* See also Rawls's critique of perfectionism in *Theory of Justice,* sec. 50, and Frankena's discussion in *Ethics,* pp. 14–16, 79–94.
35. P. F. Strawson, "Social Morality and Individual Ideal," *Philosophy* 36 (1961): 1. For a reply to which I am indebted, see Pincoffs, *Quandaries and Virtues,* pp. 108–9.
36. The same holds for the three additional objections discussed further on. In general, I do not think most perfectionists are guilty of the views critics attribute to them. Rather, there seems to be something about the word *perfectionism* that invites misunderstanding.
37. Rawls, *Theory of Justice,* p. 325.
38. Friedrich Nietzsche, *Untimely Meditations,* trans. R. J. Hollingdale (New York: Cambridge University Press, 1983), pp. 161–62. (A slightly different translation of this passage is cited by Rawls, *Theory of Justice,* p. 325, n.51.) As is well known, Nietzsche's outlook owes much to the Greeks. Aristotle's conception of *eudaimonia* does not go quite this far in requiring some people to sacrifice their lives for the sake of others. But unfortunately, the difference is only one of degree; for he tells us that "*eudaimonia* is thought to depend on leisure [*scholē,* whence *scholar*]" (*NE* 1177b4) and that it requires "external goods" such as good birth and physical beauty (1099a31; cf. 1098b26, 1101a14–16). Furthermore, "some men are by nature free, and others slaves, and . . . for these latter slavery is both expedient and right [*dikaion*]" (*Pol* 1255a1–2). Women are not quite as bad off as slaves, but Aristotle's assessment of their intellectual capacities makes it very clear that he believes they can never acquire the crucial virtue of practical wisdom: "The slave has no deliberative faculty [*bouleutikon*] at all; the woman has, but it is without authority [*akuron*]" (*Pol* 1260a12–13). Kant's conception of moral maximization is egalitarian.
39. Sullivan, *Immanuel Kant's Moral Theory,* p. 109. Cf. Sullivan's remarks on this same page concerning Kant's "rejection of the ancient Greek ideal of the leisured life and his scorn for social discriminations that favor an aristocratic nobility, . . . his profound respect for ordinary people, however uneducated they may be."
40. Rawls, *Theory of Justice,* p. 327.
41. Pincoffs, *Quandaries and Virtues,* p. 110. I am indebted in this paragraph to Pincoffs's critique of what he calls "arbitrary perfectionism" (see pp. 110–12). As I have noted earlier (p. 52), the constraints placed upon our choice of ideals and principles by the duties of justice and respect are much stricter than are those of the principles of beneficence and cultivation of our own powers. Certain specific actions (e.g., murdering innocent people) are prohibited in all circumstances. This particular set of constraints may strike certain extreme act-utilitarians as arbitrary; but here, too, it would seem that the burden of proof is on their side.
42. Bradley, for instance, argued that "the general end" of ethics "is self-realization, the making real of the ideal self" (*Ethical Studies,* p. 230). At the same time, I do not think the narcissism charge holds for his version of perfectionism, since he also states that "man is a social being; he is real only because he is social, and can realize himself only because it is as social that he realizes himself. The mere individual is a delusion of theory; and the attempt to realize it in practice is the starvation and mutilation of human nature" (*Ethical Studies,* p. 174).
43. This is true of *maximization* itself. My own conception of moral maximization is quite different from other contemporary versions with which I am familiar, and in certain circles it may even be objected that what I am advocating is not the maximization of

morality. (See, e.g., Stocker's dismissal of nonmathematical understandings of maximization in *Plural and Conflicting Values,* pp. 299–300). My reply to such charges is simply that I have tried in this chapter to defend the claim that more morality is always preferable to less and that this does seem to me to be a maximizing view.

Chapter 4

1. Slote, *Goods and Virtues,* p. 84. See also Hare, *Freedom and Reason,* pp. 168–69; Kurt Baier, "Moral Reasons and Reasons to Be Moral," in *Values and Morals,* ed. Alvin I. Goldman and Jaegwon Kim (Dordrecht: Reidel, 1978); and Neil Cooper, *The Diversity of Moral Thinking* (Oxford: Clarendon Press, 1981), p. 105. Philippa Foot's writings on this topic have also been extremely influential. See her *Virtues and Vices,* chaps. 11, 13, and "Morality and Art."

2. D. Z. Phillips, "In Search of the Moral 'Must': Mrs. Foot's Fugitive Thought," *Philosophical Quarterly* 27 (1977): 156–57. Cf. his "Do Moral Considerations Override Others?" *Philosophical Quarterly* 29 (1979): 251: "The whole notion of 'pursuing morality', as if morality is listed among men's interests, itself obscures the way moral considerations impinge on our activities." These two articles will be included in Phillips's collection of essays, *Interventions in Ethics* (Albany: State University of New York Press, 1992). Several of the essays in this volume (e.g., "The Presumption of Theory") are also relevant to the antitheory debate. For related discussion, see Neil Cooper, "Morality and Importance," in *The Definition of Morality,* ed. G. Wallace and A. D. M. Walker (London: Methuen, 1970), and his *Diversity of Moral Thinking,* chap. 6.

3. Lawrence Becker, *Reciprocity* (New York: Routledge & Kegan Paul, 1986), p. 23.

4. Slote, *Goods and Virtues,* p. 86. See also Baron, "On Admirable Immorality," for a critical analysis of this example.

5. Foot, *Virtues and Vices,* p. 167. See also her similar charges of "fictions" surrounding morality on p. 174 and in "Morality and Art," pp. 12, 22, along with her remarks on the alleged "inescapablity" of morality in *Virtues and Vices,* pp. 160, 162–63, 171.

6. However, Bradley himself seems to be somewhat inconsistent when he identifies morality with the voluntary. In the longer passage cited at the beginning of this chapter, he includes the activity of *sleeping* as coming under the purview of the moral. But in what respects does it make sense to hold that the activity of sleeping "has been brought under the control of the will?" It is not only insomniacs who are unable to fall asleep whenever and wherever they might try to do so.

7. Stuart Hampshire, *Thought and Action* (New York: Viking Press, 1967), p. 249. The first thought that Hampshire claims to be associated with the concept of morality is that it is "important and worth serious attention, not trivial" (p. 249).

8. Scheffler, "Morality's Demands," p. 535.

9. L. A. Kosman, "Being Properly Affected: Virtues and Feelings in Aristotle's Ethics," in *Essays on Aristotle's Ethics,* ed. A. Rorty, p. 112. As Aristotle remarks: "Perhaps a man is the kind of man not to take care. Still they are themselves by their slack lives responsible for becoming men of that kind. . . . To the unjust and to the self-indulgent man it was open at the beginning not to become men of this kind, and so they are unjust and self-indulgent voluntarily; but now that they have become so it is not possible for them not to be so" (*NE* 1114a3–4, 1114a19–22).

10. Adams himself, in "Involuntary Sins," articulates these same basic distinctions between directly and indirectly voluntary states, between indirectly voluntary states of mind and indirectly voluntary physiological conditions, and between indirectly voluntary states of mind that are directed toward objects and those that are not. I make no claim to originality here: the preceding analysis is deeply derivative from Adams's. It may be that our quarrel

is merely semantic; for again, it is the use of the plain, unqualified *involuntary* to which I am objecting.

11. It might be said that this example trivializes the aesthetic in focusing on hairstyles and that if a broader conception of the aesthetic (as that which is concerned with the character and quality of our experiences) were substituted for it, the example would not work. I accept the first part of the criticism, but not the second; that is, I grant that the spotlight on coiffure may suggest to some that aesthetic considerations concern only optional, add-on features of life and agree that this is a faulty conception of the aesthetic. But the central point of the example is simply that some voluntary activities strongly resist aesthetic assessment for reasons indicated. This remains true, I believe, regardless of how broad a conception of the aesthetic one assumes. (I would like to thank Mark Johnson for bringing this point to my attention.)

12. A. Rorty, *Mind in Action*, p. 289.

13. Scheffler, "Morality's Demands," p. 534.

14. Williams, *Moral Luck*, p. 18. Williams borrows the example from Charles Fried, *An Anatomy of Values* (Cambridge: Harvard University Press, 1970), p. 227.

15. Williams, *Moral Luck*, p. 18. Cf. Wolf, "Moral Saints," p. 145. Of course, there are other possibilities. He might save her because she is his wife. Suppose two women are drowning: one is his lover, the other is his wife. Does he do the right thing in saving his wife rather than the woman he loves, because he occupies a special role with respect to his wife? (I would like to thank Robert C. Roberts for bringing this issue to my attention.)

16. I am indebted here to Barbara Herman's criticism of Williams's example in "Integrity and Impartiality," *Monist* 66 (1983): 245–46.

17. But not all. For instance, conceptual explorations of categories such as "citizen," "executive power," "voter behavior," and the like, which refrain from making normative judgments concerning how people should live, belong exclusively to political theory. Also, not all shoulds are moral shoulds; and so not all normative judgments issuing from, say, an analysis of political authority will necessarily be moral judgments.

18. There are several textual problems at 1094b4. Is Aristotle claiming that *all* of the arts and sciences fall under (*hupo*) politics and are used (*chrōmenēs*) by it or only that some of them (i.e., practical ones such as rhetoric and strategy) are? Bywater, in the Oxford text, puts square brackets around the word *praktikais* at 1094b4 and writes *seclusi* in the textual apparatus, meaning that he has decided to exclude the word *praktikais* because he does not think it was written by Aristotle. If *praktikais* is regarded as being in Aristotle's original text, then Aristotle is claiming that only the practical arts fall under politics. If *praktikais* is viewed as being the insertion of a later editor, then Aristotle is making the stronger claim that all of the arts and sciences fall under politics. Also, one of the manuscripts on which Bywater's text is based omits the word *loipais* (rest), though in Bywater's view it should be retained. With this omission—and retaining *praktikais*—we would have: "Politics uses the practical sciences." Ross, in his translation, says that politics "uses the rest of the sciences" and so is following Bywater. I also agree with Bywater's reading. See, further, John Burnet's note on this passage in *The Ethics of Aristotle* (Methuen: London, 1900), p. 10, where he observes that politics "regulates" the theoretical sciences even if it does not "make use of" all of them. For an alternative reading, see Kraut, *Aristotle on the Human Good*, p. 222, n.19.

19. Chief among these is the suspicion that Aristotle is not always consistent regarding what he says about the authority of politics or morality over all other sciences. We saw earlier that he says that politics, the "most authoritative [*kuriōtatēs*] art," "uses the rest of the sciences" (1094a26–27, 1094b4). Later, we are told that practical wisdom (the same state of mind as politics represents, 1141b23–24) "does not have authority [*oude kuria*] over philosophic wisdom" (1145a6–7, cf. 1141a20–22). How can politics be the most authoritative science if it does not have authority over all the other sciences? Kraut makes

1094b4 consistent with 1145a8 simply by asserting that "politics does not govern the theoretical sciences"—the "other sciences" referred to by Aristotle at 1094b4 including only crafts such as bridlemaking and shipbuilding (*Aristotle on the Human Good*, p. 222, n.19). But this is not the way that most people, myself included, read 1094b4. See n.18.

20. I am indebted here to Kraut's comments on Aristotle's use of the verb *periechein* (to embrace or encompass) in *Aristotle on the Human Good*, pp. 223–25 (cf. *NE* 1094b6), as well as to Lawrence Becker's defense of "the 'general' conception of morality," a conception holding that "the moral point of view is the most inclusive one we can manage—the one we use when we say 'All things considered, here is what we should do' " (*Reciprocity*, p. 5).

21. Norman Kemp Smith, *A Commentary to Kant's "Critique of Pure Reason"* (Atlantic Highlands, N. J.: Humanities Press, 1962), p. xxii. Cf. W. H. Walsh, *Kant's Criticism of Metaphysics* (Chicago: University of Chicago Press, 1975), p. 38.

22. Sullivan, *Immanuel Kant's Moral Theory*, p. 329, n. 6. Fortunately, this lacuna in Kant scholarship is something that Sullivan himself addresses in chap. 8. I am much indebted to his account throughout the present section.

23. Kant's claims that belief in God and immortality are indispensable postulates of practical reason if it is to carry out its project of realizing the highest good have found few contemporary defenders. G. J. Warnock notes that these two "supposed 'postulates' would probably be regarded by many as singularly dispensable" and recommends complete dismissal of the doctrine of the primacy of the practical on the ground that "reason in its practical use lies under the logical disability of leaving, so to speak, intellectual loose ends, of constraining us to accept what we cannot possibly show to be true" ("The Primacy of Practical Reason," *Proceedings of the British Academy* 52 [1967]: 261–262). Even among writers more favorably disposed to Kant's primacy of the practical than Warnock, skepticism concerning these two postulates remains evident. See, for example, Lucien Goldmann, *Immanuel Kant*, trans. Robert Black (London: New Left Books, 1971), pp. 200, 216; van der Linden, *Kantian Ethics*, pp. 65–91; and Yirmiahu Yovel, *Kant and the Philosophy of History* (Princeton; N. J.: Princeton University Press, 1980), pp. 287–98. Yovel, in his analysis, makes a helpful distinction between what he calls the doctrinal and methodological senses of the primacy of the practical, and argues persuasively that one can accept the latter without being forced to accept the former's heavy baggage of postulates. Van der Linden (*Kantian Ethics*, pp. 81–86) also relies on Yovel's distinction in arguing that the postulate of God is not needed to solve the antinomy of practical reason. I follow these authors in choosing to detach the issue of the postulates from the doctrine of the primacy of the practical.

24. Lewis Beck, in *Commentary on Kant's Critique of Practical Reason* (Chicago: University of Chicago Press, 1960), claims that there is "an inconsistency in Kant's use of the word 'interest' " (p. 249, n.29). One use is the definition I have cited. The second, Beck claims, is "the end of the use of a faculty." I do not see an inconsistency here. The notion of a goal or end is, indeed, part of what Kant means by an interest of reason; but so, too, is that of a limit or set of constraints. (Cf. the strong deontological constraints presupposed by his moral teleology.) One basic problem with Beck's inconsistency charge is that it forces him to reject Kant's own statement regarding the interest of speculative reason: "The interest of its speculative use consists in the knowledge of objects up to the highest a priori principles" (*C2* V 120/124). According to Beck, on the other hand, the "true interest" of speculative reason lies "solely in the restriction of speculative folly" (*Commentary on Kant's*, p. 249). Kant does, indeed, say that the interest of theoretical reason is "the restriction of speculative folly" (*C2* V 121/126, a page after the previous citation); but because these two remarks appear virtually alongside one another, it is difficult for me to believe that Kant is guilty of inconsistency. If we wish to be faithful to his text, we must assume that Kant holds that (1) interests concern aims, and (2) interests also

set limits on how such aims are to be pursued. These two propositions are not necessarily inconsistent with one another.

25. Yovel, *Kant and the Philosophy of History*, p. 14.

26. Cf. *C3* V 453/122, as well as Kant's discussions at *LE* 317–19/252–53 and *R* VI 124–36/115–28. In the *Grounding*, the *Endzweck* is articulated in terms of the kingdom of ends, "a whole both of rational beings as ends in themselves and also of the particular ends which each may set for himself" (*G* IV 433/39).

27. Goldmann, *Immanuel Kant*, p. 57. Cf. van der Linden: "Practical reason views the world in both its natural and human aspects as a field for the expression and realization of the highest good, and it holds, moreover, that our ultimate purpose and satisfaction are to be found in transformative activity directed toward this ideal" (*Kantian Ethics*, p. 13).

28. Hilary Putnam, *Reason, Truth, and History* (New York: Cambridge University Press, 1981), p. 215. See also his comments in *Realism and Reason*, pp. 245–47.

29. Charles Sanders Peirce, *The Collected Papers of Charles Sanders Peirce*, ed. Charles Hartshorne and Paul Weiss (Cambridge: Harvard University Press, 1965), vol. 5 para. 35. The priority of ethics is also evident in Peirce's remark, "That truth the conditions of which the logician endeavors to analyze, and which is the goal of the reasoner's aspirations, is nothing but a phase of the *summum bonum* which forms the subject of pure ethics" (*Collected Papers*, vol. 1, para. 575). For general discussion, see H. S. Thayer, *Meaning and Action: A Critical History of Pragmatism* (Indianapolis: Bobbs-Merrill, 1968), pp. 419–23, and Manley Thompson, *The Pragmatic Philosophy of C. S. Peirce* (Chicago: University of Chicago Press, 1953), pp. 194–201. In recent years, this Peircean position has resurfaced in the works of both Karl-Otto Apel and Jürgen Habermas. Apel, for instance, holds that "logic—and, *at the same time,* all the sciences and technologies—*presupposes* an ethic as the precondition for its possibility" (*Towards a Transformation of Philosophy,* trans. Glyn Adey and David Frisby [London: Routledge & Kegan Paul, 1980], p. 258). See also Habermas, *Moral Consciousness and Communicative Action,* trans. Christian Lenhardt and Shierry Weber Nicholsen (Cambridge: MIT Press, 1990), esp. pp. 88–90.

30. William James, *Pragmatism and the Meaning of Truth* (Cambridge: Harvard University Press, 1978), p. 42. In building upon what is essentially a pragmatic revision of Kant's doctrine of the primacy of the practical, I do not wish to exclude other philosophical traditions that likewise emphasize the priority of the moral. Perhaps the most influential statement of this doctrine is found in Plato's *Republic:* "What gives truth to the objects of knowledge, and to the knowing mind the power to know, is the Form of the Good [*ten tou agathou idean*]. As it is the cause of knowledge and truth, think of it also as being the object of knowledge. Both knowledge and truth are beautiful, but you will be right to think of the Good as other and more beautiful than they" (*Republic* 508E). See also Emmanuel Levinas's attempt to show that morality "presides over the work of truth" and "is not a branch of philosophy, but first philosophy" (*Totality and Infinity,* trans. Alphonso Lingis [Pittsburgh: Duquesne University Press, 1969], p. 304).

31. John Dewey, *The Quest for Certainty* (New York: Capricorn Books, 1960), p. 68. Cf. the following remark from his *Logic* (New York: Holt, 1949): "The conduct of scientific inquiry, whether physical or mathematical, is a mode of *practice;* the working scientist is a practitioner above all else, and is constantly engaged in making practical judgments: decisions as to what to do and what means to employ in doing it" (p. 161). As Putnam remarks, logical positivism "*produced a conception of rationality so narrow as to exclude the very activity of producing that conception*" (*Realism and Reason*, p. 244).

32. Clarence Irving Lewis, *Values and Imperatives: Studies in Ethics,* ed. John Lange (Stanford: Stanford University Press, 1969), pp. 104–5. Cf. Putnam: "The elimination of the normative is attempted mental suicide" (*Realism and Reason*, p. 246). "Exclusive descriptivism" has reared its head in recent philosophical debate under the banner of "naturalized epistemology." W. V. Quine, for instance, argues that epistemology "falls into place as

a chapter of psychology and hence of natural science" (*Ontological Relativity and Other Essays* [New York: Columbia University Press, 1969], p. 82), although he also states that our speculations "about the world remain subject to norms and caveats, but these issue from science itself as we acquire it.... The norms can change somewhat as science progresses" (*Theories and Things* [Cambridge: Belknap Press, 1981], p. 181). In his recent book, *The Pursuit of Truth* (Cambridge: Harvard University Press, 1990), Quine denies that the normative element of epistemology "goes by the board"; but he does state that "normative epistemology gets naturalized into a chapter of engineering: the technology of anticipating sensory stimulation" (p. 19). Less ambiguous are the following eliminativist remarks of Paul Churchland: "The claim that the enterprise of epistemology should be conducted along the lines of any other natural science renders problematic the status of what we would call *normative* epistemology. 'Ought's not being derivable from 'is's, it would seem that normative epistemology cannot be a purely empirical science" (*Scientific Realism and the Plasticity of Mind* [New York: Cambridge University Press, 1979], p. 124). For further discussion to which I am indebted, see Robert N. McCauley, "Epistemology in an Age of Cognitive Science," *Philosophical Psychology* 1 (1988): 143–52, and Paul A. Roth, *Meaning and Method in the Social Sciences* (Ithaca; N. Y.: Cornell University Press, 1987), pp. 25–43.

33. Lewis, *Values and Imperatives,* p. 107. (This passage also reflects the strong Kantian orientation of Lewis's thinking. Unlike William James, who holds that truth is what is *good* in the way of belief, Lewis argues that the normative character of warranted beliefs is not tied to their good results but rather to the fact that they issue from "nonrepudiable demands." Lewis thus substitutes the word *right* for the word *good* in James's maxim.)

34. Lewis, *Values and Imperatives,* p. 108. Cf. the opening remarks of Lewis, *An Analysis of Knowledge and Valuation* (La Salle, Ill.: Open Court, 1946): "Knowledge, action, and evaluation are essentially connected. The primary and pervasive significance of knowledge lies in its guidance of action: knowing is for the sake of doing. And action, obviously, is rooted in evaluation" (p. 3).

35. Charles Taylor, *Sources of the Self: The Making of Modern Identity* (Cambridge: Harvard University Press, 1989), p. 47. See also Martha Nussbaum, Review of *Sources of the Self,* by Charles Taylor, *New Republic,* 9 April, 1990, pp. 27–34. Taylor's strident criticisms of Kant and of "Kant-derived moral theories" notwithstanding (see, e.g., pp. 79–88, 94), his own emphasis on the inescapability of moral frameworks bears a striking resemblance to Kant's doctrine of the primacy of the practical.

36. Taylor, *Sources of the Self,* p. 28.

37. Taylor, *Sources of the Self,* p. 58. See also Taylor's discussion of what he calls the "BA [best account] principle" (pp. 58–59, 68–69, 71–74). The best account, he notes, "is trumps" within scientific argumentation (p. 58). Moral categories, in other words, have primacy.

38. Cf. Putnam: " 'Theory of the good' ... is not only programmatic, but is itself dependent upon assumptions about human nature, about society, about the universe (including theological and metaphysical assumptions). We have had to revise our theory of the good (such as it is) again and again as our knowledge has increased and our world-view has changed" (*Reason, Truth, and History,* p. 215).

39. Sullivan, *Immanuel Kant's Moral Theory,* p. 111. Cf. O'Neill's attempt to show why the categorical imperative is the supreme principle of reason in *Constructions of Reason,* chap. 1. As she notes, the categorical imperative is "a strategy for avoiding principles of thinking, communicating and acting that cannot be adopted by all members of a plurality whose principles of interaction, let alone actual interaction (let alone coordination!), are not established by any transcendent reality" (p. 24).

40. Cf. Sullivan, *Immanuel Kant's Moral Theory,* p. 109. These two issues also receive extensive treatment in Kant's essay, "An Answer to the Question: What Is Enlightenment?"

41. I am indebted here to Christine Korsgaard ("Aristotle and Kant on the Source of Value,"

Ethics 96 [1986]: 486–505), who uses this passage to contrast Aristotle's defense of *theoria* with Kant's candidate of moral praxis as the sole source of unconditioned value.

42. I will be saying much more about "theory" in part II, but it is worth pointing out now that (1) "theory" need not and should not always be understood in a narrow contemplation-of-unchanging-truths sense, and (2) for Kant, theorizing remains an integral part of the project of moral praxis.

43. Cf. Kant's claim in the *Grounding* that we must admit that the command "Thou shalt not lie" "does not hold only for human beings [*Menschen*], as if other rational beings had no need to abide by it, and so with all the other moral laws properly so called" (IV 389/2).

44. Bentham, *Introduction to the Principles*, chap. 17, sec. 4, n.1 (p. 311). Bentham equates suffering with the mere capacity to sense pain, but what makes suffering a morally relevant capacity is that it implies an ability to respond emotionally to painful stimuli. Some organisms (e.g., amoebas) sense pain, but they do not respond emotionally to it. Also, suffering is a larger concept than pain: there are many more ways of injuring organisms than by causing pain. For further discussion, see Erich H. Loewy, *Suffering and the Beneficent Community* (Albany: State University of New York Press, 1991), chap. 1.

Chapter 5

1. *Oxford Classical Dictionary*, 2d ed., S.V. *theoroi;* cf. Nicholas Lobkowicz, *Theory and Practice: History of a Concept from Aristotle to Marx* (Notre Dame, Ind.: University of Notre Dame Press, 1967), pp. 1–9. See also the numerous textual references in Liddell and Scott's *Greek–English Lexicon*, S.V. *theōreō, theōria*, and *theōros*, on which the following account is based.

2. Wlad Godzich, foreword to *The Resistance to Theory*, by Paul de Man (Minneapolis: University of Minnesota Press, 1986), p. xiv.

3. Some people (and many antitheorists) regard theory's sole, rightful home as being within the field of the natural sciences, supposedly because only here can theories truly attain "convergence" on an answer by being guided by the way the world is in itself. However, even within the supposedly "theory-friendly" terrain of science one finds occasional antitheoretical rumblings. See, for example, Paul Feyerabend, *Against Method* (London: New Left Books, 1975). Ideas concerning the structure and aims of scientific theories have, of course, strongly influenced theory development within the humanities and social "sciences"; but there is also a long tradition—beginning at least with Aristotle's distinction between theoretical and practical science and extending through Vico's *Scienza nuova* (1725) and Dilthey's late-nineteenth-century arguments concerning the differences between *Naturwissenschaften* and *Geisteswissenschaften*—that urges caution here. Had we listened more carefully to these warnings, we might not be in as much trouble today. Ironically, most contemporary moral theorists and antitheorists continue to share with one another a model of theory lifted from outdated philosophy of science discussions. As Arthur Caplan remarks: "[The dominant] model of what constitutes a theory in ethics seems to have been inherited from early and mid–20th century discussions in the philosophy of science concerning the nature of theory structure and explanation. There are, however, serious problems with this view" ("Moral Experts and Moral Expertise: Do Either Exist?" in *Clinical Ethics: Theory and Practice,* ed. Barry Hoffmaster, B. Freedman, and G. Fraser [Clifton, N.J.: Humana Press, 1989], p. 79).

4. For antitheory sentiment within literature, see Mitchell, *Against Theory*. An earlier antitheory essay in aesthetics that also reveals the Wittgensteinian influence behind much antitheory writing is Morris Weitz, "The Role of Theory in Aesthetics," in *Philosophy Looks at the Arts,* rev. ed., ed. Joseph Margolis (Philadelphia: Temple University Press,

1978). See also John Fisher, "Against Theory, Again," *Journal of Aesthetic Education* 20 (1986): 50–53. For antitheory arguments applied to law, see, for example, Stanley Fish, *Doing What Comes Naturally: Change, Rhetoric, and the Practice of Theory in Literary and Legal Studies* (Durham, N.C.: Duke University Press, 1989).

In a broader sense, much postmodernist writing is antitheoretical in tone, and many canonical modernist texts are theoretical in outlook. Thus, Jean-François Lyotard argues that "the grand narrative has lost its credibility" in postmodern culture (*The Postmodern Condition: A Report on Knowledge* [Minneapolis: University of Minnesota Press, 1984], p. 37). By "grand narrative" he means, among other things, any broad-scale social or moral theory that seeks to legitimate or critique existing practices and institutions. Similarly, Foucault informs us that his aim is "not to formulate the global systematic theory which holds everything in place." Rather, he is a "specific" as opposed to a "universal" intellectual—a critic who does not pretend to offer an account and critique of society as a whole but seeks instead "to analyze the specificity of mechanisms of power [and] to build little by little a strategic knowledge" (*Power/Knowledge: Selected Interviews and Other Writings, 1972–1977,* ed. Colin Gordon [New York: Pantheon Books, 1980], pp. 145, 126). Stephen Toulmin, in *Cosmopolis: The Hidden Agenda of Modernity* (New York: Free Press, 1990), refers to seventeenth-century European philosophy as "a 'theory-centered' *style* of philosophizing—i.e., one that poses problems, and seeks solutions, stated in timeless, universal terms" (p. 11, cf. pp. 24, 34–35). The primary focus in part II of this book concerns the arguments of contemporary antitheorists *in ethics*. However, as I slowly find my way through the bulging literature on modernity and postmodernity, I become more and more convinced that the antitheory debate in ethics is a chapter of a much larger story.

5. For appropriate warnings on this point, see Stanley Fish, "Consequences," in *Against Theory,* ed. Mitchell, pp. 115–18 and *Doing What Comes Naturally,* p. 378.

6. For analyses and assessments of these arguments, see Clarke, "Anti-Theory in Ethics," and my "Virtue Ethics," 93–102. Several antitheory arguments against moral theory are evaluated in detail in chapter 8.

7. Annette Baier, "Doing Without Moral Theory?" in *Anti-Theory in Ethics,* ed. Clarke and Simpson, pp. 33, 36 (also in *Postures of the Mind,* pp. 232, 235). The distinction between normative and nonnormative theory is central to Baier's critique of moral theory and will be examined in more detail.

8. John McDowell, "Virtue and Reason," in *Anti-Theory in Ethics,* ed Clarke and Simpson, pp. 87, 105.

9. Hampshire, *Morality and Conflict,* p. 8.

10. Martha Nussbaum, " 'Richly Aware and Finely Responsible': Literature and the Moral Imagination," in *Anti-Theory in Ethics,* ed Clarke and Simpson, pp. 122, 126; Nussbaum, *Love's Knowledge Essays on Philosophy and Literature* (New York: Oxford University Press, 1990), pp. 157, 160. The thesis of the priority of the particular is asserted repeatedly in *Love's Knowledge.* See, for example, pp. 37–40, 66–75, 177–82, 197–98, 360–63.

11. The term *particulars* occasionally appears to be used in two different ways by antitheorists: (1) specific, noninferential moral perceptions of individual agents and (2) local moral practices and conventions within a given moral community that are not instantiations of universal principles.

12. Steven Knapp and Walter Benn Michaels, "Against Theory," in *Against Theory,* ed. Mitchell p. 30.

13. Fish, "Consequences," p. 110. Cf. his *Doing What Comes Naturally,* pp. 14–15, 25–28, 380–98.

14. Williams, *Moral Luck,* p. 2. Cf. Blum, *Friendship, Altruism,* p. 44.

15. Williams, *Ethics and the Limits of Philosophy,* pp. 16–17. According to Williams, the pattern or patterns by means of which theorists seek to reduce ethical considerations involves

highly abstract or "thin" terms such as *right* and *good*. As a result, garden-variety "thick" terms such as *courage* or *jealousy* are misunderstood by ethical theorists. For a critical discussion of this distinction, see my "Through Thick and Thin: Moral Knowledge in Skeptical Times," *Logos* 10 (1989): 57–72.

16. Cheryl N. Noble, "Normative Ethical Theories," in *Anti-Theory in Ethics,* ed. Clarke and Simpson, p. 50.

17. Nussbaum, *Love's Knowledge* p. 58, cf. pp. 36, 56–66, 106–24. See also her *Fragility of Goodness,* pp. 294–98, where she defends the claim that Aristotle viewed the values that are constitutive of a good human life as being "plural and incommensurable."

18. Taylor, "Diversity of Goods," in *Anti-Theory in Ethics,* ed. Clarke and Simpson, p. 237.

19. Pincoffs, *Quandaries and Virtues,* p. 5. The attack on reductivism is a major theme of Pincoff's book. Part 1 is entitled "Reductivism in Ethical Theory," part II, "Toward a Nonreductive Virtue Ethics."

20. Nagel, *Mortal Questions* pp. 131–32, 137. Nagel's opposition to moral theory is much more moderate than, say, Williams's. Nagel *does* recommend ethical theory "as an essential resource for making decisions," but he does not recommend it "as a decision procedure" (p. 141). Other influential defenses of the plurality and irreducibility of moral values include David Wiggins, "Truth, Invention, and the Meaning of Life," in *Essays in Moral Realism,* ed. Geoffrey Sayre-McCord (Ithaca, N. Y.: Cornell University Press, 1988), esp. pp. 157–60; and Stocker, *Plural and Conflicting Values.*

21. Mitchell, *Against Theory,* p. 7. As the introduction subtitle "Pragmatic Theory" suggests, Mitchell himself defends a less formalist and more pragmatic conception of theory that rejects the unity thesis. For more on the relationship between pragmatism, theory, and antitheory, see Horace Fairlamb, "Pragmatism and Anti-Theory: The Consequences of Theory," *MLN* 101 (1986): 1216–25. I agree with Fairlamb's claim that "though the 'anti-theorists' are part of the 'new pragmatists', pragmatism originated as a theory that theory and practice are inseparable" (p. 1217). I explore the distinction between pragmatic theory and antitheory (and the need for a more pragmatic moral theory) in chapter 7.

22. Hampshire, *Morality and Conflict,* p. 152. As his title indicates, the existence of irresolvable conflict within morality is the central theme of Hampshire's book. See, especially, the concluding chapter, "Morality and Conflict," from which the above quotation is taken. A good sourcebook on the moral conflict literature is Gowans, ed., *Moral Dilemmas.*

23. Hampshire, *Morality and Conflict,* p. 155.

24. Larmore, *Patterns of Moral Complexity,* pp. 10–11, 149. Cf. Pincoffs, *Quandaries and Virtues,* p. 35. Larmore emphasizes in his conclusion, "[My intention] has not been to deny the possibilities or the importance of moral theory. I do not believe that the complexity of morality is so great, so boundless, that it baffles any attempt at systematization. . . . My hope has not been that we should put the task of moral theory behind us, but rather that we should pursue it with less blinkered expectations" (*Patterns of Moral Complexity,* pp. 151–52).

25. For example, by Nussbaum, when she states: "If an agent ascribes intrinsic value to, and cares about, more than one activity, there is always a risk that some circumstances will arise in which incompatible courses of action are both required; deficiency therefore becomes a natural necessity. The richer my scheme of value, the more I open myself to such a possibility" (*Fragility of Goodness,* p. 7). Like Hampshire, Larmore, and others, Nussbaum is a strong advocate of the irresolvable conflict thesis, as well as a critic of moral theories that allegedly deny the possibility of irresolvable conflict (see, e.g., her criticisms of Plato and Kant in *Fragility of Goodness,* pp. 31–32, 48–49, 107–11, and 155–16, and throughout part II. However, unlike Hampshire, she holds that Aristotelian ethics is a type of ethical theory that does recognize the reality of irresolvable conflict (see *Fragility of Goodness,* part III, esp. pp. 294–97; cf. Hampshire, *Morality and Conflict,*

pp. 150–53). The general issue of whether or not Aristotle was guilty of engaging in acts of moral theorizing, as well as the specific issue of whether or not he allows for irresolvable moral conflicts, will be discussed in chapter 6.

26. See Ruth Barcan Marcus, "Moral Dilemmas and Consistency," in *Moral Dilemmas*, ed. Gowans, for more on this argument concerning "single-value conflicts." See also Gowans, *Moral Dilemmas*, p. 19.

27. Aristotle, on some readings, is a particularist who denies there are cases where the practically wise man will not be able to determine the correct course of action. Practical wisdom is concerned with particulars that are objects of perception (*NE* 1142a26–27), but *phronēsis* "is an unerring guide to action. The *phronimos* knows what to do in any practical situation" (Troels Engberg-Pedersen, *Aristotle's Theory of Moral Insight* [Oxford: Clarendon Press, 1983], p. 189); cf. *NE* 1141b10–12. See also Stocker, who argues at length that while "plurality and conflict are absolutely commonplace and generally unproblematic features of our everyday choice and action," they are not "a bar to sound judgment, resolute and informed action, and a sound and rational ethics" (*Plural and Conflicting Values*, p. 2).

28. Hampshire, *Morality and Conflict*, p. 163. Michael Oakeshott's emphasis on moral life as "a habit of affection and behavior" is also relevant here. As Oakeshott notes, this form of the moral life is one which "there is nothing that is absolutely fixed" and that "is capable of change as well as of local variation" ("The Tower of Babel," in *Anti-Theory in Ethics*, ed. Clarke and Simpson, pp. 189, 90; also in Oakeshott's *Rationalism in Politics and Other Essays* [London: Methuen, 1962]). For further discussion, see Clarke and Simpson, eds., *Anti-Theory Ethics*, pp. 8–9.

29. I would like to thank Norman Dahl for conversation on this issue.

30. Williams, *Ethics and the Limits of Philosophy*, pp. 100–101.

31. Baier, *Postures of the Mind*, p. 226.

32. Larmore, *Patterns of Moral Complexity*, p. ix, cf. p. 4.

33. Clarke and Simpson, eds., *Anti-Theory in Ethics*, p. 2. The question of who exactly is guilty of moral theorizing is an intriguing one that will be explored in more detail in chapter 6. The inclusion of Nagel's name in their list, for instance, is somewhat problematic; for we have seen already (n.20) that he accepts both the plurality of values and irresolvable conflict theses. They also include John Rawls in their list, but only "with qualifications." However, Rawls is criticized much more often in antitheory literature than any of the aforementioned authors.

34. Pincoffs, *Quandaries and Virtues*, p. 3. Cf. Baier's criticisms of "the prejudice in favor of formulated general rules," as well as of the assumption "that a genuine morality must be codifiable" (*Postures of the Mind*, pp. 234–35, 214); McDowell's defense of the "uncodifiability thesis" ("Virtue and Reason," pp. 93, 100, 102); C. Taylor's criticisms concerning "a procedure of determining what is right that takes no account" of qualitative contrasts in our moral sensibility ("Diversity of Goods," p. 233); A. Rorty's comments on "the myth of justificatory judicialism," (*Mind in Action*, pp. 283–88); and Stocker's claim that he sees "no theory, much less an algorithmic one, which solves" the problems generated by plurality and conflict (*Plural and Conflicting Values*, pp. 1–2).

35. Plato, *Protagoras* 356D–E; a translation by Nussbaum appears in *Fragility of Goodness*, p. 109. See *Fragility of Goodness*, chap. 4, as well as *Love's Knowledge*, chap. 3, for more on this issue. See also Socrates' remarks in Plato's *Euthyphro* 7B–D, where he points out that we can "turn to measurement" when we differ "about the larger and the smaller" but seem unable to turn to measurement when we disagree about "the just and the unjust, the beautiful and the ugly, the good and the bad." Here he seems to speak against the possibility of a science of moral measurement.

36. Fish, "Consequences," pp. 107–8. Cf. E. D. Hirsch, Jr., *The Aims of Interpretation* (Chicago: University of Chicago Press, 1976), p. 18. Fish's favorite example of theory is Noam Chomsky's "competence model" in linguistics. Once constructed, a successful

competence model would allegedly assign, without any interpretive activity on the part of the applier, the same description to a sentence that would be assigned by a hypothetical ideal language user. See Noam Chomsky, *Aspects of the Theory of Syntax* (Cambridge: MIT Press, 1965), and Fish, "Consequences," pp. 108–11.

37. Fish, *Doing What Comes Naturally,* p. 121. Of course, the claim that rules themselves always need to be interpreted is one that Kant made two centuries earlier. In the first *Critique,* he notes:

> Judgment will be the faculty of subsuming under rules; that is, of distinguishing whether something does or does not stand under a given rule (*casus datae legis*). General logic contains, and can contain, no rules for judgment.... If it sought to give general instructions how we are to subsume under these rules, that is, to distinguish whether something does or does not come under them, that could only be by means of another rule. This in turn, for the very reason that it is a rule, again demands guidance from judgment...Judgment is a peculiar talent which can be practised only, and cannot be taught. (*CI* A132–33/B171–72)

For further discussion, see O'Neill, *Constructions of Reason,* pp. 167–69.

38. Noble, "Normative Ethical Theories," p. 53. Similarly, she claims that because "philosophers separate the task of moral criticism from that of social analysis, their conception of the kind of knowledge and insight needed to shed light on moral issues is unavoidably inadequate" ("Ethics and Experts," *Hastings Center Report* 12 [1982]: 8). See also Harry Redner, "Ethics in Unethical Times—Towards a Sociology of Ethics," in *The Institution of Philosophy: A Discipline in Crisis?* ed. Avner Cohen and Marcelo Dascal (LaSalle, Ill.: Open Court, 1989), where he criticizes the "unspoken traditional assumption of moral philosophers that there is an area of social life demarcated throughout history as the 'ethical' and that all ethical writings, no matter from what period, are about this same thing" (p. 306). These criticisms echo earlier-voiced concerns of Alasdair MacIntyre. For instance, in *After Virtue,* MacIntyre reprimands "the dominant philosophies of the present, analytical or phenomenological," for being "powerless to detect the [present] disorders of moral thought and practice" because they do not "understand its history" (pp. 2–3). However, since the subtitle of *After Virtue* is *A Study in Moral Theory,* we are again reminded of the fact that there exists no univocal definition of moral theory at present.

39. Baier, *Postures of the Mind,* p. 138. Cf. her remarks concerning Hume (her favorite moral philosopher): "I contrasted Hume's approach to ethics with the post-Kantian and post-Benthamite moral philosophy that went in for theory construction. Hume's way involves no normative theory—it involves a psychological theory, of course, and it also involves a political–economic theory, about the actual workings of human right-determining institutions. But no *normative* theory" (p. 236).

40. However, a given moral theory need not have all three of these normative aims. Most deontological and consequentialist theories seek to be action-guiding and pay much less attention to character guidance. Virtue theories, on the other hand, are primarily interested in character guidance and tend to underemphasize action guidance.

41. Williams, *Ethics and the Limits of Philosophy,* p. 72. Williams calls the first kind of theory "positive"; the second, "negative." Benthamite utilitarianism is a paradigm case of a positive ethical theory; emotivism is the most infamous example of a negative theory. An antitheory is neither a positive nor a negative theory, since antitheory "*leaves open* the question whether there could be such tests" (p. 74). What positive and negative theories share in common is a belief in the power of theory and philosophy to stand back and judge existing moral beliefs. A positive theorist stands back and judges moral beliefs to be either correct or incorrect; a negative theorist stands back and announces that moral beliefs are neither correct nor incorrect, arguing instead that this is the wrong question to ask about them. The antitheorist, on the other hand, does not believe that philosophy

and theory are this powerful, at least in the arena of ethics (hence Williams's title, *Ethics and the Limits of Philosophy*). A similar distinction between positive and negative theory comes up frequently in the antitheory writings of literary critics. See Knapp and Michaels, "Against Theory," p. 25 (esp. n.17); Knapp and Michaels, "Reply to Our Critics," in *Against Theory*, ed. Mitchell, p. 100; and Fish, "Consequences," p. 112. Paul de Man and Jacques Derrida are frequently cited as examples of negative theorists in this area; E. D. Hirsch, Jr., is an alleged positive theorist. (However, Hirsch himself, in "Against Theory?" states, "We antitheorists should stick together" [p. 48].) See also Knapp and Michaels, "Against Theory II: Hermeneutics and Deconstruction," *Critical Inquiry* 14 (1987): 49–68.

42. Williams, *Ethics and the Limits of Philosophy*, p. 74. Cf. p. 17, where he remarks that one of the primary aims of ethical theory is "to tell us how we should think about" the ethical. This comment immediately precedes the first epigraph for our present chapter—"Philosophy should not try to produce ethical theory."

43. Baier, "Doing Without Moral Theory?" in *Anti-Theory in Ethics*, p. 33 (*Postures of the Mind*, p. 232).

44. Baier, "Doing Without Moral Theory?" in *Anti-Theory in Ethics*, p. 33 (*Postures of the Mind*, p. 232). As to why Baier thinks it is a fatal blow for a moral theory to "tend to merge with moral action" or for a moral theorist to wind up "becoming a moral reformer" (p. 33), she seems to be assuming that genuine theory is always objective and descriptive and that normative claims are never objective. Although my present concern is with the former assumption, it may be worth noting that I do not accept the latter one, either. Ironically, she cites with approval MacIntyre's remark that "every piece of theorizing is a political and moral action"; but, as we saw earlier (n.38), MacIntyre himself is a supporter of (historically informed) moral theory, not an antitheorist.

45. Baier, "Doing Without Moral Theory?" in *Anti-Theory in Ethics*, p. 34 (*Postures of the Mind*. p. 233).

46. Fish, "Consequences," p. 110. Cf. his characterization of theory: "I reserve [the word *theory*] for an abstract or algorithmic formulation that guides or governs practice from a position outside any particular conception of practice. A theory, in short, is something a practitioner consults when he wishes to perform correctly" (*Doing What Comes Naturally*, p. 378, cf. p. 14).

47. What follows is the *possibility* that such persons may exist, not their actual existence.

48. Pincoffs, *Quandaries and Virtues*, p. 3. Cf. p. 55: "There are . . . no moral experts, as there should be if there were a theory from which decisions and particular cases could be deduced."

49. Noble, "Ethics and Experts," pp. 7–8. See also the replies to Noble's article by Peter Singer, Jerry Avron, Daniel Wikler, and Tom L. Beauchamp, as well as Noble's response on pp. 9–15. Barry Hoffmaster, in "Philosophical Ethics and Practical Ethics: Never the Twain Shall Meet," in *Clinical Ethics*, ed. Hoffmaster, Freedman, and Fraser, pp. 201–30, develops Noble's claims into a broad-scale attack on the alleged pertinence of ethical theory to actual moral problems. "Philosophical ethics," he claims, "is objectionable because it imposes a view of what morality is on the real world, rather than constructing an account of morality that is informed by the real world" (p. 225). See Caplan, "Moral Experts," and Ruth Macklin, "Ethical Theory and Applied Ethics: A Reply to the Skeptics" in this same volume for defenses of the claims that ethical theories are useful in resolving moral problems and that moral experts do exist.

50. For further discussion to which I am indebted, see Anthony Weston, *Toward Better Problems: A Contemporary Deweyan Practical Ethics* (Philadelphia: Temple University Press, forthcoming), chap. 2.

51. Hoffmaster, "Philosophical Ethics," pp. 204–5. Cf. Noble: "The overwhelming failure of any normative ethical theory to gain anything approaching universal acceptance is not

promising" ("Normative Ethical Theories," p. 52), and Baier: "The villain, as I see it, is the rationalist, law-fixated tradition in moral philosophy, which . . . breeds multiple and in the end frivolous systems and their less frivolous, more dangerous applications" ("Doing Without Moral Theory?" in *Anti-Theory in Ethics,* p. 37 [*Postures of the Mind,* p. 236]).

52. This strategy has also been employed repeatedly in the end-of-philosophy literature, in an attempt to show that those who proclaim the end of philosophy are themselves guilty of philosophizing when they defend this assertion. For a good discussion to which I am indebted, see Marcelo Dascal, "Reflections on the 'Crisis of Modernity'," in *Institution of Philosophy,* ed. Cohen and Dascal, pp. 220–21. My example of a tu quoque argument applied to Williams is adopted from Samuel Scheffler, "Morality Through Thick and Thin: A Critical Notice of *Ethics and the Limits of Philosophy,*" *Philosophical Review* 96 (1987): 423–27. For related discussion, see pp. 148–52. This example of a tu quoque argument directed against Fish was suggested to me by Norman Dahl. Other examples of tu quoque arguments directed against antitheorists in literary criticism can be found in Adena Rosmarin, "On the Theory of 'Against Theory'," in *Against Theory,* ed. Mitchell, p. 86; Daniel T. O'Hara, "Revisionary Madness: The Prospects of American Literary Theory at the Present Time," in *Against Theory,* ed. Mitchell, p. 33, n.4; and Steven Mailloux, "Truth or Consequences: On Being Against Theory," in *Against Theory,* ed. Mitchell, p. 71.

Chapter 6

1. Quotation marks, the word *so-called,* or the context will indicate when the specific antitheorist conception of theory analyzed in chapter 5 is referred to.
2. Baier, "Doing Without Moral Theory?" in *Anti-Theory in Ethics,* p. 33; cf. pp. 37–38 (*Postures of the Mind,* p. 232; cf. pp. 236, 223, 138).
3. Since Pincoffs claims that "ethical theory is essentially a modern invention" (*Quandaries and Virtues,* p. 2), it follows that Aristotle, on his view, had no ethical theory. McDowell announces at the beginning of "Virtue and Reason" that "moral theory [is] a discipline which seeks to formulate acceptable principles of conduct" (p. 87) and argues later that on Aristotle's view "one knows what to do (if one does) not by applying universal principles but by being a certain kind of person: one who sees situations in a certain distinctive way" (p. 105). On his view, moral theory is concerned primarily with the nature and justification of principles of behavior; but he does not believe Aristotle's ethics reveals any indication of these concerns.
4. Nussbaum, *Fragility of Goodness,* p. 10. See also p. 11, where she mentions briefly "important rival [ethical] conceptions, above all Kant's." On her view, both Aristotle and Kant offer moral theories; but Kant's is unacceptable. Nussbaum's claims (1) that Aristotle has an ethical theory and (2) that she relies on this theory and defends it in her own work together raise the question of how antitheoretical her own considered views are. On the other hand, her strong commitment to the view that "only the style of a certain sort of narrative artist (and not . . . the style associated with the abstract theoretical treatise) can adequately state certain important truths about the world" (*Love's Knowledge,* p. 6; cf. pp. 5, 7–8) has a definite antitheoretical ring to it.
5. Hampshire, *Morality and Conflict,* esp. chap. 2, on Aristotle and Spinoza; Williams, *Ethics and the Limits of Philosophy,* esp. chap. 3. Williams does hold that Aristotle offers "a richer and more determinate view" of rational agency than does Kant (p. 29) and that "very old philosophies may have more to offer than moderately new ones" (p. 198). However, he concludes his survey of Aristotle's ethics by remarking that "we [today] have no reason to believe in" the Aristotelian view that a proper account of human nature can "adequately determine one kind of ethical life as against others" (p. 52). Similarly, Hampshire begins

by announcing that "Aristotle and Spinoza's moral philosophies . . . have seemed to me the most credible and the most worth developing of all moral theories in the light of modern knowledge and of contemporary philosophy" (*Morality and Conflict,* p. 10) but concludes by noting that "Aristotle has repelled many by the implication in his theory that there is a fixity in human nature, and therefore in the virtues, which justifies the complacent thought that the ends of action are immutable and fully known once and for all. This is the tidiness, and the limitedness, which have often been found both unrealistic and also morally repugnant" (p. 43).

6. An analogous distinction between pure and empirical divisions occurs in Kant's writings about natural science. Natural science presupposes metaphysics, since the concept "nature" carries with it the idea of universal and necessary laws—an idea that cannot be derived from experience. The metaphysics of nature always concerns nonempirical principles, but Kant subdivides it into a *general* or transcendental part that treats "the concept of a nature in general [*überhaupt*] without any reference to any determinate object of experience" and a *special* part that "occupies itself with the special [*besondern*] nature of this or that kind of things, of which an empirical concept is given in such a way that besides what lies in this concept, no other empirical principle is needed for cognizing the things" (*Science* IV 469–70/6; cf. *G* IV 388/1–2). Physics is an example of a *special* metaphysical science; Kant's discussion of the "analytic of principles" in first *Critique* (*CI* A131/B170–A260/B315) is an example of general or transcendental metaphysics of science.

7. Extensive empirical knowledge will also be required in order to apply the categorical imperative to the deliberative situations of any nonhuman rational agents. For each species of rational being, a corresponding "species-specific" kind of empirical knowledge is needed in order to apply effectively an a priori principle to that group's contingent moral situation.

8. Sullivan, *Immanuel Kant's Moral Theory,* p. 57. Cf. O'Neill:

> We can obtain only negative instruction [from the Categorical Imperative]. The Categorical Imperative is only a strategy for avoiding principles of thinking, communicating and acting that cannot be adopted by all members of a plurality whose principles of interaction, let alone actual interaction (let alone coordination!) are not established by any transcendent reality. The supreme principle of reason does not fix thought or action in unique grooves; it only points to limits to the principles that can be shared. (*Constructions of Reason,* p. 24)

My own view is that we can also obtain *positive* instruction from the categorical imperative (e.g., "Discipline your emotions so that they obey reason cheerfully")—but only instruction of a very general kind that still falls far short of fixing "thought or action in unique grooves."

9. Cf. Richard Rorty, *Consequences of Pragmatism* (Minneapolis: University of Minnesota Press, 1982), chap. 2. For an opposing view, see Allen W. Wood, "Unsociable Sociability: The Anthropological Basis of Kantian Ethics," *Philosophical Topics* 19 (1991). Wood argues that Kantian ethics is "founded on an anthropology, a conception of human nature. . . . Even in a theory based on an a priori principle, that account will be based on a definite empirical conception of human nature." I do not think it is correct to claim that Kant's moral theory is "based" on anthropology, in part because Kant believes his moral theory is applicable to nonhuman as well as to human rational agents. But I do believe that Kant holds that it is necessary to bring in empirical considerations whenever we try to apply his moral theory to human life.

10. R. Rorty writes: "In recent decades Anglo-American moral philosophers have been turning against Kant. Annette Baier, Cora Diamond, Philippa Foot, Sabina Lovibond, Alasdair MacIntyre, Iris Murdoch, J. B. Schneewind, and others have questioned the basic Kantian assumption that moral deliberation must necessarily take the form of deduction from general, preferably 'nonempirical', principles" (*Contingency, Irony,* p. 193). Anglo-

American moral philosophers may well be turning against someone; but if the argument of this section is correct, they are not turning against Kant. Contra Rorty, it is simply false to assert that "the basic Kantian assumption" is that human moral deliberation must necessarily take the form of deduction from nonempirical principles. On the contrary, Kant's explicit position is that human moral deliberation must always involve extensive empirical considerations.

11. Both Williams and Hampshire criticize Aristotle on this point (Williams, *Ethics and the Limits of Philosophy*, pp. 35, 52; Hampshire, *Morality and Conflict*, pp. 150–52).

12. Louden, "Aristotle's Practical Particularism."

13. David Wiggins, "Weakness of Will, Commensurability, and the Objects of Deliberation and Desire," in *Essays on Aristotle's Ethics*, ed. A. Rorty, p. 255.

14. Burnyeat, "Aristotle on Learning to Be Good," in *Essays on Aristotle's Ethics*, ed. A. Rorty, p. 91, n.29; Nussbaum, *Fragility of Goodness*, p. 294; *Aristotle's "De motu animalium"* (Princeton, N.J.: Princeton University Press, 1978), pp. 216–17; Stocker, *Plural and Conflicting Values*, pp. 51–84.

15. Cf. 1096b23–26: "But of honor, wisdom, and pleasure, just in respect of their goodness, the accounts are distinct and diverse. The good, therefore, is not something common answering to one idea."

16. Aquinas, *Summa Theologiae* 1–2.65 ad 1.

17. In calling *phronēsis* an unerring guide to action, I am following Troels Engberg-Pedersen's analysis (*Aristotle's Theory*, pp. 189–91).

18. This is not to say that we deliberate only about means and not ends (see, e.g., *NE* 1111b26, 1112b11–12, 1113a14–15, 1113b3–4, where Aristotle is sometimes read as asserting otherwise). I agree with Wiggins and others who argue that the Greek phrase *ta pros ta telē*, often translated as "means," is better rendered as "things that pertain to or contribute to the end." But substituting this broader translation for the narrower does nothing to diminish the fact that agents do, according to Aristotle, consider all values and choices with respect to *eudaimonia*. For further discussion, see Wiggins, "Deliberation and Practical Reason,"; John M. Cooper, *Reason and Human Good in Aristotle* (Cambridge: Harvard University Press, 1975), esp. pp. 19–22; Hardie, *Aristotle's Ethical Theory*, p. 256; and Nussbaum, *Fragility of Goodness*, p. 297.

19. See, for example, J. L. Ackrill, "Aristotle on Eudaimonia," in *Essays on Aristotle's "Ethics,"* ed. A. Rorty, and W. F. Hardie, "The Final Good in Aristotle's *Ethics*," in *Aristotle: A Collection of Critical Essays*, ed. J. M. E. Moravcsik (Garden City, N.Y.: Anchor Books, 1967). For an opposing view, see Kraut, *Aristotle on the Human Good*.

20. I am indebted to Eugene Garver for articulating this distinction for me. As I read them, antitheorists, in their strong opposition to the unity assumption, reject both the theoretical and the practical senses of value commensurability.

21. Cf. Kant's discussion in *LE* 7–13/6–11. In both texts he is primarily concerned with Epicurean and Stoic thought, but I think it is clear that he holds Aristotle to be guilty of the same fundamental error (see, e.g, C2 V 127–28n./132, n.2). As is often the case with great philosophers, Kant's reading of his predecessors is not a model of historical scholarship. But it is clear that he views ancient ethical theories as being reductionistic in a way that his own theory is not and that he believes also that the presence of such reductionism constitutes a major defect in any ethical theory.

22. Cf. Sullivan, *Immanuel Kant's Moral Theory*, p. 219, and Yovel, *Kant and the Philosophy of History*, pp. 54–55. See also van der Linden's discussion of happiness as a harmony of ends in *Kantian Ethics*, pp. 69–73.

23. For further discussion of Kant's doctrine of the highest good, see Yovel, *Kant and the Philosophy of History*, chap. 1, and Sullivan, *Immanuel Kant's Moral Theory*, pp. 218–29. See also chapter 4.

24. Yovel, *Kant and the Philosophy of History*, pp. 6–7, 29, 39.

25. In discussing conflicts of duties, Kant uses a variety of German terms that all tend to get translated as "conflict," for example, *Kollision, Widerstreit,* and *zwei einander entgegengesetze Regeln.* While I think the context indicates that he is using these terms synonymously in the passage I shall quote, it is worth pointing out that he has no one technical term for "conflict."

26. The Latin phrases *Fortior obligatio vincit* and *Fortior obligandi ratio vincit* translate into "The stronger obligation conquers" and "The stronger ground or principle of obligation conquers." Note that although the two Latin phrases are quite similar in vocabulary, Kant employs different German expressions in his own translations of them (*die Oberhand behalte,* "holds the upper hand" vs. *behält den Platz,* "holds the field").

27. See, for example, Alan Donagan, "Consistency in Rationalist Moral Systems," in *Moral Dilemmas,* ed. Gowans (see also Gowans, *Moral Dilemmas,* pp. 6–7); Nussbaum, *Fragility of Goodness,* pp. 31–32; Onora Nell (O'Neill), *Acting on Principle* (New York: Columbia University Press, 1975), pp. 132–37; Bruce Aune, *Kant's Theory of Morals* (Princeton, N.J.: Princeton University Press, 1979), pp. 191–97; Herman, Practice of Moral," pp. 420–22; and Sullivan, *Immanuel Kant's Moral Theory,* pp. 72–75.

28. Donagan, "Consistency in Rationalist Moral Systems," p. 274; Nussbaum, *Fragility of Goodness,* p. 32; Gowans, *Moral Dilemmas,* p. 6.

29. Williams, *Problems of the Self,* p. 175.

30. Herman, "Practice of Moral Judgment," p. 422.

31. This is also the way Aune reads the passage (*Kant's Theory of Morals,* p. 193). Cf. Sullivan, *Immanuel Kant's Moral Theory,* p. 324, n.38. Granted, Kant is asking a question here rather than making an assertion. His "casuistical questions" are intended as problems for the individual reader's judgment, and he does not answer them directly. But the spirit of his remarks concerning "pedantry in the observance of duty" clearly suggests that he is leaning toward an affirmative answer to his own question.

32. In addition to Aune and Sullivan, the only other writer who to my knowledge makes the connection is Gregor. In her analysis of Kant's "casuistical questions" regarding suicide, she notes: "Under special conditions, there could arise questions of a collision between grounds of obligation, in which we might allege a duty (and hence a right) to suicide on the grounds that our continued existence would imply a violation of another duty" (*Laws of Freedom,* p. 135; cf. *DV* VI 423–24/86–87). For a recent attempt to revive the casuistical tradition in ethics, see Albert R. Jonsen and Stephen Toulmin, *The Abuse of Casuistry: A History of Moral Reasoning* (Berkeley: University of California Press, 1988). The authors include a brief discussion of Kant's place in this tradition on pp. 286–88, arguing, as I have been, that Kant's ethics is too often misread as a formalist program: "We cannot see Kant, any more than Aquinas or Aristotle himself, as a philosopher who dreamed of turning Ethics into a formal branch of *epistemē*" (p. 286).

33. Sullivan, *Immanuel Kant's Moral Theory,* pp. 73–75.

34. Mary Gregor, Translator's Introduction to *The Doctrine of Virtue,* by Kant (Philadelphia: University of Pennsylvania Press, 1964), pp. xviii–vxix. Gregor's claim that the scope of *The Doctrine of Virtue* prevents Kant "from considering the circumstances in which a 'collision of grounds of obligation' might occur" may appear to contradict my earlier assertion that Kant does imply that conflicts of duty exist in the work's "casuistical questions." However, I believe the two statements are consistent with one another. In *The Doctrine of Virtue,* Kant does not "consider the circumstances" in which conflicts of duty occur—rather, he merely draws attention to them and poses questions about them for readers to consider on their own. As Gregor herself notes, "In the *Metaphysic of Morals* itself such problems [cases involving specific individual circumstances] can only be handled by way of 'casuistical questions', with a view to the exercise and training of moral judgment" (Introduction, p. xviii).

35. I would like to thank Norman Dahl for suggesting this argument to me.

36. Larmore, *Patterns of Moral Complexity*, p. 10; Hampshire, *Morality and Conflict*, p. 152.
37. McDowell, "Virtue and Reason," pp. 105–6; Stocker, *Plural and Conflicting Values*, pp. 51–84; Nussbaum, *Fragility of Goodness*, pp. 294–98, 343–45. See also Nancy Sherman's brief discussion of Aristotelian conflict in *Fabric of Character*, pp. 30–31, 104–6.
38. Stocker, *Plural and Conflicting Values*, pp. 53–59. Aristotle gives three examples: the case in which a tyrant holds one's family hostage (1110a5–7) jettinsoning cargo in a storm in order to save a ship (1110a9–12), and Alcmaeon's act of matricide (1110a28–29).
39. Cf. Sherman's remark that though the virtuous individual "will have all the virtues (*NE* 1145a2), and though these cannot conflict essentially or in principle, contingent conflicts can arise" (*Fabric of Character*, p. 30).
40. Another passage that is often cited as evidence of Kant's commitment to moral decision procedures occurs in a note to the preface of the second *Critique:* "Those who know what a formula [*eine Formel*] means to a mathematician, in determining what is to be done in solving a problem without letting him go astray, will not regard a formula which will do this for all duties as something insignificant and unnecessary" (*C2* V 8n./8n.; see also Sullivan, *Immanuel Kant's Moral Theory*, p. 74). I do not believe that any of these passages confirms the claim that Kant's goal in ethics was to produce a decision procedure. In the first passage (*C1* A 328/B 385), he is contrasting the role that transcendental ideas play in the theoretical and practical spheres of reason. In the theoretical sphere, such ideas can never be entirely empirically verified and thus remain problems "to which there is no solution." However, in the practical sphere, transcendental ideas are "always in the highest degree fruitful," since they can be given "*in concreto*" and serve to guide action. In the second passage (*C1* A 476/B 504), his point is simply that we cannot have moral obligations in regard to things of which we cannot have any knowledge: any answer to a moral problem must come from within the bounds of what is presently known (basically, an epistemological variant on the "Ought implies can" maxim). And in the passage from the second *Critique,* Kant is replying to a criticism put forward by his contemporary G. A. Tittel, who complained that "the entire Kantian reform of ethics" had limited itself "just to a new formula." His main point here is that he never claimed to be the inventor of a *new principle* of morality, for he believes the common reason of humanity already subscribes to the categorical imperative (see pp. 116–20). True, he does go on to speak of a formula that can determine "all duties"; but I do not think he believes that a formula that determines all duties is at all equivalent to a decision procedure which tells one what to do in all cases. Determining general principles of duty is not the same as knowing what to do in specific situations.
41. Nell, *Acting on Principle*, p. 43. I believe her views on this matter have changed. As noted earlier (chap. 2, n.61) in her more recent *Constructions of Reason* (1989) she states, "The Categorical Imperative is a fundamental strategy, not an algorithm" (p. 59, cf. p. 24). But even the *Acting on Principle* passage is not as pro-decision-procedure as it may appear to be. We need to distinguish between a decision procedure for "maxims of duty" and the "moral status of acts" on the one hand and one that professes to tell people what to do in every specific situation on the other. They are not equivalent notions. In the *Acting on Principle* passage, Nell interprets Kant as aiming only at the former. However, when antitheorists argue against decision procedures, they have the latter project in mind. One could, for example, determine by means of the categorical imperative that the general course of action one is considering falls under the broad category of a "morally worthy" act and still lack a formula that gives one a detailed "solution" to the moral issue at hand.
42. I would like to thank Robert C. Roberts for conversation on these topics. See also John Benson, "Who Is the Autonomous Man?" in *The Virtues*, ed. Kruschwitz and Roberts. For more on the necessity of judgment in moral deliberation, see Mark Johnson, "Imagination in Moral Judgment," *Philosophy and Phenomenological Research* 96 (1985): 265–80.

43. Like many post-Kantian thinkers, I am doubtful that there is such a thing as "ordinary moral consciousness" if by this phrase is meant a set of universal, timeless moral concepts that determines in a detailed manner moral thinking in all times and places. Moral concepts, like other concepts, are subject to cultural change, though many self-proclaimed moral genealogists have exaggerated the extent and degree of such change (cf. pp. 34–44). The attempt to construct an accurate conceptual map of people's moral beliefs, if it is truly a descriptive undertaking, would seem inevitably to generate the problem of the cultural context of the population whose views are to be systematized. Accordingly, I believe the moral theorist's topographical task needs to be historicized: part of the the-orist's job is to map the conceptual contours of moral outlooks in different times and places and to be on the lookout for conceptual changes within and among these outlooks. (For further discussion, see pp. 146–48.) Kant, of course, would not accept the claim that the topographical task needs to be historicized, at least as regards the a priori dimension of his ethical theory. But as we have seen (pp. 100–4), "morality requires anthropology in order to be applied to humans." Furthermore, more radically contingent empirical knowledge of a less than species-wide nature must be brought in whenever we are dealing with circumstances that do not concern "men considered merely as men."

44. Sullivan, *Immanuel Kant's Moral Theory,* p. 29.

45. Cf. Paton, *Categorical Imperative,* pp. 25–26.

46. The clearest instances of a "perceptual data" use of *ta phainomena* occur at *Cael* 303a22–23 and 306a13–17, where Aristotle argues that scientific principles must ultimately be judged by perceptual facts and not conceptual arguments. There is still much debate at present as to whether Aristotle's method in science is empirical or dialectical. See, for example, G. E. L. Owen, "Tithenai ta phainomena," in *Aristotle,* ed. Moravcsik; Robert Bolton, "Definition and Scientific Method in Aristotle's *Posterior Analytics* and *Generation of Animals,*" in *Philosophical Issues in Aristotle's Biology,* ed. Allan Gotthelf and James G. Lennox (New York: Cambridge University Press, 1987), esp. pp. 121–30; and Nuss-baum, *Fragility of Goodness,* chap. 8. However, all parties in the dispute agree that at least in the ethical treatises, *ta phainomena* refer to beliefs or opinions and not simply to perceptual data.

47. Nussbaum, *Fragility of Goodness,* p. 247. Again, though, since she regards Kant's con-ception of ethical theory as being the most important "rival" conception to Aristotle's (p. 11), she would presumably deny that Kant and Aristotle agree on this point.

48. A more democratic Aristotle seems at first to be evident in the *Eudemian Ethics,* when he states that "every person [*hekastos*] has some contribution to make to the truth" (1216b31). But this passage is consistent with *Top* 100b21–23 and *NE* 1145b6. Each person does have *some* contribution to make to the truth in ethics; "For we say that which everyone thinks really is so; and the man who attacks this belief will hardly have anything more credible to maintain instead" (*NE* 1172b35–73a1). But when moral theorists fail to find agreement among everyone's *endoxa,* the scale is then to be tipped toward the beliefs of educated males. Kant, on the other hand, when faced with a similar dilemma of inconsistent moral beliefs, would tip the scale against the aristocratic elite and toward working people.

49. Burnyeat, "Aristotle on Learning," p. 81. Cf. *NE* 1179b1–3, where Aristotle asserts that "with regard to virtue, then, it is not enough to know, but we must try to have and use it, or try any other way there may be of becoming good." See also 1105b2–5, 1143b18–1145a11; *EE* 1214b6–12, 1215a8–11.

50. Sullivan, *Immanuel Kant's Moral Theory,* p. 318, n.24. See also his earlier article, "The Kantian Critique of Aristotle's Moral Philosophy: An Appraisal," *Review of Metaphysics* 28 (1974): 24–53, esp. pp. 52–53.

51. Strictly speaking, formal education is not even a necessary condition for expertise in the technocratic sense. Someone who could demonstrate (say, by passing a standardized

examination) that she or he possessed the requisite knowledge—however acquired—
ought to be allowed into the expert guild. However, the earnest credentialism in all of
the professions and academic disciplines at present does mean that as a practical matter,
the right degree from an approved institution is essential.

52. It is worth noting that the wisdom model of moral expertise is etymologically closer to
the original meaning of *expert* than is the technocratic model (Latin *expertus,* p.p. of
expiriri, "to make full trial of," whence also *experience*). However, etymology is not
everything; and most contemporary usages of the word *expert* are closer to the technocratic
model.

53. Nussbaum, *Fragility of Goodness,* p. 248. *Meta.* 1010b3–14, 1011a3–13 form the textual
basis for her interpretation of Aristotle's views about expertise. See also pp. 479–80,
n.22, where she addresses the question of whether Aristotelian method can offer help in
cases where there exists serious disagreement as to who possesses expertise and what
procedures make for expertise.

54. Pietism was a branch of Protestant Christianity that began as a reaction against the
growing formal tendencies that began to appear in Protestantism in the aftermath of the
Reformation. In stressing experience, feeling, and personal participation, it was clearly
lay-oriented and somewhat antiestablishment in spirit. As a child, Kant attended Pietist
schools, and the University of Königsberg itself was a center of Pietist thought when he
enrolled there. See *Encyclopedia of Philosophy,* s.v. "pietism"; John Dillenberger and Claude
Welch, *Protestant Christianity Interpreted Through Its Development* (New York: Scribner,
1954), pp. 123–27; and Ernst Troeltsch, *The Social Teachings of the Christian Churches,* trans. Olive Wyon (New York: Harper & Row, 1960), vol. 2, esp. pp. 714–19,
784–88.

Chapter 7

1. Cf. Bernard Gert: "My vain hope is that with the advent of applied ethics the interest in
a clear, coherent, comprehensive, and useful account of morality will outweigh the traditional philosophical interest in obscure, incoherent, schematic, and useless accounts"
(*Morality: A New Justification of the Moral Rules* [New York: Oxford University Press,
1988], p. xiv).

2. See, for example, Owen Flanagan and Amelie Rorty, eds., *Identity, Character, and Morality*
(Cambridge: MIT Press, 1991); Owen Flanagan, *Varieties of Moral Personality* (Cam-
bridge: Harvard University Press, 1991); Lawrence Thomas, *Living Morally: A Psychology
of Moral Character* (Philadelphia: Temple University Press, 1989); G. E. Scott, *Moral
Personhood: An Essay in the Philosophy of Moral Psychology* (Albany: State University of New
York Press, 1990).

3. See, for example, Joshua Cohen, *The Moral Arc of the Universe: Justice and the Demise of
Slavery* (London: Basil Blackwell, forthcoming). Foucault's work is also important here,
since his neo-Nietzchean commitment to moral genealogy stems from a strong belief that
there is no fixed, ahistorical moral order and that in order to understand what we should
do, we must first understand how we have constituted ourselves. See Foucault, *Foucault
Reader,* pp. 340–72, and John Rajchman, "Ethics After Foucault," *Social Text* 13–14
(1986): 165–83. At the same time, I am in agreement with Charles Taylor's criticism of
this type of neo-Nietzchean moral theory for "not coming quite clean about its own
moral motivations. . . . It claims a kind of distance from its own value commitments, which
consists in the fact that it alone is lucid about their status as fruits of a constructed order,
which lucidity sets it apart from other views and confers the advantage on itself of being
free from delusion in a way that [other moral theories] aren't" (*Sources of the Self,* p. 100).
Finally, much recent feminist work in ethics also has a strong historical orientation. As

Nancy Fraser and Linda Nicholson note: "*Contra* Lyotard, . . . postmodern critique need forswear neither large historical narratives nor analyses of societal macrostructures. This point is important for feminists, since sexism has a long history and is deeply and pervasively embedded in contemporary societies" ("Social Criticism Without Philosophy," in *Institution of Philosophy,* ed. Cohen and Dascal, p. 298). See also Eva Feder Kittay and Diana T. Meyers, eds., *Women and Moral Theory* (Totowa, N.J.: Rowman & Littlefield, 1987).

4. Arthur L. Caplan, "Ethical Engineers Need Not Apply: The State of Applied Ethics Today," *Science, Technology, and Human Values* 6 (1980): 31. At the same time, theorists continue to debate how much (and what sorts of) empirical knowledge applied and professional ethicists actually need. See, for example, Michael Bayles, "Moral Theory and Application," *Social Theory and Practice* 10 (1984): 97–120.

5. These issues are explored in more detail (and with particular reference to Williams's opposition to general moral principles) in my essay "Through Thick and Thin." See also Samuel Scheffler's critical notice of Williams's *Ethics and the Limits of Philosophy* ("Morality Through Thick and Thin"), esp. pp. 421–29); Michael Walzer, *Interpretation and Social Criticism* (Cambridge: Harvard University Press, 1987), chap. 2.

6. Cf. Walzer, *Interpretation and Social Criticism,* p. 39.

7. Cf. John Dewey and James H. Tuft, *Ethics,* rev. ed. (New York: Holt, 1922), p. 175.

8. Willard Van Orman Quine, *From a Logical Point of View,* 2d ed., rev. (Cambridge: Harvard University Press, 1980), p. 42. I am also indebted here to Lawrence C. Becker's interesting discussion in *Reciprocity,* pp. 52–72.

9. Noble, "Normative Ethical Theories," p. 50.

10. I am indebted here to Robert N. McCauley's discussion of selectivity in his essay "A Comparative Model of Knowing," *Metaphilosophy,* forthcoming.

11. Samuel Scheffler, *The Rejection of Consequentialism* (Oxford: Clarendon Press, 1982), pp. 5–6; Derek Parfit, *Reasons and Persons* (New York: Oxford University Press, 1986), pp. 24–28. See also Scheffler, *Consequentialism and Its Critics,* pp. 4–11.

12. Amartya Sen, "Rights and Agency," in *Consequentialism and Its Critics,* ed. Scheffler, esp. sec. 4.

13. T. M. Scanlon, "Rights, Goals, and Fairness," in *Consequentialism and Its Critics,* ed. Scheffler, p. 75. Scanlon's position seems reminiscent of Rawls's argument in "Two Concepts of Rules," in *Ethics,* ed. Thomson and Dworkin, pp. 104–35. In this early article, Rawls maintained that utilitarian considerations work best when used to justify institutional practices, and that nonutilitarian considerations work best when used to justify particular actions that fall under practices.

14. John L Mackie, "Can There Be a Right-Based Moral Theory?" *Midwest Studies in Philosophy,* vol. 3, *Ethical Theory,* ed. Peter A. French and Theodore E. Uehling, Jr. (Minneapolis: University of Minnesota Press, 1978), p. 358. Ronald Dworkin, *Taking Rights Seriously* (Cambridge: Harvard University Press, 1975), pp. 171–72.

15. Jeremy Waldron, ed., *Nonsense upon Stilts: Bentham, Burke and Marx on the Rights of Man* (New York: Methuen, 1987), p. 194. See also Waldron, "A Right to Do Wrong," *Ethics* 92 (1981): 36–37. I defend a similar position in "Rights Infatuation and the Impoverishment of Moral Theory," *Journal of Value Inquiry* 17 (1983): 87–102. Responsible libertarians are also coming around to the view that moral theory involves more than rights. Thus, Loren Lomasky begins his *Persons, Rights, and the Moral Community* (New York: Oxford University Press, 1987) by announcing: "Rights are not the whole of moral value, nor is respect for rights the highest of moral virtues. Unsophisticated generosity and compassion may take one a good bit higher on the ladder of moral worth than does a well-schooled punctiliousness in not overstepping the boundaries set by the rights of others" (p. 3).

16. Gregory W. Trianosky, "Supererogation, Wrongdoing, and Vice: On the Auton-

omy of the Ethics of Virtue," *Journal of Philosophy* 83 (1986): 40. See also Louis P. Pojman, *Ethics: Discovering Right and Wrong* (Belmont, Calif.: Wadsworth, 1990), pp. 128–31.

17. Louden, "On Some Vices," p. 78. My views on this topic were influenced by Nagel, *Mortal Questions,* and Taylor, "Diversity of Goods."

18. Williams, *Ethics and the Limits of Philosophy,* p. 17. Cf. Scheffler, "Morality Through Thick and Thin." (In my doctoral dissertation, "The Elements of Ethics: Toward a Topography of the Moral Field" [University of Chicago, 1981], which predates Williams's book by four years, I, too, attempted to show "that the prevailing reductionist strategies in ethical theory cannot account for certain fundamental judgements about moral experience" [p. 190].)

19. Walzer, *Interpretation and Social Criticism,* p. 32.

20. See pp. 113–16 for my attempt to exonerate Kant from the decision procedure charge. Classical Benthamite utilitarianism is probably the most promising candidate for those who are determined to find a guilty party in the history of moral theory. For instance, in *Introduction to the Principles of Morals and Legislation,* chap. 4, Bentham lays out explicit guidelines for measuring pains and pleasures and concludes his presentation by recommending that his "process" "always be kept in view," in order that activity of moral and political decision making should "approach to the character of an exact one" (p. 31). However, Fred Berger disputes the claim that Bentham construed utilitarianism as a decision procedure, suggesting instead that Bentham saw his "calculus" more as a general device of strategy for planning future actions than as a tool that could always provide one correct answer (*Happiness, Justice, and Freedom* [Berkeley: University of California Press, 1984], pp. 73–77). As David Brink notes, "It is almost entirely opponents of utilitarianism who make [the] assumption" that utilitarianism claims to offer a decision procedure (*Moral Realism and the Foundations of Ethics* [New York: Cambridge University Press, 1989], p. 256, n.30).

21. See chap. 6, n.41. Cf. David Brink's distinction between decision procedures and criteria of rightness in *Moral Realism,* pp. 216, 256. Brink defends a version of utilitarianism that eschews decision procedures and provides only criteria of rightness.

22. I have borrowed the concept "strong evaluator" from Charles Taylor, "Responsibility for Self," in *The Identities of Persons,* ed. Amelie Rorty (Berkeley: University of California Press, 1976), pp. 287–88.

23. Antitheorists often accuse moral theorists of showing a strong bias toward very general or "thin" moral concepts such as "ought" and "right." See, for example, Williams, *Ethics and the Limits of Philosophy,* pp. 17, 128; Mark Platts, *Ways of Meaning* (London: Routledge & Kegan Paul, 1979), chap. 10. In my view both so-called thick, as well as thin, criteria of moral assessment can and should be offered for both acts and agents.

24. I have borrowed this term from Onora O'Neill, although, in what follows, I do not quite follow her usage of it. See her discussion of algorithms vs. strategies in *Constructions of Reason,* pp. 180–86.

25. Cf. Rawls, "Outline of a Decision Procedure for Ethics," in *Ethics,* ed. Thomson and Dworkin. The first step, Rawls argued, is to define a class of competent moral judges; the second, to define a class of considered judgments concerning which the judges are most likely to make correct judgments; the third, to "explicate" these judgments—that is, to determine which principles the judges used in arriving at their considered judgments. Note that I am not assuming here that *every* aspect of a competent moral judge's reasoning processes can be codified, only that *some* of them can be.

26. Cf. Hubert L. Dreyfus and Stuart E. Dreyfus's description of the RECONSIDER program, developed by Marsden Blois and others at the California Medical Center in San Francisco, in *Mind over Machine: The Power of Human Intuition and Expertise in the*

Era of the Computer (New York: Free Press, 1986), p. xv. I discuss some of the problems raised by such programs (and their possible relevance to ethics) in more detail further on.

27. Cf. Sabina Lovibond:

> Our experiential grasp of the moral institutions of our community is enough to equip us with a moral imagination which transcends the range of concrete experience that can be had within a community dominated by institutions such as those. Our acquisition of the concepts we shall use as participants in *Sittlichkeit,* or customary ethics, also provides us with all the intellectual resources we need for the purposes of *Moralität*—that part of ethics which concerns our obligation to bring about, not what already exists, but what ought to exist. (*Realism and Imagination in Ethics* [Minneapolis: University of Minnesota Press, 1983], pp. 195–96)

28. Cf. Terrance C. McConnell, "Objectivity and Moral Expertise," *Canadian Journal of Philosophy* 14 (1984): 194–95, where the opposing technocratic conception of moral expertise is defended. On McConnell's view, a moral expert need not be "a model of virtue" but need only be someone "who knows what people ought to do or is at least capable of helping people see more clearly . . . what they have good moral reasons for doing."

29. See, for example, J. Ross Quinlan, ed., *Applications of Expert Systems* (Reading, Mass.: Addison–Wesley, 1987), and Donald Mitchie, "Current Developments in Artificial Intelligence and Expert Systems," *Zygon* 20 (1985): 375–89.

30. Dreyfus and Dreyfus, *Mind over Machine,* p. 101. The literature on expert systems is enormous. For more optimistic accounts than that found in *Mind over Machine,* see Edward Feigenbaum and Pamela McCorduck, *The Fifth Generation: Artificial Intelligence and Japan's Computer Challenge to the World* (Reading, Mass.: Addison–Wesley, 1983), and Donald A. Waterman, *A Guide to Expert Systems* (Reading, Mass.: Addison–Wesley, 1986).

31. J. B. Schneewind, "Moral Knowledge and Moral Principles," in *Revisions: Changing Perspectives in Moral Philosophy,* ed. Stanley Hauerwas and Alasdair MacIntyre (Notre Dame, Ind.: University of Notre Dame Press, 1983), p. 126. Needless to say, the author is not discussing the possibility of moral expert systems in this essay.

32. Fish, "Consequences," pp. 115–16. Cf. his *Doing What Comes Naturally,* p. 378.

33. Fish, *Doing What Comes Naturally,* p. 378: "My argument here is that to include such activities under the rubric of theory is finally to make everything theory, and if one does that there is nothing of a *general* kind to be said about theory." Cf. p. 14.

34. Norwood Russell Hanson, *Patterns of Discovery* (Cambridge: Cambridge University Press, 1958), chaps. 1–2; Karl R. Popper, *Conjectures and Refutations: The Growth of Scientific Knowledge* (New York: Harper Torchbooks, 1968), p. 388. (Note that I am not suggesting that postpositivist philosophers of science are guilty of calling everything theory; rather, their point is that nearly everything has *a theoretical aspect,* including all of our observations. But I do believe that acceptance of maxims such as "All facts are theory-laden" has led many people to be less concerned than they should be about where theory begins and where it ends.) For a helpful survey of the theory versus observation issue, see William Bechtel, *Philosophy of Science: An Overview for Cognitive Science* (Hillsdale, N.J.: Erlbaum, 1988), pp. 44–48. Fish tries to finesse the issue by making a sharp distinction between *beliefs* and *theories.* He acknowledges the truth of "the chief lesson of antifoundationalism," namely, "that there are no unmediated facts nor any neutral perception and that everything we know and see is known and seen under a description or as function of some paradigm" ("Consequences," p. 116). But

he then asserts that what mediates facts are beliefs rather than theories and that "beliefs are not theories" (p. 116). Theories, he continues, "are something you can have—you can wield them and hold them at a distance; beliefs have *you*, in the sense that there can be no distance between them and the acts they enable" (p. 116). Unfortunately, this distinction between beliefs and theories raises more questions than it answers. First of all, beliefs themselves are sometimes caused by, and often strongly influenced by, theories. The beliefs we hold are often a function of the theories we subscribe to (or, at least, of the theories our teachers held). Second, it is just not the case that all beliefs possess, or "have," their subjects; nor is it the case that all subjects possess, or "have," their theories. We have both weak and strong beliefs, and we also subscribe to theories fervently or not-so-fervently. People can and do change their beliefs, and some theories do have a very strong grip on some people. Whatever distinctions between beliefs and theories may exist (and I believe there are some), Fish has not succeeded in articulating them.

35. Cf. Becker, who argues that moral theory "is as changeable as the conditions of human life. It is as indeterminate and unfinished as it is partial" (*Reciprocity*, p. 144) and R. Rorty: "There is nothing called 'the aim of writing' any more than there is something called 'the aim of theorizing' " (*Contingency, Irony*, p. 145).

36. But not necessarily moral agents *überhaupt*. A moral theorist may well wish to restrict personal efforts to reflecting about moral agents who live on his or her own planet or even within his or her own society as it currently exists. While I have no objections to responsible reflection concerning "moral agency as such," I do believe that moral theories that focus directly on subjects concerning which we have solid empirical knowledge are likely to produce more fruitful results.

37. Here I am essentially following Becker, *Reciprocity*, p. 37. See also Kant's definition of "theory" in *TP* VIII 275/61.

38. Fish, "Consequences," p. 117.

39. I am indebted to Robert McCauley for several points in this paragraph.

40. The subtitle of Michell's anthology *Against Theory* is *Literary Studies and the New Pragmatism*. And the antitheoretical position Clarke and Simpson label "moral conservativism" is often discussed (as they themselves note in *Anti-Theory in Ethics*, p. 298) under the heading of "moral pragmatism." See, for example, Jeffrey Stout, *Ethics After Babel* (Boston: Beacon Press, 1988), chap. 11.

41. W. James, *Pragmatism and the Meaning of Truth*, p. 32. For more on some distinctions between pragmatism and antitheory, see Fairlamb, "Pragmatism and Anti-Theory"

42. John Dewey, *Early Works of John Dewey*, (Carbondale: Southern Illinois University Press, 1975), vol. 3, pp. 94–95. Richard Rorty endorses this Deweyan conception of moral theory when he writes, "We need to see moral theory as Dewey saw it, as 'all one with moral *insight*, . . . the recognition of the relationships at hand' " ("Method and Morality," in *Social Science as Moral Inquiry*, ed. Norman Haan, Robert N. Bellah, Paul Rabinow, and William M. Sullivan [New York: Columbia University Press, 1983], p. 173). On my reading, Rorty should not be construed as an antitheorist in ethics, despite the strong influence of his work on many of those who so style themselves. See also his essay "Philosophy Without Principles," in *Against Theory*, ed. Mitchell, where he writes: "In its unobjectionable sense, 'theory' just means 'philosophy'. One can still have philosophy even after one stops arguing deductively and ceases to ask where the first principles are coming from, ceases to think of there being a special corner of the world—or the library—where they are found" (p. 136). However, as we shall see later (p. 155), Rorty does suffer from more-than-occasional lapses into antitheory in his recent book *Contingency, Irony, and Solidarity*.

43. Dewey, *Early Works*, p. 95.

Chapter 8

1. For a classic logical empiricist account, see Carl G. Hempel, *Aspects of Scientific Explanation and Other Essays in the Philosophy of Science* (New York: Free Press, 1965), chap. 12. For a recent survey of explanation issues within the philosophy of science, see Bechtel, *Philosophy of Science*, pp. 22–29, 38–41. Hempel's "deductive–nomological" model of scientific explanation involves sets of covering laws and initial conditions in the explanans and an event-to-be-explained in the explanandum. For example, "A building made of materials a and b, located distance x from the epicenter of a quake of intensity y, will fall during such a quake. Bookshop Santa Cruz was made of materials a and b, and was located distance x from the epicenter of a quake of intensity y. Therefore, the Bookshop fell."

2. See Gilbert Harman, *The Nature of Morality* (New York: Oxford University Press, 1977), chaps. 1–2, and John L. Mackie, *Ethics: Inventing Right and Wrong* (New York: Penguin Books, 1977), chap. 1. Recent defenses of moral theory's explanatory role include Nicholas Sturgeon, "Moral Explanations," and Geoffrey Sayre-McCord, "Moral Theory and Explanatory Impotence," both in *Essays in Moral Realism*, ed. Sayre-McCord.

3. Sturgeon, "Moral Explanations," p. 244. Bernard De Voto, *The Year of Decision: 1846* (Boston: Little, Brown, 1943), pp. 426, 442.

4. Cohen, *Moral Arc;* John W. Blassingame, ed., *Slave Testimony: Two Centuries of Letters, Speeches, Interviews, and Autobiographies* (Baton Rouge: Louisiana State University Press, 1977), p. 437.

5. Sayre-McCord, "Moral Theory," p. 276.

6. See chap. 5, n.41. Williams discusses negative versus positive ethical theories in *Ethics and the Limits of Philosophy*, p. 72. A similar distinction is also common in the antitheory writings of literary critics. See, for example, Mitchell, *Against Theory*, pp. 25, 100, 112.

7. Williams, *Ethics and the Limits of Philosophy*, p. 74.

8. For further discussion to which I am indebted, see E. Thomas Lawson and Robert N. McCauley, *Rethinking Religion: Connecting Cognition and Culture* (New York: Cambridge University Press, 1990), chap. 1. Lawson and McCauley defend an "interactionist" position that "champions the positive values" of both hermeneutic interpretation and scientific explanation without allowing either one to exclude or subordinate the other (p. 22).

9. Richard Rorty, *Consequences of Pragmatism* (Minneapolis: University of Minnesota Press, 1982), p. 16.

10. It is generally assumed that Kant, in his moral theory, successfully engaged in precisely this act of will. True, his writings on ethics do reveal a particular fondness for the project of "pure practical philosophy"—the project of uncovering moral principles that are "free from everything empirical," "not grounded on the peculiarities of human nature," and valid for all rational beings. But as we have seen, he also insists that substantial empirical knowledge is needed whenever a priori moral theory is applied to the human situation. Furthermore, the Hegelian conviction that human nature is a historical product may itself have Kantian origins. In the *Anthropology*, Kant states that man "has a character which he himself creates, insofar as he is capable of perfecting himself according to the ends that he himself adopts" (VII 321/183). If human beings do develop their own nature through history, there will be conceptual change at this level as well. For further discussion, see Wood, "Unsociable Sociability," sec. 2.

11. Isaiah Berlin, *Concepts and Categories: Philosophical Essays* (New York: Penguin Books, 1981), p. 159. See also pp. 7–8, where Berlin acknowledges the Kantian origins of this way of understanding theory's task. Bernard Williams, in his introduction to this volume, comments briefly on Berlin's suggestion that the primary task of theory is to offer an

account "of various models or presuppositions which men have brought to their experience, and which have helped, indeed, to form that experience" (p. xiii); but he does
not state whether, according to his own view, *moral* theories are needed to help carry it
out. At the same time, a premonition of Williams's subsequent attack on moral theory
(and a hint that the attack owes more than a little to Berlin's own views concerning the
irreducible plurality of value) is present in the allusion to "the demands of another kind
of theory, moral theory, which aims to systematise and simplify our moral opinions" (p.
xvii).

12. Berlin, *Concepts and Categories,* p. 167. In this passage, Berlin appears to be assuming a
    conception of the moral that confines itself to individuals. This is a narrower conception
    of the moral than I advocate. See pp. 69–70.
13. Walzer, *Company of Critics,* p. 17. See also Brian Barry's review essay, "Social Criticism
    and Political Philosophy," *Philosophy and Public Affairs* 19 (1990): 360–73, esp. pp. 363–
    64. Barry argues that a "critic of institutions" needs a theory but that a "critic of conduct"
    does not. For reasons I have indicated, my position is that both kinds of criticism even-
    tually require support from theory.
14. Kupperman, "Character and Ethical," p. 122.
15. Walzer, *Company of Critics,* p. 229.
16. Clarke and Simpson, eds., *Anti-Theory in Ethics,* p. 15. Opponents of antitheory in lit-
    erature have also claimed that antitheory necessarily has conservative implications. For
    instance, Jeffrey Malkan asserts that Fish's position "is skewed toward conservatism be-
    cause, by removing external reference points, Fish discredits the power and energy of
    radicalism: its belief in a transcendent theory of history" (" 'Against Theory,' Pragmatism
    and Deconstruction," *Telos* 71 [1987], p. 137). Fish denies that both theory and antithe-
    ory have consequences (radical or conservative) in "Consequences," as well as in *Doing
    What Comes Naturally,* pp. 27–29.
17. Cf. Max Horkheimer:

> The hostility to theory as such which prevails in contemporary public life is really
> directed against the transformative activity associated with critical thinking. . . .
> Among the vast majority of the ruled there is the unconscious fear that theoretical
> thinking might show their painfully won adaptation to reality to be perverse and
> unnecessary. Those who profit from the status quo entertain a general suspicion
> of any intellectual independence. The tendency to conceive theory as the opposite
> of a positive outlook is so strong that even the inoffensive traditional type of
> theory suffers from it at times. (*Critical Theory: Selected Essays,* trans. Matthew
> J. O'Connell [New York: Seabury Press, 1972], p. 232)

18. Williams, *Ethics and the Limits of Philosophy,* p. 115.
19. Williams, *Ethics and the Limits of Philosophy,* pp. 116, 198. Cf. p. 112: "It is quite wrong
    to think that the only alternative to ethical theory is to refuse reflection and to remain
    in unreflective prejudice. Theory and prejudice are not the only possibilities for an in-
    telligent agent, or for philosophy."
20. Williams, *Ethics and the Limits of Philosophy,* p. 112. Cf. his remarks about "reflective social
    knowledge" (p. 199). For evidence of Williams's debt to critical theory, see pp. 166–67,
    esp. nn.11, 12. Jürgen Habermas announces that his aim is "to recover the forgotten
    experience of reflection" (p. vii); and the concept of reflection plays a central—albeit not
    always clear—role in much of his work (*Knowledge and Human Interests,* trans. Jeremy
    J. Shapiro [Boston: Beacon Press, 1971]). See also Raymond Geuss, *The Idea of a Critical
    Theory* (New York: Cambridge University Press, 1981), pp. 61–63, 70, 79, 91–94.
21. Williams, *Ethics and the Limits of Philosophy,* p. 114. Cf. Scheffler, "Morality Through
    Thick and Thin," p. 422. As Scheffler points out, Williams uncharacteristically suggests
    that justice may be one moral concept that "transcends the relativism of distance" (*Ethics*

and the Limits of Philosophy, p. 166), thus allowing us to appraise societies as just or unjust that are temporally or spatially quite distant from us. If this is so, on Williams's view we can appraise *some* aspects of moral practices from a standpoint external to them. However, it is hard to see what the force of these "justice appraisals" could be. Since the concept of justice is also (on Williams's view) a thin term that is not world-guided, it follows that such appraisals must, according to Williams, ultimately lack an objective basis.

22. Cf. Habermas's distinction between *reflexive learning* and *nonreflexive learning* in *Legitimation Crisis,* trans. Thomas McCarthy (Boston: Beacon Press, 1973), p. 15. Reflexive learning involves defending or rejecting practical claims "on the basis of arguments"; nonreflexive learning takes place when practical claims "are naively taken for granted and accepted or rejected without discursive consideration." I am grateful to Tony Smith for conversation on this point.

23. Habermas, *Knowledge and Human Interests,* pp. vii, 317. Habermas seems to have softened his position in recent years in the sense that he now accepts the claim "that philosophy has no business playing the part of the highest arbiter in matters of science and culture." However, he continues to hold that philosophy ought to concern itself with justificatory discourse in all areas of life and with the validity claims raised in all conversations. Philosophy's proper role is thus that of interpreter or "stand-in" as opposed to judge. See his *Moral Consciousness,* esp. pp. 14, 19.

24. Cf. Sheldon Wolin's discussion of imaginative vision and political theory in *Politics and Vision* (Boston: Little, Brown, 1960), pp. 17–21, 35–37, and in "Political Theory as a Vocation," *American Political Science Review* 63 (1969): 1073–76, 1082. Wolin's assertion that "at the center of the enterprise of [classical] political theory was an imaginative element, an ordering vision of what the political system ought to be and what it might become" (*Politics and Vision,* p. 35), suggests that political imagination also involves normative moral concerns. However, this is not to say that political theory is in any danger of being swallowed up by moral theory; for many questions (e.g., the meaning of the public interest, the nature of political authority) will remain distinctively political in nature.

25. R. G. Collingwood, *The Principles of Art* (Oxford: Clarendon Press, 1938), p. 286. See also Sabina Lovibond's development of this idea within the context of ethics in *Realism and Imagination,* pp. 76, 194–200. Collingwood's directive to construct possible worlds also anticipates one of the major themes of Nelson Goodman's work. See, for example, *Ways of Worldmaking* (Indianapolis: Hackett, 1978).

26. For further discussion, see Mark Johnson, *The Body in the Mind: The Bodily Basis of Meaning, Imagination, and Reason* (Chicago: University of Chicago Press, 1987), esp. chap. 6. See also Lovibond, *Realism and Imagination,* p. 198; and *Encyclopedia of Philosophy,* s.v. "imagination."

27. Johnson, "Imagination in Moral Judgment," pp. 275–76. In this essay Johnson argues that Kant "recognized the need for imagination in order to apply moral rules to specific cases" but also faults Kant for failing to give "an adequate account of how imagination operates" (p. 265). See also Johnson's criticism of Kant's account of the imagination in *Body in the Mind,* pp. 147–70.

28. Cf. Iris Murdoch's remark that as moral agents "we have to try to see justly, to overcome prejudice, to avoid temptation, to control and curb imagination" (*The Sovereignty of Good* [London: Routledge & Kegan Paul, 1970], p. 40). Lovibond seeks to defuse the conservative tendencies of this variety of moral realism by construing moral imagination as a linguistic capacity—"a product of our ability to manipulate a finite repertoire of concepts and syntactic rules in creative ways" (*Realism and Imagination,* p. 198). Even though the repertoire of concepts and syntactic rules is finite, it can be applied in an infinite number of ways. The possibility of novelty is thus built in.

29. Nussbaum, *Love's Knowledge,* p. 148, cf. pp. 5–8. Kant, on the other hand, argues ve-

hemently against the use of novels in moral education, asserting at one point that "all novels should be taken away from children" (*Ed* IX 473/73). His rationale for this claim seems to be the assumption that novel-reading causes a weakening of the memory, which eventually leads to habitual distraction and absent-mindedness. We lose the ability to think critically about the actual world if we seek refuge too often in the possible worlds constructed by novelists (*Ed* IX 473/73; cf. *A* VII 185/59, 208/79). I do not find this particular argument of Kant's compelling, but it is worth noting how radically it differs from Nussbaum's. On her view, only novels can teach us moral vision. On Kant's view, novels are the chief destroyer of moral vision. My own view is that there is nothing about the nature of novels per se that necessarily makes them either heroes or villians in the pursuit of moral vision.

30. Nussbaum, *Love's Knowledge,* p. 5. Again though, her position is complicated by the fact that she explicitly endorses an Aristotelian conception of ethical theory throughout all of her writings and is thus clearly not opposed to *all* ethical theory programs (see, e.g., *Fragility of Goodness,* p. 10 and my earlier discussion at chap. 5, n. 25, and chap. 6, n. 4). However, in another essay she states that even Aristotle holds that the central claims of his own views about moral imagination and practical excellence "can be clarified only by appeal to life and to works of literature" (*Love's Knowledge,* p. 141). We can infer from this latter statement that even Aristotelian ethical theory, at least on Nussbaum's reading, must itself always be subordinate to literature. As Hilary Putnam remarks in his response to Nussbaum, "For Martha Nussbaum, Aristotle gets high marks; after that, it seems that novels are the works of choice in 'moral philosophy' " (*Realism with a Human Face* [Cambridge: Harvard University Press, 1990], p. 193).

31. Nussbaum, *Love's Knowledge,* p. 142. Her characterization of philosophical style as hard or plain echoes a similar remark of Iris Murdoch's in an interview with Brian Magee in the latter's edited *Men of Ideas* (New York: Viking Press, 1979), p. 265. Nussbaum comments at greater length on philosophical versus literary style in *Love's Knowledge,* chaps. 10, 11, and *Fragility of Goodness,* pp. 16–17.

32. Nussbaum, *Fragility of Goodness,* p. 15. Cf. *Love's Knowledge,* pp. 40–43.

33. Diamond, "Anything but Argument?" pp. 25, 41.

34. R. Rorty, *Contingency, Irony,* p. xvi. Cf. Charles Larmore: "Theory can carry us only so far in our attempt to grasp the nature of moral judgment. To go further, we must turn above all to the great works of imaginative literature" (*Patterns of Moral Complexity,* p. 21).

35. Cora Diamond, "Having a Rough Story About What Moral Philosophy Is," *New Literary History* 15 (1983): 162, 164. The expression "texture of being" is borrowed from Iris Murdoch, "Vision and Choice in Morality," *Proceedings of the Aristotelian Society: Supplement* 30 (1956): 39. Nussbaum states that "we must have some rough story about what moral philosophy and the job of moral philosophy are"; and after her customary dismissal of "the Kantian account," she proposes as a starting point the "Aristotelian idea that ethics is the search for a specification of the good life for a human being" (*Love's Knowledge,* pp. 138–39). Diamond allows that Nussbaum's Aristotelian specification of ethics, like Murdoch's emphasis on the texture of a person's being, is sufficiently broad, and thus is following her on this point (p. 163).

36. What about the contributions of popular music, film, dance, and other art forms to the enlargement of moral imagination? Ironically, philosophers' biases toward the printed word and toward high culture manifest themselves even in antitheoretical polemics against philosophy and theory.

37. Cf. C. Wright Mills's list of seven ways to stimulate the sociological imagination in *The Sociological Imagination* (New York: Oxford University Press, 1959), pp. 212–18. None of them involves any necessary exposure to either art or theoretical discourse. Mills's definition of *sociological* imagination—"the capacity to range from the most impersonal and remote transformations to the most intimate features of the human self—and to see

the relations between the two" (p. 7)—is also relevant to *moral* imagination, since moral deliberation always involves the capacity to envision how one's actions and policies will effect others and/or oneself. *The Sociological Imagination* can also be read as a classic early antitheory treatise in its own right: two of Mills's central targets are overly systematic social theorists who seek to manipulate historical evidence "into a trans-historical strait-jacket" (e.g., Auguste Comte; see p. 22) and overly formalist "grand theorists" who seek systematic theories concerning "the nature of man and society" (e.g., Talcott Parsons; see p. 23). For a recent reply, see Quentin Skinner, ed., *The Return of Grand Theory in the Human Sciences* (New York: Cambridge University Press, 1985), intro.

38. Percy Bysshe Shelley, *A Defense of Poetry*, ed. Albert S. Cook (Boston: Ginn, 1890), p. 6.

39. Jacques Derrida, *Margins of Philosophy*, trans. Alan Bass (Chicago: University Press, 1982), pp. 292–94. (I am indebted here to Christopher Norris's discussion in *Derrida* [Cambridge: Harvard University Press, 1987], pp. 22–25.)

40. Shelley, *Defense of Poetry*, p. 9.

41. "Nor are those supreme poets, who have employed traditional forms of rhythm on account of the form and action of their subjects, less capable of perceiving and teaching the truth of things, than those who have omitted that form. Shakespeare, Dante, and Milton . . . are philosophers of the very loftiest power" (Shelley, *Defense of Poetry*, pp. 9–10).

42. Hilary Putnam, "Literature, Science, and Reflection," in *Meaning and the Moral Sciences* (Boston: Routledge & Kegan Paul, 1978), p. 89. *Tested* is not the word I would choose here (the insights of novelists—not to speak of philosophers—cannot always be tested). But so long as the term is not construed in an overly verificationist manner, the point is well taken.

43. Shelley, *Defense of Poetry*, p. 13.

44. Richard Wollheim, "Flawed Crystals: James's *The Golden Bowl* and the Plausibility of Literature as Moral Philosophy," *New Literature History* 15 (1983): 190. Nussbaum's essay "Flawed Crystals" appeared originally in this same journal, later in *Love's Knowledge*. In her "Reply to Richard Wollheim, Patrick Gardiner, and Hilary Putnam," *New Literary History* 15 (1983): 201–8 (not reprinted in *Love's Knowledge*), she concedes Wollheim's point about the necessity of commentary; and in several subsequent works she has sought to incorporate it by promoting "the idea of a philosophical style that is the ally of literature, one that is not identical to the styles of the literary works, but directs the reader's attention to the salient features of those works, setting their insights in a perspicuous relation to other alternatives, other texts" (*Love's Knowledge*, p. 49, cf. pp. 283–85). Her current project of making moral philosophy an ally of literature is much closer to the position I am advocating, and her warning that moral philosophy "must adopt forms and procedures that do not negate the insights of literature" if it is to be an ally is well taken (*Love's Knowledge*, p. 284). However, I am doubtful whether this more recent "ally" position is consistent with the earlier "theory vs. literature" position.

45. Cf. John Cooper, Review of *The Fragility of Goodness*, by Martha Nussbaum, *Philosophical Review* 97 (1988): 543–64. He accuses Nussbaum of confusing philosophical arguments with emotional appeals: "Emotional appeals are never *part* of philosophical argument, however necessary and valuable they may be in moral training (a very different thing)" (p. 563). In my view, Cooper's statement errs too far in the opposite direction. Emotional appeals frequently do have a legitimate place in moral argument. Suppose I am deciding whether to give political support to an administration which is funding a guerrilla warfare movement against a democratically elected regime in a small Central American country. My friend reminds me of the horrors of modern warfare, of the innocent civilians who will be killed, of the devastation that such a war will wreak upon an already impoverished country. These appeals to emotion are legitimate in this specific context. Granted, the amount of weight that should be given to the appeals is itself open to debate (perhaps the administration's policy is nevertheless morally justifiable—perhaps I cannot see this

because I am presently ignorant of all the relevant facts); but the appeals themselves are not out of place. In moral argument, we must frequently consider actions and policies that will effect ourselves or others for good or for ill, and one kind of consideration that is often relevant is just *how* well or *how* badly we or others will be affected. (The example and explanation are adopted from Jerry Cederblum and David W. Paulsen, *Critical Reasoning,* 2d ed. [Belmont, Calif.: Wadsworth, 1986], pp. 113–14.)

46. Oscar Wilde, *The Picture of Dorian Gray,* in *The Portable Oscar Wilde,* ed. Richard Arlington (New York: Viking Press, 1974) p. 138. For recent replies to the claim that literary works can be judged properly only by "intrinsic," aesthetic categories, see Christopher Clausen, *The Moral Imagination: Essays on Literature and Ethics* (Iowa City: University of Iowa Press, 1986), esp. chap. 1, and Wayne Booth, *The Company We Keep: An Ethics of Fiction* (Berkeley: University of California Press, 1988). See also Tobin Siebers, *The Ethics of Criticism* (Ithaca, N.Y.: Cornell University Press, 1988), who announces in his opening sentence, "Literary criticism is inextricably linked to ethics" (p. 1). Clearly, there are several issues lurking in Wilde's remark. One is whether or not literature has important moral effects, a second is whether aesthetic values are more important than moral values. For some remarks on the second issue, see pp. 19–23, 58, 65–66.

47. John Dewey, *Art as Experience* (New York: Capricorn Books, 1958), p. 348. Cf. Shelley, *Defense of Poetry,* p. 14.

48. Shelley, *Defense of Poetry,* p. 37. (Cf. the Iris Murdoch epigraph cited at the beginning of this chapter.)

49. John Plamenatz, *Man and Society* (New York: McGraw-Hill, 1963), vol. 1, pp. xix–xx. See also his earlier essay, "The Use of Political Theory," in *Political Philosophy,* ed. Anthony Quinton (New York: Oxford University Press, 1967), pp. 19–31. Alasdair MacIntyre offers his own elaboration on Plamenatz's claim in "The Indispensability of Political Theory," in *The Nature of Political Theory,* ed. David Miller and Larry Siedentop (Oxford: Clarendon Press, 1983), pp. 17–34. See also Hilary Putnam's concluding remarks concerning "the desire for integration" in *Realism and Reason,* p. 303.

50. Not to mention other branches of philosophy and science. Cf. Karl Popper: "For me the interest of philosophy, no less than of science, lies solely in its bold attempt to add to our [cosmological] knowledge of the world, and to the theory of our knowledge of the world. . . . For me, both philosophy and science lose all their attraction when they give up that pursuit—when they become specialisms and cease to see, and to wonder at, the riddles of our world" (*Conjectures and Refutations,* p. 136).

51. I am paraphrasing Hume here: "If the importance of truth be requisite to compleat the pleasure, 'tis not on account of any considerable addition, which of itself it brings to our enjoyment, but only because 'tis, in some measure, requisite to fix our attention" (*A Treatise of Human Nature,* 2d ed, ed. L. A. Selby-Bigge) (Oxford: Clarendon Press, 1978), p. 451. See also his analogy between hunting and philosophy on this same page. Amélie Rorty makes interesting use of this analogy in her essay "Socrates and Sophia Perform the Philosophic Turn," in *Institution of Philosophy,* ed. Cohen and Dascal, pp. 277–78.

52. Cf. Mitchell, *Against Theory:* "My point . . . is that the central thesis of 'Against Theory' is no more or less 'theoretical', no more or less 'pragmatic', or intuitive, than its antithesis" (p. 8). See also my earlier remarks concerning the tu quoque argument on pp. 97–98, 164 n. 12.

53. Frank Lentricchia, *Ariel and the Police: Michael Foucault, William James, Wallace Stevens* (Madison: University of Wisconsin Press, 1988), p. 125.

54. Cf. Ludwig Wittgenstein, *Philosophical Investigations,* trans. G. E. M. Anscombe (New York: Macmillian, 1953), no. 133.

55. Hume, *Treatise of Human Nature,* pp. 270–71.

Bibliography

Ackrill, J. L. "Aristotle on Eudaimonia." In *Essays on Aristotles Ethics,* ed. Amélie O. Rorty. Berkeley: University of California Press, 1980.

Adams, Robert Merrihew. "Motive Utilitarianism." *The Philosophical Review* 73 (1976): 476–81.

———. "Involuntary Sins." *Philosophical Review* 94 (1985): 3–31.

———. *The Virtue of Faith and Other Essays in Philosophical Theology.* New York: Oxford University Press, 1987.

Adkins, Arthur W. H. *Merit and Responsibility: A Study in Greek Values.* Oxford: Clarendon Press, 1960.

Allan, D. J. *The Philosophy of Aristotle.* 2d ed. New York: Oxford University Press, 1970.

———. "The Fine and the Good in the *Eudemian Ethics.*" In *Untersuchungen zur Eudemischen Ethik,* ed. Paul Moraux and Dieter Harlfinger. Berlin: de Gruyter, 1971.

Anscombe, G. E. M. "Modern Moral Philosophy." In *Ethics,* ed. Judith J. Thompson and Gerald Dworkin. New York: Harper & Row. 1968.

Anton, John, and Anthony Preus, eds. *Essays in Ancient Philosophy.* Vol. 4, *Aristotle's Ethics and Politics.* Albany: State University of New York Press, 1991.

Apel, Karl-Otto. *Towards a Transformation of Philosophy.* Trans. Glyn Adey and David Frisby. London: Routledge & Kegan Paul, 1980.

Aristotle. *The Complete Works of Aristotle.* 2 vols. Ed. Jonathan Barnes. Princeton, N.J.: Princeton University Press, 1984.

Aune, Bruce. *Kant's Theory of Morals.* Princeton, N.J.: Princeton University Press, 1979.

Baier, Annette. *Postures of the Mind: Essays on Mind and Morals.* Minneapolis: University of Minnesota Press, 1985.

———. "Doing Without Moral Theory?" In *Anti-Theory in Ethics and Moral Conservation,* ed. Stanley Clarke and Evan Simpson. Albany: State University of New York Press, 1989.

Baier, Kurt. *The Moral Point of View.* Ithaca, N. Y.: Cornell University Press, 1958.

———. "Moral Reasons and Reasons To Be Moral." In *Values and Morals,* ed. Alvin I. Goldman and Jaegwon Kim. Dordrecht: Reidel, 1978.

Barnes, Jonathan, Malcolm Schofield, and Richard Sorabji, eds. *Articles on Aristotle.* Vol. 2, *Ethics and Politics.* New York: St. Martin's Press, 1977.

Baron, Marcia. "On the Alleged Repugnance of Acting from Duty." *Journal of Philosophy* 81 (1984): 179–219.

———. "On Admirable Immorality." *Ethics* 96 (1986): 557–66.

Barry, Brian. "Social Criticism and Political Philosophy." *Philosophy and Public Affairs* 19 (1990): 360–73.

Bayles, Michael. "Moral Theory and Application." *Social Theory and Practice* 10 (1984): 97–120.

Bechtel, William. *Philosophy of Science: An Overview for Cognitive Science*. Hillsdale, N.J.: Erlbaum, 1988.

Beck, Lewis White. *A Commentary on Kant's "Critique of Practical Reason."* Chicago: University of Chicago Press, 1960.

Becker, Lawrence C. "The Neglect of Virtue." *Ethics* 85 (1975): 110–22.

———. *Reciprocity*. New York: Routledge & Kegan Paul, 1986.

Benson, John. "Who is the Autonomous Man?" In *The Virtues*, ed. Robert B. Kruschiwitz and Robert C. Roberts. Belmont, Calif.: Wadsworth, 1987.

Bentham, Jeremy. *The Works of Jeremy Bentham*. Ed. J. Bowring. 11 vols. Edinburgh: Tait, 1838–43.

———. *An Introduction to the Principles of Morals and Legislation*. New York: Hafner, 1948.

———. *Bentham's Political Thought*. Ed. Bhiku Parekh. New York: Barnes & Noble, 1973.

Berger, Fred. *Happiness, Justice, and Freedom*. Berkeley: University of California Press, 1984.

Berlin, Isaiah. *Concepts and Categories: Philosophical Essays*. New York: Penguin Books, 1981.

Blassingame, John W., ed. *Slave Testimony: Two Centuries of Letters, Speeches, Interviews, and Autobiographies*. Baton Rouge: Louisiana State University Press, 1977.

Bloom, Allan. *The Closing of the American Mind*. New York: Simon and Schuster, 1987.

Blum, Lawrence A. *Friendship, Altruism, and Morality*. London: Routledge & Kegan Paul, 1980.

Bok, Sissela. *Lying*. New York: Vintage Books, 1979.

Bolton, Robert. "Definition and Scientific Method in Aristotle's *Posterior Analytics* and *Generation of Animals*." In *Philosophical Issues in Aristotle's Biology*, ed. Allan Gotthelf and James G. Lennox. New York: Cambridge University Press, 1987.

Booth, Wayne. *The Company We Keep: An Ethics of Fiction*. Berkeley: University of California Press, 1988.

Bradley, F. H. *Ethical Studies*. 2d ed. New York: Oxford University Press, 1962.

Brandt, Richard. "The Concepts of Obligation and Duty." *Mind* 73 (1964): 374–93.

———. *A Theory of the Right and the Good*. Oxford: Clarendon Press, 1979.

Brink, David. *Moral Realism and the Foundations of Ethics*. New York: Cambridge University Press, 1989.

Burnet, John. *The Ethics of Aristotle*. London: Methuen, 1900.

———. *Plato's Euthyphro, Apology of Socrates and Crito*. Oxford: Clarendon Press, 1924.

Burnyeat, Myles. "Aristotle on Learning To Be Good." In *Essays on Aristotle's Ethics*, ed. Amélie O. Rorty. Berkeley: University of California Press, 1980.

Caplan, Arthur L. "Ethical Engineers Need Not Apply: The State of Applied Ethics Today." *Science, Technology, and Human Values* 6 (1980): 24–32.

———. "Moral Experts and Moral Expertise: Do Either Exist?" In *Clinical Ethics*, ed. B. Hoffmaster, B. Freedman, and G. Fraser. Clifton, N.J.: Humana Press, 1989.

Carritt, E. F. *Theory of Morals*. Oxford: Clarendon Press, 1928.

Cederblum, Jerry, and David W. Paulsen. *Critical Reasoning*. 2d ed. Belmont, Calif.: Wadsworth, 1986.

Chomsky, Noam. *Aspects of the Theory of Syntax*. Cambridge: MIT Press, 1965.

Churchland, Paul. *Scientific Realism and the Plasticity of Mind*. New York: Cambridge University Press, 1979.

Clarke, Stanley G. "Anti-Theory in Ethics." *American Philosophical Quarterly* 24 (1987): 237–44.

Clarke, Stanley G., and Evan Simpson, eds. *Anti-Theory in Ethics and Moral Conservatism.* Albany: State University of New York Press, 1989.

Clausen, Christopher. *The Moral Imagination: Essays on Literature and Ethics.* Iowa City: University of Iowa Press, 1986.

Cleary, John, ed. *Proceedings of the Boston Area Colloquium in Ancient Philosophy.* Washington, D.C.: University Press of America, 1985.

Cohen, Avner, and Marcelo Dascal, eds. *The Institution of Philosophy: A Discipline in Crisis?* La Salle, Ill.: Open Court, 1989.

Cohen, Joshua. *The Moral Arc of the Universe: Justice and the Demise of Slavery.* London: Basil Blackwell, forthcoming.

Collingwood, R. G. *The Principles of Art.* Oxford: Clarendon Press, 1938.

Conly, Sarah. "Flourishing and the Failure of the Ethics of Virtue." In *Ethical Theory,* ed. Peter French, Theodore Uehling, Jr., and Howard Wettstein. Notre Dame, Ind.: Notre Dame University Press, 1988.

Cooper, John M. *Reason and Human Good in Aristotle.* Cambridge: Harvard University Press, 1975.

———. "Aristotle on Friendship." In *Essays on Aristotle's "Ethics,"* ed. Amélie O. Rorty. Berkeley: University of California Press, 1980.

———. "Aristotle on the Goods of Fortune." *Philosophical Review* 94 (1985): 173–96.

———. Review of *The Fragility of Goodness,* by Martha Nussbaum. *Philosophical Review* 97 (1988): 543–64.

Cooper, Neil. "Morality and Importance." In *The Definition of Morality,* ed. G. Wallace and A. D. M. Walker. London: Methuen, 1970.

———. *The Diversity of Moral Thinking.* Oxford: Clarendon Press, 1981.

Dancy, Jonathan. "Ethical Particularism and Morally Relevant Properties." *Mind* 92 (1983): 530–47.

Dascal, Marcelo. "Reflections on the 'Crisis of Modernity'." In *The Institution of Philosophy,* ed. Avner Cohen and Marcelo Dascal. LaSalle, Ill.: Open Court, 1989.

Davidson, Donald. *Inquiries into Truth and Interpretation.* Oxford: Clarendon Press, 1984.

Derrida, Jacques. *Margins of Philosophy.* Trans. Alan Bass. Chicago: University of Chicago Press, 1982.

De Voto, Bernard. *The Year of Decision: 1846.* Boston: Little, Brown, 1943.

Dewey, John. *Human Nature and Conduct.* New York: Holt, 1922.

———. *Logic: The Theory of Inquiry.* New York: Holt, 1938.

———. *Art as Experience.* New York: Capricorn Books, 1958.

———. *The Quest for Certainty.* New York: Capricorn Books, 1960.

———. *The Early Works of John Dewey.* Vol. 3, *1889–1892.* Carbondale: Southern Illinois University Press, 1975.

Dewey, John, and James H. Tuft. *Ethics.* Rev. ed. New York: Holt, 1932.

Diamond, Cora. "Anything but Argument?" *Philosophical Investigations* 5 (1982): 23–41.

———. "Having a Rough Story About What Moral Philosophy Is." *New Literary History* 15 (1983): 171–77.

Dillenberger, John, and Claude Welch. *Protestant Christianity Interpreted Through Its Development.* New York: Scribner, 1954.

Donagan, Alan. *The Theory of Morality.* Chicago: University of Chicago Press, 1977.

————. "Consistency in Rationalist Moral Systems." In *Moral Dilemmas,* ed. Christopher Gowans. New York: Oxford University Press, 1987.

Dreyfus, Hubert L., and Stuart E. Dreyfus. *Mind over Machine: The Power of Human Intuition and Expertise in the Era of the Computer.* New York: Free Press, 1989.

Dryer, D. P. "Aristotle's Conception of *Orthos Logos." Monist* 66 (1983): 106–19.

Dworkin, Ronald. *Taking Rights Seriously.* Cambridge: Harvard University Press, 1975.

Engberg-Pedersen, Troels. *Aristotle's Theory of Moral Insight.* Oxford: Clarendon Press, 1983.

Fairlamb, Horace. "Pragmatism and Anti-Theory: The Consequences of Theory." *MLN* 101 (1986): 1216–25.

Falk, W. D. "Morality, Self, and Others." In *Morality and the Language of Conduct,* ed. Hector-Neri Castaneda and George Naknikian. Detroit: Wayne State University Press, 1963.

————. *Ought, Reasons, and Morality.* Ithaca, N.Y.: Cornell University Press, 1986.

Feigenbaum, Edward, and Pamela McCorduck. *The Fifth Generation: Artificial Intelligence and Japan's Computer Challenge to the World.* Reading, Mass.: Addison–Wesley, 1983.

Feinberg, Joel, ed. *Moral Concepts.* New York: Oxford University Press, 1970.

Feyerabend, Paul. *Against Method.* London: New Left Books, 1975.

Finley, M. I., ed. *The Legacy of Greece.* New York: Oxford University Press, 1981.

Fish, Stanley. "Consequences." In *Against Theory,* ed W. J. T. Mitchell. Chicago: University of Chicago Press, 1989.

————. *Doing What Comes Naturally: Change, Rhetoric, and the Practice of Theory in Literary and Legal Studies.* Durham, N.C.: Duke University Press, 1989.

Fisher, John. "Against Theory, Again." *Journal of Aesthetic Education* 20 (1986): 50–53.

Flanagan, Owen. "Admirable Immorality and Admirable Imperfection." *Journal of Philosophy* 83 (1986): 41–60.

————. *Varieties of Moral Personality.* Cambridge: Harvard University Press, 1991.

Flanagan, Owen, and Amélie O. Rorty, eds. *Identity, Character, and Morality.* Cambridge: MIT Press, 1991.

Foot, Philippa. *Virtues and Vices.* Berkeley: University of California Press, 1978.

————. "Morality and Art." In *Philosophy as It Is,* ed. Ted Honderich and Myles Burnyeat. New York: Penguin Books, 1979.

————. "Utilitarianism and the Virtues." In *Consequentialism and Its Critics,* ed. Samuel Scheffler. New York: Oxford University Press, 1988.

Fortenbaugh, W. W. "Aristotle on Slaves and Women." In *Articles on Aristotle,* vol. 2, ed. Jonathan Barnes, Malcolm Schofield, and Richard Sorabji. New York: St. Martin's Press, 1977.

Foucault, Michael. *Power/Knowledge: Selected Interviews and Other Writings 1972–77.* Ed. Colin Gordon. New York: Pantheon Books, 1980.

————. *The Foucault Reader.* Ed. Paul Rabinow. New York: Pantheon Books, 1984.

Frankena, William. *Ethics.* 2d ed. Englewood Cliffs; N.J.: Prentice–Hall, 1973.

Frankfurt, Harry. *The Importance of What We Care About.* New York: Cambridge University Press, 1988.

Fraser, Nancy, and Linda Nicholson. "Social Criticism Without Philosophy." In *The Institution of Philosophy,* ed. Avner Cohen and Marcelo Dascal. LaSalle, Ill.: Open Court, 1989.

French, Peter A. Theodore E. Uehling Jr., and Howard K. Wettstein, eds. *Midwest Studies in Philosophy,* vol. 13, *Ethical Theory: Character and Virtue.* Notre Dame, Ind.: University of Notre Dame Press, 1988.

Fried, Charles. *An Anatomy of Moral Values*. Cambridge: Harvard University Press, 1970.

Gauguin, Paul. *Noa Noa: Voyage to Tahiti*. Trans. Jonathan Griffin. New York: Reynal, 1962.

Gauthier, David. "Reason and Maximization." *Canadian Journal of Philosophy* 4 (1975): 411–33.

———. *Morals by Agreement*. Oxford: Clarendon Press, 1986.

———, ed. *Morality and Rational Self-Interest*. Englewood Cliffs, N.J.: Prentice–Hall, 1970.

Gauthier, R. "On the Nature of Aristotle's *Ethics*." In *Aristotle's Ethics: Issues and Interpretations,* ed. H. L. Shapiro and J. J. Walsh. Belmont, Calif.: Wadsworth, 1967.

Gert, Bernard. *Morality: A New Justification of the Moral Rules*. New York: Oxford University Press, 1988.

———. "Rationality, Human Nature, and Lists." *Ethics* 100 (1990): 279–300.

Geuss, Raymond. *The Idea of a Critical Theory*. New York: Cambridge University Press, 1981.

Godzich, Wlad. Foreword to *The Resistance to Theory,* by Paul de Man. Minneapolis: University of Minnesota Press, 1986.

Goldman, Alvin I., and Jaegwon Kim, eds. *Values and Morals*. Dordrecht: Reidel, 1978.

Goldmann, Lucien. *Immanuel Kant*. Trans. Robert Black. London: New Left Books, 1971.

Goodman, Nelson. *Ways of Worldmaking*. Indianapolis: Hackett, 1978.

Gotthelf, Allan, and James G. Lennox, eds. *Philosophical Issues in Aristotle's Biology*. New York: Cambridge University Press, 1987.

Gowans, Christopher W., ed. *Moral Dilemmas*. New York: Oxford University Press, 1987.

Grant, Alexander. *The Ethics of Aristotle*. 2 vols. 3d ed. London: Longmans, Green, 1874.

Grant, C. K. "Akrasia and the Critique of Assent to Practical Principles." *Mind* 65 (1956): 400–407.

Gregor, Mary J. *Laws of Freedom*. New York: Barnes & Noble, 1963.

———. Translator's Introduction to *The Doctrine of Virtue,* by Immanuel Kant. Philadelphia: University of Pennsylvania Press, 1964.

Habermas, Jürgen. *Knowledge and Human Interests*. Trans. Jeremy Shapiro. Boston: Beacon Press, 1971.

———. *Legitimation Crisis*. Trans. Thomas McCarthy. Boston: Beacon Press, 1973.

———. *Moral Consciousness and Communicative Action*. Trans. Christian Lenhardt and Shierry Weber Nicholsen. Cambridge: MIT Press, 1990.

Hallie, Philip. *Lest Innocent Blood Be Shed*. New York: Harper Torchbooks, 1985.

Hampshire, Stuart. *Thought and Action*. New York: Viking Press, 1967.

———. *Morality and Conflict*. Cambridge: Harvard University Press, 1983.

Hanson, Norwood Russell. *Patterns of Discovery*. Cambridge: Cambridge University Press, 1958.

Hardie, W. F. "The Final Good in Aristotle's *Ethics*." In *Aristotle,* ed. J. M. E. Moravcsik. Garden City, N.Y.: Anchor Books, 1967.

———. *Aristotle's Ethical Theory*. 2d ed. Oxford: Clarendon Press, 1980.

Hare, R. M. *Freedom and Reason*. Oxford: Clarendon Press, 1963.

Harman, Gilbert. *The Nature of Morality*. New York: Oxford University Press, 1977.

Harsanyi, John C. "Morality and the Theory of Rational Behavior." In *Utilitarianism and Beyond,* ed. Amartya Sen and Bernard Williams. New York: Cambridge University Press, 1982.

Hauerwas, Stanley, and Alasdair MacIntyre, eds., *Revisions: Changing Perspectives in Moral Philosophy*. Notre Dame, Ind.: University of Notre Dame Press, 1983.

Hempel, Carl G. *Aspects of Scientific Explanation and Other Essays in the Philosophy of Science*. New York: Free Press, 1965.

Herman, Barbara. "On the Value of Acting from the Motive of Duty." *Philosophical Review* 90 (1981): 359–82.

———. "Integrity and Impartiality." *Monist* 66 (1983): 233–50.

———. "The Practice of Moral Judgment." *Journal of Philosophy* 82 (1985): 414–36.

Hirsch, E. D., Jr. *The Aims of Interpretation*. Chicago: University of Chicago Press, 1976.

———. "Against Theory?" In *Against Theory,* ed. W. J. T. Mitchell. Chicago: University of Chicago Press, 1985.

Hoffmaster, Barry. "Philosophical Ethics and Practical Ethics: Never the Twain Shall Meet." In *Clinical Ethics,* ed. Barry Hoffmaster, B. Freeman, and G. Fraser. Clifton, N.J.: Humana Press, 1989.

Hoffmaster, Barry, B. Freedman, and G. Fraser, eds. *Clinical Ethics: Theory and Practice*. Clifton, N.J.: Humana Press, 1989.

Hollis, Martin. *The Cunning of Reason*. New York: Cambridge University Press, 1987.

Horkheimer, Max. *Critical Theory: Selected Essays*. Trans. Matthew J. O'Connell. New York: Seabury Press, 1972.

Hume, David. *A Treatise of Human Nature*. Ed. L. A. Selby-Bigge. 2d ed. Oxford: Clarendon Press, 1978.

Irwin, Terence. "Aristotle's Concept of Morality." In *Proceedings of the Boston Area Colloquium in Ancient Philosophy,* vol. 1, ed. John J. Cleary. Washington, D.C.: University Press of America, 1985.

———. *Aristotle's First Principles*. Oxford: Clarendon Press, 1988.

James, William. *Pragmatism and the Meaning of Truth*. Cambridge: Harvard University Press, 1978.

Johnson, Mark. "Imagination in Moral Judgment." *Philosophy and Phenomenological Research* 96 (1985): 265–80.

———. *The Body in the Mind: The Bodily Basis of Meaning, Imagination, and Reason*. Chicago: University of Chicago Press, 1987.

Jonsen, Albert R., and Stephen Toulmin. *The Abuse of Casuistry: A History of Moral Reasoning*. Berkeley: University of California Press, 1988.

Kalin, Jesse. "In Defense of Egoism." In *Morality and Rational Self-Interest,* ed. David Gauthier. Englewood Cliffs, N.J.: Prentice–Hall, 1970.

Kant, Immanuel. *Kants gesammelte Schriften*. Ed. Königliche Preussische Akademie der Wissenschaften. 29 vols. Berlin: de Gruyter, 1902–

———. *Anthropology from a Pragmatic Point of View*. Trans. Mary J. Gregor. The Hague: Martinus Nijhoff, 1974.

———. *Critique of Judgment*. Trans. James Creed Meredith. Oxford: Clarendon Press, 1952.

———. *Critique of Practical Reason*. Trans. Lewis White Beck. Indianapolis: Bobbs-Merrill, 1956.

———. *Critique of Pure Reason*. Trans. Normal Kemp Smith. London: Macmillian, 1933.

———. *The Doctrine of Virtue*. Trans. Mary J. Gregor. Philadelphia: University of Pennsylvania Press, 1964.

———. *Education*. Trans. Annette Churton. Ann Arbor: University of Michigan Press, 1960.

————. *Eine Vorlesung Kants über Ethik*. Ed. Paul Menzer. Berlin: Rolf Heise, 1924.

————. *Grounding of the Metaphysics of Morals*. Trans. James W. Ellington. Indianapolis: Hackett, 1981.

————. *Kant's Political Writings*. Trans. Hans Reiss. New York: Cambridge University Press, 1977.

————. *Lectures on Ethics*. Trans. Louis Infield. New York: Harper & Row, 1961.

————. *Logic*. Trans. Robert S. Hartman and Wolfgang Schwarz. Indianapolis: Bobbs-Merrill, 1974.

————. *Metaphysical Foundations of Natural Science*. Trans. James W. Ellington. Indianapolis: Bobbs-Merrill, 1970.

————. *Perpetual Peace and Other Essays*. Trans. Ted Humphrey. Indianapolis: Hackett, 1983.

————. *Religion Within the Limits of Reason Alone*. Trans. Theodore M. Green and Hoyt H. Hudson. New York: Harper & Row, 1960.

Kittay, Eva Feder, and Diana T. Meyers, eds. *Women and Moral Theory*. Totowa, N.J.: Rowman & Littlefield, 1987.

Knapp, Steven, and Walter Benn Michaels. "Against Theory." In *Against Theory*, ed. W. J. T. Mitchell. Chicago: University of Chicago Press, 1985.

————. "Against Theory II: Hermeneutics and Deconstruction." *Critical Inquiry* 14 (1987): 49–68.

Korsgaard, Christine. "Aristotle and Kant on the Source of Value." *Ethics* 96 (1986): 486–505.

Kosman, L. A. "Being Properly Affected: Virtues and Feelings in Aristotle's *Ethics*." In *Essays on Aristotle's "Ethics,"* ed. Amélie O. Rorty. Berkeley, University of California Press, 1980.

Kraut, Richard. *Aristotle on the Human Good*. Princeton, N.J.: Princeton University Press, 1989.

Kruschwitz, Robert B., and Robert C. Roberts, eds. *The Virtues: Contemporary Essays on Moral Character*. Belmont Calif.: Wadsworth, 1987.

Kupperman, Joel J. "Character and Ethical Theory." In *Ethical Theory,* ed. Peter French, Theodore Uehling, Jr., and Howard Wettstein. Notre Dame, Ind.: Notre Dame University, Press, 1988.

Lakoff, George. *Women, Fire, and Dangerous Things: What Categories Reveal About the Mind*. Chicago: University of Chicago Press, 1987.

Larmore, Charles E. *Patterns of Moral Complexity*. New York: Cambridge University Press, 1987.

Lawson, E. Thomas, and Robert N. McCauley. *Rethinking Religion: Connecting Cognition and Culture*. New York: Cambridge University Press, 1990.

Lentricchia, Frank. *Ariel and the Police: Michael Foucault, William James, Wallace Stevens*. Madison: University of Wisconsin Press, 1988.

Levinas, Emmanuel. *Totality and Infinity*. Trans. Alphonso Lingis. Pittsburgh: Duquesne University Press, 1969.

Lewis, Clarence Irving. *An Analysis of Knowledge and Valuation*. LaSalle, Ill.: Open Court, 1946.

————. *Values and Imperatives: Studies in Ethics*. Ed. John Lange. Stanford: Stanford University Press, 1969.

Lobkowicz, Nicholas. *Theory and Practice: History of a Concept from Aristotle to Marx*. Notre Dame, Ind.: University of Notre Dame Press, 1967.

Loewy, Eric H. *Suffering and the Beneficent Community*. Albany: State University of New York Press, 1991.

Lomasky, Loren. *Persons, Rights, and the Moral Community*. New York: Oxford University Press, 1987.

Louden, Robert B. "The Elements of Ethics: Toward a Topography of the Moral Field." Ph.D. diss., University of Chicago, 1981.

———. "Rights Infatuation and the Impoverishment of Moral Theory." *Journal of Value Inquiry* 17 (1983): 87–102.

———. "Kant's Virtue Ethics." *Philosophy* 61 (1986): 473–89.

———. "On Some Vices of Virtue Ethics." In *The Virtues,* ed. Robert B. Kruschwitz and Robert C. Roberts. Belmont, Calif.: Wadsworth, 1987.

———. "Can We Be Too Moral?" *Ethics* 98 (1988): 361–78.

———. "Through Thick and Thin: Moral Knowledge in Skeptical Times." *Logos* 10 (1989): 57–72.

———. "Virtue Ethics and Anti-Theory." *Philosophia* 20 (1990): 93–114.

———. "Aristotle's Practical Particularism." In *Essays in Ancient Greek Philosophy,* vol. 4, ed. John P. Anton and Anthony Preus. Albany: State University of New York Press, 1991.

———. "Go-Carts of Judgment: Exemplars in Kantian Moral Education." *Archiv für Geschichte der Philosophie,* Forthcoming.

Lovibond, Sabina. *Realism and Imagination in Ethics*. Minneapolis: University of Minnesota Press, 1983.

Lyotard, Jean-François. *The Postmodern Condition: A Report on Knowledge*. Minneapolis: University of Minnesota Press, 1984.

McCauley, Robert N. "Epistemology in an Age of Cognitive Science." *Philosophical Psychology* 1 (1988): 143–52.

———. "A Comparative Model of Knowing." *Metaphilosophy,* forthcoming.

McConnell, Terrance C. "Objectivity and Moral Expertise." *Canadian Journal of Philosophy* 14 (1984): 193–216.

McDowell, John. "Virtue and Reason." In *Anti-Theory in Ethics and Moral Conservatism,* ed. Stanley Clarke and Evan Simpson. Albany: State University of New York Press, 1989.

MacIntyre, Alasdair. *A Short History of Ethics*. New York: Macmillan, 1966.

———. "The Indispensability of Political Theory." In *The Nature of Political Theory,* ed. David Miller and Larry Siedentop. Oxford: Clarendon Press, 1983.

———. *After Virtue: A Study in Moral Theory*. 2d ed. Notre Dame, Ind.: University of Notre Dame Press, 1984.

Mackie, John L. *Ethics: Inventing Right and Wrong*. New York: Penguin Books, 1977.

———. "Can There Be a Right-based Moral Theory?" In *Midwest Studies in Philosophy,* vol. 3, *Ethical Theory,* ed. Peter A. French and Theodore E. Uehling, Jr. Minneapolis: University of Minnesota Press, 1978.

MacPherson, C. B. *Democratic Theory: Essays in Retrieval*. Oxford: Clarendon, 1973.

Magee, Brian, ed. *Men of Ideas*. New York: Viking Press, 1979.

Mailloux, Steven. "Truth or Consequences: On Being Against Theory." In *Against Theory,* ed. W. J. T. Mitchell. Chicago: University of Chicago Press, 1985.

Malkan, Jeffrey. " 'Against Theory', Pragmatism and Deconstruction." *Telos* 71 (1987): 129–54.

Marcus, Ruth Barcan. "Moral Dilemmas and Consistency." In *Moral Dilemmas,* ed. Christopher W. Gowans. New York: Oxford University Press, 1987.

Margolis, Joseph, ed. *Philosophy Looks at the Arts*. Rev. ed. Philadelphia: Temple University Press, 1978.

Mill, John Stuart. *On Liberty*. Ed. Elizabeth Rapaport. Indianapolis: Hackett, 1978.

Mills, C. Wright. *The Sociological Imagination*. New York: Oxford University Press, 1959.

Mitchell, W. J. T., ed. *Against Theory: Literary Studies and the New Pragmatism*. Chicago: University of Chicago Press, 1985.

Mitchie, Donald. "Current Developments in Artificial Intelligence and Expert Systems." *Zygon* 20 (1985): 375–89.

Montaigne, Michel de. *The Complete Essays of Montaigne*. Trans. Donald M. Frame. Stanford: Stanford University Press, 1958.

Moravcsik, J. M. E., ed. *Aristotle: A Collection of Critical Essays*. Garden City, N.Y.: Anchor Books, 1967.

Moulton, Janice. "A Paradigm of Philosophy: The Adversary Method." In *Discovering Reality,* ed. Sandra Harding and Merrill B. Hintikka. Dordrecht: Reidel, 1983.

Mulgan, R. G. *Aristotle's Political Theory*. Oxford: Clarendon Press, 1977.

Murdoch, Iris. "Vision and Choice in Morality." *Proceedings of the Aristotelian Society: Supplement* 30 (1956): 32–58.

———. *The Sovereignty of the Good*. London: Routledge & Kegan Paul, 1970.

Nagel, Thomas. *Mortal Questions*. New York: Cambridge University Press, 1979.

Nell (O'Neill), Onora. *Acting on Principle*. New York: Columbia University Press, 1975.

Nietzsche, Friedrich. *Untimely Meditations*. Trans. R. J. Hollingdale. New York: Cambridge University Press, 1983.

Noble, Cheryl. "Ethics and Experts." *Hastings Center Report* 12 (1982): 7–15.

———. "Normative Ethical Theories." In *Anti-Theory in Ethics and Moral Conservatism,* ed. Stanley Clarke and Evan Simpson. Albany: State University of New York Press, 1989.

Norris, Christopher. *Derrida*. Cambridge: Harvard University Press, 1987.

Norton, David L. "Moral Minimalism and the Development of Moral Character." In *Ethical Theory,* ed. Peter French, Theodore Uehling, Jr., and Howard Wettstein. Notre Dame, Ind.: University of Notre Dame Press, 1988.

Nozick, Robert. *Anarchy, State, and Utopia*. New York: Basic Books, 1974.

———. *Philosophical Explanations*. Cambridge: Harvard University Press, 1981.

Nussbaum, Martha C. *Aristotle's De Motu Animalium*. Text with translation, commentary, and interpretive essays. Princeton, N.J.: Princeton University Press, 1978.

———. "Reply to Richard Wollheim, Patrick Gardiner, and Hilary Putnam." *New Literary History* 15 (1983): 201–8.

———. *The Fragility of Goodness: Luck and Ethics in Greek Tragedy and Philosophy*. New York: Cambridge University Press, 1986.

———. " 'Richly Aware and Finely Responsible': Literature and the Moral Imagination," In *Anti-Theory in Ethics and Moral Conservatism,* ed. Stanley Clarke and Evan Simpson. Albany: State University of New York Press, 1989.

———. *Love's Knowledge: Essays on Philosophy and Literature*. New York: Oxford University Press, 1990.

———. Review of *Sources of the Self,* by Charles Taylor. *New Republic,* 9 April 1990, pp. 27–34.

Oakeshott, Michael. *"Rationalism in Politics" and Other Essays*. London: Methuen, 1962.

———. "The Tower of Babel". In *Anti-Theory in Ethics and Moral Conservatism,* ed. Stanley Clarke and Evan Simpson. Albany: State University of New York Press, 1989.

O'Hara, Daniel T. "Revisionary Madness: The Prospects of American Literary Theory at the Present Time," In *Against Theory,* ed. W. J. T. Mitchell. Chicago: University of Chicago Press, 1985.

O'Neill, Onora. *Constructions of Reason: Explorations of Kant's Practical Philosophy.* New York: Cambridge University Press, 1989.

Owen, G. E. L. *"Tithenai ta phainomena."* In *Aristotle: A Collection of Critical Essays.* Ed. J. M. E. Moravcsik. Garden City, N.Y.: Anchor Books, 1967.

Owens, Joseph. "The *Kalon* in Aristotelian Ethics." In *Studies in Aristotle,* ed. Dominic J. O'Meara. Washington, D.C.: Catholic University of America Press, 1981.

Parfit, Derek. *Reasons and Persons.* New York: Oxford University Press, 1984.

Paton, H. J. "Kant on Friendship." *Proceedings of the British Academy* 42 (1956): 45–66.

———. *The Categorical Imperative: A Study in Kant's Moral Philosophy.* Philadelphia: University of Pennsylvania Press, 1971.

Peirce, Charles Sanders. *The Collected Papers of Charles Sanders Peirce.* 6 vols. Ed. Charles Hartshorne and Paul Weiss. Cambridge: Harvard University Press, 1931–35.

Phillips, D. Z. "In Search of the Moral 'Must': Mrs. Foot's Fugitive Thought." *Philosophical Quarterly* 27 (1977): 140–57.

———. "Do Moral Questions Override Others?" *Philosophical Quarterly* 29 (1979): 247–54.

———. *Interventions in Ethics.* Albany: State University of New York Press, 1992.

Pincoffs, Edmund L. *Quandaries and Virtues.* Lawrence: University of Kansas Press, 1986.

Piper, Adrian M. "Moral Theory and Moral Alienation." *Journal of Philosophy* 84 (1987): 102–18.

Plamenatz, John. *Man and Society.* 2 vols. New York: McGraw-Hill, 1963.

———. "The Use of Political Theory." In *Political Philosophy,* ed. Anthony Quinton. New York: Oxford University Press, 1967.

Platts, Mark. *Ways of Meaning.* London: Routledge & Kegan Paul, 1979.

Pojman, Louis P. *Ethics: Discovering Right and Wrong.* Belmont, Calif.: Wadsworth, 1990.

Popper, Karl R. *Conjectures and Refutations: The Growth of Scientific Knowledge.* New York: Harper Torchbooks, 1968.

Putnam, Hilary. *Meaning and the Moral Sciences.* Boston: Routledge & Kegan Paul, 1978.

———. *Reason, Truth, and History.* New York: Cambridge University Press, 1981.

———. *Realism and Reason: Philosophical Papers.* Vol. 3. New York: Cambridge University Press, 1983.

———. *Realism with a Human Face.* Cambridge: Harvard University Press, 1990.

Quine, Willard Van Orman. *Ontological Relativity and Other Essays.* New York: Columbia University Press, 1969.

———. *From a Logical Point of View.* 2d ed., rev. Cambridge: Harvard University Press, 1980.

———. *Theories and Things.* Cambridge: Belknap Press, 1981.

———. *The Pursuit of Truth.* Cambridge: Harvard University Press, 1990.

Quinlan, J. Ross, ed. *Applications of Expert Systems.* Reading, Mass.: Addison–Wesley, 1987.

Railton, Peter. "How Thinking About Character and Utilitarianism Might Lead to Rethinking the Character of Utilitarianism." In *Ethical Theory,* ed. Peter French,

Theodore Uehling, and Howard Wettstein. Notre Dame, Ind.: Nortre Dame University Press, 1988.

Rajchman, John. "Ethics After Foucault." *Social Text* 13–14 (1986): 165–83.

Rawls, John. "Outline of a Decision Procedure for Ethics." In *Ethics,* ed. Judith J. Thompson and Gerald Dworkin. New York: Harper & Row, 1968.

———. "Two Concepts of Rules." In *Ethics,* ed. Judith J. Thompson and Gerald Dworkin. New York: Harper & Row, 1968.

———. *A Theory of Justice.* Cambridge: Harvard University Press, 1971.

———. "Social Unity and Primary Goods." In *Utilitarianism and Beyond,* ed. Amartya Sen and Bernard Williams. New York: Cambridge University Press, 1982.

Rist, J. M. "An Early Dispute About *Right* Reason." *Monist* 66 (1983): 39–48.

Roberts, Robert C. "Virtues and Rules." *Philosophy and Phenomenological Research* 51 (1991): 325–43.

Rorty, Amélie O. *Mind in Action.* Boston: Beacon Press, 1988.

———. "Socrates and Sophia Perform the Philosophic Turn." In *The Institution of Philosophy,* ed. Avner Cohen and Marcelo Dascal. LaSalle, Ill.: Open Court, 1989.

———, ed. *Essays on Aristotle's Ethics.* Berkeley: University of California Press, 1980.

Rorty, Richard. *Consequences of Pragmatism.* Minneapolis: University of Minnesota Press, 1982.

———. "Method and Morality." In *Social Science as Moral Inquiry,* ed. Norma Haan, Robert N. Bellah, Paul Rabinow, and William M. Sullivan. New York: Columbia University Press, 1983.

———. "Philosophy Without Principles." In *Against Theory,* ed. W. J. T. Mitchell. Chicago: Chicago University Press, 1985.

———. *Contingency, Irony, and Solidarity.* New York: Cambridge University Press, 1989.

Rosmarin, Adena. "On the Theory of 'Against Theory'." In *Against Theory,* ed. W. J. T. Mitchell. Chicago: University of Chicago Press, 1985.

Ross, W. D. *The Right and the Good.* Oxford: Clarendon Press, 1930.

Roth, Paul A. *Meaning and Method in the Social Sciences.* Ithaca, N. Y.: Cornell University Press, 1987.

Sabini, John, and Maury Silver. "Emotions, Responsibility, and Character." In *Responsibility, Character, and the Emotions,* ed. Ferdinard Schoeman. New York: Cambridge University Press, 1989.

Sankowski, Edward. "Responsibility of Persons for Their Emotions." *Canadian Journal of Philosophy* 7 (1977): 829–40.

Sartre, Jean-Paul. "Existentialism Is a Humanism." In *Existentialism from Dostoevsky to Sartre,* ed. Walter Kaufmann. Cleveland: Meridian Books, 1956.

Sayre-McCord, Geoffrey, ed. *Essays in Moral Realism.* Ithaca, N.Y.: Cornell University Press, 1988.

———. "Moral Theory and Explanatory Impotence." In *Essays in Moral Realism,* ed. Geoffrey Sayre-McCord. Ithaca, N.Y.: Cornell University Press, 1988.

Scanlon, Thomas M. "Rights, Goals, and Fairness." In *Consequentialism and Its Critics.* New York: Oxford University Press, 1988.

Scheffler, Samuel. *The Rejection of Consequentialism.* Oxford: Clarendon Press, 1982.

———. "Morality's Demands and Their Limits." *Journal of Philosophy* 83 (1986): 531–37.

———. "Morality Through Thick and Thin: A Critical Notice of *Ethics and the Limits of Philosophy.*" *Philosophical Review* 96 (1987): 411–34.

———, ed. *Consequentialism and Its Critics.* New York: Oxford University Press, 1988.

Schneewind, J. B. "Moral Knowledge and Moral Principles." In *Revisions,* ed. Stanley
    Hauerwas and Alasdair MacIntyre. Notre Dame, Ind.: Notre Dame University
    Press, 1983.
———. "The Misfortunes of Virtue." *Ethics* 101 (1990): 42–63.
Schoeman, Ferdinand, ed. *Responsibility, Character, and the Emotions.* New York: Cam-
    bridge University Press, 1989.
Scott, G. E. *Moral Personhood: An Essay in the Philosophy of Moral Psychology.* Albany: State
    University of New York Press, 1990.
Sen, Amartya. "Rights and Agency." In *Consequentialism and Its Critics,* ed. Samuel
    Scheffler. New York: Oxford University Press, 1988.
Sen, Amartya, and Bernard Williams, eds. *Utilitarianism and Beyond.* New York: Cam-
    bridge University Press, 1982.
Shelly, Percy Bysshe. *A Defense of Poetry.* Ed. Albert S. Cook. Boston: Ginn, 1890.
Sherman, Nancy. "Commentary on Irwin." In *Proceedings of the Boston Area Colloquium
    in Ancient Philosophy,* vol. 1, ed. John J. Cleary. Washington, D.C.: University
    Press of America, 1985.
———. "Common Sense and Uncommon Virtue." In *Ethical Theory,* ed. Peter French,
    Theodore Uehling, Jr., and Howard Wettstein. Notre Dame, Ind.: University of
    Notre Dame Press, 1988.
———. *The Fabric of Character: Aristotle's Theory of Virtue.* Oxford: Clarendon Press,
    1989.
———. "The Place of Emotions in Morality." Georgetown University, 1990.
    Mimeographed.
Sidgwick, Henry. *The Methods of Ethics.* 7th ed. New York: Dover, 1966.
Siebers, Tobin. *The Ethics of Criticism.* Ithaca, N.Y.: Cornell University Press, 1988.
Simon, Herbert A. "A Behavioral Model of Rational Choice." *Quarterly Journal of Eco-
    nomics* 69 (1955): 99–118.
Singer, Marcus. *Generalization in Ethics.* New York: Knopf, 1961.
Singer, Peter. *Practical Ethics.* New York: Cambridge University Press, 1989.
Skinner, Quentin, ed. *The Return of Grand Theory in the Human Sciences.* New York:
    Cambridge University Press, 1985.
Slote, Michael. *Goods and Virtues.* Oxford: Clarendon Press, 1983.
———. "Utilitarian Virtue." In *Ethical Theory,* ed. Peter French, Theodore Uehling, Jr.,
    and Howard Wettstein. Notre Dame, Ind.: University of Notre Dame Press,
    1988.
———. *Beyond Optimizing: A Study of Rational Choice.* Cambridge: Harvard University
    Press, 1989.
Smart, J. J. C., and Bernard Williams. *Utilitarianism: For and Against.* New York:
    Cambridge University Press, 1973.
Smith, J. A. "Aristotelica." *Classical Quarterly* 14 (1920): 18–22.
Smith, Norman Kemp. *A Commentary to Kant's "Critique of Pure Reason."* Atlantic
    Highlands, N.J.: Humanities Press, 1962.
Stocker, Michael. "The Schizophrenia of Modern Moral Theories." *Journal of Philosophy*
    73 (1976): 453–66.
———. *Plural and Conflicting Values.* Oxford: Clarendon Press, 1990.
Stocks, John L. "On the Aristotelian Use of *Logos:* A Reply." *Classical Quarterly* 8 (1914):
    9–12.
———. *Morality and Purpose.* Ed. D. Z. Phillips. New York: Schocken Books, 1969.
Stout, Jeffrey. *Ethics After Babel.* Boston: Beacon Press, 1988.
Strawson, P. F. "Social Morality and Individual Ideal. *Philosophy* 36 (1961): 1–17.

Sturgeon, Nicholas. "Moral Explanations." In *Essays in Moral Realism*, ed. Geoffrey Sayre-McCord. Ithaca, N.Y.: Cornell University Press, 1988.

Sullivan, Roger J. "The Kantian Critique of Aristotle's Moral Philosophy: An Appraisal." *Review of Metaphysics* 28 (1974): 24–53.

———. *Immanuel Kant's Moral Theory*. New York: Cambridge University Press, 1989.

Taylor, Charles. "Responsibility for Self." In *The Identities of Persons*, ed. Amelie O. Rorty. Berkeley: University of California Press, 1976.

———. "The Diversity of Goods." In *Utilitarianism and Beyond*, ed. Amartya Sen and Bernard Williams. New York: Cambridge University Press, 1982. Also in *Anti-Theory in Ethics and Moral Conservatism*, ed. Stanley Clarke and Evan Simpson. Albany: State University of New York Press, 1989.

———. *Sources of the Self*. Cambridge: Harvard University Press, 1989.

Taylor, Richard. "Ancient Wisdom and Modern Folly." In *Ethical Theory*, ed. Peter French, Theodore Uehling, Jr., and Howard Wettman. Notre Dame, Ind.: Notre Dame University Press, 1988.

Thayer, H. S. *Meaning and Action: A Critical History of Pragmatism*. Indianapolis: Bobbs-Merrill, 1968.

Thomas, Lawrence. *Living Morally: A Psychology of Moral Character*. Philadelphia: Temple University Press, 1989.

Thompson, Manley. *The Pragmatic Philosophy of C. S. Peirce*. Chicago: University of Chicago Press, 1953.

Thomson, Judith J., and Gerald Dworkin, eds. *Ethics*. New York: Harper & Row, 1968.

Toulmin, Stephen. *Cosmopolis: The Hidden Agenda of Modernity*. New York: Free Press, 1990.

Trianosky, Gregory W. "Supererogation, Wrongdoing, and Vice: The Autonomy of the Ethics of Virtue." *Journal of Philosophy* 83 (1986): 26–40.

———. "What Is Virtue Ethics All About?" *American Philosophical Quarterly* 27 (1990): 335–44.

Troeltsch, Ernst. *The Social Teachings of the Christian Churches*. Trans. Olive Wyon. 2 vols. New York: Harper & Row, 1960.

van der Linden, Harry. *Kantian Ethics and Socialism*. Indianapolis: Hackett, 1988.

Waldron, Jeremy. "A Right To Do Wrong." *Ethics* 92 (1981): 21–39.

———, ed. *Nonsense upon Stilts: Bentham, Burke, and Marx on the Rights of Man*. New York: Methuen, 1987.

Wallace, James D. *Virtues and Vices*. Ithaca, N.Y.: Cornell University Press, 1978.

Walsh, W. H. *Kant's Criticism of Metaphysics*. Chicago: University of Chicago Press, 1975.

Walzer, Michael. *Interpretation and Social Criticism*. Cambridge: Harvard University Press, 1987.

———. *The Company of Critics*. New York: Basic Books, 1988.

Warnock, G. J. "The Primacy of Practical Reason." *Proceedings of the British Academy* 52 (1967): 253–66.

Waterman, Donald A. *A Guide to Expert Systems*. Reading, Mass.: Addison-Wesley, 1986.

Weitz, Morris. "The Role of Theory in Aesthetics." In *Philosophy Looks at the Arts*, rev. ed., ed. Joseph Margolis. Philadelphia: Temple University Press, 1978.

Weston, Anthony. *Toward Better Problems: A Contemporary Deweyan Practical Ethics*. Philadelphia: Temple University Press, forthcoming.

Whitely, C. H. "On Duties." In *Moral Concepts*, ed. Joel Feinberg. New York: Oxford University Press, 1980.

Wick, Warner A. "More About Duties to Oneself." *Ethics* 70 (1960): 158–63.

————. Introduction to *Ethical Philosophy,* by Immanuel Kant. Trans. James W. Ellington. Indianapolis: Hackett, 1983.

Wiggins, David. "Deliberation and Practical Reason." In *Essays on Aristotle's Ethics,* ed. Amelie Rorty. Berkeley: University of California Press, 1980.

————. "Weakness of Will." In *Essays on Aristotle's Ethics,* ed. Amélie O. Rorty. Berkeley: University of California Press, 1980.

————. "Truth, Invention, and the Meaning of Life." In *Essays in Moral Realism,* ed. Geoffrey Sayre-McCord. Ithaca N.Y.: Cornell University Press, 1988.

Wilde, Oscar. *The Portable Oscar Wilde.* Ed. Richard Arlington. New York: Viking Press, 1974.

Williams, Bernard. *Morality: An Introduction to Ethics.* New York: Harper Torchbooks, 1972.

————. *Problems of the Self.* New York: Cambridge University Press, 1973.

————. Introduction to *Concepts and Categories,* by Isaiah Berlin. New York: Penguin Books, 1981.

————. *Moral Luck.* New York: Cambridge University Press, 1981.

————. "Philosophy." In *The Legacy of Greece,* ed. M. I. Finley. New York: Oxford University Press, 1981.

————. *Ethics and the Limits of Philosophy.* Cambridge: Harvard University Press, 1985.

Wilson, J. Cook. "On the Meaning of *Logos* in Certain Passages in Aristotle's *Nicomachean Ethics.*" *Classical Review* 27 (1913): 113–17.

Wittgenstein, Ludwig. *Philosophical Investigations.* Trans. G. E. M. Anscombe. New York: Macmillan, 1953.

Wolf, Susan. "Moral Saints." In *The Virtues,* ed. Robert B. Kruschwitz and Robert C. Roberts. Belmont; Calif.: Wadsworth, 1987.

Wolin, Sheldon. *Politics and Vision.* Boston: Little, Brown 1960.

————. "Political Theory as a Vocation." *American Political Science Review* 63 (1969): 1062–82.

Wollheim, Richard. "Flawed Crystals: James's *The Golden Bowl* and the Plausibility of Literature as Moral Philosophy." *New Literary History* 15 (1983): 185–91.

Wood, Allen W. "Unsociable Sociability: The Anthropological Basis of Kantian Ethics." *Philosophical Topics* 19 (1991).

"Work on Virtue," special issue. *Philosophia* 20 (1990).

Wright, Georg Henrik von. *The Varieties of Goodness.* New York: Routledge & Kegan Paul, 1963.

Yovel, Yirmiahu. *Kant and the Philosophy of History.* Princeton, N.J.: Princeton University Press, 1980.

Index